D1212661

THE RISE OF ENGLISH LITERARY PROSE

George Philip Krapp

FREDERICK UNGAR PUBLISHING CO.
New York

Republished 1963

First published 1915

Printed in the United States of America

Library of Congress Catalog Card No. 63-12909

CONTENTS

1948 64 Baker and Taylor 760

53189

PREFACE

This book covers the period of discovery in the history of English literary prose. It begins with the latter half of the fourteenth century, when the writing of prose first assumed importance in the life of the English people, and it ends with the first quarter of the seventeenth century, when practice and experiment had made of English prose, in the reigns of Elizabeth and James, a highly developed and efficient means of expression.

The origins of English prose come relatively late in the development of English literary experience. This apparently is true of most prose literatures, and the explanation seems to lie in the nature of prose. Even in its beginnings the art of prose is never an unconscious, never a genuinely primitive art. The origins of prose literature can consequently be examined without venturing far into those misty regions of theory and speculation, where the student of poetry must wander in the attempt to explain beginnings which certainly precede the age of historical documents, and perhaps of human record of any kind. Poetry may be the more ancient, the more divine art, but prose lies nearer to us and is more practical and human.

Being human, prose bears upon it, and early prose especially, some of the marks of human imperfection. Poetry of primitive origins, for example the ballad, often attains a finality of form which art cannot better, but not so with prose. Perhaps the explanation of this may be that poetry is concerned primarily with the emotions, and the emotions are among the original and perfect gifts of mankind, ever the same; whereas prose is concerned with the reasonable powers of man's nature, which have been and are being only slowly won by painful conquest. Whether this be a right explanation or not, it is certainly true that in its first efforts English prose is uncertain and faltering, that it often engages our sympathies more by what it attempts to do than by what it actually accomplishes.

In this book the purpose has been to show how the English mind approached the practical problem of the invention of prose, to point out what things seemed appropriately to be expressed in prose and what devices of language appropriately employed in the expression of them. The process was obviously one of the adaptation of language, a genuinely primitive inheritance like the traditions of poetry, to many differing and present needs. It was indeed closely bound up with the effort of the English people to find for itself the golden mean of expression between ephemeral colloquial discourse and the special and often highly conventionalized forms of poetic expression. The study of the origins of English prose is consequently concerned not only with the growth of the English mind, but, in the broadest sense, with the development of the English language.

Since literary prose is very largely the speech of everyday discourse applied to special purposes, it is in a way true that the origins of English prose are to be sought in the origins of English speech. No student of the speech would be content to pause short of the earliest English records in the four centuries which preceded the Norman Conquest. From the days of the first Teutonic conquerors of Celtic Britain, the English speech has continued in an unbroken oral tradition to the present time. But obviously English literary prose in its various stages has not been merely the written form, the echo, of this colloquial speech.

The bonds which unite the two are close, but their courses are not parallel. English literary prose has had no such continuous history as the language, and there are sufficient reasons for regarding the prose of Alfred and his few contemporaries and successors as a chapter in the life of the English people which begins and ends with itself. For its antiquity and for its importance in preserving so abundantly the early records of the language, Old English prose is to be respected; but it was never highly developed as an art, nor was its vitality great enough to withstand the shock of the several conquests which brought about a general confusion of English ideals and traditions in the tenth and eleventh centuries. It is consequently in no sense the source from which modern English prose has sprung. It has a separate story, and when writers of the early modern period again turned to prose, they did so in utter disregard and ignorance of the fact that Alfred and Ælfric had preceded them by several centuries in the use of English for purposes of prose expression. Nor did the later writers unwittingly benefit by the inheritance of a previous discipline of the language in the writing of prose. In the general political and social cataclysm of the eleventh century, the literary speech of the Old English period went down forever, leaving for succeeding generations nothing but the popular speech upon which to build anew the foundations of a literary culture.

After the Conquest came the slow process of establishing social order. Laws must first be formulated, Normans, Scandinavians, and Saxons must learn to live in harmony with one another, above all must learn to communicate with one another in a commonly accepted speech, before literature could again lift its head. During all this period of the making of the new England, verse remained the standard form for literary expression. Such prose as was written was mainly of a documentary character, wills, deeds of transfer and gift, rules for the government of religious houses, and similar writings of limited appeal. In the lack of a standard vernacular idiom, more serious efforts, such as histories and theological treatises, were composed in Latin, and to a less extent, in French. It was not until towards the middle of the fourteenth century that the various elements of English life were fused into what came to be felt more and more as a national unity. A wave of popular patriotism swept over the country at this time, clearing away the encumbering foreign traditions by which the English had permitted themselves to become burdened. This new national feeling showed itself in various ways, in a renewed interest in English history, in the special respect now shown to English saints, and above all in the rejection of French and in the cultivation of the English language as the proper expression of the English people. At the same time men of riper and broader culture made their appearance in the intellectual life of the people. An age which produced three such personalities as those of Chaucer, Langland, and Wiclif cannot be regarded as anticipatory and uncertain of itself. Economic conditions also forced upon the humbler classes of people the necessity of thinking for themselves and of setting forth and defending their interests. In the larger world of international affairs the dissensions and corruptions of the church, culminating in the great schism of the last quarter of the century, compelled account to be taken of that whole order of theocratic government which the medieval world had hitherto accepted almost without question.

In this combination of circumstances, one man stands out pre-eminently in England as realizing the drift of events and the kind of action needed to regulate them. This man was Wiclif, a scholar and theologian, but not merely a man of the study or the lecturer's chair. Wiclif's practical wisdom is particularly apparent in his deliberate choice of the English language as a means of exposition and persuasion. If English prose must have a father, no one is so worthy of this title of respect as Wiclif. Not a great master of prose style himself, Wiclif was the first Englishman clearly to realize the broad principles which underlie prose expression. He made a sharp distinction between prose and verse, and he foresaw, at least, the ends to be attained by a skillful use of the mechanism of daily colloquial speech for broader and less ephemeral purposes than those to which it had hitherto been applied. In a word, Wiclif was the first intelligent writer of English prose, a discoverer in the truest sense of the word. With him begins the long and unbroken line of English writers who have striven to use the English tongue as a means of conveying their message as directly and as forcibly as possible to their hearers and readers. The spirit of Wiclif is the spirit of Sir Thomas More, of Tindale, of Hooker, of Milton, of Burke, of Carlyle, of all the great masters of expositional and hortatory prose in the English language. Technical details have changed, exterior ornaments have varied, but the fundamental purpose and method have remained the same. With Wiclif and his period, therefore, we begin our study of the rise of English literary prose.

The later limits of the present undertaking have not so easily determined themselves. It would have been interesting to carry the discussion down to the masters of prose in the seventeenth century, to Milton, Clarendon, Jeremy Taylor, Burton, Dryden, for they are indeed the fruit of the sixteenth-century flower. But the close of the sixteenth century and the opening of the seventeenth century mark the end of the great originating period in the development of English prose. The tentative beginnings of Wiclifite prose are by that time fully realized in models of the plain style not surpassed by any later writers. The literary and more narrowly artistic interests have entered, and experimentation in this direction has been carried almost to the extreme limits of the possibilities of the language. Scarcely any side of human activity remains unexpressed in English prose at the end of the reign of Elizabeth, and though it by no means follows that the prose of later times is less admirable, it is nevertheless different from the prose of this first fresh and tremendously energetic age of invention and experimentation.

Since that is the subject of the whole volume, it manifestly falls outside the province of these prefatory remarks to discuss the various processes and developments of this first formative period of English prose. It may be worth while to put down, however, as a kind of preliminary scaffolding, the opinions of one of the greatest of the early moderns, of one who from the vantage-ground of the end of a long life, cast his eye backward and formulated what seemed to him the prime moving causes and tendencies of writing in his day. Starting with the discussion of the origins of the fantastic or ornate literary style in Europe, Bacon continues with an analysis which, whether true for the whole European awakening or not, certainly applies in a peculiar degree to England, where the Renascence was from the first so largely a religious and theological movement:

"Martin Luther, conducted (no doubt) by an higher Providence, but in discourse of reason finding what a province he had undertaken against the Bishop of Rome and the degenerate traditions of the church, and finding his own solitude, being no ways aided by the opinions of his own time, was enforced to awake all antiquity, and to call former times to his succors to make a part against the present time, so that the ancient authors, both in divinity and in humanity, which had long time slept in libraries, began generally to be read and revolved. This by consequence did draw on a necessity of a more exquisite travail in the languages original wherein those authors did write, for the better understanding of those authors and the better advantage of pressing and applying their words. And thereof grew again a delight in their manner of style and phrase, and an admiration of that kind of writing; which was much furthered and precipitated by the enmity and opposition that the propounders of those (primitive but seeming new) opinions had against the schoolmen; who were generally of the contrary part, and whose writings were altogether in a differing style and form; taking liberty to coin and frame new terms of art to express their own sense and to avoid circuit of speech, without regard to the pureness, pleasantness, and (as I may call it) lawfulness of the phrase or word. And again, because the great labor then was with the people, (of whom the Pharisees were wont to say, *Execrabilis ista turba, quæ non novit legem,*) [the wretched crowd that has not known the law,] for the winning and persuading of them, there grew of necessity in chief price and request eloquence and variety of discourse, as the fittest and forciblest access into the capacity of the vulgar sort. So that these four causes concurring, the admiration of ancient authors, the hate of the schoolmen, the exact study of languages, and the efficacy of preaching, did bring in an affectionate study of eloquence and copie of speech, which then began to flourish. This grew speedily to an excess; for men began to hunt more after words than matter; and more after the choiceness of the phrase, and the round and clean composition of the sentence, and the sweet falling of the clauses, and the varying and illustration of their works with tropes and figures, than after the weight of matter, worth of subject, soundness of argument, life of invention, or depth of judgment. Then grew the flowing and watery vein of Osorius, the Portugal bishop, to be in price. Then did Sturmius spend such infinite and curious pains upon Cicero the orator and Hermogenes the rhetorician, besides his own books of periods and imitation and the like. Then did Car of Cambridge, and

Ascham, with their lectures and writings, almost deify Cicero and Demosthenes, and allure all young men that were studious unto that delicate and polished kind of learning. Then did Erasmus take occasion to make the scoffing echo: *Decem annos consumpsi in legendo Cicerone,* [I have spent ten years in reading Cicero:] and the echo answered in Greek, *one, Asine.* Then grew the learning of the schoolmen to be utterly despised as barbarous. In sum, the whole inclination and bent of those times was rather toward copie than weight." [1]

Bacon closes his survey with the generation which immediately preceded his own. The detachment with which he viewed the refinements of the artificial writers shows that he at least had accepted different standards and ideals of writing. To complete the sketch, it would be necessary to add certain developments of English prose in the direction of order and moderation of which Bacon's own writings are signally illustrative. And it is with these developments that the survey undertaken in the following pages will come to an appropriate conclusion.

The limits of the present undertaking imply certain exclusions. This book is neither a bibliographical nor a biographical history of English literary prose, nor is it a dictionary of reference to all prose monuments for the period it covers. No attempt has been made to give a critical survey of the paper wars that have centered about debated points, though it will be found, it is hoped, that the references given supply the clew to all the rest. Thus the earlier bibliography of Euphuism may be derived from the studies mentioned in the text or notes. Biographical details are included only when they seemed useful for the better understanding of such writings as are discussed, and titles are mentioned only for the purpose of indicating with certainty the sources of the various passages cited or

[1] Bacon, *Works,* VI, 118-120.

quoted in the text. Passages within double quotation marks are quoted exactly—except that, for the sake of consistency, the modern custom in the use of u and v has been followed. Passages within single marks are the author's literal modernizations. The temptation to quote more frequently and at greater length has been strong, but a single volume of reasonable size cannot be both history and anthology. Quotation can never take the place of the reading of texts, and fortunately, for those who have not access to large libraries and for students in college classes, several collections of illustrative extracts are available.

The author has assumed the liberty of saying nothing about works and about writers that, to his mind, required no mention. It might be a satisfaction to put down all the results of one's investigations, if one could only be sure in so doing that the reader's share in this pleasure would be as great as the author's. But it would be unkind for the literary critic or historian to attempt to rescue insignificant names from the "poke of oblivion" where time in its mercy has permitted them to rest in peace. In such names the sixteenth century was as rich as any other, though mere antiquity does often seem to lend a specious importance to writings otherwise not important. But the author has endeavored to choose his materials always with an eye to the main point, which has been to trace the growth of a temper and attitude of mind towards the use of speech, to show the development of taste and feeling for prose expression by directing attention to those writings which reveal some skill and originating power in the practice of the art of prose composition.

GEORGE PHILIP KRAPP.

COLUMBIA UNIVERSITY,
August, 1915.

I

INTRODUCTION

THE FOURTEENTH CENTURY—CHAUCER'S PROSE—LANGLAND—MAUNDEVILE—TREVISA—ARTIFICIAL WRITERS: TAYSTEK, RICHARD ROLLE, THOMAS USK

THE second half of the fourteenth century in England was a period rich both in realization and in anticipation. At such happy times, not one but many kinds of thought and action occupy men's attention. The pageant of chivalry was then still being displayed upon the stage of the great world, and was finding in Froissart a worthy chronicler. Crécy and Poitiers were living memories of young men when Edward III died. Though the changes abroad were many, at home English laws and government were rapidly assuming forms which were to be permanent. The place of the commons in the control of affairs was becoming more clearly defined, and the nation at large was entering upon a new era of patriotism and national self-consciousness. Architecture, especially domestic architecture, flourished, and the comforts and luxuries of life were increasing. Gower, Chaucer, Langland, and the unknown author of *The Pearl* and other remarkable poems, were lending luster to the newly-prized English language. In the humbler walks of life, the voice of the people was making itself heard, and the last remnants of medieval serfdom were disappearing as new conceptions of personal liberty came into being. Wiclif and his followers were spreading doctrines of almost incalculable importance for the future growth of the English nation. And not least in importance among these shadowings of the future, English prose was coming to be applied to English thought in ways more effective and intimate than had ever before been necessary or possible.

By the middle of the fourteenth century, the various Scandinavian and Romance additions which had enriched at the same time that they had disintegrated the old England, built up by the successive kings of the West Saxons from the time of Egbert, had united with the English base to form a new nation. During the time of disturbance the English speech had passed through a period of popular degradation. It had lost literary caste, but now, under the influence of a new national feeling and a renascence of culture, it had recovered all that had been lost and was gaining more. By the assimilation of a host of Romance words, it had acquired possibilities of expression beyond the reach of the language of the Old English period. The English were no longer an isolated people. Their intellectual life was more vigorous and more varied, and their social life was more gracious, than either had been in the most flourishing days before the Conquest. The English writer of the later fourteenth century had a richer body of thought and sentiment to express than his Anglo-Saxon ancestor, and he had a more effective medium in the language of his day to serve the purposes of expression. The Anglo-Saxon poets had seldom passed beyond the simple themes of war and religion; and the prose of Alfred, of Wulfstan, of Ælfric, was limited almost entirely to the second of these themes. Religion and theology remain, indeed, the principal concern of prose even into the sixteenth century, but with a very great difference. Scarcely a trace of popular insurgence is to be found in English writing before the days of Wiclif. The newest, the most disturbing, and for the history of English prose, the most important element in the life of England in the fourteenth century was just this awakening of the underworld of the people. Men now first began to realize that their political and spiritual salvation lay not in the hands of overlords and ecclesiastics, but in their own. New impulses within demanded new modes of external expression. Literature could not continue to be merely artistic and courtly, learning could not expend itself entirely in theological exegesis or the formulation of dogma. The pallid legends and the summary repetitions of officially approved information and doctrine which constitute so large a part of medieval writing in the vernacular began now to disappear and their place to be taken by a fresher literature, addressed not merely to the memory, but directly to the reason and the hearts of mankind.

It was only gradually, however, that English writers acquired the courage to use prose. Long custom had established verse as the only accredited form of literary expression. From the point of view of literary art, the two most significant writers of the latter half of the fourteenth century were Chaucer, courtly, polished, and reasonable, and Langland, something of a mystic and enthusiast, a fellow-sufferer with the people, whose hard life he so intimately describes, and certainly less an artist than his greater contemporary. Chaucer's prevailing interest being in men and manners, one might suppose that prose would have been for him a more appropriate form of expression than verse. And in truth, we may suppose that the use of metrical form by Chaucer was largely an accident of time. He wrote in verse because the literary conventions of his time imposed the metrical form upon all writing of artistic pretension. Perhaps it was fortunate for Chaucer that he accepted these conventions. In his day and hour it was easier to realize the ideals of simplicity, clarity, and control which his verse exhibits by following the conventional custom of metrical composition than it would have been if he had chosen to experiment in prose. But Chaucer was not temperamentally an experimenter or innovator. He followed clearly defined paths of literary tradition, changing and improving greatly in detail, but seldom departing widely from the practice of his predecessors and masters. He seems to have felt no impulse, therefore, to invent prose for English literature, to become an English Boccaccio.

Chaucer did not neglect altogether the writing of prose, although by universal consent his prose writings are regarded as the least interesting of all his works. They are four in number, and all of considerable length. The only one which can be dated certainly is the latest, the *Treatise on the Astrolabe,* written in 1391. The others were written probably within the decade preceding this year, and it is interesting to note, therefore, that Chaucer's prose works were produced at about the same time that Wiclif began to write in English. Of these four prose efforts of Chaucer, the most important is his translation of the *De Consolatione Philosophiae* of Boethius, made probably in entire ignorance of the fact that it had already been translated into English by King Alfred almost five hundred years before. The *De Consolatione* is mentioned in the *Romance of the Rose*[1] as "Boece," and the original author of this section of the famous allegory, Jean de Meun, declares that he would confer a great benefit on the unlearned folk who should translate this work for them. It is not unlikely that Chaucer found in this statement of the much admired French poet the suggestion which led him to undertake his translation into English.

The original work of Boethius is divided into five books,

[1] Ll. 5052-5056.

and each book is sub-divided into alternating metrical and prose sections, commonly known as Metres and Proses, all of which, however, Chaucer translated into prose. In general Chaucer's translation attempted to give the content of the original, but it is by no means a literal translation, such not being the custom of Chaucer's day. Neither is it altogether a true translation, for Chaucer's scholarship was not always sufficient to save him from blunders. An instructive comparison may be made between Chaucer's prose version of Boethius and those passages of the same work which he versified in *Troilus and Cressida*[2] and in *The Former Age*. Such a comparison will show that the metrical versions are decidedly more idiomatic and natural than the prose—another proof, if any were needed, that Chaucer had mastered more completely the discipline of verse than that of prose.

The main defects of the translation are crudity and awkwardness, even at times obscurity, of expression, due to imperfect adaptation of the thought to the English idiom. Chaucer's difficulties arose from the embarrassment caused by the necessity of striking a balance between a Latin and an English phrasing. In general the translations of the Proses are more idiomatic and less complicated than the translations of the Metres, obviously due to the fact that the Metres are more compact and involved in expression in the original. Chaucer wisely made little effort to introduce specifically English ornaments of style. Riming passages occur occasionally, but they are not frequent or long enough to disturb the prose intention. Alliteration is used, sometimes rather markedly, as in the phrase "fortroden under the feet of felonous folk,"[3] but is never carried through long passages. The only notable mannerism of style is the omission of the definite article where the

[2] Bk. IV, ll. 958-1078.

[3] *Works,* II, 93.

English idiom requires it. This is an obvious Latinism, found not only in Chaucer but in Wiclif and many other writers of this time who wrote English under the influence of Latin.[4]

Two of Chaucer's prose writings were distinguished by inclusion within the framework of the Canterbury Tales. One of these is Chaucer's own contribution to the entertainment of the pilgrims, the *Tale of Melibeus,* narrated by Chaucer after he has been 'stinted' of his *Tale of Sir Thopas* by the disgusted Host. The other is the *Parson's Tale,* a long and weary treatise on the vices and virtues which serves as the pious ending to the whole series of the Canterbury Tales. It is not certain that Chaucer wrote either of these tales, granting them this title by courtesy, for the express purpose of including them in the Canterbury group. Quite possibly they were early works written when he was more deeply interested in the composition of pious prayers and other works of devotion than he was later, which were thriftily turned to account in the elaboration of the plan of the Canterbury Tales. The two prose tales have very little dramatic appropriateness. One does not expect a conventional medieval sermon on the vices and virtues from the parson, the brother of the ploughman, who is described in the Prolog in terms that suggest Wiclif's poor priests. Here was Chaucer's opportunity to give that pic-

[4] One or two examples will illustrate: Empted of light of his thought, *Works,* II, 5, translates *effeto lumine mentis,* Bk. I, Metr. II; comen to corage of a parfit man, ibid., translating *in uirilis animi robur,* Bk. I, Prose II; on allone is fader of thinges, *Works,* II, 65, translating *unus enim rerum pater est,* Bk. III, Metr. VI; thus, whan that night was discussed and chased awey, derknesses forleften me, *Works,* II, 5, translating *Tunc me discussa liquerunt nocte tenebrae,* Bk. I, Metr. III. The use of several synonomous words to translate a single Latin word is not uncommon. The literal translation of the plural *tenebrae* was not English idiom.

ture of actual popular movements in his day which we miss so much in his writings and which, without question, he consciously avoided giving. And the other prose tale, the *Tale of Melibeus,* is equally inappropriate to Chaucer, who tells it. Chaucer apparently assigned this tale to himself in a moment of ironic humor. At the same time it must be kept in mind that the modern reader's impatience with these two tales is likely to be much greater than was that of Chaucer's contemporaries. In the fourteenth century both the materials and the method of them were familiar and approved, and many of Chaucer's readers doubtless received them as highly respectable and meritorious performances.

Both of these prose tales are really translations. The *Tale of Melibeus* is a translation of a French treatise, *Le Livre de Melibee et de dame Prudence,* probably made by Jean de Meun, on the basis of a Latin work, *Liber Consolationis et Consilii,* by Albertano of Brescia. The *Tale* is not much more than a bundle of quotations of a generally moral and sententious character, bound together by a simple thread of allegorical narrative. Melibeus is a rich man of the world who finds himself ill-treated by his enemies and who is elaborately counseled by his wife, Dame Prudence, on such topics as the choice of friends and advisers, on avenging wrongs, on the use of riches. The characters are not realistically conceived, and the wife of Melibeus is the source of all wisdom in the story because Prudentia, Justitia, Philosophia, and the other virtues were traditionally allegorized as feminine. The *Tale* has some resemblance to the type of didactic romance made popular in the sixteenth century by Guevara's *Dial of Princes,* the quotations being derived not merely from scriptural and patristic sources, but many of them from classical and post-classical literature. But the romantic and narrative interests of the *Tale* are held severely in hand and the main purpose of the story was to serve as a container for numerous aphoristic and sententious quotations. From the point of view of Chaucer as a writer of prose, the chief interest of the *Tale* lies in the fact that it is freely and idiomatically written, and that it thus shows how much easier Chaucer found it to translate from French than from Latin.

The other of Chaucer's two pious tales is not unlike the *Tale of Melibeus*. It likewise is obviously a translation, but the immediate source is not known.[5] Whatever this immediate source may have been, it was almost certainly written in French and was closely followed by Chaucer in his translation. Like the *Tale of Melibeus,* the *Parson's Tale* is idiomatically expressed in a simple, straightforward, and unmannered style. Like the *Melibeus* in another respect, it is quite without personal or dramatic coloring in the body of text, although occasionally, as in the satirical passages on extravagance in dress, the conventional themes of medieval sermonizing are treated with some vivacity. But the main personal interest of the *Tale* lies in the fact that it is followed by the well-known retractions of Chaucer, in which he revokes his " Endytinges of worldly vanitees," and calls attention to his " othere bokes of Legendes of seintes and omelies and moralitee and devocioun." [6]

Both the *Melibeus* and the *Parson's Tale* come safely under the head of medieval works of devotion, and it is quite probable that a good many similar pious writings of Chaucer have been lost. If so, some of them were pretty certainly written in prose, for in this kind of writing, prose had established for itself an unquestioned position.

[5] See Hammond, *Chaucer Bibliography,* p. 320.
[6] *Works,* IV, 644.

Chaucer's remaining English prose work is a kind of medieval text-book, written for his little son Louis, who was at the time of the "tendre age of ten yeer" and who had shown evidences of ability to "lerñe sciencez touchinge noumbres and proporciouns."[7] This *Treatise on the Astrolabe,* like Chaucer's other prose writings, is merely a translation, or adaptation, the original in this case being a Latin version of a text in Arabic. Chaucer has omitted parts of his Latin source and has re-arranged the materials to suit himself, but his translation of the Latin is often literal. Although the exigencies of the subject-matter compelled him to use a good many Latinized technical words, the style on the whole, thanks perhaps to Chaucer's efforts to adapt it to a child of ten, is simple and much more idiomatic than the style of the translation from Boethius. The work was popular in Chaucer's day, as is shown by the unusual number of twenty-two early manuscripts still extant in various libraries.

More interesting, however, to the student of Chaucer's prose than the body of this translation is an original preface by Chaucer, which is addressed to his little son Louis, and which, short as it is, constitutes the longest piece of original prose we have from Chaucer's hand. Chaucer declares it to be his purpose to set forth his treatise under "ful lighte rewles and naked wordes in English; for Latin ne canstow yit but smal, my lyte sone." He continues with a more general address to his readers in which he asks them to excuse his "rewde endyting" and his "superfluite of wordes," the first because "curious endyting and hard sentence is ful hevy atones for swich a child to lerne," and the second because it seems to him better "to wryten unto a child twyes a good sentence than he forgete it ones." In conclusion Chaucer points out that he makes no claim to

[7] *Works,* III, 175.

the original authorship of his book, but confesses that he is merely "a lewd compilatour of the labour of olde Astrologiens," whose work he has translated: "And with this swerd shal I sleen envye." The whole passage is instructive as showing that the quaint simplicity and humor which constitute the main charm of his verse writings were not impossible to Chaucer in prose. Had he chosen to do so, Chaucer might have written prose tales for some of his Canterbury pilgrims, the Shipman or the Miller for example, which would have been more than deserving of a place in that series. But prose in Chaucer's mind must have seemed entirely inappropriate for writing of an entertaining or artistic character, and he therefore uses it only for practical and pious purposes. Chaucer's attitude towards prose was generally the attitude of his contemporaries. The first English prose was written under the hard necessity of instructing and edifying men, not of pleasing them, as Chaucer was mainly endeavoring to do. The art of prose begins with the effort to adapt language to useful ends, to find some means of communication whereby men may inform or persuade each other in the thousand and one complications of everyday life. Chaucer's perfunctory use of prose shows on the one hand how little interested he was in the complexities of the life of his day from the point of view of direct exposition or of persuasion, and it shows on the other hand how little impressed he was with the possibilities of prose as an art of fine writing. Limited though this attitude towards prose may seem to the modern student, it was natural in Chaucer's day and represents undoubtedly the best literary feeling of his time. For the development of the technic of English writing in verse, Chaucer is important; for the development of the technic of English prose, he is almost negligible.

By the side of Chaucer stands his greatest literary contemporary, Langland. Thanks to his connections with the court and with the higher official life of his time, public records have preserved a considerable body of information with respect to Chaucer. All that is known of Langland, on the other hand, is derived from the various manuscripts of his writings, and the information thus obtained is meager and often uncertain. It is fairly sure that the author of *Piers Plowman* was of Midland origin, that he lived for some time in London, that he was married and therefore not eligible to any of the higher offices of the church, that he himself had known the miseries of poverty which he so feelingly describes, and that his Christian name was William. The exact form of his surname is doubtful, but tradition has firmly established Langland in general use. The poem which passes under Langland's name is not a single, systematically organized work, but rather a group of closely related poems centering more or less about the figure of the Plowman. It is recorded in three quite distinct versions, the earliest composed about 1362, the second a revision and enlargement of this version made some fifteen years later, and the third a second revision probably made in the last decade of the fourteenth century. Certain interesting questions of technical scholarship have been raised by the existence of these three versions, the most important being whether the three versions are to be regarded as the work of a single poet or of two or more poets who revised and expanded the original theme as it was first developed by Langland. It is quite certain that Piers Plowman came to be in time a type figure about whom there gathered a considerable number of writings of generally similar style and purpose. He became thus in a way the eponymous hero of popular political and theological discussion of the times.[8] But that the three versions of the poem known as *Piers*

[8] See below, p. 60.

Plowman were the work of a school of popular alliterative poets, writing perhaps under the direct inspiration of Langland very much as Wiclif's poor priests preached and taught under the leadership of their master, though not inherently impossible, seems on the ground of the evidence less probable than that Langland himself revised and enlarged his own work. Whether the poem be regarded as the work of one or of several authors, however, the significant point is that the three versions exemplify a homogeneous and fully thought out method of literary expression.

Both the similarities and the differences of *Piers Plowman* as compared with the writings of Chaucer are significant. Like Chaucer, Langland accepted verse unquestioningly as the proper medium of literary expression and for general, popular appeal. He viewed life at a different angle from the courtly Chaucer, but he also in his degree was a literary artist, and in his art, the child of his own generation. Both poets used the standard literary speech of their day, for Chaucer's style was not pedantically learned, nor was Langland's extravagantly archaic or popular. The most striking characteristic of Langland which distinguishes him from Chaucer, the characteristic also which connects him directly with the study of the origins of English prose, is his use of metrical form. Chaucer wrote in the strictly regulated meter of numbered syllables and of rime which English borrowed from French and which the traditions of English poetry have established as the prevailing English meter. But Langland followed a different and native style of metrical composition, moribund but temporarily revived in his day and effectively employed by a number of different poets. This was the alliterative long line which came by direct descent from the Old English line of Cædmon and Cynewulf. It differs from the Old

English line, however, in that the latter, in standard Old English poetry, is maintained more rigorously and in accordance with the rules of a more narrowly defined metrical system than in Langland's long line. With the later poet, we observe clearly the operation of that breaking down tendency which led ultimately to a complete loss of feeling for the alliterative long line as in any way a metrical form distinguished from prose. Even in the latter part of the Old English period, the pure tradition of Old English versification was not maintained, and Ælfric, in many respects possessed of a fine literary feeling, was guilty of a kind of prose poetry compounded of legitimate prose and degenerate Old English verse. With the obscuring and loss of native customs in general which attended the Danish and Norman conquests, the strict system of Old English meter disappeared, never again to be restored in the practice of English poetry. At no time, however, did the composition of alliterative English verse cease altogether. Side by side with the regular meter of Romance origin, which took upon itself the character of the standard literary meter, a corrupted form of the older alliterative long line continued to be used, especially as the meter appropriate to popular and patriotic writing. This popular alliterative meter was cultivated, at least in one or two regions of England, with special enthusiasm in Langland's own day, as evidenced not only by Langland's preference for it, but also by the writings of his contemporary, the unknown but highly accomplished author of *Sir Gawayne and the Green Knight* and other poems.

Structurally the old alliterative long line consisted of two approximately equal half-lines, each with its own independent scansion, which were held together as one line by the possession of a common alliterating sound. Each half-line contained two metrically stressed syllables, sometimes also a third secondarily stressed syllable, and a varying but on the whole rather narrowly limited number of unstressed syllables, the two kinds of syllables being arranged according to a small number of fixed patterns. The alliterating sounds were always the initial sounds of metrically stressed syllables, which at the same time must also bear a logical stress, and each half-line contained at least one, though either or both might contain two. Alliteration other than that between metrically stressed syllables did not count in the metrical scheme, and where it occurs is to be regarded as accidental. It was a fixed rule in this strict system of scansion that the first metrically stressed syllable of the second half-line must bear the alliteration and thus serve as a kind of key-word to the alliterative scheme of the line as a whole.

Many lines will be found in Langland which satisfy the demands of the strict system of Old English alliterative verse. The following, for example, are as regular as any written in the Old English period:

> "And also Job the gentel   what Joye hadde he on erthe,
> How bittere he hit bouhte   as the book telleth!"[9]

Such lines are not uncommon in the poem, but the poet usually preserves the general rhythm of the style without paying much attention to the strict rules of Old English scansion. Sometimes the alliteration is altogether lacking, sometimes it falls on words so lightly stressed that they fail to take their place in the metrical structure of the line. Frequently the two half-lines contain separate and independent alliterating sounds. Many half-lines are found which can be read only with three and sometimes more

[9] Skeat, *Piers the Plowman,* I, 352, Passus XIV, ll. 15-16, C-version.

heavy stresses, and the unstressed syllables are frequently so numerous and so disposed as to destroy altogether the feeling for the few type patterns of scansion characteristic of regular alliterative verse. The result of these various irregularities is to produce a line which often is without strict metrical structure, and when several of these lines come together the effect is not distinguishable from prose with a sprinkling of alliteration. It is true that the swing of the lines in *Piers Plowman* usually carries the reader over these unmetrical passages without a violent sense of interruption. But it is apparent that in the hands of a more careless versifier than Langland the meter would suffer still more and the distinction between prose and verse become completely effaced. As it is, often a slightly unusual order of words is all that distinguishes Langland's verse rhythm from prose rhythm.[10]

The free alliterative line, as treated by Langland, is admirably suited to his somewhat rambling, often turgid and colloquial subject-matter. The style is not that of the scholar or the refined artist. Langland probably never submitted himself to the severe discipline in versification which Chaucer's early experiments in ballades and complaints illustrate. Discipline was not necessary to write the kind of verse he was trying to write. The main requisites were a feeling for rhythm, a vocabulary extensive enough to provide alliterating words, and, finally, volubility of expression.

Perhaps this last is the most persistent and striking characteristic of Langland's style, a characteristic which again connects him with the popular feeling for prose expression. Although many lines of admirable compression occur, they are usually proverbial in tone, or are short sum-

[10] See the long passage in the latest version (C. Passus I, 107-124) in which alliteration has almost completely disappeared.

maries of moral wisdom. The poem is not infrequently powerful, but it attains its effects by a tumultuous heaping of details rather than by the carefully weighed style of a classic artist, like Chaucer, who uses every word with a sense of its fullest effect and meaning. His own moral earnestness and the unfailing gift of a concrete and highly poetic imagination are all that save Langland from falling into rant and bombast. This quality of improvisation in the poem appears throughout in the selection of detail. Everything that came into the author's mind is included, the coarsest pictures of popular life standing side by side with poetical and profoundly spiritual allegorical imagery. Personal allusions abound, to Wat and to Tom Stowe, to Bet and to Beton the brewster, to Hick the hackneyman, and to dozens of others, who may or may not stand for real persons of Langland's acquaintance, but who are effectively real in the poem. Frequent references to places in London, to Cornhill, Westminster, Shoreditch, Southwark, Tyburn, and others, also often lend an air of easy familiarity to the narrative. The speech, even of very dignified characters, is often colored with the colloquialism of conversation. Truth responds to Mercy when the latter expounds the plan of the resurrection, that her story is " bote a tale of Walterot," a piece of nonsense.[11] And the version of the sentiment, *Dentem pro dente, et oculum pro oculo,* which is put into the mouth of the Lord himself, picturesquely declares that whoso hitteth out a man's eye or else his front teeth or maimeth or hurteth any other limb, he shall suffer the same sore.[12]

Langland was fond of making up long fantastic compound names, such as Dame Work-when-time-is, the name of the wife of Piers, or Do-right-so-or-thy-dame-shall-thee-beat, the name of his daughter. Some of these names, as

[11] C. Passus, XXI, 146. [12] Ibid., 386 ff.

for example the name of Piers' son, are several lines in length and so unwieldy as to become grotesque. Picturesque words of popular color occur, and the main difference between the vocabulary of Langland and that of Chaucer consists in the presence of a certain number of outlandish words, as they seem to the modern reader, in the writings of Langland, which have been lost altogether to the language or have fallen from the literary speech to the dialects. Undoubtedly the alliteration, demanding as it does a wide range of vocabulary, is partly responsible for Langland's popular words, alliteration and the popular style naturally going together. Broad picturesque phrases abound, as in the description of Sir Harvey, the covetous man, "bitelbrowed and baberlipped," his beard beslobbered, like a bondman's, with his bacon;[13] or when Langland calls Christ's disciples God's boys, merry-mouthed men, the minstrels of heaven.[14] When occasion calls for them, Langland even uses freely words not to be repeated for modern readers. Plainness of speech is inherent in his mode of thought, and if plainness becomes vulgarity, Langland feels no necessity for apologizing, as Chaucer does when he defends his broad style on the artistic grounds that the manner must be appropriate to the matter. On the other hand, Langland is equally free in introducing learned Latin and French into the body of his narrative, not systematically in the manner of the later Macaronic writing, as in Skelton, but apparently as the fancy struck him.

The spirit of Langland's verse was not that of the school. Although the style was not without its technic, it was a free and easy technic. It called for the readiness and copiousness of the improviser, rather than the care and forethought of the literary artist. If impassioned prose had been possible in his day, Langland might well have chosen

[13] B. Passus V, 190 ff.

[14] C. Passus X, 127-128.

to write in that form, but lacking such a medium, he developed in his free metrical rhythms a form that approaches prose. By means of this form he expressed himself with an astonishing ease and abundance. There is a power in the mere sweep of his thought which would have been impossible in the regular rimed meters of Chaucer. And yet Langland's eloquence seldom reaches the lofty heights of great poetry. His art is crude, grotesque, and unformed, as compared with the art of later masters of the serious style, like Hooker in prose or Milton in verse. Lacking Langland's earnestness of thought, his style in the hands of his successors often degenerated into the blustering, robustious, but formless writing of a host of popular rimesters, pamphleteers, and preachers of the Tudor and Elizabethan periods. Even with Langland, the form of *Piers Plowman* occupied a position of unstable equilibrium between verse and prose, and not infrequently the free alliterative verse of this tradition passed over into popular alliterative prose. In its looseness of form and its picturesqueness and homely vigor this prose resembles the degraded survival of the older alliterative long line known as 'tumbling verse,' and perhaps no better name can be found for it than 'tumbling prose.' With all its crudities, this prose played a not inconspicuous part in the development of literary style in the fifteenth and sixteenth centuries, and more must be said of it later.

The latter half of the fourteenth century presents no writers of equal eminence to Chaucer and Langland. Verse, as has already been pointed out, occupied almost the whole field of literary activity, and such prose as was written had usually an immediate practical or documentary purpose. Simple narration, however, was not beyond the powers of fourteenth-century prose, and the famous *Voiage and Travaile of Sir John Maundevile* and Trevisa's numerous translations, especially his version of Higden's *Polychronicon,* are the best representatives of this naïve and rudimentary prose which had as yet hardly lifted itself to the literary level. The *Voiage and Travaile* is also a translation, preserved in three versions by unknown translators, which are all more or less freely adapted from the French original. Under the guise of a manual of directions for pilgrims making the journey to the Holy Land, the original author or compiler of the work, who also is unknown, really wrote a traveler's book, filled with all manner of picturesque misinformation about man and nature. How much faith the compiler of the book and its translators may have had in the marvelous stories it contained it is difficult to say. Everything is told with a most profound seriousness, equal to that of Defoe or Swift, which gives even the most absurd descriptions an air of verisimilitude. That a fourteenth-century reader would realize to some extent the contrast between the matter and the manner can hardly be questioned, but it is not probable that his attitude in general would be very skeptical. In fact, mixed with the other matters, the book contains a number of Bible stories which can scarcely have been told in any other than a spirit of simple belief. To the modern reader the book seems much more of an artistic feat than it would have seemed to the reader of the time of its compilation. And the same applies to the style in which the narrative is written. The distinguishing characteristic of this style is its utter, its guileless simplicity. The sentences are short and direct, never complex. Few connectives are used and those of the most obvious kind. The words are all familiar and never merely ornamental. The whole tone of the expression is naïve, the language of a grown-up child:

"Also beyonde that Flome, more upward to the Desertes, is a gret Pleyn alle gravelly betwene the Mountaynes; and in that Playn every day at the Sonne risynge begynnen to growe smale Trees, and thei growen til mydday, berynge Frute; but no man dar taken of that Frute, for it is a thing of Fayrye. And aftre mydday thei discrecen and entren ayen in-to the Erthe; so that at the goynge down of the Sonne thei apperen no more; and so thei don every day: and that is a gret marvaylle."[15]

And so it continues, the tone never rising, never falling. The simplicity of the book is the simplicity of nature, not of art. Much of its quaintness is imparted to it by the modern reader who feels keenly the contrast between its childlike and effortless style and the more mature manner of modern English expression. But no such contrast could have been intended in the last quarter of the fourteenth century, and the style is consistent because it reflects the naïve simplicity of the medieval mind.

Though John de Trevisa was an industrious writer, he can scarcely be called a man of letters. A student and fellow of Oxford, he later became chaplain and vicar to Thomas, fourth baron Berkeley, at whose request his various translations were made. These consisted of a translation of Bartholomew de Glanville's *De Proprietatibus Rerum,* of Vegetius' *De Re Militari,* of Ægidius' *De Regimine Principum,* and of various other works interesting to his master, besides the most important of all, a version of Higden's *Polychronicon.* As a preface to the *Polychronicon,* Trevisa composed a *Dialogue between a Lord and a Clerk upon Translation,*[16] in which he discusses interestingly the principles of the art of translation. Diversity of speech, says the lord, has brought it about that men of different nations understand each other "no more than gagling of geese."

[15] Chapter XXVII, Cotton version.

[16] Reprinted in Pollard, *Fifteenth Century Prose and Verse,* pp. 203-208.

Interpreters are therefore necessary, especially out of Latin, in which so many important books are written. The clerk presents various reasons why translations should not be made, one of them being that "a great deal of these books standeth much by holy writ, by holy doctors, and by philosophy," which should not be translated into English. The lord responds with arguments frequently used by the reformers of the sixteenth century, that St. Jerome translated from Hebrew into Latin, that the gospel and the faith must be preached to men who know no Latin, that "English preaching is very translation, and such English preaching is good and needful." The clerk finally sees the necessity of translation, as was fore-ordained, and asks the lord if he would "liefer have a translation of these chronicles in rhyme or in prose?" "In prose," answers the lord, "for commonly prose is more clear than rhyme, more easy and more plain to know and understand."

The translation was accordingly made in prose, carried through and finished on the 18th of April, 1387. "In some place I shall set word for word," says Trevisa,[17] "and active for active, and passive for passive, a-row right as it standeth, without changing of the order of words. But in some place I must change the order of words, and set active for passive and again-ward. And in some place I must set a reason for a word and tell what it meaneth. But for all such changing, the meaning shall stand and not be changed." To this program Trevisa faithfully adhered. His translation is usually close, though not literal, and his additions are few and unimportant. Occasional errors occur, due to misunderstanding of the original Latin. The most notable characteristic of Trevisa's English as compared with the compact and well-constructed Latin of the original, is its looseness of form and its verbosity. A

[17] *Epistle of Sir John Trevisa,* in Pollard, ibid., p. 208.

single English word is seldom allowed to count as the equivalent of a Latin word. The simple Latin phrase of Higden, *in signum quod minoris virtutis est quaerere quam quaesita tueri,* became in Trevisa, "in tokeynge þat þis is lasse maistrie to wynne and to conquere þan it is to kepe and to save þat þat is conquered and i-wonne."[18] The more earnest and the more careful he is, the more cumbersome Trevisa becomes. An unfamiliar allusion always calls for elaboration, as in the following sentence of Higden: *Cujus negotii, velut Daedalini labyrinthi, inextricabilem attendens intricationem, rogata sum veritus attemptare.* This is rendered by Trevisa as follows: "Þoo toke I hede þat þis matir, as laborintus, Dedalus hous, haþ many halkes and hurnes, wonderful weies, wyndynges and wrynkelynges, þat wil nouȝt be unwarled, me schamed and dradde to fynde so grete and so gostliche a bone to graunte."[19] Awkward as this translation of Trevisa's is, however, it is better than that of the later fifteenth-century translator of the *Polychronicon,* who speaks in his Latin English of "the intricacion inextricable of this labor" and of "the obnubilous and clowdy processe of this matter." Trevisa, with all his faults, retains his feeling for native and familiar English. It had not yet occurred to him that English words could be made out of Latin by the simple process of bodily transference. His struggle was to render his original into intelligible English, not to write a high style or to create a new literary vocabulary. His attitude towards English is not that of the Renascence but of the Medieval mind. He uses the language naturally, crudely, laboriously, with no higher quality than occasionally the unconscious and naïve charm of a simple-minded man writing as he speaks.

[18] *Polychronicon,* Roll's Series, I, 233-235.
[19] Ibid., pp. 8-9.

The latter fourteenth century was not, however, without more ambitious writers who attempted to develop a higher literary type of prose than the simple medieval narrative of Maundevile and Trevisa. These experimenters, like the earliest Greek prose stylists, endeavored to raise prose to the literary level by giving it some of the characteristics of verse. Or perhaps it would be truer to say that a kind of prose was derived by abstracting some of the most marked features of verse, leaving something which stood half-way between colloquial discourse and regular verse. An instructive example of this type of English prose is a didactic treatise written about 1357 on the basis of a Latin original by John Thoresby, archbishop of York. The name of the translator, or paraphraser, was John de Taystek (Tavistock?), a monk of St. Mary's Abbey at York, a name which seems to have been corrupted in later transcripts of the text to Gaytrigge, Gaytrik, Gaytringe, and other forms.[20] The treatise was intended to be preached, as a manual of instruction, by parsons and vicars to their parishioners. It has been printed in three versions, one from the official records preserved at York, another from the manuscript of a Wiclifite version of Taystek's translation, and one from a later copy of it. The work treats of the ten commandments, the seven sacraments, the seven deadly sins, the seven virtues, and the seven works of mercy, and similar material, and it serves, so far as content goes, as a good example of popular discourse in the fourteenth century. The most notable stylistic feature of the treatise is its semi-metrical character. The metrical characteristics easily become obscured, however, and in the Wiclifite version many passages pass over into unqualified prose. In

[20] See "Dan Jon Gaytrigge's Sermon," *Religious Pieces in Prose and Verse,* ed. Perry, E.E.T.S., XXVI[a], 1-14; *Lay Folks Catechism,* ed. Simmons and Nolloth, E.E.T.S., CXVIII, 1-99.

the version known as *Dan Jon Gaytrigge's Sermon,* the editors have felt so little the metrical elements in the text that they have simply printed it as prose. There can be no doubt, however, that Taystek in his paraphrase of Thoresby's original intended to produce a style which would be a safe compromise between plain prose and out-and-out verse. The metrical feature which survives most distinctly is the feeling for the cadence of the four-stress long line of alliterative verse. Occasional lines occur which are quite regular in scansion, both with respect to rhythm and alliteration. In general, however, alliteration is not well maintained, and apparently what Taystek endeavored to do was to discard alliteration and retain the general rhythmical structure of the alliterative long line. Rime occurs scarcely at all. Sometimes the rhythm of the line has been satisfied at the expense of an unusual word-order, but otherwise there is little in the text to warn the reader that he is not reading prose but verse. We can scarcely suppose that Taystek refrained from writing his treatise in a more regular verse style either from ignorance or inability. Quite probably he felt that ordinary alliterative verse, familiar to all in secular romance and story, was not appropriate for official instruction in the serious concerns of the religious life. And to have spoken to his audience merely as man to man, in the language of daily communication, was of course not to be thought of. It would be vain to seek for evidences of a genuinely creative attitude towards prose style in so crude a stylist as Taystek. To the worn-down verse which he employed, he added nothing in the way of stylistic ornament, except perhaps the frequent use of synonymous word-pairs, such as *of witt and of wisdome* (p. 2), *withouten travaile or trey* (p. 4), *to knowe and to kun* (p. 4), *comandes and biddes* (p. 20), *ordayned and bidden* (p. 22), *hiding or helyng* (p. 50).

This was a trick of style not unknown to prose writers of the Old English period, and one which became almost a constant feature of oratorical and artistic prose of the fifteenth and sixteenth centuries. Needless to say these word-pairs were used because of their appropriateness to the rotund oratorical style which the various writers affected, not at all for the sake of logical clearness or with any theories of the etymological origins of the words thus paired.

A much more skillful writer of prose and of prose poetry than Taystek was Richard Rolle, called of Hampole from the place of his death and burial. Although Richard Rolle died in the year 1349 at about the age of fifty, his influence was especially strong in the last quarter of the fourteenth century. At that time a revival of his fame took place, and with the popular growth of interest in religion and theology, Rolle was annexed by the reformers to their party. In one of the transcriptions of Rolle's English Psalter, dating from this time, the writer complains that the Psalter has been Lollardized and thus "ymped in with eresy." Various disciples who followed Rolle's methods in writing became active in the last quarter of the century. Of these the most important were William Nassyngton, Walter Hylton, and Juliana of Norwich. Doubtless there were other members of this group whose names have been lost, and whose works, if they have survived, are not distinguishable from the writings of the better known representatives of the school.[21]

Rolle began his career in a dramatic manner. He had left Oxford at the age of nineteen, having spent his time

[21] See Horstman, *Richard Rolle of Hampole and his followers*, I, 1895, II, 1896. The contents of these two volumes are in need of sifting in order to determine their authorship, but however numerous the authors may be, they are all of the school of Hampole.

there mainly in the study of the Bible and having become dissatisfied with the scholasticism which at that time held sway in the university. He returned home, and shortly after, dressing himself up in a costume made from a white and a gray gown of his sister's and a hood of his father's, and frightening off his sister, who thought that he had gone mad, he ran away and became a hermit. For the rest of his life Rolle led the life of a recluse, occupying himself with preaching, writing, and meditation, and according to his own testimony, passing through the various formal stages of mystical experience. He was not in holy orders, was not a priest or a monk, and though his whole life was passed in pious and religious activities, in the eyes of the church he was a layman. At first he appears to have attempted to spread his views by oral preaching, but perhaps he was limited in these endeavors because he was not a priest and so could not preach from church pulpits. Quite probably, however, he preached anyway, very much as Wiclif's poor priests did later, speaking to the people wherever he found them. Later he turned to writing, and in the composition both of verse and of prose treatises, he seems to have found a congenial and effective mode of expression.

As a thinker, Rolle makes no pretensions to a philosophic system. "His system is religious life, not theory." [22] His prose pieces, consisting of prayers, meditations, sentences, epistles, tracts, translations from Bonaventura, Richard of St. Victor, and other mystics, are generally structureless and unrelated to each other, except as they all breathe the same feeling of pious and fervid devotion. The longer pieces are made up merely of a succession of spiritual reflections and ejaculations, especially on divine love. Few allusions to contemporary life occur, and the

[22] Horstman, II, xiv.

satirical note is altogether absent. Rolle has little of the righteous indignation of the reformer, and though the punishments of hell are eloquently described, his most frequent subject is the love of God.

It was a fervid and lyrical temperament which Rolle brought with him to the composition of his prose. His feeling for prose was by no means artless, although on the other hand, the use of his various devices of style is not persistent and regular enough to give him a carefully thought out and consistent style. At times he wrote quite simply. One of his most popular tracts was his *Form of Perfect Living,* addressed to Margaret, an anchoress, who was Rolle's disciple and with whom he seems to have enjoyed much spiritual communion. The tract recounts the various temptations to which one leading the lonely life of the hermit is subjected and also the ways by which the perfect love of God may be attained. Now thou hast heard, he says, a part of the subtle crafts of the devil, and if thou wilt thou shalt destroy his traps, and 'burn in the fire of love all the bands that he would bind thee with.'[23] 'For that thou hast forsaken the solace and the joy of this world, and taken thee to solitary life, for God's love to suffer tribulation and anguish here, and sithen [afterwards] come to that bliss that nevermore blins [ceases]: I trow truly that the comfort of Jesus Christ and the sweetness of his love, with the fire of the Holy Ghost that purges all sin, shall be in thee and with thee, how thou shalt think, how thou shalt pray, what thou shalt work, so that in a few years thou shalt have more delight to be alone and speak to thy love and to thy spouse Jesus Christ, that high is in heaven, than if thou were lady here of a thousand worlds.' Many suppose, he continues, that we hermits

[23] Vol. I, 9. The modernization is literal, as in all passages within single quotation marks.

are in pain and great penance. 'They see our body, but they see not our heart, where our solace is. If they saw that, many of them would forsake all that they have, for to follow us.' The love of God is the perfection of the religious life. 'Amore langueo. These two words are written in the book of love, that is called the song of love, or the song of songs.' The special gift of the solitary is to love God. 'In heaven the angels that are most burning in love are nearest God.'[24] 'If thou love him mickle, mickle joy and sweetness and burning thou feelest, that is thy comfort and strength, night and day.'[25]

The *Form of Perfect Living* is an example of Rolle's simpler prose style, the purpose of it being mainly expositional. Even here, however, there is considerable alliteration, some use of the metrical cadences of the long line, of oratorical, ejaculatory devices, in short a general tendency to fall into a dithyrambic kind of expression suited to the mood of the prose-poet. The sentences often have a fullness and roundness of phrasing which remind one of the cadences of later liturgical literature. Always one feels that Rolle's written style is merely a transference of the impassioned expression of the orator to the more permanent record of the manuscript page.

More characteristic of Rolle's popular style in its admixture of prose and verse is the tract *Ego dormio et cor meum vigilat.*[26] In general this tract is similar in method to Taystek's sermon, and is representative of a kind of preaching and writing which Wiclif expressly condemned. At times, passages can be scanned as alliterative verse, though the piece is intended in the main to be prose. It is a disquisition, a kind of rhapsody, on divine love, and naturally the subject lends itself to a more lyric treatment than the *Form of Perfect Living:*

[24] P. 29. [25] P. 30. [26] Vol. I, 49-61.

"All perisches & passes þat we with eghe see. It wanes in to wrechednes, þe welth of þis worlde. Robes & ritches rotes in dike. Prowde payntyng slakes in to sorow. Delites & drewryse stynk sal ful sone. Þaire golde & þaire tresoure drawes þam til dede. Al þe wikked of þis worlde drawes til a dale, þat þai may se þare sorowyng whare waa es ever stabel. Bot he may syng of solace þat lufed Jhesu Criste: þe wretchesse fra wele falles in to hell." [27]

The tract continues with a passage of plain exposition in a more normal prose style, until it reaches a *Meditatio de passione Cristi,* where it again breaks out into a kind of rimed prose.

From the point of view of ingenuity of technic Rolle is without question the most effective writer of prose in the fourteenth century, though it cannot be said that he accomplished much in the development of a practicable art of prose style. The distinction between prose and verse is not clearly maintained by him, and of prose dignified by thought and wisdom, he had no conception. Good English prose has generally appealed primarily to the reason, but Rolle's appeal is almost altogether to emotion. When his prose is normal it is least distinguished. It is only when his heart is kindled by the fire of love that a kind of vatic enthusiasm colors and exalts his expression, and at the same time lifts it into regions where only those equally inspired can follow him.

One further experiment in the writing of artistic prose in this period must be noted. This is Thomas Usk's *Testament of Love,*[28] made about 1387, and formerly often attributed to Chaucer. The treatise is in fact based upon Chaucer's translation of Boethius, and is an attempt to

[27] Vol. I, 53.
[28] See Skeat, *Chaucerian and other Pieces,* pp. 1-45.

give a testament, or witness, of the divine love in relation to a symbolic Margaret, the pearl beyond all price, who stands for various ideas, the Church, the grace of God, and others. The author of the treatise endeavored to write mystically, but being without genuine mystical fervor, he succeeded merely in furnishing an instructive illustration of what must happen when an uninspired writer tries to write an inspired style. Usk comments in some detail on his own theories of style. Many men, he says, so much swallow the deliciousness of gests and of rime by quaint knitting colors,[29] that they take little heed of the goodness or badness of the thought. But such craft of enditing, he continues, will not be of my acquaintance. He puts his trust in "rude wordes and boystous." Many delight in French and Latin, but Englishmen will do better to write in English, for "the understanding of Englishmen wol not strecche to the privy termes in Frenche, what-so-ever we bosten of straunge langage."[30] He frequently speaks of his 'lewdness,' and his desire to write plainly in order to be easily understood. The reader of his *Testament* soon realizes, however, that this is all false modesty and affectation of simplicity, for the style of the work is highly artificial and ambitious. Although there is some use of alliteration, of rime, of puns, of violent antitheses, and of ingenious figures, Usk depends mainly for his stylistic effects upon an obscure and tortuous form of expression, derived apparently by taking the crudities of word-order and of unidiomatic phrasing found in Chaucer's *Boece* (and due there merely to Chaucer's difficulty in rendering the text of his original) and making these inadequacies of the *Boece* the marks of his own distinction of style. That Usk was striving after a literary prose style is apparent. He deserves some credit for rejecting the dithyrambic

[29] P. 1.

[30] P. 2.

style of Rolle, but his own style, though different, is little better. His theme he felt to be lofty, but without a genuine or deep desire to express himself truly and lacking a model to follow, he invented a literary prose which saved itself from being merely colloquial and natural by being unidiomatic and unintelligible.

II

WICLIF

Wiclif's Career—Latin Writings—Theories of Prose Style—English Works—Literary Technic

In the survey of Wiclif's life, the first feeling is one of disappointment at its seeming futility. Though he stands as the representative English scholar and thinker of the latter half of the fourteenth century, what he accomplished for his immediate generation seems very little. His life was, in Milton's phrase, "but a short blaze, soon damped and stifled."[1] He wrote no great works, he achieved no apparent and dramatic reforms, only once or twice does he appear in the arena of the higher public life of his day. And after his death when civil and ecclesiastical authority had done its best to destroy the seeds of his teaching, it might well have seemed to a contemporary that Wiclif belonged to that class of ephemerally troublesome spirits, the Wat Tylers, the John Balls of the time, who fought their brief fight against the world and then were swallowed up by it. Only a later generation could see that the defeat was but apparent, and that at the pure flame of Wiclif's life "all the succeeding reformers more effectually lighted their tapers."[2]

Wiclif received the benefit of the best intellectual training of his day. Born about the year 1320, he became in

[1] "Of Reformation in England," *Prose Works,* ed. Symmons, I, 4.
[2] Ibid.

due time a student at Oxford University, perhaps in Balliol College, of which college he was later made master. The greater part of his life was passed at Oxford, in teaching and preaching before large bodies of students. On several occasions he took part in the public affairs of the time, but then as the ally of John of Gaunt and others, rather than as an independent leader. But Wiclif's life, though that of the scholar, was by no means the life of the hermit or recluse. He was not a mystic, nor was Oxford in Wiclif's day, still under the spell of the scholastic philosophy, a congenial place for the development of mysticism. It was a stirring life that Wiclif led and one that brought him into close contact with the living issues of the time. For the most part he appears to have been permitted to express his views without restraint. Indeed it was not until the later years of his life that he passed from criticism of the abuses of the church to hostility towards the pope himself and the whole system of the ecclesiastical hierarchy. After the election of the two popes in 1378, Urban VI and the anti-pope Clement VII, Wiclif's hostility towards papal authority was intensified. It was about this time, also, that his opposition to the friars led to the organization of his informal order of "poor priests," in a way a new order of friars who were to live and teach according to the rules which the friars were supposed to follow. A few years earlier, in 1374, Wiclif had received a Crown appointment to the rectory of Lutterworth, in Leicestershire, and here he went to live altogether when in 1382 he was expelled from the University of Oxford. His heretical opinions, especially his denial of that mystery of mysteries, the doctrine of transubstantiation, separated him more completely than ever from the traditional and conservative party both in church and state during the last five or six years of his life. So far as the English authorities are concerned, he seems to have been allowed to dwell at Lutterworth in peace. He was cited to Rome, however, to answer the charges of heresy preferred against him, but his physical infirmities made such a journey impossible, and he died on December 31, 1384, without ever having been actually excommunicated.

The motive power of Wiclif's life was a strong personal sense of justice, guided and supported by a powerful and fearless logic. Although he was trained in and himself followed the system of scholasticism, Wiclif was not dominated by it. On the contrary, he used his scholastic methods to make more effective his own personal convictions. This is not the place to discuss in detail what these convictions were, how he began with the arraignment of the patent abuses of ecclesiastical authority and privilege, how his hostility to the older religious orders led to a new and profound conception of the rights of property and dominion, of the inter-relation of civil and ecclesiastical authority, of the control which one person may exert over the conscience of another, in short to the elaboration of a system of Christian democracy far in advance of even the enlightened opinion of his own day. The general trend of his teaching was to discount the authority of priests and officially designated directors of the spiritual life. A priest who preaches good doctrine and does not follow it in practice, so he says in his *Opus Evangelicum,* is like a cow that gives plenty of good milk but immediately afterward kicks over the milking-pail. The futility of faith without works and of merely formal ceremonies was one of his strongest convictions. His theology thus had always a distinctly practical side. In the later years of his life, when he had passed beyond the authority of the pope and beyond the control of his patron, John of Gaunt, these doctrines were preached with an apostolic fervor and directness which lift Wiclif far above the level of the mere logician and philosopher, or even that of the practical reformer. His vision became that of the prophet, and thus ceased to be the program of the practical statesman.

The attempt to find the real test of the worth of a man from within, to establish the standard of truth in the individual's personal sincerity was not only novel, but also heretical teaching in the fourteenth century. It is not remarkable, therefore, that as Wiclif's views became more and more positive, he found himself compelled to break completely with the official party in church and state. In the hope of finding a more fertile soil for his teaching, he was impelled to address himself to the humbler people of England whose minds were not bound by interest and privilege to the established order of society. It was the necessity of reaching this humbler public that caused Wiclif to reflect on the capabilities of language for exposition and argument, and for the first time in the history of the English people, to exemplify the ideal of an honest man speaking his convictions on questions of conduct and belief without authorization from official sources and in plain language, intelligible to all men.

During the years of his activity as teacher and preacher at Oxford, Wiclif naturally wrote in Latin, the established language of learning and theology in the time. He wrote abundantly, his extant Latin works consisting of several hundred short sermons and a number of longer essays and treatises. His only attempts at what might be called an artistic form in Latin are his dialogues, and even these betray some impatience with the limitations which literary form may place upon the free expression of the mind of the writer. His first treatise in the form of dialogue was his *Speculum Ecclesie Militantis,*[3] in which the speakers are

[3] Edited by A. W. Pollard, London, 1886.

Veritas and Mendacium, the first supposed to stand for Christ and the second for the Devil. At the beginning of the first chapter Wiclif remarks that he makes use of dialogue because many persons take pleasure in *loquela dialogi*. In fact, however, the dialogue soon ceases to have any dramatic significance. In the first three chapters the characters speak with some respect to the parts which they are supposed to take, but after that "Veritas is Wiclif and Wiclif only, and we have him frequently professing the purity of his motives and his readiness to confront the Pope or to endure persecution for the truth." [4] Mendacium in the same way becomes merely a mouthpiece for stating the existing abuses of the church, a man of straw, frequently, for Wiclif to knock down. Veritas soliloquizes often at inordinate length. His opening speech fills fourteen pages, and his last three speeches are nine, four and eleven pages long, while Mendacium is allowed only short speeches. The *Trialogus* [5] is another of Wiclif's experiments in what might be called a dramatic form. He again comments on the greater interest of discussions in which concrete persons are supposed to take part as compared with general and impersonal address, and describes the persons of his *Trialogus* as Alithia, a *solidus philosophus,* Pseustis, *infidelis captiosus,* and Phronesis, *subtilis theologus et maturus*. The work, which was very popular, is a compendium of theological doctrine, but practically no attempt is made to put dramatic life into it. The speakers are not given character, the speeches frequently run through pages without interruption, and to all intents, are nothing more than paragraph divisions. Wiclif never attempted the dialogue form in English, and the examples of it in Latin are interesting mainly as showing how little his mind concerned itself with artistic literary form. They followed the

[4] Pollard, ibid., p. vi.

[5] Edited by Lechler, Oxford, 1867.

traditions of the lifeless medieval dialogue and owe nothing to Plato or Cicero, or even to contemporary colloquial discourse.[6] In the minor technical details of expression also, Wiclif cultivated a natural and unornamented rather than an artificial style. From the time of Tertullian, theological discussion and preaching had made use of a highly ingenious prose rhetoric, based mainly on antithesis and balance in phrasing, the use of alliteration, rime, and punning, and of various other formal devices derived ultimately from the Greek rhetoric of Gorgias and his successors. All this literary artifice, which even affected early attempts to write prose in the vernacular and which was certainly highly admired by most medieval Latinists, Wiclif expressly rejected in theory and never illustrated in practice.[7]

Of the Latin *Sermones* of Wiclif, some two hundred are extant.[8] They were evidently composed for a general but learned public, and many of them were doubtless delivered at Oxford, probably at St. Mary's, where Wiclif often preached. Most of the sermons date from a rather late period of Wiclif's life, and those that were of earlier composition are more or less revised. It was probably during the last five years of his life that Wiclif collected and revised the sermons. His reasons for doing so are given in an interesting *Praefatio* in which he says that now at the end of his days, being freed from academic occupations and desiring to employ his leisure to the advantage of the

[6] Wiclif agrees with the frequently expressed medieval opinion that the first element in the word *dialogue* means two, and that therefore a dialogue is a conversation between two persons. On the analogy of this interpretation, he invented his title *Trialogus,* a discussion in which three take part.

[7] For a fuller statement of the technical development of Latin Christian prose in the Middle Ages, reference must be made to Norden, *Die Antike Kunstprosa,* pp. 512 ff.

[8] Edited by Loserth, 4 vols., London, 1887-1890.

church, he has collected his *sermones rudes ad populum* in order that all that is in them accordant to the true teaching of Christ may be approved and all that varies from the catholic truth may be rejected. The collection was evidently intended, as were Wiclif's English sermons written about the same time, to serve as models for other preachers, and it is so arranged, according to the calendar, as to provide a sermon for each important feast of the year. Wiclif thus composed a book to take the place of the popular festival books of his day, the legendaries and collections of exempla and anecdotes against the use of which he constantly preached. For though Wiclif calls his sermons rude and popular, the description applies only in the sense that he strove to present in them definite instruction for the people, not to amuse and distract them by literary artifice or with tales of wonder and romantic adventure.

The *Sermones* are deserving of special consideration, for in them Wiclif has set forth more fully and frankly than elsewhere his theories of the art of preaching and of the art of literary composition in general. Preaching is frequently recommended, in a way that reminds one of the later Puritans, as the first and most important duty of the pastor. With equal positiveness, Wiclif insists that the preaching must be adapted to the needs of the hearers.[9] What the preacher requires is above all a sincere desire in his heart to help the people. He must avoid the *pomposam eloquenciam* of the grammarian.[10] And the subtleties of logic, the laborious observations of natural philosophy, and the demonstrations of mathematics are all useless to him.[11] All he need know is the life, the teaching, and the acts of Christ. Too much learning is not to be imported into

[9] See *Sermones*, I, 35, 107, 128, 130, 133, 197; II, 79.
[10] Ibid., I, 209.
[11] Ibid., II, 18.

the study of the scriptures. Christ and his apostles, *hominum sapientissimi,* did not insist on any such learning, which indeed savors too much of curiousness and pride. Let us know the sacred scriptures and nothing beyond them, says Wiclif, for thereby man's spiritual life is regulated.[12] Many books indeed might well be destroyed, the New Testament remaining, for then priests, imitating Christ, might the more effectively preach the truths contained within these books.[13]

To this theme of the necessity of simplicity and sincerity, Wiclif returns again and again. Rhetoric is not needed by the preacher, however pleasing it may be to him and his audience,[14] for the preacher must not preach for his own honor or profit, or pay too much heed to what is merely pleasing to his audience.[15] On the contrary the preacher must speak plainly at all times, and even follow Christ's boldness in reproving when necessary.[16] Prelates must not allow themselves by reason of their high station to lose patience with the people or to become chilled by the wind of pomp which blows upon them. The people think that a high mountainous place is warmer because it is nearer the sun, whereas in truth it is colder for that reason.[17]

In one of the *Sermones,* on the text *Semen est verbum dei,* Wiclif entered into a more specific statement of his views on preaching and on the proper style in writing. Christ often taught in parables, the sermon begins, and of all the parables none is better suited for instructing the people than the parable of the sower. From this text Wiclif de-

[12] *Sapiamus ergo scripturam sacram et nichil extra illam, cum in hoc consistit sobrietas hominis spiritualis, Sermones,* III, 83.

[13] Ibid., III, 265.

[14] Ibid., II, 230-231.

[15] Ibid., II, 279, 448.

[16] Ibid., I, 281.

[17] Ibid., II, 220.

rives, in scholastic fashion, three themes for the edification of his hearers.[18] The first concerns the nature of the seed, the second of the sower, and the third the results of the sowing. The word is the seed, and it has as its material nature, the voice of the preacher. In it there resides a certain seminal power given from above capable of producing a new creature, by which Wiclif means the new man, in the hearts of the hearers. But the effectiveness of the word is impaired nowadays by the abuse of the material (that is of the manner of preaching), which becomes thus the seed of death rather than of life. For the preacher now preaches not the words of God, but gests, poems, and fables; or if he preaches the sacred scripture, he first dismembers it and then binds it up again by means of rhythmical ornament so that it seems no longer the text of the scripture but the very speech of the preacher himself and his own invention. Various excuses are given by such preachers for these novelties. Some say that if you do not admit certain artifices of speech, it will be impossible to distinguish between the preaching of the subtle theologian and that of the ignorant country priest.[19] But it is mere vain-glory, Wiclif declares, to seek after rhetorical distinctions and curious weavings of words, in order that the preacher may be considered ingenious by his audience.

A second excuse often made for the ornamental style was that it is a law of nature that the forms of things should be accordant to the matter. Since then the matter of theology is the most perfect of all, it should be given the most noble and the most beautiful form. This must be

[18] His words show that he was addressing a band of his priests: *Ex quibus verbis elicio michi tria fraternitati vestre per ordinem declaranda, Sermones,* IV, 263.

[19] *Inter theologum quantumcunque subtilem in seminando verbum Dei et sacerdotem ruralem quantum libet exiliter literatum, Sermones,* IV, 266.

done by means of rhetorical ornament and of rhythmical combinations, for so, these authors say, eloquence perfects wisdom. But such arguments, answers Wiclif, are erroneous. They are wrong because those who defend them assume that the form of wisdom consists in the beauty of words, and that they speak wisdom, which comes from God alone, when they affect a meretricious form. All this is nothing other than adulteration of the word of God.[20] 'What else is it, I ask, but adulteration of the word of God, when the preacher wraps himself in cloaks and other meretricious ornaments, extraneous to the scripture, and employed for his own ostentatious delight and to the destruction of the flower and the fruit of preaching, which is the honor of God and the conversion of our fellow man? And what is sincere speaking, except to utter the truth which edifies with clear intention, plainly and aptly?'[21] Still another excuse offered for fine style was that certain books of the Bible are in meter, and why not also sermons? To this Wiclif answers that it is one thing to sing a song of praise or a prophecy and another thing to set forth the words of an exhortation. Ornaments of style obscure the understanding of the thought, for the hearer, perceiving the author's intentness on his meter, pays more heed to the sensible signs of the thought than to those things for which the signs stand. Like those listening to musical melodies, for the most part the audience of a popular preacher carry nothing away with them except the tickling delight of the moment, unless perchance the cleverness of the preacher calls forth also their windy praises.

Philosophy teaches us, says Wiclif in conclusion of this part of the sermon, that the most effective means to an end are the ones properly to be employed. Since the sowing of the word of God is the means ordained for the

[20] II Cor. ii, 17.

[21] *Sermones,* IV, 267-268.

honor of God and the instruction of mankind, it follows that the more compendiously and fully this is done, the more suitable it is; and since there can be no doubt that plain speech on all that concerns the salvation of man is the most effective, it follows that plain speech should be used and all heroical declamation set aside. Of all the works of the militant church, the faithful sowing of the seed is the one most pleasing to God, and so, on the other hand, fraud in the sowing of the seed is most harmful, and in consequence, most hateful in the sight of God.[22]

Thus fully and clearly Wiclif presented the fundamental principles of prose discourse. That he should look at the matter mainly from the point of view of spoken language was inevitable in his day. But the principles which he has so clearly and so completely stated are intended to apply equally to all forms, spoken or written, of literary prose composition. At bottom Wiclif's demand is that prose shall be addressed primarily to man's reasonable understanding. He distinguishes clearly and firmly between verse and its conventions, which indeed he allows in their proper place, and the fitting means which prose must use to attain its ends. He raises the standard of the honest man trying first of all to express himself sincerely, to find the measure of truth not in artifice and external ornament, but in his own inner sense of conviction. If he is true to himself, he need not be greatly concerned about what others think of his efforts.[23] On the other hand Wiclif does not neglect the just demands which the author's public may make upon him. Discourse which is not adapted to attain its end is bad. The task of the author is to express himself sincerely, and at the same time effectively and persuasively. Later generations of ingenious experimenters sometimes disregarded the principles which Wiclif has here laid down,

[22] *Sermones,* IV, 270-271.

[23] Ibid., II, 279.

have obscured the distinctions between prose and poetry, and have made the art of prose to consist merely in the art of pleasing; but in the main Wiclif's principles, doubtless set forth many a time to his disciples, have persisted from Wiclif's time to the present day. English prose, through all its changes, has always demanded a basis of truth and plain reason, and its highest forms have always resulted from the efforts of honest and sincere men to address plainly and convincingly an audience of their equals and fellow-men.

Although Wiclif wrote abundantly in English, he never attained the same degree of skill in the management of his native tongue as he had acquired through long years of experience in the writing of Latin. His early, and his more learned works in general, were all written in Latin, the strong, easy, free medieval Latin of his day. Later in life, as his attention and hopes centered on the people and their support, Wiclif made use of English, partly perhaps because Chaucer, Gower, Langland, and others were making English better known as a literary language, but mainly because he attached himself more and more closely to the strong national movement of the times and because his own interests and the appeal which he wished to make were becoming less scholastic and academic and increasingly popular. The success of the contemporary English translation of the scriptures, which will be discussed in a later chapter, may also have encouraged him in the use of the vernacular. But the use of the native idiom was a logical and necessary consequent of Wiclif's opinions, and all through his writings he defends the use of English not only for purposes of preaching and popular teaching, but also as the language of the services of the church, of the Bible, and of instruction in theological doctrine. That Wiclif found some difficulty in expressing himself in

English is evident not only from his writing but also from his own statement. In a passage in which he answers certain questions on the nature of the love of God, he remarks that it is hard to answer these questions truly in English, but that 'charity drives men to tell them somewhat in English so that men may best know by this English what is God's will.'[24] He realized the difficulty of his task, and the imperfection of his execution of it. He wrote in English not for his own satisfaction, but because charity towards his fellow-men drove him to tell them what he could in their native tongue.

The authorship of the English writings attributed to Wiclif is not always definitely determinable. Owing to the uncritical habit which scholars and historians of the fourteenth century have had of attributing all writings of Wiclifean color to Wiclif himself, many texts have certainly been assigned to him which he did not write. As a matter of fact there must have been a considerable school of writers who followed in general Wiclif's method, but who in many instances made use of devices of style never found in the certain works of Wiclif.[25] Of the assured writings of Wiclif, the most considerable body is to be found in his English sermons, and in a number of miscellaneous treatises which may be extracted from a medley of writings of various origin which his editors have assigned to him.[26] From these sermons and treatises one may form an adequate conception of Wiclif's methods and

[24] Arnold, *Select English Works,* III, 183.

[25] For some discussion of the canon of Wiclif's writings, see an essay by E. D. Jones, in *Anglia,* XXX.

[26] The sermons are published in Arnold's *Select English Works of John Wyclif,* Oxford, 1871, 3 vols., especially Vols. I and II; other treatises appear in Matthew's *English Works of Wyclif, hitherto unprinted,* London, 1880. E.E.T.S., LXXIV.

ability as a writer of English. Though not so numerous as the surviving Latin sermons, the English sermons resemble the Latin in purpose and content. They are almost exclusively expositional, argumentative, or invective in character, never meditative or lyric, ejaculatory or hortatory. There is little expression of Richard Rolle's favorite theme, the love of God, and not much of the terror of him. The evangelical side of the religious life is on the whole slightly represented in Wiclif. On the other hand, he frequently delays to discuss scientific or learned matters, as for example the nature of thunder,[27] or of salt,[28] although these digressions are less extensive in the English than they are in the Latin sermons. His method is usually to begin with a text, given in Latin and translated into English, then to explain the literal meaning of the text, then its spiritual significance. The sermon ends often with an application of the text, especially to the friars, whose faults Wiclif never tires of describing. Sometimes the sermon closes with what Wiclif calls an elucidation of the doubts, that is, a discussion of the various ideas suggested by the sermon, and Wiclif frequently shows his good sense by dismissing subtleties or uncertainties or insignificant matters by saying that it is not worth while spending time over them. Sometimes the sermons are not fully developed, but are preserved only as suggestive notes for further elaboration. That they were intended to serve as model sermons, doubtless for the poor priests, is shown by the fact that Wiclif frequently gives direct instructions to preachers. "In this Gospel," he says, "may priests tell of fals pride of riche men"; [29] or again, "Here may men touche of alle manner of sin"; [30] or, "Here after this wit [interpretation] men may large this Gospel and treat what matter that they ween should profit

[27] Arnold, I, 186.
[28] Ibid., I, 266.
[29] Ibid., I, 3.
[30] Ibid., I, 6.

to the people." [31] The sermons are, therefore, intended as a kind of *liber festivalis,* like the Latin *sermones,* to be used by the poor priests in place of similar books prepared by the friars.

The themes of the Latin sermons recur in the English writings. Wiclif's bitter hostility towards the friars has already been mentioned. He frequently preaches against warfare and civil dissension, charging the prelates with assuming temporal authority in order to encourage and to participate in warfare.[32] But the priest, though he must be peaceful, need not always be mild. Scornful words and 'snibbing' are permitted by the example of Christ, as well as of Paul and others. 'But it is said commonly that three things are hard to men, to scorn meedfully, or meedfully plead with men, or else to fight with man, by the way of charity. But all this may be done, as wise men think. But for they are perilous, many men suppose that Christ used them never, but went the king's highway.' [33] As Wiclif points out, snibbing is prevented in the 'orders' (that is, the orders of the friars), because when one reproves them, the friars say they have a superior to whom reproof belongs; one brother may not freely reprove another, but only the superior may reprove. To this Wiclif objects that 'Christ reproved where most was need, and so should men do to-day.' [34] Wiclif availed himself frequently of this

[31] Arnold, I, 133.
[32] See Arnold, II, 43, 44, 166, 190, and frequently elsewhere.
[33] Ibid., I, 114; see also II, 76.
[34] Ibid., II, 202. Cf. Chaucer's 'poor priest' in the Canterbury Tales, Prolog, ll. 519-523:

> "To drawen folk to heven by fairnesse
> By good ensample was his besinesse:
> But it were any persone obstinat,
> What-so he were, of high or lowe estat,
> Him wolde he snibben sharply for the nones."

Cf. also Chaucer's *Gentilesse* as an expression of possible Wiclifean or Lollard doctrine.

privilege of freedom of speech, which appears to be here for the first time in the history of the English people openly and fully defended. And as one finds in examining the history of Lollardy, his successors were no less slow in seizing their opportunity. Freedom of speech, with the popular Bible-men and Lollard enthusiasts of the early fifteenth century often degenerated into license of speech, but a new privilege is almost certain to be abused before it is properly used, and perhaps the world to-day has not fully learned how to 'fight with man by the way of charity.'

Wiclif earnestly advises his hearers to stick to the Gospel. The love that Christ taught is enough for this life.[35] 'To some men it pleaseth to tell the tales that they find in saints' lives or without Holy Writ, and such things please often more the people. But we hold this manner good,—to leave such words and trust in God, and tell surely his law, and specially his Gospels; for we know that they came of Christ, and so God saith them all. . . . And thus these feasts of these saints have this good beside other, that men may well tell in them the understanding of the Gospel.'[36] The use of English Wiclif defends in the English sermons with a broad common sense which Tindale, Cranmer, and the other reformers of the sixteenth century scarcely surpassed. Truth consists not in words but in wit, that is, in the understanding. 'Whoever liveth best, teacheth best, pleaseth most God, of what language ever he be.'[37] As the Holy Ghost gave to the apostles the gift of tongues at Pentecost, so God desires that the law be taught in different languages. St. Jerome translated the Bible into Latin so that it might be afterwards translated into other tongues. The French have a translation of the Bible and Gospels into French. Why should not the English have one

[35] Arnold, I, 310. [36] Ibid., I, 332. [37] Ibid., III, 98.

in their own language? As the lords of England have this Bible in French, so it is not unreasonable that the people should have the same in English. Even the friars in England have taught the Pater Noster in English, as for example, in the play of York; and since the Pater Noster is part of St. Matthew's Gospel, why not turn the whole Gospel into English? Mistakes may be made in translating into English, but so may there be in translating from Hebrew into Greek, or Greek into Latin. Study alone will prevent error.[38]

The general tone of Wiclif's English writing is simple, and Wiclif frequently declares that he is striving to write simply. But as has already been pointed out, the sermons are not popular in the usual manner of medieval sermons. The stock exempla of sermonizing are altogether lacking, and there is very little exhortation. Scripture texts are quoted sparingly, and the fathers and the authorities still less frequently. Each sermon is a compact and unified discussion of a single theme, not generally dry and scholastic, though logical and psychological subtleties sometimes appear in spite of Wiclif's endeavor to avoid them. The references to current life are numerous, though explicit mention of persons is not often made. Wiclif makes little effort to be eloquent, his most spirited passages being his invectives against the friars. He is without humor, except occasionally a grim kind of irony, as, for example, when he explains why Christ loved fishermen more than hunters. Fishermen, he says, are humbler men than hunters, hunting being a "more gentil craft," and being humbler, fishers are nearer the state of innocence than hunters. Gentlemen, he

[38] Matthew, *English Works,* pp. 429-430. The treatise, *De Officio Pastorali,* from which this defense of English is taken, is a free English version of one of Wiclif's Latin tracts, but it is uncertain whether the translation was made by Wiclif himself.

notes regretfully, often hunt even in Lent. Moreover the flesh of fish is nearer the elements and not so like to man's flesh, and 'thus fish is nearer to meat that man should have in Paradise, and slaying of fish is farther from slaying of men than is slaying of earthly beasts.' But the friars have no scruples against slaying of beasts, and (by implication) none against slaying of men. And now there is used a 'new craft to slay men commonly' (gunpowder?), and priests especially are to use this craft, since they are to be lords over men. 'But what men they should kill, whether their brethren or aliens, they hold yet in their purse, although they practice on their brethren. But this people (i.e. the friars) is wide scattered,—some in England and some without. And these more friars without say that men should kill English; and so less error at the beginning groweth to mickle and perilous.[39] Following the general tradition of his time, Wiclif was much given to the tropological or anagogical interpretation of the scriptures. He insists, as positively as Tindale does later, that the literal sense of the scriptures is the most important and that traditional interpretations and moralizations have no authoritative value. One man's interpretation is as good as another's, and the final appeal must be made in all cases to the letter of the scriptures themselves.[40] But all the scriptures and all the acts of Christ have also a mystical meaning which the preacher may properly search out.[41] Thus the ship into which Christ entered may be understood to signify, according to the mystical sense, the body of the Virgin Mary or Christ's own body which he took from her.[42]

[39] Arnold I, 307-8.

[40] See *Sermones,* I, 83; Arnold, II, 343; *Trialogus,* ed. Lechler, p. 266.

[41] *Sermones,* I, 14.

[42] Ibid., I, 336.

The man sick of the palsy signifies 'unstableness of belief.'[43] These interpretations are often worked out ingeniously and at great length, but obviously they were not regarded by Wiclif as ornaments, not as *grammaticorum pomposam eloquenciam,*[44] but as an essential and valuable part of the scriptures themselves. We shall see them later as medieval survivals, for example in the sermons of Bishop Fisher, cultivated for their own sake.

As to details of expression, one naturally finds in Wiclif's English writings much that is crude and experimental, although on the other hand Wiclif never sinks to the level of Maundevile's naïve and medieval simplicity. His sentences are short but well constructed, and usually have unity. The many-membered, sprawling sentence, found in most early writers of English prose, is not characteristic of Wiclif. The feeling which he had acquired for a varied and logically compact sentence structure in writing Latin was carried over into English when he began to write in his native speech. The logical connections of sentences are also more varied than one usually finds in the simple medieval style, with its monotonous sequence of *ands, whens, thens,* and *buts.* Practically no attempts at ornamental diction of any kind are made by Wiclif. He uses new words only as they are needed to express his thought, never from admiration for fine diction in itself. Even the very general fifteenth and sixteenth century rhetorical device of word-pairs is lacking in Wiclif. He uses no alliteration, except such as is accidental, no heaping or cataloguing passages, none of the popular tricks of the tumbling style characteristic of the oratorical prose discourse of the period. Figures and similes occur frequently, but they always arise naturally from the text. The question of figurative or metaphorical expression, as has already been indicated, was

[43] Arnold, I, 47.

[44] *Sermones,* I, 209.

an important one in Wiclif's eyes, and he frequently distinguishes between 'literal wit' and 'ghostly wit.'[45] He shows none of the rhetorician's interest, however, in the classification of figures of speech.

Even in the expression of new and abstract ideas, Wiclif exercised the scholar's right of invention in matters of vocabulary very sparingly. It is interesting to note that the Wiclifean translation of the Bible contains many more newly borrowed Latin words than Wiclif's English writings, the obvious reasons being that the Latin of the Vulgate offered immediate models for the formation of new English words, and that the text of the Vulgate being regarded as specially sacred, the effort was made to translate it into English with as little change as possible. The general feeling, however, that English as a language ought to be elevated and enriched by the consistent borrowing of words from Latin had not yet arisen in Wiclif's day. On the contrary, Wiclif often stretches an English word to make it express his meaning. He uses *bigginge* (buying) in the sense of 'salvation,' or 'redemption,'[46] and *waishe* (wash) in the sense of 'baptize,'[47] although the words baptize and baptism also frequently occur. The use of *wit,* meaning 'understanding,' 'interpretation,' has already been illustrated in passages quoted. Other examples are *bekenyng,* 'confession,'[48] *boruhed,* 'surety,'[49] *furþerhedis, hynderhedis,* 'things which precede,' 'things which follow.'[50] A constant feature of Wiclif's vocabulary is his fondness for substantives in *-ing,* as for example, 'knowing of the day of doom';[51] 'by chasing (i.e. expulsion) of these fiends';[52] 'after general doing,'[53] and so frequently. The free use of

[45] Arnold, II, 343.
[46] Ibid., I, 69; II, 281.
[47] Ibid., I, 72.
[48] Ibid., II, 79.
[49] Ibid., III, 10.
[50] Ibid., III, 78.
[51] Ibid., II, 407.
[52] Ibid., I, 118.
[53] Ibid., I, 83.

this verbal substantive is directly due to Wiclif's familiarity with Latin, the supine, the gerund, and the verbal noun in *-io* being all represented by words in *-ing*. The motive which led Wiclif to the extensive use of these verbal substantives in *-ing* was the necessity of finding English words that would express the abstract verbal ideas of words like *cognitio, visio,* etc. He might indeed have taken over the Latin words 'cognition,' 'vision,' etc., but this method of language enrichment was commonly employed only after the Renascence. Instead Wiclif preferred to develop a native resource of the language by adapting it to Latin models. Another Latinism frequently to be noticed in Wiclif's English style is the omission of the definite article, not only when he is translating directly from the Latin, but at any time. This feature of style often gives his English an unidiomatic and abrupt appearance, e.g. 'Time of this reaping is clept the day of doom,' [54] or, 'For when winds of men's boast make us to dread of worldly harms, and floods of tribulation come to us, they make us dread and cry on Christ to have help for failing in our belief.' [55] This unidiomatic treatment of the article seems to be due to an unconscious and instinctive imitation of Latin usage on the part of Wiclif, not to any desire to refashion English into a literary language on the basis of Latin models of style.

With Wiclif the sole purpose in the use of words was to be clear and intelligible, and the question which occupied so much of the thought of theologians and translators of the sixteenth century, whether words should be used in their etymological or in their acquired traditional senses, had not yet arisen to trouble the writer and thinker of Wiclif's day.

[54] Arnold, I, 97.

[55] Ibid., I, 94. Other characteristic examples, I, 98, 99, 103, 104, 120, 139, 406; II, 398; III, 160, 175, 180, 203.

With all his endeavor to be simple and clear, however, Wiclif's English vocabulary is not adequate to save him from falling into obscurity. When he wishes to speak of general conduct which serves as a public example, he has only the words 'general doing,' cited above, to express the idea. The distinction between a corporate body and the individuals who compose the corporation is intended when he speaks of the teaching of the friars 'to feign poverty in each person but to ground (i.e. establish) riches in the great person.' [56] Priests, we are told, 'charge behests of winning, and they charge not more behests,' [57] which means that priests command those things to be done which redound to their own profit or winning, but more important things they command not at all. Such inadequate forms of expression as these cited often make Wiclif's meaning difficult to grasp and show how his vigorous mind was compelled to yield to the insufficiencies of the language. They suggest also what has already been indicated, that Wiclif's importance in the development of English prose style consists in the ideas which he promulgated and which succeeding generations made effective, rather than in his own example and practice in the art of writing.

[56] Arnold, II, 410.

[57] Ibid., II, 381.

III

CONTROVERSY AND FREE SPEECH

DEVELOPMENT OF FREE SPEECH—OLDCASTLE AND THE LOLLARDS—PIERS PLOWMAN AND JACK UPLAND—REGINALD PECOCK—POPULAR REFORMERS—SIMON FISH—MORE AND TINDALE—OTHER CONTROVERSIES—JOHN FOXE—CARTWRIGHT AND WHITGIFT—MARTIN MARPRELATE—HOOKER'S "ECCLESIASTICAL POLITY"

I

IT was perhaps Wiclif's greatest service to mankind that he opened the search for truth to all earnest seekers and inquirers. In the fourteenth century, and for centuries before, it had been an established and unquestioned rule, with learned and unlearned, that the truth was the special charge of the church, that it was to be formulated by those whom the authority of the church recognized, and was to be distributed and imparted to others in the manner and in the degree approved by the conservers of truth thus ordained. To the authority of the church scholastic philosophy added the sanction of Aristotelian logic, human reason being thus supposedly united with divine revelation. Doubly safeguarded in this way, the truth was held firmly in the hands of its accredited interpreters, and it was formulated not as the tentative and mutable opinions of a growing and developing body of truth, but as final and absolute dogmas, not again to be questioned after they had been passed upon by the highest possible witnesses and judges of truth. This strong position of dogmatic authority Wiclif, himself both divine and logician, was the first effectively to attack. Every serious and pious man, cleric or layman, according to this new teaching, had the right of individual opinion. The scriptures were a sufficient and an authoritative revelation of truth, and it was each man's privilege and duty to know the scriptures for himself, and from them to draw the rules which should govern his conduct in all the concerns, spiritual, intellectual, and practical, of his personal life.

Wiclif, in short, took truth out of the hands of authoritative dogmatists, and put it into the hands of all those who were earnestly seeking for truth. He removed it from the regions of the fixed and the absolute, and placed it on the battlefield of popular debate and opinion, where the measure of its validity was to be found in the degree to which it satisfied the general sense of truth, where its acceptance or rejection was to depend only upon the free and voluntary choice of the seekers after the truth. Debate, which had hitherto been carried on only in the high altitudes of technical and disciplined scholarship, was now to descend to the level of the popular speech and of the popular mind, undrilled and untaught in the subtleties of logic, but often making up for these deficiencies by earnestness of purpose, by breadth of human interest, and by a vivacity of feeling which somehow seems often to evaporate at the higher levels. For two centuries after Wiclif's death the spirit of controversy was to rage over the questions which he had raised, and from this controversial warfare the English mind and its expression in English prose were to emerge with a surer sense of personal values, with a power of strong and vivid self-expression that would never have been possible under the older medieval rule of docile and tranquil submission.

The development of free public discussion was not unimpeded or rapid. Although Wiclif himself never counseled violence or sedition, to a contemporary observer there must have seemed a dangerous and close connection between the social disturbances which culminated in the Peasants' Revolt and the new teaching of the poor priests. Established society could not be expected to welcome enthusiastically a reform which threatened its own safety, and the protected interests of property and money therefore combined with the official party of the church to suppress the apostles of unrest. Without any systematic organization or any code of belief, the Lollards came to be regarded as a popular party in both church and state which was seeking the overthrow of established authority and the acceptance of radical reforms in political and social theory. With all the forces of authority arrayed against it, Lollardy tended to become more and more a movement of the unlearned and the submerged. In 1401 was passed the notorious act authorizing the burning of heretics. A few years later a synod was held at Oxford at which twelve censors were appointed to examine Wiclif's writings, with the result that nearly three hundred propositions found in them were condemned.[1] Even his own followers failed to realize the greatness of Wiclif's teachings. The story of Sir John Oldcastle, 'the good Lord Cobham' of tradition and of Tennyson's poem, tells dramatically the rebellious state of Lollardy at this time. A just appraisal of the character of Sir John Oldcastle was not possible in his own day when the enthusiasm of his followers made of him a kind of Messiah, sent to lead them out of their bondage, and the hostility of his enemies saw nothing but fanaticism and sedition in his troublesome activities. At a still later time the desire of the reformers of the sixteenth century to appropriate to their

[1] Gairdner, *Lollardy and the Reformation,* I, 65.

party all earlier advocates of anything that savored of Protestant doctrine from the time of Ælfric down, led to a further idealization of the character of Oldcastle, who now became, in the eyes of Foxe and similar zealots, a martyr for the faith. In fact, Oldcastle seems to have been the kind of leader doomed to failure from the beginning, representing an impracticable combination of moral earnestness with unrestrained zeal in action. It is not difficult to see why the protectors of law and order felt that they must condemn him, as they did in the year 1417, as a traitor to the king, and as a notorious heretic and a traitor to God.

It was Oldcastle's rank perhaps as much as his specific opinions which made his case particularly famous and significant in his own day. For here was a Lollard who was not a poor plowman, but a knight with money and the resources of a distinguished social position at his command. By his own class he was regarded as a renegade and as untrue to the obligations which his rank entailed. Thomas Occleve, a faithful defender of the church, expresses the attitude of his contemporaries in a poem written in 1415 for the purpose of recalling Oldcastle to a sense of what Occleve conceived to be his duty.[2] Occleve writes more in sorrow than in anger, his attempt being to recall a good man from a bad cause. Oldcastle, he says, has drunk of "heresies galle," has "lost the style of cristenly prowesse," and should now "Ryse up a manly knyght out of the slow of heresie." The right duty of a man, according to Occleve, is to defend what has come down from past times, just as one who is heir to an heritage would defend it against any who should strive to gain possession of it or to destroy it. Oldcastle moreover troubles himself over matters that do not concern him. The church is the authority which has power

[2] Published by L. T. Smith, *Anglia,* V, 9-42.

to dispute of doctrine, not the bailiff or reeve or man of craft:

> "Lete holy chirche medle of the doctryne
> Of Crystes lawes, and of his byleeve,
> And lete all othir folke therto enclyne,
> And of our feith noon argumentis meeve.
> For if we mighte our feith by reson preeve,
> We sholde no meryt of our feith have.[3]
> But now a dayes, a Bailiff or Reeve
> Or man of craft, wole in it dote or rave.
> Some wommen eeke thogh hir wit be thynne
> Wole argument[e]s make in holy writ;
> Lewde calates! sittith down and spynne,
> And kakele of sumwhat elles, for your wit
> Is al to feeble to despute of it!"[4]

Let Oldcastle beware, continues Occleve, and climb not so high in Holy Writ. If he will read, let him read the story of Launcelot de Lake, or "Vegece of the aart of Chivalrie," or the siege of Troy or Thebes, such things as pertain to the order of a knight. Or if he will read "thing of auctoritee," that is, stories of authentic fact, not fable, let him go to "Judicum, Regum, and Josue, To Judith and Paralipomenon and Machabe," and there as sure as a stone he will find "autentik thing" and "pertinent to Chivalrie." As it is, Oldcastle and the Lollards meddle with all things—they try to shoe the goose. Too free by far are they in the charges they make:

> "Presumpcion of wit and ydilnesse,
> And covetyse of good, tho vices three
> Been cause of al your ydil bysynesse."[5]

[3] An idea which rests upon the authority of St. Gregory: "Gregorie seith, in his IIIe Omelie, in the beginnyng: *Feith hath no merit, to which mannys resoun geveth other sure proof or experience.*" Pecock, *Book of Faith,* p. 145. Langland expresses the same opinion in *Piers Plowman,* B. X, 246.

[4] P. 27.

[5] P. 36.

The only way for Oldcastle to rehabilitate himself, says Occleve, is to renounce his connection with the rabble of heretics, Bible-men, and malcontents, to flee to the king, and to show his manhood by serving his rightful leader and lord. " Cest tout."

Several other contemporary poems have been preserved which likewise express clearly the attitude of established society towards the insurging populace, with its " unstedefast speryte of indyscrecioun." [6] In one of these Oldcastle is again indirectly mentioned. It is no " gentel mannes game " [7] for a knight who should keep his castle for the king to forsake his spear and bow, to creep from knighthood into clergy, and to " jangle of Job or Jeremye ":

> " Hit is unkyndly for a kniȝt
> That shuld a kynges castel kepe,
> To bable the Bibel day and niȝt
> In restyng tyme when he shuld slepe." [8]

Although Oldcastle must have had some sympathizers among those of his own rank, the attitude of the writers of the poems from which these quotations have been made is typical of the average well-regulated opinion of the times. Great as the evils which needed correction might confessedly be, it was felt that the program offered by the Lollards was too ideal, too crude and radical, to deserve the consideration of serious men. And anyway it was not a gentleman's business to discuss such matters.

The gap between the higher administrative and intellectual life of the times and the popular life of strong feeling

[6] " How Mischaunce regnythe in Ingeland," in Wright, *Political Poems and Songs,* II, 242.
[7] "Against the Lollards," in Wright, ibid., II, 245.
[8] Ibid., p. 244.

and intuitive, somewhat blundering sense of justice was too great to be easily bridged. The questions raised by the Lollards were thrown back more and more upon the popular mind, there to be debated, clarified, and developed until, when the favorable moment came, which indeed was not until a century later, they should have that most powerful of all supports, a tradition which had established and finally justified itself in the general consciousness of the people. For the time being, however, the fires of free thinking and of free expression of thought, if not extinguished, were at least smothered beneath the blanket of oppressive authority.

Lacking the support of the accredited leaders of opinion, the new doctrines found their characteristic defender in the traditional plowman, the plain man of the people, as typical representative of the Lollards. The plowman is not of course a cleric, but rather the type of a good man who feels himself to be rightly master over his own conscience. The tradition was set by *Piers Plowman,* and Chaucer in his Plowman, the brother of the Parson, in whom the Host 'smells a Loller,'[9] presents a typical picture of simple and whole-hearted piety. The tradition was continued in a number of writings, such as the *Prayer and Complaint of the Ploughman,* which was re-issued by Tindale as a Reformation document,[10] in *Pierce the Plowman's Creed,*[11] written about 1394 in the alliterative verse of Langland, and in the so-called *Plowman's Tale,*[12] incorrectly ascribed by some of Chaucer's early editors to Chaucer, in order to provide the Plowman in the Canterbury Tales with a tale,

[9] *Canterbury Tales,* in the Shipman's Prolog, l. 10.

[10] See Foxe, *Acts and Monuments,* ed. Cattley, II, 727-747, for the text of this *Prayer.* The author of the work is not known, and the character of the plowman is not dramatically maintained.

[11] *Pierce the Ploughmans Crede,* ed. Skeat, Oxford, 1906.

[12] Skeat, *Chaucerian and other Pieces,* pp. 147-190.

but probably written by the author of the *Plowman's Creed.* The animated dialogue of *John Bon and Mast Parson,* of the early years of the Reformation, continues the fiction.[13] John Bon, plowing in the field, converses with the Parson, who is passing by. With elaborate display of simplicity, John asks "what Saint is Copsi Cursty, a man or a woman," and cunningly leads the priest on to explain the sacrament of the communion as he understands it. But when John reveals his own opinions, the priest leaves him with a prayer that God may bring him to a better mind. "But pray not so for me," says John as he turns to his horses and his plowing, "for I am well enough." The dialogue is well maintained, with the character of John, and in less degree, that of the Parson, consistently and realistically drawn.

In an interesting group of writings of the first decade of the fifteenth century, the name of the protagonist of the popular party changes from Piers Plowman to Jack Upland. The character remains the same, however, an 'uplandish man' being merely a man from the country. Jack Upland puts a series of some fifty questions to a friar, who replies under the name of Friar Daw Topias, and the debate closes with a rejoinder by Jack.[14] On the side of form, the compositions are noteworthy because they are written in a rhythmical kind of alliterating prose, especially Friar Daw's reply and Jack Upland's rejoinder, printed as verse by the editor but really the kind of tumbling prose which so often resulted from the popular and loose treatment of the older

[13] *Tudor Tracts,* ed. Pollard, pp. 161-169. It was first printed in 1548 and probably written not long before.

[14] The text of *Jack Upland* is printed by Skeat, *Chaucerian and other Pieces,* pp. 191-203. It is also printed, together with the reply of Friar Daw Topias (whose real name we learn at the end of the reply is John Walsingham), and the rejoinder by Jack Upland, in Wright, *Political Poems and Songs,* II, 16 ff.

alliterative long line. The questions which Jack addresses to the friar are chosen with a view to pointing out the main abuses with which the orders were usually charged. Simply, plainly, bitingly, though without railing or scurrility, Jack's questions are effectively expressed. Although he speaks in the character of the countryman, Jack is of course acquainted with the traditions of his subject, and he even quotes Latin, especially in his rejoinder to Friar Daw Topias. On the whole, however, the simplicity of the character in Jack's questions is fairly well maintained. 'Go now forth,' he says in his final admonition to Friar Daw, 'and study God's law and give Jack an answer; and when thou hast assoiled me that I have said sadly in truth, then I shall assoil thee of thy orders and save thee to heaven.'[15] Friar Daw's reply is much more alliterative, as well as more abusive, than is Jack in his questions. He also assumes simplicity, and says that though Jack may think his questions hard, it needs no master or no 'man of school' to answer them, 'but a lewd friar that men call Friar Daw Topias, as lewd as a leek,' will suffice.[16] Friar Daw frequently gives Jack the lie direct, although occasionally he varies the formula: 'God wot, Jack, thou sparest here the sooth.' His answers to Jack's questions are not much to the point, being weak in logic and strong in abuse. With a fine show of frankness, he declares it great folly for either him or Jack to meddle with the scripture. 'For as lewd am I as thou. God wot the sooth; I know not an A from the wind-mill, nor a B from a bull-foot, I trow, nor thyself either.'[17] This fiction of simplicity on the part both of Jack and Friar Daw wears a little thin when they both begin to quote Latin and 'holy doctors.' After one such passage, Friar Daw explains his Latin by saying that he was once a manciple at Merton hall and

[15] Wright, p. 38. [16] Ibid., p. 43. [17] Ibid., p. 57.

that there he learned Latin by rote from the clerks. Friar Daw has various popular epithets for Jack, such as Jakke Jospinel, Jak Jawdewyne, but Jack returns the favor with Dawe Dotypolle, an epithet which was to see much service for the next century and half. In general the two parties to the combat maintain the tone of good-humored, vivacious raillery, but Jack defends his master bravely when Friar Daw attacks Wiclif, and once or twice Friar Daw himself rises to an expression of serious and sincere feeling. Both in Friar Daw's reply and in Jack's rejoinder, the dialogue is dramatic and well-sustained, and the works are interesting as early illustrations of that animation and homely vigor which develops most effectively in the free air of popular discussion.

Many such debates as this between Jack Upland and Friar Daw were doubtless continually taking place at ale-houses, fairs, and all places of public meeting among those whose humble position offered some degree of protection from the prelatical party. Both the wits and the tongues of the people were sharpened by these encounters. It could hardly be expected that an undisciplined laity with what it regarded as a profound grievance should express itself moderately. "The essence of heresy," it has been said, "was not erroneous thinking—for all men are liable to that—but arrogance, tending to contempt of the decisions of learned councils and the most approved judgments of ancient fathers." [18] It was perhaps necessarily characteristic of this popular and liberal movement of the fifteenth century, that it should deny the final authority of learned councils and ancient fathers. The radicals of the time were seeking new and more immediately personal tests of truth, and it was inevitable that their newly acquired freedom of speech and criticism should lead them into extravagance and

[18] Gairdner, *Lollardy and the Reformation,* I, 507-8.

license, and also into a contemptuous scorn for ways of thinking which they could not understand or practice. So effective was the opposition to the new movement that all this ferment of popular debate can now be viewed only indirectly in the efforts which were made to suppress it. Imprisonment, punishment, even burning at the stake were freely resorted to, with the only result, however, of causing the disturbers of the established order of things to devise secret and, perhaps for that reason, more seductive means of publishing their doctrine. Only one important effort was made in the fifteenth century to control this flood of popular and radical argument by meeting it on its own ground of discussion in the language of the vernacular. This attempt was made by Reginald Pecock, himself a bishop of the church, who assuming the task of defending the church and of convicting her Lollard enemies of false belief, by a strange irony of fate was finally denounced by his own party and ended his career under conviction of the charge of heresy.

Pecock was a learned man and a voluminous writer, both in Latin and English. He was born in the last decade of the fourteenth century, was a student and fellow of Oriel College, Oxford, and later proceeded to the doctor's degree in divinity. Soon after this he was summoned to the court, where he found a patron in Humphrey, Duke of Gloucester, and was made master of Whittington College in London. In the year 1447 he preached a sermon at Paul's Cross in which he undertook the defense of the 'unpreaching prelates,' that is, those high dignitaries in the church whose time and interests were so entirely taken up with secular matters of state or with the official and financial affairs of the church that they found no opportunity to provide instruction or sympathetic counsel for the people. The popular party was naturally offended at Pecock for what seemed to the laity a shameless defense of one of the most patent abuses of ecclesiastical opportunity, and the prelates, on the other hand, must have regarded Pecock's effort as at least untimely, since they felt themselves to be in a position doubtfully tenable and at the moment under particularly heavy and effective fire. There can be no question, however, of Pecock's entire sincerity in this defense, for he continued it later at greater length and even more uncompromisingly. Three years before the delivery of the sermon, he had been appointed bishop of St. Asaph, in Wales, his native country, and three years later he was made bishop of Chichester. He led an active life, both as writer and as public preacher, for though theoretically he declared preaching not to be an essential part of the priestly office, he himself in practice frequently expounded his views before popular audiences. In the year 1457 came the trial for heresy and the abject recantation which ended his public career. The few remaining years of his life were spent in confinement in the abbey of Thorney, in Cambridgeshire, part of the heavy sentence imposed upon him being "that he have nothing to write with, no stuff to write upon." [19]

In his general principles, Pecock doubtless considered that he had safely established himself upon the solid foundation of the accredited system of theological belief as set forth by Thomas Aquinas. Thomas had made the distinction between truth which was solely accessible by faith and that which was likewise accessible by reason. The former was the more important truth and was imparted to mankind by revelation in the scriptures. Though not out of harmony with reason, this truth could never be attained by the unaided reason, nor could it ever be challenged by the reason. The church, with the pope at its head, determined what

[19] Babington, I, lvii.

the matters of faith contained in the scriptures were, and these were ultimate truths not in need of proof and never to be questioned by the reason. On a lower plane of the theological and religious life, however, there were truths which might legitimately be examined and tested by the rules of disciplined reasoning. This second kind of truth overlapped to some extent the first; that is, God in his goodness made certain truths accessible by process of reasoning also matters of explicit revelation in the scriptures. And he had done so, because the methods of determining truth by the logical proofs of reasoning were seldom acquired by the plain man, incapable of philosophic thought and too much occupied with the business of this world to be able to undergo the preliminary discipline necessary to the application of a sound philosophic method. To save him from utter confusion, therefore, the scriptures present to the unlearned man certain truths which he might also attain, if his abilities or learning were greater, by the exercise of reason.

This in general was the sub-structure upon which Pecock reared his system of theology and practical morals. But the change of emphasis which he introduced into the scholastic scheme, made of his own system something very different. For it is the reason and its workings through the forms of logic that stirred Pecock to the greatest enthusiasm and admiration. Nothing seemed so excellent in his eyes as the operation of a syllogism. Given two premisses "openli trewe and to be grauntid," he declares that we have an instrument so mighty in all kinds of matters that though all the angels in heaven should say that its conclusion was not true, yet "we schulde leeve the aungels seiyng, and we schulden truste more to the proof of thilk sillogisme, than to the contrarie seiyng of alle the aungels in hevene, for that alle Goddis creaturis musten nedis obeie to doom of resoun, and such a sillogisme is not ellis than doom of resoun." [20] And elsewhere he says that if any law or statement of the scriptures is at variance with the "doom of resoun" with respect to any moral virtue, then the scriptures must be brought into accord with the judgment of reason, not the reverse.[21] Pecock's unwillingness to accept mere literal authority is also shown in his brusque treatment of the fathers and doctors of the church, one of the most serious charges brought against him in his trial for heresy. The statements of the fathers have significance in Pecock's eyes only as they have reasonable significance in themselves. Such opinions seem in no way startling to a mind of the nineteenth century, hardened to rational ways of thinking, but to many of Pecock's contemporaries the skeptical boldness of them was disturbing. And what made them more disturbing was the harsh self-confidence with which Pecock expressed his opinions and rejected all others. He had a profound conviction of the validity of the disciplined reason in attaining truth and an equally profound distrust of the undisciplined reason. By the exercise of reason only could mankind attain to a true understanding of the moral virtues, but it must always be the reason as governed by the laws of formal logic, the laws of "groundly disputing." Much the greater part of man's conduct in life, according to Pecock, must be governed solely by the reason, since the scriptures present no practical and complete guide to conduct. Pecock thus takes issue with the Lollards or Bible-men, who maintained that the Bible was in itself a sufficient source of all truth, both the truth which is a matter of faith and which lies beyond the power of reason, as well as the more prac-

[20] *Book of Faith,* pp. 174-5.

[21] *Repressor,* I, 25, Cap. V. This may be contrasted with Purvey's opinion, which is the more orthodox of the two, that if any statement of the scriptures does not harmonize with 'honesty of virtues,' the statement is to be taken only figuratively (see p. 228).

tical truth which has to do with moral conduct. Instead of one source of truth, that is divine inspiration as recorded in the Bible and conserved and expounded by its authorized interpreters, or as the Lollards would have it, by each devout layman for himself, Pecock proposed two sources of truth, divine inspiration as revealed through the church and rationally confirmed by mankind, and natural reason as revealed through the operation of the laws of logic. And of these two sources of truth, the emphasis is always upon the latter. There is very little place in Pecock's system for the direct union of the mystic with the divine, and very little sympathy for those human habits and customs which may not be logically impeccable, but which warm and console the hearts of men by their familiarity. Like Hooker in the outlines and in many of the details of his thought, Pecock is unlike the gentle scholar of Elizabeth's day in his uncompromising insistence upon the adequacy of his formal method to satisfy all the needs of the religious and the practical life.

In his various writings, English and Latin, Pecock planned a comprehensive system of popular instruction, embracing doctrinal theology and morals in general. Of his English writings, only six have survived, and of these only two have been printed. The printed works are *The Repressor of over much blaming of the Clergy,*[22] the most important of all his writings, and *The Book of Faith.*[23] The unprinted works are briefer summaries of principles contained in *The Repressor* and *The Book of Faith.* They are *The Donet,* a compendium of theological doctrine for popular use, the title, from the name Donatus, being explained by Pecock himself as meaning the grammar or key of Christian religion; a continuation of *The Donet,* called *The Follower to the Donet;*

[22] Edited by Babington, 2 vols., London, 1860.
[23] Edited by J. L. Morison, Glasgow, 1909.

and two similar works, *The Book or Rule of Christian Religion,* and *The Poor Men's Mirror,* the latter being an 'outdraught from the first part of the said Donet.'[24] *The Donet, The Follower to the Donet, The Poor Men's Mirror,* and *The Book of Faith* are all in the form of a dialogue between a father and his son. Pecock rarely exerted himself to make his writing interesting, but he calls attention to his use of dialogue as deserving the favor which "such dialogazacioun or togider talking and clatering" ought to have, "which favour, peraventure, sum hasty unconsiderers schulen not aspie, and schulen therfore peraventure the soner impugne."[25]

The title which Pecock himself gave to his most important book was *The Repressing of over miche wyting of the Clergie,* but the name by which it has become more generally known is a version of Pecock's title supplied by a later hand, *The Represser of over myche blamyng the Clergie.* The purpose of the book, which appeared about the year 1450, was avowedly to offer, in formal fashion, a complete defense of the clergy, and in the way of such defense, to overthrow the teachings of the Lollards and Bible-men. More specifically, Pecock promises to vindicate the church against eleven charges which have been brought against it by the Lollards; but before he begins this detailed defense, he presents at length a statement of his general position. The fundamental tenet of the Bible-men was not only that all truth necessary to man's welfare was contained in the scriptures, but also that any good man seeking for the truth need only go to the scriptures and interpret them for himself. If he did this in an humble and earnest spirit, the right meaning of the scriptures would be revealed to him, if not completely and infallibly, at any rate, sufficiently for his own needs. As Milton phrased this principle after

[24] Babington, I, lxxi.

[25] *Book of Faith,* p. 122.

it had passed through two centuries of debate, the scriptures only "can be the final judge or rule in matters of religion, and that only in the conscience of every christian to himself," "the holy spirit so interpreting that scripture as warrantable only to ourselves."[26] When, therefore, a principle of belief or action was proposed to the Bible-men, their first demand was for literal authority, and their first question was, Where find you it grounded in the Holy Scripture? And to this Pecock answers that many truths must be accepted about which the Bible says nothing:

'They that will ask and say thus, "Where findest thou it grounded in Holy Scripture?" as though else it is not worthy to be taken for true, whenever any governance or truth sufficiently grounded in law of kind and in moral philosophy is affirmed and ministered to them (as are many of those xj. governances and truths which shal be treated after in this present book: which are setting up of images in high places of the bodily church, pilgrimages done privily and pilgrimages openly by laymen and by priests and bishops unto the memorials or mind-places of saints, and the endowing of priests by rents and by unmoveable possessions, and such other) ask the while in like manner unreasonably and like unskilfully and like reproveably, as if they would ask and say thus,—"Where findest thou it grounded in Holy Scripture?" when a truth and a conclusion of grammar is affirmed and said to them: or else thus, "Where findest thou it grounded in tailor craft?" when that a point or a truth and a conclusion of saddler craft is affirmed, said and ministered to them: or ellis thus, "Where findest thou it grounded in butchery?" when a point or truth and conclusion of masonry is affirmed and said and ministered to them.

This present thirteenth conclusion may be proved thus: Even as grammar and divinity are two diverse faculties and cunnings, and therefore are unmeddled [unmixed], and each of them hath his proper to him bounds and marks, how far and no farther he shall stretch himself upon mat-

[26] *Prose Works,* ed. Symmons, III, 320, 321.

ters, truths and conclusions, and not to entirmete nor entermeene [interfere] with any other facultie's bounds, and even as saddlery and tailoring are two diverse faculties and cunnings, and therefore are unmeddled, and each of them hath his proper to him bounds and marks, how far and no farther he shall stretch himself forth upon matters, truths and conclusions, and not intercommune with any other craft or faculty in conclusions and truths: so it is that the faculty of the said moral philosophy and the faculty of pure divinity or the Holy Scripture are two diverse faculties, each of them having his proper to him truths and conclusions to be grounded in him, as the before set six first conclusions shew.' [27]

From this statement, characteristically involved and cumbersome, it will be apparent on what grounds Pecock bases his defense when he endeavors to answer the criticisms which the people made against the holding of property by the clergy, the worship of images, going on pilgrimages, and the various other customs of the church which the Bible-men were inclined to sweep aside as superstitions and unauthorized traditions. Strong as his arguments are, however, they could not have been satisfying even to the sounder instincts of the popular party. For in the first place, Pecock with his logic proves entirely too much. A custom which may have essentially good uses, as for example going on pilgrimages and the worshiping of images, cannot be made to seem good by theoretical reasoning after it has become corrupt in practice. The Lollards had not the logical skill to answer the arguments of Pecock, but they had a strong personal conviction of error somewhere which enabled them to persist, obstinately, blindly, arrogantly as it may have seemed, in the attitude they had taken. The Lollard doctrine that the plain honest man is an adequate judge of truth may be a sophistical one, for the

[27] Vol. I, 48-49, Pt. I, Cap. X.

approach to truth may often be by the way of technical knowledge which the plain man does not possess. A reasonable defense of the doctrine, however, may be made on the ground that the truth stripped of its technicalities and presented in intelligible language is appreciated with equal readiness by all men of good sense, lay or learned.

It was just this difficulty of finding a form of communication common to all men of good sense that Pecock could not surmount, and it was this lack which made him in the end an ineffective advocate of his cause. He consented to address the people in their native tongue, but he did so for the purpose of proving to them that they must put their trust not in native wisdom, but in something which they did not possess, in an esoteric science of formal logic. For the people in general, says Pecock, going on pilgrimages and the worshiping of images are to be approved and encouraged, since these, though rudimentary kinds of expression, are the only ones adapted to their undeveloped minds. On the other hand, preaching is of little service, since if sermons are intelligible to the people and are liked by them, they are sure to be the empty mouthings of 'pulpit-bawlers,' [28] of no value whatever in proving or disproving the doctrines under discussion. Preaching may be profitable "into the end of exhortation and remembrancing," but it is of little value "into the end of best teaching." Therefore this matter of repressing errors must be taken in hand in another way than by wearing a doctor's hat in the pulpit, by cunning and savory preaching, or "by great plenteous outhilding [outpouring] of texts written in the Bible or in Doctors." It is easy, says Pecock, to repeat texts and narrations and parables and likenesses, and thus to preach "full gloriously into pleasaunce of the people." And yet

[28] So Babington, I, lxxxii, translates Pecock's *clamitatores in pulpitis*.

if such preachers were "apposed" in any of their texts and parables, "they could not defend and maintain any one of them, neither could put out sufficiently the very and full duest understanding of any one of them." [29]

It is strange to hear Wiclif's enemy denouncing almost in Wiclif's words the eloquence of popular pulpit orators. But Pecock's scorn of popular preaching is merely part of his general contempt for the popular mind. If the Lollards were guilty of the arrogance of ignorance, Pecock was certainly guilty of the pride of intellect. The qualities of lightness, of geniality and of humor, the warmth of personal feeling, and even of piety, all of which a genuine sympathy with the people might have given him, or at least have encouraged in him, he sacrificed for the sake of an unconvincing formal method. The details of his style in writing naturally exhibit the defects of his general attitude of mind. He makes little effort to realize any of the effects of beauty or of vivacity in expression. All is heavy and repetitious without being dignified. He formed himself not upon the long cadences of the Ciceronian period, but upon a legal and syllogistical style. The result is that his sentences, though long, are logically clear but never stylistically limpid. Occasionally he falls into a semi-colloquial and familiar vein, but he never becomes simple and picturesque. His main concern is to be comprehensive and exact, and it is the effort to be so which makes his style so often labored and tediously verbose. He lacked the technical skill of a writer like Hooker, who was able to bear up and combine, and at the same time to animate, the various qualifications of a many-sided thought.

One of the definite charges brought against Pecock in his trial for heresy was that he had ventured to address the people on matters of weight in their vulgar tongue. But

[29] Vol. I, 88-89, Pt. I, Cap. XVI.

Pecock was thoroughly persuaded that the only way to convince the people of error was to place before them books which they could read and re-read. It is not enough, he declares, that these books "be writen and made and leid up or rest in the hondis of clerkis," even though "fame and noise" be made to the lay people that such books exist in which their errors are confuted.[30] But the books should be sent abroad among the people who must "sadli and oft overrede" them until they are fully acquainted with the arguments the books contain. In other words, Pecock seems to have been as unwilling to force the popular mind to submit blindly to authority as he himself was unwilling to accept such submission. But though he accepted the vernacular for popular instruction Pecock found great difficulty in adapting English to his purposes. It was, to be sure, a difficult undertaking to address the people on learned subjects in the English language of the middle of the fifteenth century, and the popular and the learned tendencies continually clash in Pecock's writing. An air of quaint vernacular idiom often results from his use of native English words or compounds of mixed origin for which the custom of the language in later periods has substituted Latin equivalents. Thus he employs *follower* in the sense of 'sequel' or 'successor'; *sayer,* meaning 'speaker'; *unobediencers,* meaning 'disobedient persons'; *knowingal,* 'that which is matter of knowledge,' or to give Pecock's equivalent term, 'sciential'; *outdraught* for 'extract'; *before-crier* for 'herald'; *mind places of saints,* for 'memorials' or 'shrines.' The Latin suffix *-able* is freely united to roots of native origin, as in "birewable and wepeable"; verbs are made from nouns and adjectives, e.g. "thou infirmyst and feblist," thou makest infirm and feeble; and many similar usages are employed which show

[30] *Book of Faith,* p. 116.

an independent and constructive attitude of mind in questions of English style. But in this as in other respects, Pecock is characteristically half-hearted. His style in the main is a highly Latinized style, and his use of native words and constructions is not due to any consistent or puristic respect for the English language. It is due largely to an incomplete realization on the part of Pecock of the value of the Latin vocabulary as a source for the enrichment of the English vocabulary. It was not until the Renascence had made itself felt in England in the early sixteenth century that the bilingual character of the English language became finally established. The Romance element which had been added to the language in Chaucer's time and before had indeed started the tendency towards the introduction of Latin words, but a writer of Wiclif's or Pecock's day could scarcely have foreseen that their efforts to create a learned and technical vocabulary from the native elements of the language was soon to be replaced by another which made the very words archaic and often unintelligible, even though of native origin, which they used for the sake of their clearness and simplicity. If Pecock had been more consistent in his style, if he had written altogether in popular language or had invented a thoroughly Latinized style, his influence as a writer might have been greater. As it is he stands halfway, and he provided for his own day neither a model of idiomatic English, suitable for popular discussion, nor yet a consistent literary style for the scholar and thinker. The really powerful forces in the making of English style in Pecock's day were those forces of popular debate and dissension which Pecock scorned and which seldom reached the level of literary expression. As a writer Pecock consequently exerted but little influence upon his own or upon succeeding generations.

Suppressed so far as surface indications go, Lollardy with

its accompanying vigor and picturesqueness of expression continued to flourish in secret until such time as the self-will of Henry VIII should set not only the tongues but also the pens of men free. Of this hidden life one finds clear evidence in the reports of trials and the sayings of popular leaders preserved in Foxe and other contemporary historians of the fifteenth and sixteenth centuries. The homely vivid rhetoric of John Ball, and doubtless many of Wiclif's poor priests, was continued by an unbroken line of successors, whose utterances can be illustrated here only by a few typical examples, most of which are taken from the pages of Foxe. John Ashton (1382) when asked whether after the words of consecration there remained "material bread, particular bread, or universal bread," answered that the matter passed his understanding, "but amongst other things, he spoke in deriding wise against this word 'material,' saying, 'you may put that in your purse, if you have any.'"[31] William Sawtrey (1400) is also arrogant and answers the questions of his examiners deridingly.[32] John Badby (1409) said "that John Rakier of Bristol had as much power and authority to make the like body of Christ as any priest had."[33] Foxe's account of the trial of Oldcastle preserves many vivid passages. When his examiners attempted to prove to Oldcastle the propriety of worshiping the cross, "then said the Lord Cobham, and spread his arms abroad, 'This is the very cross, yea, and so much better than your cross of wood, in that it was created of God, yet will not I seek to have it worshipped.'"[34] John Claydon, under examination in 1415, confessed that he had sundry English books in his possession, one of which was the *Lanthorn of Light,* a summary of Lollard doctrine.[35] Master Robert, parson of Heggely, examined about the same

[31] Foxe, III, 32.
[32] Ibid., III, 224.
[33] Ibid., III, 235.
[34] Ibid., III, 334.
[35] Ibid., III, 532.

time, answered "mockingly and doubly."[36] The charge was brought against Richard Belward (1424) that he blamed certain of his neighbors for refusing his doctrine, saying to them, "Truly ye are fools that deny to learn the doctrine of my sect, for your neighbours who are of my sect are able to confound and vanquish all others that are of your sect."[37] Margery Backster (1429) testified that she thought "that it were better to eat the fragments left upon Thursday at night on the fasting days than to go to the market to bring themselves in debt to buy fish."[38] Because he smoked the beard and chin of an image of St. John Baptist at Newport in Devonshire and addressed abusive words to it, Hugh Knight was excommunicated and fined in 1441.[39] William Barlowe (1467) would not make confession, "but oonly unto God, and sayde that no pryste had noo more pouer to hyre confessyon thenn Jacke Hare." When "Docter Mayster Hewe Damlet" reasoned with him, Barlowe answered, "Bawe! bawe! bawe! What menyth thys pryste?" with much other irreverent speech.[40]

Coming down to the years immediately preceding the outbreak of the Reformation, one finds this same note of practical commonsense, mingled often with the grossest irreverence of a people intoxicated with the new wine of unrestrained expression. Elizabeth Sampson (1508) declared that Our Lady of Wilsdon was but "a burnt tailed elf and a burnt tailed stock"; she also called the image of St. Saviour, "Sim Saviour with kit lips," and maintained

[36] Foxe, III, 538.
[37] Ibid., III, 585.
[38] Ibid., III, 595.
[39] *Transactions of the Royal Historical Society,* Third Series, VIII, 116.
[40] *Historical Collections of a Citizen of London,* ed. Gairdner, pp. 233-234.

that she could make as good bread as that the priest occupied.[41] Of the image of Our Lady, John Falks (1509) asked "What is it but a block? If it could speak to me, I would give it an halfpenny worth of ale."[42] John Higges declared "that while he was alive he would do as much for himself as he could, for after his death he thought that prayers and almsdeeds could little help him."[42a] It was charged against Joan Sampson that she called St. Saviour at Bermondsey "St. Sawyer," and said "that it was better to eat the altar-cloth," since it might be eaten and digested as easily as the Lord's body.[43] Thomas Man, burned in 1518, said that pulpits were "priests' lying stools," and blasphemed Our Lady, calling her "Mably."[44] As old father Bartlet (1521) was threshing one day, there came a man to him and said, "God speed, father Bartlet, ye work sore." "Yea," said he, "I thresh God Almighty out of the straw." This from the testimony of Richard, father Bartlet's son.[45] Richard Vulford and Thomas Geffrey said that "the Host consecrated was not the very true body of Christ; in proof whereof they said that let a mouse be put in the pix with the Host, and the mouse would eat it up."[46] This same Richard Vulford, meeting with a man who had made a wheel with which to take fish, asked him whether "the wheel now could turn again and make him, and he said, No. 'Even so,' quoth he, 'God hath made all priests, as thou hast made the wheel; and how can they turn again and make God?'"[47]

A public nourished on such strong food as that provided in the popular discussions of which the above incidents are but a few faint echoes must have quickly developed a

[41] Foxe, IV, 126.
[42] Ibid., IV, 134.
[42a] Ibid., IX, 179.
[43] Ibid., IV, 206.
[44] Ibid., IV, 210.
[45] Ibid., IV, 222.
[46] Ibid., IV, 229.
[47] Ibid., IV, 231.

taste for picturesque personal expression. The bitter railing spirit of the popular enthusiasts cannot but seem altogether reprehensible if it be regarded as the permanent spiritual mood or temper of a people. But the fervid rhetoric of the popular reformers, of the 'hot gospellers,'[48] was merely the froth and foam on the surface of a profound national feeling. It was this feeling which determined the nature of English controversial writing when in the sixteenth century, in the works of Sir Thomas More, of Tindale and others, controversy became the concern not merely of an ignorant populace, but of the most learned and skillful writers of the time. And it may as truly be said that this feeling for a popular, yet sincere and vividly personal statement of the case has remained throughout its history the determining feature of English controversial literature. Modern taste has toned down the abusiveness of the style of the sixteenth century, but the avoidance of pedantry and the broad frank personal appeal remain the characteristics of the English public address.

II

The first shots in the classic controversy of the English Reformation were fired at a safe distance in Germany. Thither Simon Fish, a "Gentleman of Grayes Inne," had fled when he had incurred the ill-will of Cardinal Wolsey by playing a part in a comedy at Gray's Inn "whiche touched the sayd Cardinall."[49] From this retreat, in the year 1529, Fish sent forth his *Supplicacyon for*

[48] So Edward Underhill acknowledges he is called (Nichols, *Narratives of the Reformation,* p. 159).

[49] Foxe, quoted by Furnivall, in his edition of Fish's *Supplicacyon for the Beggers,* E.E.T.S., Extra Series 13, from the edition of 1576, pp. 986-991.

the Beggers,[50] a little book which set the model for a number of other supplications and which is important not only because it interested Henry VIII, but because it was answered by Sir Thomas More in his *Supplycacyon of Soulys.* It was this answer which in turn led to More's controversy with Tindale. The humble plowman of the earlier Lollard literature changes now to the poor man in general, the "poore commons" as they are called in a somewhat later supplication.[51] The main petition of Fish's *Supplicacyon,* which is directed to the king, is that the religious orders should be suppressed for the benefit of the poor people of England. The tract is written with great vigor and simple, direct logic, part of its effectiveness being due to its brevity. It is a powerful, direct charge to the king himself to act, to assume the leadership of those "poore commons" whose voice was no longer to be silenced. How much influence the book had upon Henry VIII, it would be difficult to say. Foxe speaks as though it were the king's constant companion. He tells us that when Wolsey heard that the book was abroad, he went to the king and warned him against certain copies which had reached England, "desiryng his grace to beware of them. Whereupon the kyng, puttyng his hand in his bosome, tooke out one of the bookes and delivered it unto the Cardinall." [52] Foxe also preserves the story of Henry's first reception of the book. It was brought to him by two merchants, who read it to him: "The whole booke beyng read out, the kyng made a long pause, and then sayd, if a man should pull downe an old stone wall and begyn at the lower part, the upper part thereof might chaunce to fall upon his head." [53]

[50] Printed by Foxe, and edited by Furnivall as above, and by Arber, *The English Scholar's Library,* No. 4, London, 1878.

[51] Edited by Furnivall, as above.

[52] Furnivall, l. c., p. x.

[53] Furnivall, l. c., p. viii.

Whether it influenced Henry VIII or not, the little book created great stir in England, all the greater because it was not the first of its kind to appear. Tindale had already published some of his popular books of instruction, and his translation of the New Testament had been printed four years before. Feeling that a crisis had come, the bishops made an especially vigorous effort to suppress heretical publications, and among other measures, in the year 1530, and with at least the formal consent of Henry VIII, they issued a decree prohibiting the circulation or reading of a number of books, "both detestable and damnable," among them being certain writings of Tindale, and *The Book of the Beggars,* as the *Supplicacyon* is here called.[54] Similar decrees had been issued in 1526 by Tunstall, bishop of London, and Warham, archbishop of Canterbury, especially against Tindale's New Testament and certain other offensive books which had appeared before the date of the decrees. But more effective means were taken by the bishops for the suppression of heretical literature than the issuing of formal decrees which must have been difficult of practical execution. They felt that the books of the enemy must not only be destroyed, but that their arguments must be answered on their own ground. They therefore called upon Sir Thomas More to come forth as defender of the faith, and by special permission of the bishop of London, More was given leave to read and to have by him heretical books for the purpose of answering them. "And forasmuch as you, dearly beloved brother!" runs Tunstall's letter to More, "can play the Demosthenes both in this our English tongue and also in the Latin, and have always accustomed to be an earnest defender of the truth in all assaults, you can never bestow your spare hours better

[54] Gairdner, *Lollardy and the Reformation,* II, 244.

(if ye can steal any from your weighty affairs) than to set forth something in our tongue, to declare unto the rude and simple people the crafty malice of the heretics, and to make us the more prompt against these wicked supplanters of the church." [55]

The bishops were fortunate in having such a man as More to call to their aid. Scholar, lawyer, poet, philosopher, wit, with the prestige of a wide European fame, it might seem that the mere weight of this man's utterance would be sufficient to crush to extinction the rabble of reformers who constituted the opposition. As a writer of Latin, More was widely known, not only for his *Utopia* (1516), but for his Latin poems, epistles, and other scholarly productions. Nor was he without discipline as a writer of English when he entered the field as defender of the church against her enemies. He had written a number of English poems, mainly of a serious, didactic nature, but like his friend and contemporary Erasmus, he had not spared also to treat the friars and their faults in a spirit of broad and humorous satire.[56] In prose he had made a translation from the Latin of the life of Pico della Mirandola, presented by More to his "right entierly beloved sister in Christ, Joyeuce Leigh," as a New Year's gift.[57] He had also translated a history of King Richard III, the original Latin probably being by John Morton, archbishop of Canterbury, in whose household More at one time resided, into a dignified, formal, and at times some-

[55] Foxe, IV, 697. The date of this letter was March 7, 1528.

[56] The poems are printed at the beginning, without page numbering, of *The Workes of Sir Thomas More Knyght, sometyme Lorde Chauncellour of England, wrytten by him in the Englysh tonge.* London, 1557. This book, a modern edition of which is greatly to be desired, will be referred to hereafter simply as *Workes.*

[57] *Workes,* pp. 1-34.

what Latinized style.[58] Another of More's early prose writings was *A Treatyce (unfynyshed) uppon these wordes of holye Scrypture, Memorare nouissima & in eternum non peccabis,* written about 1521, and consisting of general reflections on religious and moral topics, such as prayer, pride, wrath, envy, and similar themes. The treatise is not at all controversial in tone, and is interesting as a somewhat conventional devotional tract indicating More's early interest in serious subjects.

Much the greater part of More's English writings, and the most significant, are his polemical treatises, seven in number, which were all written between the years 1528 and 1533. These are not slight tracts, but the ample work of a great mind arrived at the fullness of its power. The first of the series, written in 1528, but not published until 1529, in the collected edition bears the following descriptive title: *A Dialogue of Syr Thomas More Knyghte: one of the counsaill of our soverayne Lorde the Kinge and Chauncellour of his Duchy of Lancaster. Wherin be treatyd divers maters, as of the veneracion & worship of ymages and relyques, prayng to saintes, and goyng on pylgrimage. With many other thinges touchyng the pestilent secte of Luther and Tyndale, by the tone bygone in Saxony,*

[58] Some uncertainty exists, both as to More's share in the translation and as to the original authorship of the book, but the weight of the evidence at least supports the ascription of the English version to More. See Churchill, *Richard the Third up to Shakespeare* (Berlin, 1900), p. 77; Kingsford, *English Historical Literature in the Fifteenth Century,* p. 190. Ascham in his *Report and Discourse of the affairs of Germany* (1553) speaks of "Sir Thomas More in that pamphlet of Richard the Thyrd" as presenting a commendable example of historical writing. The editor of the first collection of More's English writings (1557) says that he printed the history of Richard the Third from a manuscript in More's own handwriting.

and by the tother labored to be brought into England.[59] This work, by all odds the best of More's prose writings in English, was the first fruits of Bishop Tunstall's permission to More to read and have by him the writings of the heretics. Of the publications of Tindale, *The New Testament,* the *Parable of the Wicked Mammon,* and *The Obedience of a Christian Man* had appeared before More's *Dialogue* was written. The book itself is somewhat elaborately planned and constructed. More begins by saying that one business begets another, that all his writing in this book had arisen from the fact that 'a right worshipful friend' of his in the country had sent to him a messenger to make inquiries concerning certain matters much called in question of the people. At first, says More, he thought it enough to tell the messenger by word of mouth what his opinions were. After further consideration, however, certain doubts assailed him, especially whether he had done right in trusting so many and so diverse matters to the messenger's memory, and whether even with the best intentions the messenger could report him truly. He determined at length that it would be best to put down in writing the conversation he had had with the messenger, and so the *Dialogue* was written with these two persons as its characters, More, or "quod I," as Tindale facetiously calls him from the tag that always accompanies his words, and the messenger, or "quod he" or "quod your friend." Having written out the conversation, More debated with himself whether he should publish it. He decides that he must do so, for if copies of his manuscript got abroad and became corrupt, as they were bound to do, afterwards if he should make corrections in them, the heretics would say that he made them at their instigation. Before proceeding to publication, however, More says that he sought the advice of

[59] *Workes,* pp. 105-288.

various persons, because however ready he was to express himself or commune in familiar manner with any person on any deep subject, he hesitated to appear in print, "but if better lerned than my selfe shoulde thinke it eyther profitable or at the lestwise harmlesse." [60] On two points in especial More was desirous of securing advice, first, "whether it were convenient to reherse the wordes of any man so homly & in maner somtime unreverently spoken against goddes holy halowes & their reverent memories" as were the words of "quod he," and also whether "quod he" should be allowed to express at large the wrong positions of the heretics concerning whom he professed to be seeking for information. In other words, More here raises the question whether he should fully state his opponents' case, a question which the body of the *Dialogue* happily answers in the affirmative. The second point concerning which More sought advice was whether "certaine tales & mery wordes which he [i.e. the messenger] mengled with his matter, and some such on mine owne parte among" might not seem too light and wanton for the gravity of his subject. Finding that the opinions of his friends were seldom in harmony, More determines to let stand whatever two agree upon, even though others disapprove. Then follows in the elaborate machinery of this introduction the letter supposed to have been brought by the messenger, "quod he," from More's friend in the country, and a letter which More sent to his friend with the book after it was printed.

No names are given, either of More's friend or of "quod he," and no details which would identify either, and indeed it seems most probable that the whole framework of the *Dialogue* is a literary artifice.[61] Doubtless More did have

[60] *Workes,* p. 106.

[61] Gairdner, *Lollardy and the Reformation,* I, 511 ff., on the

frequent conversations with persons from various parts of England and doubtless he endeavored always to spread what he regarded as the right views in controversial questions. But one can hardly think of More on terms of friendly equality with a person who defended heretical views as extreme as those which "quod he" holds. The messenger is obviously an imaginary character, a vividly conceived type by means of which More can display the opinions which he wishes to refute. In the *Dialogue* More the artist has not yet been swallowed up by More the controversialist. "Quod he" serves a good dramatic purpose, representing the free-speaking, sometimes coarse and vulgar popular mind, a kind of Bible-man, in contrast to More himself, who appears usually as the representative of dignified and authoritative learning. This contrast shows clearly in the different manners of speech of the two participants in the *Dialogue*. The messenger is described in the friend's letter as wise and more than meanly learned, of a very merry wit and "of nature nothing tonge-tayed." More asks him to what faculty he had given most study, and "quod he" replies that he has studied Latin mainly, that "Logicke he rekened but babblinge, Musicke to serve for singers, Arithmetricke meete for marchaunts, Geometry for masons, Astronomy good for no man, and as for Philosophy, the most vanite of all." [62] Logic and philosophy, he says, have destroyed all divinity, and besides Latin, he studies only the Bible. He pays no heed to learned interpreters, but gets the meaning out for himself, mainly by comparing one text with another. After "quod he" has expressed himself at some length in this fashion, More

contrary, thinks the country friend and "quod he" are real persons and that the *Dialogue* is practically a report of a conversation actually held.

[62] *Workes,* p. 111.

begins to doubt whether he has not "fallen in to Luther's secte." Since he was endeavoring to write not only a convincing but also an entertaining work, More likewise finds it convenient to have an opponent like "quod he" upon whose shoulders he can place the responsibility for some of his jests and merry tales. In short, More uses in the *Dialogue* devices for securing realistic effect somewhat similar to those which he had previously used in the *Utopia,* and which he was to use again later in the *Dialogue of Comfort.* And if the *Dialogue,* not lacking in literary charm, had been on the winning instead of the losing side of the great intellectual debate of the time, it might have equaled the *Utopia* in the permanence and universality of its interest.

The general intent of the *Dialogue,* which is divided into four books and numerous chapters, is apparent from its title. It is an attempt to answer Lutheran heresy, especially with respect to Tindale's part in it. "Quod he" fearlessly states the position of the reformers in England, that they think many persons have been 'sore handled' by the authorities (especially one, Thomas Bilney, who is not mentioned by name, however, anywhere in the *Dialogue*), for the purpose of intimidating conscientious seekers after the truth, that "all this gere is done but onelie to stoppe mennes mouthes" who would speak of the faults of the clergy. Many men begin indeed to doubt if Luther is as "evyll as he is borne in hande," and they begin to think that "this name of a Lutherane serveth the clargy for a common clocke [cloak] of a false crime, y^t where they lacke special mater to charge one with by iugement, they labour to bringe him first in the infamy of the name that compriseth (as they make it seme) a confused heape of herisies, no man can tell what."[63] More hears "quod he"

[63] *Workes,* p. 109.

out and then summarizes his charges and doubtings under four heads, each of which he promises to consider in detail. He does not permit himself, however, to indulge in long speeches to the detriment of the dramatic illusion of the *Dialogue*. After the story of Bilney, the worship of images, and the working of miracles have all been discussed at length in a varied and interesting manner, the first book closes with one of those pleasant personal passages which lend life and verisimilitude to the whole *Dialogue*. "Quod he" says he still has one important point in mind, but as it is now twelve o'clock, he will save it until after dinner. More declares his eagerness to hear this matter. "Naye," quod he, "it were better ye dyne fyrste. My Ladye wyll, I wene, bee angrye with me, that I kepe you so longe therefro. For I holde it nowe well towarde twelve. And yet more angrye woulde waxe with me, if I should make you sit and muse at your meat, as ye woulde, I wote well, muse on the matter if ye wyst what it wer." "If I were," quod I, "lyke my wyfe, I shoulde muse more theron now and eate no meat for longing to know. But come on than, & let us dyne fyrste and ye shall tell us after."[64] If tradition does not belie Mistress More's temper, this little picture of More's domestic life is not only interesting, but also true.

In the second book, the speaker discusses first what constitutes the true church and the reasons why 'sectarians' are not of it. In the latter part of the book there is considerable repetition of subjects taken up in the first book, such as the reverence due to saints, to relics, and images. The discussion is resumed in the third book after an interval of time during which "quod he" has visited the University (i.e. Cambridge), where he has found many offended at the burning of Tindale's *New Testament,* at the official

[64] *Workes,* p. 177.

denunciation of Luther's teaching, and at the treatment which Bilney had received. More defends the burning of Tindale's *New Testament* on the ground that it was full of heretical translations, maliciously inserted. Over a thousand texts, according to More, were mistranslated, the most flagrant instances being Tindale's translations *seniors, congregation,* and *love,* for which the approved translations were *priests, church,* and *charity,* and also Tindale's *favor, knowledging,* and *repentance* instead of *grace, confession,* and *penance.* The most interesting question discussed in this book, perhaps in the whole *Dialogue,* is whether the scriptures should be translated into English at all, and if so, how this translation should be used.[65] The last book of the *Dialogue* returns to the discussion of general questions of doctrine, and of the proper way of treating heretics, whether they should be put to death or not. In general there is a good deal of repetition throughout the *Dialogue.* Topics are dropped and taken up again without much order, yet in a manner appropriate to a conversation. The friendly, urbane tone of the discussion is maintained throughout and the charm and good humor of the work never fail. "Quod he" lives up to the character of wanton which "quod I" gives him in a way which shows how More's fondness for 'merry tales' not infrequently got the better of his sense of dignity.[66] But no more serious charges can be made against the *Dialogue.* The modern reader may wonder that More should think of coolly explaining, and even defending, the cruel and barbarous methods of punishment employed against heretics, but fire

[65] Bk. III, Cap. XVI. For a fuller account of this chapter, see below, pp. 242-243.

[66] As in Bk. II, Cap. X, describing the shrine of "saint walerie" (St. Valeri) in Picardy, which Tindale in his *Answer,* p. 124, dismisses briefly as "a filthy chapter," and "meet for the author and his worshipful doctrine."

and the sword were accepted theological arguments in the sixteenth century, and More was less extreme than many of his contemporaries. The views of the reformers are fairly, even emphatically expressed, so that without intending it, and merely by the clearness of his exposition, More may have confirmed some of his readers in their heretical opinions. In general More endeavors to answer his opponents fairly and reasonably, not with mere rant and invective. The decision as to which has the better side of the argument goes back, however, to questions which are really fundamental but which are not specifically raised in the *Dialogue,* that is to the questions how far authority should operate in the control of opinion and by what means changes should be brought about. To a conservative and a lawyer, like More, committed to the maintenance of the traditional order of things, the position which he held would seem abundantly justified. It is only in the light of history that one is led to wonder that a man so wise and just should not have seen his way to a more positively constructive part in the great changes that were taking place in his day.

Scarcely was the printer's ink dry on the *Dialogue* when More appeared a second time in the lists with his *Supplication of Souls* (1529), written in answer to Simon Fish's *Supplication for the Beggars.* Fish had recommended the confiscation of church endowments and the use of the money thus obtained for the relief of the poor people of England. He had dwelt upon the immense riches of the church, the priests' neglect of duty, and above all their selfish use of the doctrine of purgatory. The answering supplication of More is supposed to come from "the sely soules in purgatory," who would be abandoned to their fate if Fish's counsels were carried into execution. But the silly souls plead not only for themselves but also for the souls of others who are still alive, since lack of belief in purgatory will bring many a good simple soul "the verye strayghte waye to helle." The *Supplication* is, therefore, first an answer to Fish's book, and secondly, a defense of the doctrine of purgatory. It is much longer than the *Supplication for the Beggars* and loses in effectiveness in proportion to its length. Fish had written with a fierce indignation that made every word tell; More's answer is wiser and ampler, but it fails to hit the mark as unerringly as the tract of his opponent.

Still less effective is the third of More's controversial writings, his *Confutation of Tindale's Answer* (1532), the longest and least interesting of all More's English writings. Tindale's *Answer* to More's *Dialogue* had appeared the preceding year. More's *Confutation* of the *Answer* fills nearly five hundred folio pages, is divided into nine books, and is unfinished at the end. The pleasant conversational tone of the *Dialogue,* still maintained to some extent in the *Supplication of Souls,* is here replaced by the harsh controversial manner of the most violent popular writers of the time. Perhaps More felt that the day for gentle dealing had gone by. At the beginning of his *Confutation* he calls attention to the fact that of late years England has had "plentuous of evill bookes," giving a list of them, which includes many besides Tindale's. As he advances, More grows more earnest, and also becomes less regardful of the artistic side of his writing. The notable attention to literary form found in the *Dialogue* is lacking in the *Confutation,* the method of which is the crude, mechanical one of quoting a passage from Tindale's *Answer* and of replying to each passage immediately and separately. The disproportion between the length of the passages quoted and More's answers is great. Perhaps More hoped to crush his opponent and his doctrines once and for all by the fullness and ponderosity of his own arguments. If so, he deceived himself, for the simplicity and directness of Tindale's presentation of his side of the case seem all the more effective and admirable when compared with More's long, repetitious, and heavy, even though learned and closely argued answers. The entire sincerity and earnestness of More in this undertaking cannot be called in question. He was deeply concerned to provide an antidote to the poison of heresy, and he felt that men should "have againe at hande suche bookes as may well arme them to resist and confute" the writings of heretics. And though he speaks modestly of his own work, he declares that he has not "shoffled it up so hasteli" but that it may stand in some good stead.

As the *Confutation* is entirely without structure, it is not susceptible of analysis. More takes up the various topics of the book scatteringly, as they are suggested to him by Tindale's *Answer*. In his general attitude towards Tindale and the reformers he is extremely harsh and condemnatory. The merry jests and pleasant humor of "quod he" have completely disappeared, and instead of the "poetry," as his critics called it, of the imaginary *Dialogue*, the *Confutation* is profoundly serious. More does not hesitate to give Tindale the lie direct. All this gear, he says at one place, is "but a fardel ful of lies, and that woteth Tindall himself well ynough,"[67]—and on the next page, "This is another fardell full of lyes." He pictures Tindalc as stricken stark blind by the devil, who has "set him in a corner with a chayne and a clogge & made him his ape to sit there & serve hym & to make him sporte, with mocking and mowing and potting the sacramentes, which yet the devil dreadeth himselfe, and dare not come anere them."[68] Answering Tindale's teaching that men should search the

[67] *Workes*, p. 397. [68] Ibid., p. 398.

causes and reasons of things, not trust to blind faith, More declares that if "our father Tindal had been in paradise in the stede of our father Adam, he should never have neded any serpent or woman either to tempt him to eate the apple of the tree of knowledge." Searching for the cause of this first commandment and not finding any, for at that time the flesh had no need of taming, "then woulde he have eaten on a good pace . . . and so would he by his own rule of searching have found out as much mischief as the woman and the serpente and the devill and all."[69] Even so dignified a person as the lord chancellor of England descends at times to puerile taunting. Tindale had asked why More had not contended with Erasmus, "whom he calleth my darling," for translating, as Tindale had done, the word *ecclesia* by *congregatio*. There had he hit me, lo, says More, save for lack of a little fault:

"I have not contended with Erasmus my derling because I found no suche malicious entente with Erasmus my derlyng as I fynde with Tyndall. For hadde I founde with Erasmus my derling the shrewde entent and purpose that I fynde in Tyndall, Erasmus my derlyng should be no more my derlyng. But I fynde in Erasmus my derlyng that he detesteth and abhorreth the errours & heresies that Tyndall playnly teacheth and abideth by, and therefore Erasmus my derlyng shalbe my dere derling stil. And surely if Tyndale had either never taughte them or yet had the grace to revoke them, then should Tyndall be my dere derling too. But while he holdeth such heresies styl, I cannot take for my derling him that the devil taketh for his derlyng."[70]

Following the *Confutation* in the sequence of More's English writings, comes a *Letter of Sir Thomas More knight, impugning the erroniouse wryting of John Frith agaynst the blessed sacrament of the aulter*,[71] a short

[69] *Workes*, p. 367.
[70] Ibid., pp. 421-422.
[71] Ibid., pp. 833-844.

treatise the purport of which is sufficiently indicated by its title. Much more interesting and important is the *Apology,* written in 1533, after More had given up the office of lord chancellor.[72] The *Apology* was written with a double purpose, first as a defense against the criticisms which various persons had made of More and the methods of his previous writings, and secondly, to answer a work called *A Treatise Concerning the Division between the Spiritualty and the Temporalty,* by Christopher St. German, after Tindale, More's most important controversial opponent. More acknowledges that there are faults in his writings which "badde brethren" will sift to the "uttermost flake of branne," but he comforts himself with the assurance that what he has written is consonant with "the common catholike fayth and determinacions of Chrystes catholike church."[73] To the objection that he had handled Tindale and others "with no fayrer woordes nor in no more courtes maner," and that in his writings he had been too "parcial towarde the spiritualtye," More responds first by giving a summary of his own position as he had stated it in his various criticisms of Tindale and of Lutheran heresy in general. Then follows a specific defense of the charge that he had handled his opponents "ungoodly and with uncomely woordes, callynge theym by the name of heretyques and fooles."[74] The defense, somewhat disingenuous, is that the heretics are wicked, that God's wrath is upon them, and that in simple honesty one must give them their proper names. Every man, says More, hath not like wit or like invention in writing. He is but a "simple playne bodye," like the Macedonians who knew no better than to call a traitor a traitor. "And in good faithe, lyke those good folke am I. For thoughe Tindall and Frithe in

[72] *Workes,* pp. 845-928.

[73] Ibid., p. 845.

[74] Ibid., p. 863.

their writinge cal me a Poet, it is but of their owne courtesye, undeserved on my part. For I canne neither so muche poetrye, nor so muche rethorique neither, as to fynde good names fer evyll thinges, but even as the Macedonies coulde not call a traitour but a traitour, so canne I not call a foole but a foole, nor an heretique but an heretique." [75] More defends himself also against another charge, "that is to wytte where they reprove that I bring in among the most earnest matters, fansies and sportes & mery tales." For, as Horace says, a man may tell the truth in game. And moreover for one who is but a layman, it may "better happely become hym merely to tell hys minde than seriously and solempnely to preach. And over thys, I can scant believe that the brethren finde anye mirthe in my bookes. For I have not much hearde that thei very merely read them." [76]

As an example of "a goodlye milde maner" of writing, More's attention had been called to St. German's *Treatise,* but he excuses himself for not having followed this example by saying that the *Book of the Division* had appeared since he wrote his own works and therefore could not have served him as a model. The greater part of the *Apology* is taken up with More's discussion of this book and its author, whom he does not mention by name, but whom he ironically calls the Pacifier, from St. German's avowed desire to bring about harmony between spiritualty and temporalty by mild and reasonable means, and to encourage in general a more charitable manner of discussing the questions which were dividing the clergy and the laity. St. German was a lawyer, with some leaning towards the side of the laity. One of his main principles, for example, was that where the common law of the land had laid down principles at variance with those of the canon law, the decisions

[75] *Workes,* p. 864.

[76] Ibid., p. 927.

of the common law must stand against those of ecclesiastical tribunals. More apparently saw in St. German an enemy to the church in the disguise of a friend, and as later events proved, the support which he gave to the policies of Henry VIII strengthened the cause of the reformers. Although frequently ironical, More's treatment of St. German is restrained, compared with his treatment of Tindale. The length at which he defends himself is some indication that More perhaps felt that he had been led into undue violence, an indication also, if any were needed, that the party of the laity was no longer made up of plowmen and rustics and beggars, but that important and intelligent people were ready to lend a willing ear to the teachings of the reformers. The *Apology* is significant, therefore, not only as a revelation of More's own opinions with respect to propriety of manner in polemical discussion, but also of the general change in the tone of controversy which was a necessary result as soon as the two parties to discussion were approximately on the same social and intellectual level. In conclusion, More says that he thinks he has adequately confuted Tindale's heresies, and that for a time now he intends to give up writing and to devote himself to something more necessary than writing, the mending of his own faults in good living. "For of newe booke makers there are now moe then ynough." [77]

The chastened spirit in which More concluded his *Apology* seems, however, to have been somewhat premature. For the *Apology* called forth an answer by St. German, *Salem and Bizance,* a dialogue in which Salem (from Jerusalem) defends the claims of the clergy and Bizance (Byzantium) stands for the authority of civil law. This book More answered in his *Debellacyon of Salem and Bizance* (1533),[78] continuing to speak of St. German as

[77] *Workes,* p. 928.

[78] Ibid., pp. 929-1034.

the Pacifier. Although milder in tone than More's earlier writings, the *Debellacyon* is by no means lacking in passages of personal aspersion and ridicule. The last of More's polemical treatises appeared in the same year as the *Debellacyon,* and is entitled *The Answer to the first part of the poysoned booke whych a nameles heretike hath named the supper of the Lord.* The " poysoned booke " is a little pamphlet, containing altogether thirty-two leaves, and divided into two parts, of which the first contains fourteen leaves.[79] More intended to answer the two parts separately, but he finished only the answer to the first part.[80] This *Answer* is a large book, twenty times as long as the *Supper of the Lord,* and More here again shows a sad lack of discretion in answering the light artillery of the enemy with such heavy cannonading. The brethren indeed might well be forgiven if they had not " very merely read " so long an answer to so short a treatise.

The works of More's last years are a pleasant relief after the storms of his controversial period. Forced by public opinion and the request of those whose wishes he respected to take up the defense of England's traditional ecclesiastical institutions, More was at heart less a controversialist than he was a philosopher, and to use the term of reproach which his enemies so frequently directed against him, a poet. A sincerely pious man himself, he was deeply shocked at the evidences of growing irreverence and iconoclasm which he beheld on all sides, and after his own duty as defender of the faith had been performed, he turned gladly to the more congenial task of mending his own faults in good living. The year before his execution, while he was a prisoner in the Tower, he wrote a *Dyalogue of Comforte*

[79] Gairdner, I, 539-540, Note.

[80] *Workes,* pp. 1035-1138, with an additional unnumbered page, making altogether 134 folio pages.

agaynste tribulacyon, made in the yere of our lorde, 1534, which is supposedly a translation of a work originally written by a Hungarian in Latin, first translated into French, and then by More from French into English.[81] The Hungarian author and the Latin and French originals existed, however, only in More's poetic imagination, the whole being his invention. The dialogue takes place between an uncle, named Anthony, and his nephew Vincent, and discusses tribulation in a highly analytic way, the kinds thereof and the remedies to be employed against it. The reader is reminded of the *De Consolatione Philosophiae* of Boethius, both being dialogues written in prison, of an elevated and dignified moral tone, by authors who suffered similar fates. It is as a philosopher, wise in the affairs of the human heart, that More speaks in this *Dyalogue,* and he here reveals those spiritual and amiable sides of his nature which represent him at his best. Two other meditative treatises were written in this last year of More's life, one entitled *A treatice to receave the blessed body of our lorde* and the other, *A treatice upon the passion of Chryste,* the latter being unfinished.[82] These treatises, together with some shorter pieces, devout instructions, meditations, and prayers, as well as a number of letters, complete the list of More's English writings.

As a controversialist More had the misfortune to be always on the defensive, and further, to have had his opinions largely determined for him by his party. He could not consequently enter into discussions with the same fire and enthusiasm as his opponents. But though he was a conservative and had turned aside from the more liberal opinions of his earlier years, More never became narrow. He perhaps did not see clearly the forward tendencies of his

[81] *Workes,* pp. 1139-1264.
[82] Ibid., pp. 1264-1404.

age, but at the same time it is unquestionably true that there lay grave danger in what More did see clearly, the contemporary violence in thought and feeling, and the disregard of traditional customs and rights. He is a fair disputant, often stating, in his self-confidence, his opponents' case better than they could do it themselves. As to his own arguments and proofs, it is not necessary to speak, since history has answered them. More's certainty of the justice of his own position led him perhaps to underestimate the strength of his opponents. He is occasionally bitter towards them, as Tindale is sometimes towards him, but on the whole is rather inclined to regard them with something of the scorn and contempt of a strong man grown insolent with his sense of power. The jests and merry tales, after all is said, also frequently strike a false note. Perhaps More did not fully realize the seriousness of the situation. He was not fighting for liberty and conscience in the same degree as the reformers, and though stronger on the side of reason and logic than his opponents, More seems lacking a little in moral earnestness. There is indeed something unseemly in answering an opponent who speaks at a white heat of moral indignation with a jest. Such a man is not to be put off with banter, nor is he to be reasoned with; he is deaf to philosophy and logic, and the only way to silence him is to meet him with a passion equal to his own. More was backed by history, by tradition, by the best scholarship of his day, but the questions of the hour were not to be solved by history, tradition, and scholarship. They were not to be solved either by literary skill, in which More was superior to all his opponents, both in the variety of his literary accomplishments and in his power of sustained workmanship. This, however, if he could have looked into the future, would have seemed to him an empty victory, for he did not write in English mainly for the sake of his art, but for the sake of the truth as he viewed it.

As a writer of English prose, More followed now one and now the other of two tendencies. The first of these was the tendency toward an informal easy style which rests directly upon colloquial discourse, and the second towards the use of a structurally elaborated form after the classical tradition. It is characteristic of the experimental stage in which English style found itself in More's day that he developed neither of these tendencies into a consistent and harmonious style of his own. But on the whole his writing stands much closer to colloquial discourse than to the artificially elaborated periods of the classical stylists. For though More was partly driven and did not voluntarily choose to use English in order to oppose a popular movement, he shows his customary wisdom and open-mindedness in his frank acceptance of the native idiom for literary purposes. His range of expression in English is consequently wide. When it suits his purpose he can assume the familiar, even the broadly popular style. And in his more literary moments, he has command over a carefully cultivated and organized form of expression. But even when he is most literary, he is not manneristic. All such tricks of style as alliteration, the use of doublets, of strange and learned words, of ingenious figures of speech, he consistently avoids. His diction is admirably simple and idiomatic and he seems to have felt no difficulty in expressing learned matters in plain English. He rises superior to the naïve medieval sentence, with its sprawling members held together by a sprinkling of temporal and co-ordinating conjunctions, and he does so by giving his sentences body and structure as well as length. But his periodic sentences are not often highly elaborated, and the order of clauses, though not always natural, is seldom stiff or mechanical. The first modern English writer to develop and to maintain a dignified literary style, without being pompous or overcharged with literary mannerism, More shows a much more certain feeling for English expression than any of his learned contemporaries.

When it comes to structure in the larger sense, it is apparent that More was not quite so sure of himself, though here again he is vastly superior to most of his contemporaries. His dialogue in answer to Tindale and his later *Dialogue of Comfort* are ample proof that More was capable of maintaining a feeling for the structure of the whole throughout an extended piece of writing, but his other works show also that the demands of structure were likely to yield under the pressure of strong feeling. It was assumed, certainly by many of More's opponents and to some extent also by More himself, that formal structure savored too much of literary artifice, of the work of the 'poet,' and that the honest man should speak and write as the spirit gave him utterance. This principle resulted well for Tindale and others of the reformers whose minds saw few things but saw them with inexorable directness and distinctness. They write as runners stripped for the race. But with More there is always more or less fumbling. He crowds his canvas, like a medieval tapestry, with a multiplicity of detail the abundance and disorder of which confuse the mind in spite of its relevancy. Doubtless also the richness of his own mind, his perception of the many aspects of every subject he examined, insensibly led him at times to discuss questions more fully than was necessary.

With all his abundance, however, More is always vivacious, holding the interest now by the picturesqueness of his phrasing, now by the direct vigor and wisdom of his thought, now by the higher charm of a gracious and kindly spirit communing at ease with his human fellows. He is sometimes quizzical, bantering, a little superior and even scornful, but his raillery never hardens into fanaticism. His weaknesses and defects are largely those of his age, and in the retrospect they seem slight in comparison with the strength and the many charms of his personality.

The David in this classic controversy of the English Reformation was William Tindale, a humble scholar and wanderer on the face of the earth, with no more powerful ally or support than the printing presses of his German friends. Of Gloucestershire family, Tindale entered Oxford in 1510, five years after Colet had brought to a close his famous lectures on the New Testament which mark a new epoch in the English method of interpreting the scriptures. On leaving Oxford he dwelt for some years at Cambridge, inheriting there the traditions of the teaching of Erasmus, who had lectured at Cambridge from 1510 to 1513. The great purpose of Tindale's life, the origin of which dates from the time of his residence at Oxford and Cambridge, or perhaps earlier, was to see the Bible translated into English and placed in the hands of the English people, and it was in the hope of accomplishing this end that he went to London in 1523 and sought the patronage of Tunstall, bishop of London. He soon found that his choice of a prospective patron was not judicious, and giving up all hope, after various endeavors, of carrying out his project in England, the following year he left England for the Continent, never to return during the few remaining years of his short life. As a voluntary exile in Germany, Tindale composed and published all of his writings. With respect to the most important of these, his translation of parts of the Bible, further details will be given in a later chapter.[83] His other extant works consist of exegetical commentary on the scriptures, covering, however, a wide field and includ-

[83] See below, pp. 233-256.

ing not only discussions of theological doctrine, but also of practical questions of contemporary politics and daily life, and of didactic and polemical treatises, summarizing the teachings of the reformers and defending them against the attacks of the Romanists. When Sir Thomas More answered the call of the church to come to its defense, Tindale had already published several doctrinal treatises, besides that prime cause of offense, his translation of the New Testament. More's *Dialogue* was published in 1529, but it was not until two years later that Tindale issued his *Answer to Sir Thomas More's Dialogue.*[84] The *Answer* exhibits the quality of straightforward sincerity found in all of Tindale's writings, and although it is not without a good deal of strong personal language, it is characterized in general by moderation and dignity of tone. Perhaps nowhere do Tindale's deep sense of justice and truth, his burning hatred of ignorance and superstition, reveal themselves more clearly than in this *Answer*. His main point, the significance of which he never allows to become obscured, is the Lutheran doctrine of justification by faith, the doctrine that the test of spiritual values is to be found in the heart of each man for himself, and not in dogma, or authority, or ceremony. As to structure, the *Answer* resembles More's *Confutation* in that it takes up the propositions of the *Dialogue* one by one and answers them thus with little realization of the effect of the argument as a whole. The *Answer* is therefore not only without structure, but also quite without the dramatic interest of the *Dialogue,* and the lightness, humor, and grace which the characters lend to it. But the *Answer* is by no means a disorderly jeremiad. It is written with the serenity of a lofty mind which, once having seen the truth, expresses itself with

[84] Edited by Walker, for the Parker Society, 1850, where Tindale's other writings will be found.

impersonal but none the less powerful conviction. On the side of clearness and coherency of thought, Tindale has the better of More; on the side of sustained literary skill and human interest, he falls short of his opponent.

It is always in detached passages that Tindale shows at his best, and then at times he attains a clarity and perfection of form, the naked simplicity of which asks nothing of the highest art. Such, for example, is the passage, an allegory in essence, called by Tindale a "pretty antithesis," in which Holy Church attempts to bully Little Flock:

"When the great multitude . . . behold Little Flock, that they come not forth in the service of God, they roar out, 'Where art thou? Why comest thou not forth and takest holy water?' 'Wherefore?' saith Little Flock. 'To put away thy sins.' 'Nay, brethren, God forbid that ye should so think; Christ's blood only washeth away the sins of all that repent and believe. Fire, salt, water, bread and oil be bodily things, given unto man for his necessity, and to help his brother with; and God that is a spirit cannot be served therewith. Neither can such things enter into the soul, to purge her, for God's word only is her purgation.' 'No!' say they, 'are not such things hallowed? And say we not in the hallowing of them, that whosoever is sprinkled with the water or eateth of the bread, shall receive health of soul and body?' 'Sir, the blessings promised unto Abraham, for all nations, are in Christ; and out of his blood we must fetch them, and his word is the bread, salt, and water of our souls. God hath given you no power to give through your charms, such virtue unto unsensible creatures, which he hath hallowed himself, and made them all clean (for the bodily use of them that believe) through his word of promise and permission, and our thanksgiving. God saith, If thou believe St. John's gospel, thou shalt be saved, and not for the bearing of it about thee with so many crosses, or for the observing of any such observances.' 'God, for thy bitter passion,' roar they out by and by, 'what an heretic is this! I tell thee that Holy Church need to allege no scripture for them; for they have the Holy Ghost, which inspireth them ever secretly, so that they cannot err, whatsoever they say, do or ordain. What, wilt thou despise the blessed sacraments of Holy Church, wherewith God hath been served this fifteen hundred years? (Yea, verily, this five thousand years, even since Cain hitherto, and shall endure unto the world's end, among them that have no love unto the truth to be saved thereby). Thou art a strong heretic and worthy to be burnt.' And then he is excommunicate out of the church. If Little Flock fear not that bug, then they go straight unto the king: 'And it like your grace, perilous people and seditious, even enough to destroy your realm, if ye see not to them betimes. They be so obstinate and tough that they will not be converted, and rebellious against God and the ordinances of his holy church. And how much more shall they so be against your grace, if they increase and grow to a multitude! They will pervert all, and surely make new laws, and either subdue your grace unto them, or rise against you.' And then goeth a part of Little Flock to pot, and the rest scatter. Thus hath it ever been, and shall ever be: let no man therefore deceive himself." [85]

This pointed, picturesque style, simple but never crudely naïve, plain but never coarse, is the standard of form which Tindale consciously strove to realize. He speaks scornfully of Bishop Fisher's "oratory," [86] and Sir Thomas More's "painted poetry, babbling eloquence." [87] Vaughan, the English envoy at Antwerp, replies to Thomas Cromwell's objection that Tindale's *Answer* to More's *Dialogue* was "unclerkly done," by saying that "so seem all his works to eloquent men, because he useth so rude and simple style, nothing liking any vain praise and commendation." [88]

[85] *Answer,* ed. Walker, for the Parker Society, pp. 109-110. Spelling and punctuation have been modernized by the editors in all the publications of the Parker Society, but no verbal changes have been made without acknowledgment.

[86] *Obedience of a Christian Man,* in *Doctrinal Treatises,* ed. Walker, p. 221, and again, ibid., p. 341.

[87] *Expositions,* ed. Walker, p. 100.

[88] Demaus, *William Tyndale,* p. 311.

Simple Tindale's style may be, but it is not rude. It is the style of a writer who knows what he wishes to say, and knows also precisely the right way of saying it. He strikes a golden mean of perfectly idiomatic expression, avoiding the extremes of popular bombast on the one side and of formal literary artifice on the other. He was deeply impressed with the necessity of the direct appeal to popular intelligence, but he saw also the necessity of scholarship and of the humanistic study of the classics. He recalls with disapproval the time when, "within this thirty years and far less," the children of darkness raged in every pulpit against Greek, Latin, and Hebrew, "some beating the pulpit with their fists for madness, and roaring out with open and foaming mouth, that if there were but one Terence or Virgil in the world, and that same in their sleeves, and a fire before them, they would burn them therein, though it should cost them their lives." [89]

This defense of the classics is of course at bottom based upon the conviction that the only proper way to interpret the language of the scriptures was to approach them with a knowledge of the meanings of words as words were used in general literature, not as they were used in later acquired and traditional ecclesiastical senses. The secondary place which Tindale assigned to all writings of a purely literary kind is indicative of the singleness as well as the limitations of his character. His appeal is mainly to commonsense, to reason, and to the average human feeling for justice and fair dealing. He does not often see the lighter half of life, the graceful, the playful, and the humorous. Nor does he often appeal to the meditative or mystical side of religious experience. He uses language mainly as a thinker intent on making his meaning clear, and thus cultivates compactness rather than variety or amplitude of expression. If he

[89] *Answer,* p. 75; see also ibid., p. 55.

is eloquent at all, it is by virtue of the deep feeling which lends warmth and color to what otherwise might seem a naked simplicity.

Tindale's sentences are usually short but well constructed and only slightly more formal than the sentences of colloquial discourse. His vocabulary is plain, but without affectation of rudeness or quaintness. The perfect sense of idiom which distinguishes his translation of the Bible, appears in his other English writings. Although nearly four hundred years have passed since his treatises were written, a reader to-day is seldom brought to a pause by an unfamiliar word or locution, certainly less often than in reading Spenser or Shakspere, or almost any of the greater Elizabethans. The reason for this is partly that Tindale's writings have been potent factors in the development of the modern feeling for English idiom, but partly also, and mainly, the explanation is to be found in the fact that Tindale identified himself, and in consequence his expression, so completely with that great central body of English people, neither scholars nor plowmen, but honest men of good sense, strong in their feeling for personal sincerity and relatively untouched by the changes of literary opinion and fashion, who have been, since his day, the determining elements in English life. The beneficent results of the ferment and turmoil of the English Reformation are typically represented in Tindale's mind and in his style. He has attained absolute clearness of thought; his mind stands alone, refusing the aid of all irrelevant and obscuring detail. And in harmony with this independence and certainty of thought, he expresses himself serenely and lucidly, firmly but not violently, with profound earnestness, but not with passion. His first and only concern in writing was to transmit his message in terms capable of conveying his meaning as clearly and deeply as he felt it himself. Literary devices which served no useful purpose to this end he ignored. Oratory he scorned. He put his faith in his own sincerity of purpose, and asked of language nothing more than that it should enable him to communicate simply, clearly, and sympathetically with his fellow Englishmen.

III

If a few more years of life had been granted to him, Sir Thomas More would not have been so confident that he had adequately confuted Tindale's heresies. For the heresies grew and controversial battles over them continued to rage. Only fifteen years after More's unhappy end, Cranmer issued, in 1550, *A Defence of the true and Catholic Doctrine of the Sacrament of the Body and Blood of our Saviour Christ,* a book which began the controversy between Cranmer and Bishop Gardiner and which raised the question in men's minds not how far Cranmer's teachings differed from the orthodox tenets of the Roman church, but how near they were to the doctrines of the more radical branches of the Continental reformed church.

Always closely related to political affairs, in the reigns of Henry VIII and his successors questions of belief and of church government became more than ever questions of state. With the exception of the brief retardation of the reign of Mary (1553-1558), the trend of public events was in the main favorable to the cause of the reformers. New and difficult problems arose, however, with the attempted establishment of a uniform national church under Elizabeth which were most fully debated in the writings of Jewel and Harding, of Cartwright and Whitgift, in the Marprelate pamphlets, and in the *Ecclesiastical Polity* of Hooker, the crowning achievement of this second great period of English controversy. In the reign of James, the attacks of Bellarmine brought forth all English learning and patriotism in defense of the throne, and at the same time introduced a more cosmopolitan tone into English controversial writing than had hitherto existed. The amount of ink spilled in defenses and confutations, in answers and counter-answers, in the course of these various paper battles is appalling to consider. Only a patient endurance of theological subtleties enables the reader to make his way through the tangled forest of debate. Nothing loses its interest so soon as controversy, especially controversy over minor details of doctrine after the main issues have been settled. Exceptional literary skill may preserve for future generations old questions of outworn significance, but the number of controversial writers who possess this skill must always be small. After a method of controversy was discovered, many of the later controversies of the sixteenth century cease to have even an historical interest from the literary point of view. They show, however, that the ability to write English of a direct and business-like kind was not a rare accomplishment.

Perhaps the most important of the controversies of the early years of Elizabeth's reign were the two polemical battles waged between Jewel, bishop of Salisbury, and Thomas Harding, one time canon of Jewel's cathedral. The first controversy began with a sermon by Jewel, preached in 1559, and several times later, on the subject of the nature of the presence in the sacrament. Harding has an *Answer to M. Juelles Challenge* (1564); this is followed by Jewel's *Reply,* and this in turn by Harding's *Rejoinder* and a second amplified *Rejoinder* the year following the first. The other controversy between Jewel and Harding began with the publication of Jewel's *Apologia Ecclesiae Anglicanae* (1562). Three years later Harding published a *Confutation of a Booke intituled an Apologie,* Jewel answering with a *Defence of the Apology.*

Harding then appeared with a *Detection of sundry foul errors uttered by M. Jewel in his Defence of the Apologie,* and in conclusion of the debate, Jewel published a new and enlarged edition of his *Defence,* taking account of the statements in Harding's *Detection.* Although both participants in the controversies exhibit great industry and learning, from the literary point of view their writings have little to distinguish them from the mass of the controversial literature of the period. Jewel was the better writer of the two, but he follows the conventional method of citing the propositions of his opponent one at a time and then answering them in turn by means of citations from learned authorities, varied by passages of personal recrimination. He writes simply and clearly, but at inordinate length, and, even when he is abusive, without vivacity or picturesqueness.

In this unsettled transitional period of many changes, when both radicals and conservatives were shifting to new positions, the one side tending towards a more stringent Presbyterianism in church government, the other entrenching itself more and more strongly within the system of Episcopalianism, appeared the stupendous work of John Foxe, *The Acts and Monuments of these latter and perilous days,* a work which purports to be a history of the church from primitive times, but which in fact turns every historical record into an argument in favor of reformation doctrine and ends in being a wild ululation of victory rather than a history. The first edition, written in Latin, was issued at Strassburg in 1559, during Foxe's residence abroad in the troubled period of Mary's reign, but an enlarged English version was printed at London in 1563, after Foxe's return to England. Four later editions within the sixteenth century and three in the first half of the seventeenth century testify to its continued popularity, and indeed Protestant

England has never ceased to draw upon *The Acts* as from an inexhaustible source of strength and encouragement.

One's first impression of the book is of amazement at its huge dimensions. Although it is conceived on a scale of epic grandeur, from sheer lack of control it ends in being big rather than great, an agglomeration rather than a structure. Its purpose was, as Foxe himself announces, to tell the tale of all the martyrs of the church, beginning with the earliest persecutions, and narrating with special fullness the events of "these latter and perilous days" in England and Scotland. It becomes thus a church history, the thread of unity being the persecutions of the saints, with digressions on the German reformation, on affairs in Italy, Spain, and Portugal, on the Turks, on Bohemia and the Bohemian reformers. There is also some attention to general history apart from ecclesiastical matters, although Foxe, when he writes historically at all, sticks fairly close to his main subject. But the story is much interrupted by matter which is not historical, by controversial discussions, by comments and sermonizings from Foxe himself. There is a plentiful display of documentary evidence, much of which is quoted literally. It is hardly necessary to state that Foxe wrote as a violent partisan, and that, for all his documents, his method was naïvely uncritical. He so misunderstands Chaucer, for example, as to call him "a right Wicklevian," adding that he knows of certain people who "were brought to the true knowledge of religion" by reading Chaucer's works. Foxe apparently thinks of Chaucer only as the author of the pseudo-Chaucerian *Testament of Love* and *The Plowman's Tale;* the genuine works of Chaucer he doubtless had never read, although he remarks that "Chaucer's works be all printed in one volume and therefore known to all men." [90]

[90] *Acts and Monuments,* edited by Townsend, IV, 248-250.

When at the end Foxe brings his work to a conclusion "not for lack of matter, but to shorten rather the matter for largeness of the volume,"[91] the reader's wonder at the tremendous energy and enthusiasm of the author is likely to be replaced by a feeling of exasperation and profound melancholy. This feeling arises not so much from the stories of bloody cruelty and persecution which the volume contains, although the monotonous succession of these is depressing enough, but from the fact that the story of every godly martyr serves merely as the occasion for the expression of Foxe's own blind and intolerant spirit. He writes with a corroding bitterness and violence of speech that deforms everything he touches; his martyrs are all incredible epitomes of goodness, and their oppressors are all unbelievably wicked. He is always the zealot, partisan, and fanatic. His soul has not come out of the fiery trial chastened and humbled, but hardened in its own anger and righteousness. One longs for a touch of the clear serenity and patient charity of Tindale, but longs in vain. Page after page, volume after volume, the reader staggers through the storm of scorn and abuse, of grotesque exaggeration, of intense but bigoted and narrow feeling, with hardly a ray of genial human sympathy to cheer him on the dark journey. Strong, personal, independent, with a mighty sense of wrong and a determination to express himself to the uttermost, Foxe is the complete summing up of the hardness and bitterness of struggling England in the battle for liberty of thought and teaching. He glories in the righteousness of his own cause, but all else is to be trodden under foot as evil and wicked.

As a writer Foxe is remarkable for the distinctness and concreteness of his expression. His pictures, though always seen through the smoke and red flame of his own burning

[91] *Acts and Monuments,* VIII, 753.

zeal, are dramatically vivid. His characters, whether butcher, baker, village prophet, or dignitary of the church, stand forth with the reality of life. The many dialogues, disputations, and examinations with which he loads his narrative are all unfailingly interesting because in them Foxe catches the very words and tones of conversation. The set portraits of persons, many of whom Foxe must have known intimately, are sketched with admirable clearness and concreteness of detail. Naturally the portraits of the enemies of reform are more vivid than those of the friends. An especially elaborate one is his picture of that arch-foe of the reformers, Stephen Gardiner, bishop of Winchester. "First this viper's bird," the passage begins, "crept out of the town of Bury in Suffolk, was brought up most part of his youth in Cambridge; his wit, capacity, memory and other endowments of nature were not to be complained of, if he had well used and rightly applied the same; wherein there was no great want in God's part in him, if he had not rather himself wanted to the goodness of his gifts."[92] Unfortunately, continues Foxe, to his good gifts were joined as great or greater vices. "He was of a proud stomach and high-minded, in his own opinion and conceit flattering himself too much; in wit, crafty and subtle; toward his superiors, flattering and fair spoken; to his inferiors, fierce; against his equal, stout and envious, namely if in judgment and sentence he any thing withstood him. . . . I will not here speak of that which hath been constantly reported to me touching the monstrous making and mis-shaped fashion of his feet and toes, the nails whereof were said not to be like other men's, but to crook downward, and to be sharp like the claws of ravening beasts." Without denying him learning or natural ability, Foxe gives Gardiner little credit for either. "But what learning or cunning soever

[92] *Acts and Monuments,* VII, 585-588.

it was he had, so it fared in him as it doth in butchers, which use to blow up their flesh. Even so he with boldness and stoutness, and especially with authority, made those gifts which he had to appear much greater than they were in very deed. Whereunto, peradventure, use also, and experience abroad, brought no little helps, rather than either quickness of wit or happiness of education." And so the portrait proceeds, adding detail after detail, but nothing that receives unqualified praise. In contrast to this and similar pictures of monsters of wickedness, one should set Foxe's glorifications of his saints and martyrs, whose virtues are often portrayed with exaggerated pathos and sweetness of feeling. Foxe is unfortunate in that at both extremes he suggests the worst sides of the narrow Puritanism of a later generation, its unctuous piety and exaltation of all within the fold and its venomous hatred and condemnation of all without.

With the accession of Elizabeth to the throne, the terms of religious controversy had changed but the spirit remained much the same. With her strong passion for order and obedience in government, Elizabeth felt no more sympathy with "sects" than Catholic Mary had done. She desired above all things to see one uniform church in England, dignified in its services and strongly managed in its government. It was inevitable under the circumstances that the form of government for this established church should be episcopal and that many details of service and of church furniture should be retained from the ancient and traditional uses of the historical church in England. And it was also inevitable that the successors of the opponents of the papacy, those reformers who since the days of Wiclif had taken the Bible as their sole guide and who had been striving to bring back the church to what they regarded as its primitive, simple forms of worship, should be as bitterly opposed to prelacy as they had been to papacy. Vague and uncertain in their beginnings, the theories and opinions of the popular party were now assuming a definite, even a rigid form. The Bible indeed had been the one recognized staff of support of the reformers after they had renounced the authority of the organized church, but the teachings of the Bible needed formulation and systematization to make them effective as a clearly defined statement of belief. The influence, therefore, of Calvin and the Genevan church, both upon the practice of dissenting sections of the church and also on many persons in the established church who were giving their minds to questions of organization and government, was profound. Although still discussed with animation, for the time being questions of ritual and observance retired to the second place, and the more important matter of the method by which order should be brought into the threatened chaos in the economy of the church received chief attention.

After the death of the mild Grindal, from whom Queen Elizabeth had withdrawn her favor because of what she regarded as a too lenient attitude towards elements of disorder in the church, Elizabeth was fortunate in finding a new archbishop of Canterbury whose zeal in the cause of uniformity was not less than her own, and who combined with this zeal the greatest steadfastness and ruthlessness of purpose. This was John Whitgift, who after many dignities and honors received at Cambridge and in the church, became archbishop of Canterbury in 1583 and held that office for the succeeding two decades. Although not hostile to Calvin's doctrinal views, Whitgift did not share with him his theories of church government. On the contrary he was a firm believer in the episcopal form of government, and both as the opponent of Presbyterianism and the patron and supporter of the defenders of the Established

Church, he perhaps more than any other man of his day was responsible for the fate of the English church in this formative period of its history. A rich man, he lived the life of a prince, dispensing liberal hospitality at his palace, where Queen Elizabeth herself often dined with her "little black husband," as she is said to have called him. When he traveled abroad, it was in great state, with a throng of attendants accompanying him. In the eyes of the Puritan advocates of simplicity, he stood as the typical representative of the proud prelate. Often arbitrary in his actions and of a violent temper, he sometimes passed the bounds of legality in the carrying out of his purposes, and indeed "little flock" might well consider that it had gained nothing if it had freed itself from the power of Rome only to fall into the clutches of such high-handed governors as Whitgift showed himself to be.

The Puritan cause was not, however, without defense, led by Whitgift's controversial opponent, Thomas Cartwright. The hostility between Cartwright and Whitgift began early. As preacher, as scholar, and as disputant, Cartwright won for himself a distinguished place in the life of Cambridge, and it was at Cambridge as defender of Calvinistic principles that he came into conflict with Whitgift. In the year 1569 Cartwright was appointed Lady Margaret professor of divinity and preached in St. Mary's church against the Anglican establishment and in favor of the simple primitive type of church organization. The following year, largely through the instrumentality of Whitgift, he was deprived of his professorship, and soon after of his other university privileges. Whitgift was also responsible for the fact that Cartwright never received his doctor's degree in divinity, a fact which Cartwright seems not readily to have forgotten, since in the controversy with Whitgift which was soon to open, he constantly refers ironically to

Whitgift as Master Doctor—" 370 times is the least," says Whitgift, who apparently took the trouble to count the instances. After a year spent at Geneva, Cartwright returned to England and resumed his defense of the Puritan cause. In this same year of Cartwright's return, 1572, there had appeared a work by two well-known Puritans, John Field and Thomas Wilcox, entitled *An Admonition to Parliament,* which occupies somewhat the same relative position in the controversial literature of the last quarter of the sixteenth century as Simon Fish's *Supplication for the Beggars* in that of the second quarter of the century. Cartwright then wrote a *Second Admonition to the Parliament,* supporting the position of Field and Wilcox. Whitgift now appeared with an answer to the first admonition, and Cartwright followed with a reply to Whitgift. The ball was sent back and forth once more, Whitgift issuing a *Defence* of his answer and Cartwright responding with a second reply, which Whitgift refrained from answering. The controversy was brought to a close by Cartwright's flight from England to escape a warrant for his arrest which had been issued at Whitgift's instigation. After twelve years of exile he returned to England, and under the patronage of the Earl of Leicester, passed the remaining years of his life in comparative quiet. Besides his writings in the controversy with Whitgift, Cartwright's most important publications were a translation of Travers's *Ecclesiasticae Disciplinae . . . Explicatio,* published at Rochelle in 1574, the recognized text-book of Puritanism, and *A Confutation of the Rhemists' Translation,* written about 1582, but not printed until 1618, fifteen years after Cartwright's death.

With the passing of the years much of the flavor of the controversy between Cartwright and Whitgift has evaporated. On both sides the personal element in the discussion is strong and the grasp of general principles is weak, or at least if general principles are clearly perceived, they are insufficiently expressed. Both Cartwright and Whitgift write adequately in a simple business-like way, though neither pays much attention to literary charm and both are likely soon to grow wearisome to readers who are no longer deeply concerned as to what kinds of vestments priests should wear or whether or not they should make the sign of the cross in baptism. For the high lights of personal abuse, one turns to the Marprelate tracts, which take up the fight where Cartwright left it, and for a defense of the cause of episcopacy and an explanation of the meaning of forms, one turns to Hooker, by the support of whom Whitgift accomplished more than by all his own writings or repressive acts of legislation.

The immediate circumstances under which the Martin Marprelate tracts were written and published are wrapped to a large extent in a cloud of uncertainty. Not one but a number of persons were concerned in the production of the tracts, and the name Martin Marprelate was something more than the pen-name of an author. Martin indeed was a dramatically conceived character, unified and consistent, like the Piers Plowman and Jack Upland of earlier periods of English religious controversy, and he sums up the spirit and tone of one large section of the Puritan party of the last quarter of the sixteenth century. It is not known who invented the character, nor is it possible to determine with any degree of certainty in most instances who wrote the various tracts that appeared during the course of the controversy. It was natural that suspicion should fall upon Cartwright, but Cartwright disavowed complicity in the production of the pamphlets and expressed his strong disapproval of the methods of the Martinists. In the interests of self-protection, every effort had to be made by the Martinists to carry on their activities in secrecy. Their program was one of direct attack, not only upon the theory of episcopacy, but upon the private lives and practices of the bishops themselves. Whitgift, the archbishop of Canterbury, Aylmer, the bishop of London, and Cooper, the bishop of Winchester, three princes of the church, were the targets at which the heaviest firing was directed. The ingenious methods by which the various writings of Martin were printed and distributed in defiance of the licensing laws of the press and the inquisition of Whitgift, as well as the mystery of the composition of the tracts themselves, have afforded one of the most intricate puzzles to which the antiquarian student of English literature can give his attention. The important facts, however, are plain enough. Seven of the Marprelate tracts have survived, which show sufficiently the methods and purpose which governed the authors in their composition, besides a considerable number of tracts, pamphlets, and books by opponents of Martin, or by favorers of the Puritan cause who were not within the inner circle of the Martinists.

Of the various writings immediately preceding the publication of the Marprelate tracts, two must be noticed because of their direct connection with the tracts themselves. One of these was John Udall's *State of the Church of England.*[93] This is a dialogue in which five characters take part: Diotrephes, a bishop, Tertullus, a papist, Demetrius, a usurer, Pandochus, an innkeeper, who is equally well inclined to all teachings, and Paul, a preacher, who defends Puritan principles. This tract appeared in April, 1588, without license, and was printed by Robert Waldegrave. It is written with considerable animation and dramatic verisimilitude, and it presents the case against the bishops and in favor of "these precise and hot preachers," as they are called by Demetrius, in the most outspoken fashion. It

[93] Edited by Arber, *English Scholar's Library,* No. 5.

appeared anonymously, but Waldegrave's connection with it soon became known, his press and types were seized and destroyed, and he himself was compelled to flee the country. Udall continued his campaign against episcopacy, and shortly afterwards was brought to trial on charge of sedition. Sentence of death was passed upon him, and though the sentence was not carried out, Udall died in prison, probably from neglect and the hardships of prison life. Udall was a distinguished scholar and a man of blameless private life. His misfortunes called forth expressions of sympathy for him and efforts on his behalf from many quarters. One of his friends was John Penry, a Welsh Puritan, who seems now to have become the main mover in the Marprelate plot. Udall provided Penry with some of the materials utilized in the first of the Marprelate tracts, but beyond this he apparently had no connection with the plot itself. Before the appearance of any of the Marprelate tracts proper, however, Penry, who compares himself to St. Paul and Jeremiah and whose known writings show that he had command over the peculiar style of invective employed in the tracts, had issued the second of the two writings mentioned above. In 1587 he published a work entitled *A Treatise containing the aequity of an humble supplication which is to be exhibited unto her gracious majesty, and this high Court of Parliament in the behalfe of the Countrey of Wales, that some order may be taken for the preaching of the Gospell among those people,* in which he called attention to the neglected state of the church in Wales. The freedom with which Penry had criticised the church and its ministers in this work immediately aroused the hostility of Whitgift. The author of it was called before the court of High Commission, was accused of heresy and treason, and was cast into prison. The charges against him, however, were never specified, nor was he at this time brought to trial. After a period of imprisonment, illegal since there was no charge against him, Penry was released, and it seems probable that soon after under the incentive of the harsh treatment which he had received, he set about the organization of the Marprelate conspiracy in which he was unquestionably one of the chief figures.[94] It is not necessary to follow Penry through the various stages of his career, but it will be sufficient to mention that in 1593, by which time the Marprelate controversy was closed but not forgotten, he was brought to trial and was condemned and hanged on a charge of having written words inciting to rebellion and insurrection during his residence in Scotland, whither he had fled to escape the dangers resulting from his suspected complicity in the Marprelate publications. If the matter had been brought to trial, doubtless a conviction could have been secured in connection with the Marprelate tracts, but the other charges were apparently preferred as being more readily susceptible of proof.

The first two of the Marprelate tracts, in abbreviated forms of their long titles called *The Epistle* and *The Epitome,* appeared in the latter part of the year 1588 and are on related subjects. *The Epistle* is announced as an introduction to Martin's proposed answer to a book by John Bridges, then dean of Salisbury and later bishop of Oxford, entitled *A Defence of the Government established in the church of England,* which had appeared the preceding year. Although Bridges, "doctor of Divillitie," is ostensibly the main object of attack in *The Epistle,* the tract is addressed to all, "whether fickers generall, worshipful paltripolitans, or any other of the holy league of subscription." [95] Martin

[94] See Wilson, "A New Tract from the Marprelate Press," *The Library,* X, 225-240, for a discussion of Penry's *Exhortation,* published under his own name in 1588. This tract is similar in tone to the anonymous Marprelate tracts.

[95] Peterham's ed., p. 1.

declares that he keeps a register of all the bishops' knaveries and that it is his intention to spare none. John Aylmer, bishop of London, "the Lord dumbe John,"[96] comes in for a special share of attention, and Thomas Cooper, then dean of Winchester, whose "face is made of seasoned wainscot and will lie as fast as a dog can trot,"[97] is not forgotten. A sample is given of the bishop of Gloucester's preaching, whose mannerism apparently it was to repeat certain words over and over: "John, John, the grace of God, the grace of God, the grace of God: gracious John, not graceless John, but gracious John. John, holy John, holy John, not John ful of holes, but holy John."[98] Dean Bridges, however, is the center to which Martin returns from all his excursions, his main endeavor being to make Bridges seem ridiculous as a writer. The Dean is assumed not to have written *Gammer Gurton's Needle,* which shows both wit and invention, because his books "seeme to proceede from the braynes of a woodcocke, as having neyther wit nor learning."[99] Martin quotes sentences from *The Defence,* which indeed are chaotic and unintelligible, declaring that "a man might almost run himself out of breath before he could come to a full point in many places in your booke."[100] He advises the bishops in general to write syllogistically if they must write, "for you shame yourselves when you use any continued speach, because your stile is so rude and barbarous."[101] Martin is evidently proud of his own style and speaks of it frequently. His command over sentence-structure, his ingenuity in subject matter, his lightness and high spirits, his willingness to do anything for the sake of vivacity and variety, give him a great advantage over his worthy but heavy adversary.

The Epistle was followed almost immediately by *The*

[96] Peterham's ed., p. 11.
[97] Ibid., p. 43.
[98] Ibid., p. 60.
[99] Ibid., p. 13.
[100] Ibid., p. 15.
[101] Ibid., p. 68.

Epitome, which professedly was to contain a summary of Bridge's arguments, with answers to them. In point of fact but a small part of the book is concerned with *The Defence,* although a few passages are quoted and answered in mock-serious fashion. In *The Epitome* as in *The Epistle,* Martin is a free lance, striking here and there wherever he sees a head, and more intent on making his opponents seem ridiculous than in answering their arguments.

Smarting under the sting of Martin's satire, an answer was attempted, though not in kind,[102] by Thomas Cooper, who in 1589, as the official representative of the bishops, sent forth *An Admonition to the People of England.* In this admonition the writer professes not to satisfy all kinds of men, but only the "moderate and godly." He consistently maintains a dignified and restrained tone. Writing with considerable good sense and wisdom, he makes no attempt to defend abuses, but discourages rash accusations and of course denies many of Martin's specific charges. He pleads, in reproof of Martin, for a charitable attitude towards the bishops, who, being spiritual fathers, should not be treated as the sons of Noah treated their father, but their infirmities should be hidden from the public gaze. "A wart in the face and a blemish in a bishop is no small disfiguring of either of them"—but it is merely the prominence of the bishop which causes his blemishes to seem so great.[103] Martin is reproved for his looseness and boldness of speech, for his "bitter stile of malicious Momus dipt in the gall of ungodlinesse."[104] But Cooper shows plainly enough that the wounds which Martin had inflicted were still burning.

[102] As Bacon approvingly noted in his *Advertisement touching the controversies of the Church of England, Letters and Life,* I, 77.

[103] Peterham's ed., p. 14.

[104] Ibid., p. 44.

As a contrast to Martin's portrait of himself with a face of "seasoned wainscot," he endeavors to show Martin his "owne ougly shape," proceeding with a portrait of Martin like a medieval allegory, with Dolus, Fraus, Insidiae, etc., as part of the machinery. Nothing could show more completely Cooper's inadequacy to meet Martin on his own ground than this labored effort, and indeed, as Hooker might have said, silence would have been a more effective answer to Martin's impertinence.

As might have been foreseen, Cooper's *Admonition,* instead of quieting Martin, stirred him to new activities. In a fantastic broadside, *Certain Mineral and Metaphysical Schoolpoints to be defended by the reverend bishops,* Martin presents a list of thirty-seven absurd propositions, supposed to be held by various of his enemies, many of which are perversions of statements made in Cooper's *Admonition.* A fuller answer to the dean of Winchester, however, appeared soon, which took its title from a London street cry, *Hay any worke for Cooper, or a briefe Pistle, directed by Waye of an hublication to the reverende Byshopps.*[105] Although the title calls this a "briefe Pistle," it is the longest, as it is the most amusing of the Marprelate tracts. The impudence, the bluster, and the abusiveness of the earlier tracts are still much in evidence. With an impish Py, hy, hy, hy, of laughter Martin pokes fun at Cooper for his mispronunciation of a Greek word in one of his sermons.[106] "Hold my cloake there somebody," he says, "that I may go roundly to work."[107] And again, after a somewhat serious passage, he recalls himself with the roar that is a regular part of his stock in trade: "Whau, whau, but where have I bin al this while. . . . Why Martin, I say,

[105] That is, *Have you any work for cooper,* etc.
[106] Peterham's ed., p. 10.
[107] Ibid., p. 23.

hast tow forgotten thy selfe?"[108] He continues then in a humorous passage in dialect: "But did I not say truely of thee y[t] thou canst cog, face and lye as fast as a dog can trot, and that thou hast a right seasoned wainscoate face of ti nowne, chwarnt tee, ti vorehead zaze hard as horne."[109] The tract, however, is not entirely made up of such ridicule and buffoonery, but many grave charges are seriously and specifically brought against the bishops, and some attempt is made to answer the arguments of Cooper's *Admonition*. One of the most interesting passages of the tract is that in which Martin for a moment speaks seriously about himself:

"Like you any of these Nuts, John Canterbury?", he says to Whitgift, "his Canterburinesse." "I am not disposed to jest in this serious matter. I am called Martin Marprelat. There be many that greatly dislike my doinges. I may have my wants I know. For I am a man. But my course I knowe to be ordinary and lawfull. I sawe the cause of Christ's government, and of the Bishops antichristian dealing to be hidden. The most part of men could not be gotten to read any thing written in the defence of the on[e] and against the other. I bethought mee therefore of a way whereby men might be drawne to do both, perceiving the humors of men in these times (especially of those that are in any place) to be given to mirth. I tooke that course. I might lawfully do it. I, for jesting is lawful by circumstances, even in the greatest matters. The circumstances of time, place and persons urged me thereunto. I never profaned the word in any jest. Other mirth I used as a covert, wherein I would bring the truth into light. The Lord being the authour both of mirth and gravitie, is it not lawfull in it selfe for the trueth to use eyther of these wayes when the circumstances do make it lawful? . . . My purpose was and is to do good. I know I have don no harme, howsoever some may judg Martin to mar al . . . I know I am disliked of many which are your enemies, that is of many which you cal puritans. It

[108] Peterham's ed., p. 53.

[109] Ibid., p. 65.

is their weaknes. I am threatened to be hanged by you. What though I were hanged, do you thinke your cause shalbe the better. For the day that you hange Martin, assure your selves, there wil 20. Martins spring in my place." [110]

This defense of his methods was continued by Martin in the tract which followed, *Theses Martinianae,* purporting to have been set forth as a posthumous work of Martin's, by a "prety stripling of his, Martin Junior, and dedicated by him to his good neame and nuncka, Maister John Kankerbury." After the *Theses* came *The just censure and reproofe of Martin Junior,* by another member of this imaginary family, "his reverend and elder brother, Martin Senior." The last of the Martinist tracts, *The Protestatyon of Martin Marprelat,* which appeared in the latter part of 1589, was written and published after the capture of the secret press which the Martinists had used hitherto, and it consists mainly of a protestation on Martin's part of his intention to continue the defense of his cause, and of a challenge to the prelates to discuss openly the questions in dispute between them.

In the wake of the genuine Marprelate tracts there followed a number of imitations and rejoinders. Recognizing the futility of any serious answer to Martin, the bishops, according to Walton with the approval of Whitgift, sought for aid among the professed literary wits of the day. In response to this call, tracts were written by John Lyly, Thomas Nashe, whose influence in silencing Martin Walton greatly exaggerates, and Richard Harvey, all of whom owe a great deal to Martin's style but never equal it. Lyly's *Pappe with a hatchet* is an obvious effort to out-Martin Martin in his own manner. The writer professes "rayling," and tries to coin words after the fashion of Martin. The

[110] Peterham's ed., pp. 33-41.

tract is much more noisy and scurrilous than Martin, lacking of course Martin's underlying seriousness of purpose and consistently substituting coarseness for Martin's wit. The author is at a disadvantage also in not knowing who Martin actually is, and consequently his personal charges must all be general and manifestly invented. *An Almond for a Parrat,* which may have been written by Nashe, is preceded by a letter addressed to "Monsieur du Kempe, Jestmonger and Vice-gerent generall to the Ghost of Dicke Tarlton," and the whole tract is a piece of rather elaborate fooling. Martin's style apparently impressed the author of this tract deeply, although he declares that "the filth of the stewes, distild into ribauldry termes, cannot confectionate a more intemperate stile then his Pamphlets."[111] Commenting on his own style, he remarks that Martin thinks no man can write but himself, adding that he is willing "to try it out by the teeth for the best benefice in England."[112] Also in a ranting style imitative of Martin is the *Plaine Percevall* of Richard Harvey, in which Plain Percevall (who is a very distant cousin indeed of the old Piers) takes the part of peacemaker. The author implies that Martin is merely the literary tool of more powerful persons. "I pray thee," he says, "make once an *auricular confession,* tell me in mine eare: is the desire of *Reformation* so deeply imprinted in thine heart, as the terme is often printed in thy papers? Is it conscience or lucre that spurgals thy hackney pen to force it take so high a hedge as thou leapest at?"[113] But these and the other imitative tracts which attended and followed the publication of Martin's own writings are all of secondary inspiration and prove that the new and original note, the one which held the attention not only of the digni-

[111] Peterham's ed., p. 11.
[112] Ibid., p. 44.
[113] Ibid., p. 10.

taries of the church and their Puritan enemies but of the literary public as well, was the one which was struck by the mysterious Martin himself.

In the development of English prose, the Marprelate tracts occupy a place in that long line of invective controversial writing which begins with Wiclif's sermons, and which finds in Martin not its final but perhaps its most picturesque and least restrained expression. Although popular in their appeal, the Marprelate tracts are not the work of an ignorant or uneducated man any more than the disquisitions of Piers Plowman or Jack Upland were. Behind the disguise of an apparently erratic popular style, one perceives in Martin not only profound feeling but also clear comprehension of the two main points of his opposition to the bishops, first that they support a false form of ecclesiastical government, and second, that they are personally corrupt, ignorant, and incompetent. In his shameless references to persons by name and in his free use of slanderous material, all under cover of anonymity, Martin indeed exceeds the limits of anything that had hitherto appeared in English invective, nor are his methods, we may think, quite justified by his excuses. The significant point is, however, that Martin here also employed his method as a trained writer, perfectly conscious of the effects which he wished to secure. Comparison with his literary opponents, Lyly, Nashe, and Harvey, shows his superiority over them. They were drawn into the controversy in part undoubtedly for mercenary reasons and perhaps in part from a desire to try their metal against so skillful a writer as Martin. They endeavored to answer wit with wit, but where Martin's charges against his enemies have the flavor of genuine incidents of real life, told with all of Martin's peculiar vivacity, his imitators were compelled to fall back upon 'merry jests' and tales of the conventional popular style. The great achievement of Martin was the creation of so real a character as Martin himself. This creation was a 'poetic' device of the kind which Tindale criticised in the writings of More. Nor did the Puritans of Martin's own day altogether approve of his methods. Cartwright and others specifically condemned them, not only because of the license of ink with which Martin taunted his enemies, but also from the feeling that Martin was lowering the tone of serious discussion by introducing too great an element of fancy and literary artifice, the tricks of the stage, as they were regarded, into his writings. Bacon in a scathing rebuke of what he characterized as the spirit of profane scoffing in the controversial writing of the day evidently alludes to Martin when he speaks of "this immodest and deformed manner of writing lately entertained, whereby matters of religion are handled in the style of the stage." [114] The proper method of controversy, as it was commonly considered, was first to state or quote, point by point, the specific opinions of your opponent, following each point by its refutation. Martin was aware of this, but he declares that such writings were not read. It is curious to find that the dignified Hooker, who also departed from the conventional method, and the flippant Martin were subjected to the same kind of criticism. As it was Hooker's merit to show that controversy need not necessarily dwell merely upon details and points but may properly concern itself with general principles, so it was Martin's particular achievement to illustrate the fact that controversial writing need not be heavy, dry, and pedantic.

The model employed by the inventor of the character of Martin may have been, as was frequently charged against him, some popular actor of the day, like Tarleton or Kemp. Martin always monologizes. He appears alone upon the

[114] *Letters and Life,* I, 76.

stage, figuratively speaking, and pours forth his torrent of invective in the ranting, huff-snuff style which had been made familiar to the public not only by comic actors but by many a dithyrambic popular preacher. He is fond of puns, of mutilated and newly invented words, of loud ejaculations and shoutings, which serve the same humorous purpose as the thwackings of the Merry Andrew or the antics of the Vice in the old comedy. But his changes are sudden. In an instant he drops the mask of Momus, delivers a quick home thrust that Dryden might envy, and then back to his buffoonery. Although the term was frequently applied to him by his victims, Martin does not deserve to be called scurrilous. Impertinent and facetious, often bitterly personal in his more serious charges, he does not descend to indecencies. He merely says in writing what many respectable Puritans doubtless said in conversation. On the other hand, neither Martin's inventor nor Puritans in general would have been willing to regard Martin as typical of their class. The character was hastily conceived as a dramatic invention fitted to arrest and hold attention by reason of its extravagance. A longer period of reflection might have given the character a greater depth and truthfulness, at the same time freeing it of some of its superabundant vivacity. The germ of an effective literary satire is contained in the creation, to which a more mature art might have given permanent form. In the circumstances under which the tracts were written, however, the mere invention of so picturesque and consistent a device as Martin Marprelate was no small literary achievement. Only the vigilance and the extreme zeal of the friends of episcopacy in suppressing the Marprelate tracts could have prevented such a character from developing into a genuinely popular hero of Puritanism.

IV

Though he was not immediately connected with the Marprelate controversy, or indeed after his early years with any controversy, it was the controversial spirit of the age which provided Hooker with the main incentive to the composition of his great work, *Of the Laws of Ecclesiastical Polity*. This book is a survey of the chief points in ecclesiastical procedure and doctrine which were under discussion in the second half of the sixteenth century, especially those points debated in the several writings of Cartwright and Whitgift. It is genuinely judicial and philosophical in tone, for Hooker temperamentally was better fitted for peaceable than for violent discussion.

After some years at Oxford, Hooker retired in 1584 to the quiet country living of Drayton Beauchamp, in Buckinghamshire. But he was not permitted to remain long in this congenial retreat. In the following year, through the influence of Whitgift, he was appointed Master of the Temple, as a compromise candidate instead of the well-known Puritan, Walter Travers, author of the *Ecclesiasticae Disciplinae et Anglicanae Ecclesiae . . . explicatio*. Travers was already afternoon reader in the Temple and was being strongly recommended by his friends and followers for the mastership. Unwillingly Hooker left his country living where, in his own words as quoted by Walton in his *Life of Hooker*, he might "see God's blessing spring out of the earth and be free from noise, and eat that bread which he might more properly call his own in privacy and quietness," for the more dignified but less peaceful post of preacher in the Temple. As Master of the Temple, Hooker found himself under the necessity of expressing fully and clearly the position he wished to occupy in the engrossing questions of the day concerning ecclesiastical discipline and government. His own opinions were by no means uncertain, and opposed as they were in most respects to those of Travers, the Temple soon became the scene of a vigorous debate. In the familiar words preserved by Fuller and Walton, "the pulpit spoke pure Canterbury in the morning and Geneva in the afternoon, until Travers was silenced." The silencing of Travers was not long delayed. Although the discussion between Hooker and Travers was earnest, it seems to have been conducted in a dignified manner and with little of the personal abuse characteristic of most debates of the times.[115] At the close of it, the rare spectacle is presented of two theological controversialists who separated with respect for each other, and with their self-respect maintained. In the eyes of Whitgift, however, any such discussion, no matter how dignified, was unseemly, and in his usual way, he brought it to an end by inhibiting Travers from preaching, mainly on the ground of irregularity in his ordination.

Though the immediate discussion was over, Hooker's mind was by no means at rest. He was already revolving the project of a great work in which the nature and authority of laws and government should be fundamentally examined. This work was begun at the Temple, but Hooker soon found the atmosphere of the place uncongenial to the carrying out of his task. He therefore wrote to the archbishop that he was weary of the "noise and oppositions" of the place, that God and nature did not intend him for contentions, but for "study and quietness," and he concluded with a request that he might be removed to some quiet charge where he could proceed with the treatise already begun, on "the justification of the laws of our ecclesiastical polity." This modest request was granted, and

[115] Hooker and Travers were related by marriage, Travers' brother having married Hooker's sister.

in the year 1591 he entered into the living of Boscombe, near Salisbury, exchanging this in 1595 for the living of Bishopsborne, near Canterbury. There are no startling or dramatic events in the life of Hooker. Walton presents a charming picture of him, in which his humility, however, is somewhat exaggerated at the expense of his sagacity, and the testimony of all his contemporaries is at one in finding in him the perfect type of the learned but benign and gentle scholar. As a preacher, Hooker was lacking in animation, and being short-sighted, "where he fixt his eyes at the beginning of his sermon, there they continued till it was ended."[116] Fuller preserves the report that when Hooker and Travers were both preaching at the Temple, "the congregation ebbed in the morning and flowed in the afternoon."[117] But it was "the happy pen of this humble man" that expressed his character most fully, and it is by means of these writings that later generations of Englishmen have been led to understand and to admire his real greatness of mind and of soul.

The design of Hooker's monumental book was carefully considered, and, it seems probable, almost completely carried out by the author. The whole was to consist of eight parts or books, but unfortunately only the first five were printed at the time of Hooker's death in 1600. The remaining three books, probably nearly ready for publication as Hooker left them, have suffered both from the carelessness and the editorial interference of Hooker's friends. The original sixth book, indeed, is generally thought to have been altogether lost, that which is now published as the sixth book being made up from other of Hooker's writings which formed no part of his original plan. The seventh and eighth books, as printed, are probably revisions of Hooker's own manuscript. Those books which appeared in

[116] Walton's Life. [117] Fuller, Bk. IX, 216.

Hooker's lifetime were issued in two sections. The first four, published without date, appeared, according to Walton, in 1594, having been entered in the Stationers' Register the preceding year. The fifth book was published by itself in 1597. The fifth book is the longest, equaling in length the first four books, and together with the first book, is that part of Hooker's work which is now most generally read.

The first book, which is introductory to the whole work, presents a broad philosophic discussion of "laws and their several kinds in general." It is Hooker's purpose here, following his consistent practice of stating general principles before proceeding to specific details, to discover "the grounds and first original causes" of all laws. It is his fundamental position that all things work according to law, by which he means in accordance with reason and purpose. The supreme all-comprehending law is the law of God, whose nature it is to work only according to the reasonable mandates of his will. Reason, therefore, there always must be in the working of God, although man in his weakness may not be able to discern this reason. As Hooker understands the term, law means not merely the "rule of working which superior authority imposeth," but any kind of rule or canon "whereby actions are framed." [118] The rule of the working of God is therefore the framing of his actions in harmony with his will. That part of God's law which acts through natural agents is called usually "nature's law"; the law of reason "bindeth creatures reasonable in this world," divine law is known to man only by special revelation from God, and human law is that which men, "out of the law either of reason or of God probably gathering to be expedient," [119] make to be a law. The law of God's being by which he must work in accord with the reasonable dictates of his will Hooker calls "the first eternal

[118] Bk. I, ed. Church, p. 11.

[119] Ibid., p. 11.

law," and the law which regulates the actions of all God's creatures he calls "the second eternal law." Nothing therefore stands outside the rule of law. God himself cannot act by caprice, since all his actions must spring from his will, which is governed by the dictates of reason and of the good. And inasmuch as all creatures of God act by consent of God, the workings of the second eternal law are "in some sort ordered by the first eternal law."[120] Hooker then proceeds in a passage of great beauty to distinguish between those natural agents whose actions are involuntary, the winds, the sun, and the rain, all of them under the guidance of a director of infinite knowledge, and those creatures of God who are endowed with the power of voluntary action. Of these, the highest in order are the angels, in whom the desire to resemble God in goodness, "maketh them unweariable and even unsatiable in their longing to do by all means all manner good unto all the creatures of God, but especially unto the children of men, in the countenance of whose nature, looking downward, they behold themselves beneath themselves, even as upward, in God, beneath whom themselves are, they see that character which is nowhere but in themselves and us resembled."[121] Like the angels, man is free in his actions, and again like them, the motive force of his action is the desire of goodness. But man differs from the higher powers in that the latter "already have full and complete knowledge in the highest degree that can be imparted to them,"[122] whereas man continually strives towards that which, by the limits of his nature, is unattainable. Man's reach exceeds his grasp, in the words of a modern poet.

As the guide and director in the discovery of the good, man is governed by reason. "For the laws of well-doing are the dictates of right reason. Children, which are not as

[120] Church, p. 11. [121] Ibid., p. 19. [122] Ibid., p. 24.

yet come unto those years whereat they may have; again, innocents, which are excluded by natural defect from ever having; thirdly, madmen, which for the present cannot possibly have the use of right reason to guide themselves, have for their guide the reason that guideth other men, which are tutors over them to seek and to procure their good for them. In the rest there is that light of reason, whereby good may be known from evil, and which discovering the same rightly is termed right." [123] Evil in man's actions results not from an inherent love of evil, but from the choice of the less good in preference to the greater good, and the causes why man sometimes chooses the less good are mainly ignorance and sloth. "Goodness doth not move by being, but by being apparent; and therefore many things are neglected which are most precious, only because the value of them lieth hid." [124] And again custom or habit, "inuring the mind by long practice, and so leaving there a sensible impression, prevaileth more than reasonable persuasion what way soever. Reason therefore may rightly discern the thing which is good, and yet the will of man not incline itself thereunto, as oft as the prejudice of sensible experience doth oversway." [125]

Having laid this preliminary foundation of general principles, Hooker then proceeds to the practically more important task of showing by what signs and tokens man may know the good. Of these the most certain proof of the good is that "all men do so account it." [126] "The general and perpetual voice of men is as the sentence of God himself. For that which all men have at all times learned, nature herself must needs have taught; and God being the author of nature, her voice is but his instrument." [127] Action in harmony with the nature of its being is the surest

[123] Church, pp. 29-30.
[124] Ibid., p. 31.
[125] Ibid., p. 31.
[126] Ibid., p. 35.
[127] Ibid., pp. 35-36.

test of the good for every creature. By this test man as an individual aspires towards the goodness of God which is reflected in him, and as a social being, living in congregation with other men, he governs himself in such a way as neither to occasion injury to others nor suffer it himself. This is righteousness, the reasonable duty of man to God and his fellow-man, just as transgression of these laws of his being is sin. Nature herself is the great teacher of laws and statutes whereby men are to live. And formal laws, such as are fashioned by social and political bodies, are merely outdraughts from this great law of nature, formulated in various ways as expediency teaches in order that men may live with least hindrance in harmony with the law of their nature. No one form of government, therefore, has divine right, but the choice is left arbitrary, according as circumstances shall dictate. And since the choice of governments is free, manifestly also the forms of social and political laws may be altered as experience shows how they may be brought into closer harmony with the laws of nature and reason. Laws which men thus formulate Hooker calls positive laws, and declares that they are not universally binding, being but man's fallible and occasional interpretation of the law of nature. On the other hand a genuine law of nature, whether formulated or not, is eternal and universally binding.

In the search for perfection, mankind is led to seek three kinds of good, first a sensual, which is concerned with the physical accompaniments of life, second an intellectual, which is concerned with such "knowledge and virtue as doth most commend men"[128] to each other in the social human relations, and third a spiritual, which has to do with man's imperfect apprehension of things spiritual and supernatural, the eternal law of God's being. What, then, are

[128] Church, p. 73.

the signs and tokens of right reason on the part of man in this third and most important of his aspirations? It is in answering this question that Hooker makes clear the fundamental difference between his own way of thinking and the narrow Puritanism of the Bible-men which for two centuries it had been their endeavor to force upon the English mind. Accepting the scriptures as a divinely inspired gift of God, the necessary position to take in that day, Hooker looks upon them as only one of the ways in which the law of God's being is revealed to man. In them there are contained many laws or truths of universal and eternal value, but they also contain many positive laws, "but personally expedient to be practised of certain men."[129] To raise such expedient laws to the position of eternal laws, that is, to take every statement of the scriptures as a direct command of God to all men, in the manner of many Puritan thinkers, would be to impose upon man a tyranny irrational and intolerable. Every positive law, even of the scriptures, must first be tested by its agreement or disagreement with the eternal laws of nature before it can be accepted as of general value. But more than this. The scriptures contain many eternal laws or truths necessary to salvation. How are we to know these truths, except by the aid of natural reason, "when of things necessary the very chiefest is to know what books we are bound to esteem holy, which point is confessed impossible for the scripture itself to teach?"[130] Supplementing, completing every law of the scriptures, every law or tradition of the church, every law of states and other bodies and every custom of society, the law of reason, implanted in man by God as one of the means of revealing himself, must help man to the knowledge of those things which he is capable of knowing. Revealed religion is an aid to the natural understanding, not, with responsible

[129] Church, p. 84. [130] Ibid., p. 86.

beings, a substitute for it. Rites and customs are merely expedient practices which justify themselves only as they help in the perception of truth. Over all, guiding all, is the will of man making for goodness and the intelligent understanding of man whereby he examines into the causes, reasons, and grounds of the good in order that he may accept it.

In this spirit of earnest and wise endeavor it was that Hooker set about his great task of finding some "method of reducing the laws whereof there is present controversy unto their first original causes," for, he continues, "Is there any thing which can either be thoroughly understood or soundly judged of, till the very first causes and principles from which originally it springeth be made manifest?"[131] But though such is briefly the manner in which Hooker approaches his subject in this first book, it is only fair to add that no summary abstract can do justice to the firmness and the breadth of his hold upon ideas, to the wealth of suggestion and illustration he displays in expounding them, to the admirable clearness of his exposition, or to the deep and serene love of law, whose "seat is the bosom of God, her voice the harmony of the world," that lends life and color to the most abstract of his general principles.

The second book discusses in detail a question to which a general answer had already been given in the first book, that is, whether "scripture is the only rule of all things which in this life may be done by men." But here also, Hooker keeps himself free, as far as possible, from controversy with specific persons. His endeavor is to answer a general position, not to overcome an opponent in an argument. Opening with a discussion of the real nature of the church, the true members of which are clearly known only to God, "who seeth their hearts and understandeth all their secret cogitations,"[132] the third book continues with the discussion begun

[131] Church, p. 98.

[132] *Works,* ed. Keble, I, 219.

in the second by inquiring whether "in scripture there must be of necessity contained a form of church polity, the laws whereof may in nowise be altered." Hooker's answer to this question is, obviously, that forms of church polity are merely the positive and expedient practices of men, that no one form of church government is necessary to salvation, and that the government of the church is to be determined as experience and reason dictate. The fourth book opens with a general discussion of the use of ceremonies in the church, and considers then in detail the charge that the established church had retained many rites and ceremonies from the Roman church which it should have followed the example of certain reformed churches in discarding.

The famous fifth book, although it really continues the subject of the fourth, its theme being announced as the alleged superstitions and corrupt practices which survived in the Established Church, takes a fresh start and treats its subject with a fullness and independence which give the book somewhat the character of a separate work. One notes with pleasure that with the passing of time, Hooker's spirit has not become harsh or bitter towards his opponents, but if anything, his charity and his serene wisdom are greater than ever. The wits of the multitude he perceives are not naturally perverse, but "being possesst with some notable either dislike or liking of any one thing whatsoever, sundry other in the mean time may escape them unperceived."[133] This loose regard of circumstances is the nurse of vulgar folly.[134] For his own part Hooker declares his purpose to be to help men to think soundly and on all sides of subjects. He cares little for "sharp and subtile discourses of wit," and his endeavor is not so much to overthrow his opponents, as "to yield them just and reasonable

[133] Bk. V, ed. Bayne, p. 8. [134] Ibid., p. 15.

cause of these things, which for want of due consideration heretofore, they misconceived." [135] He reprehends that art of contradiction by scorn and mockery, with its "wanton superfluity of wit, too much insulting over the patience of more virtuously disposed minds." [136] His own patience seldom gives way. Sometimes he feels that if it were not "to satisfy the minds of the simpler sort of men," many of the contemporary questions of controversy would not be worth the labor required to answer them.[137] "We are still persuaded," he says again, "that a bare denial is answer sufficient to things which mere fancy objecteth; and that the best apology to words of scorn and petulancy is Isack's apology to his brother Ishmael, the apology which patience and silence maketh. Our answer therefore to their reasons is no; to their scoffs, nothing." [138]

The specific subjects which Hooker discusses in the fifth book are many and varied. With characteristic Elizabethan feeling for stately ceremony, he argues for a certain degree of sumptuousness in church structures and furniture. The exaggerated importance of the sermon and the comparative neglect of prayer in the Puritan discipline he notes with disapproval, and of course defends the use of fixed forms in the church service, both for the sake of dignity and as the best expression of social religious feeling. In a noble passage, which Milton must have read with pleasure, he justifies the art of music, not only for its general human interest, but also as an effective means of divine worship. But nowhere, perhaps, does Hooker rise to greater heights of dignity and eloquence than in the carefully constructed chapter, Of the Cross in Baptism, with its admirable balance between superstition and genuine reverence, or in that chapter of even profounder feeling, Of the Sacrament of the Body and

[135] Bayne, p. 14.
[136] Ibid., p. 21.
[137] Ibid., p. 54.
[138] Ibid., p. 150.

Blood of Christ, where without evading the theoretical sides of this most engrossing theological question of the times, Hooker reveals both practical wisdom and the piety of a genuinely religious nature in the expressed wish that "men would more give themselves to meditate with silence what we have by the sacrament, and less to dispute of the manner how."[139]

Of the three remaining books it will be sufficient to note that, in the form in which they have been preserved, the sixth treats mainly of the Puritan contention that the scriptures themselves establish the particular form of church government by lay elders advocated in the Puritan discipline, that the seventh is a formal defense of the episcopal form of church government, and that the eighth discusses the general question of the relation of church and state and the degree and nature of the king's authority in ecclesiastical matters.

With Hooker's claims to distinction as a philosopher and theologian we are not here primarily concerned. That he owed much to Aristotle, to the Greek fathers, to St. Augustine, to Thomas Aquinas, and to others, is sufficiently evident from the annotations with which the labors of his editors have illustrated his writings. But whether or not Hooker was great or original as a thinker, he was both regarded as a temper of mind revealing itself through the technic of literary expression. His book, in the first place, has Elizabethan largeness of conception and of execution. It is a work of the age of giants, worthy of its place in the rank with the writings of Bacon, Shakspere, and the other great Elizabethans. Nor does Hooker's name suffer when it is coupled with that of Aristotle, "the patriarch of philosophers," as he is called by the writer of *A Christian Letter of Certain English Protestants,*[140] in which under the

[139] Bayne, p. 373. [140] Ibid., *Eccles. Polity,* p. 627.

cover of general approval much fault is found both with Hooker's personality and style. The resemblance to Aristotle, in the eyes of the writer of this letter and of others in that day, seemed not altogether to Hooker's credit. His book seemed long and tedious, "in a style not usual and (as we verily think) the like hard to be found, far differing from the simplicity of the holy scripture, and nothing after the frame of the writings of the reverend and learned Fathers of our Church, as of Cranmer, Ridley, Latimer, Jewel, Whitgeeft, Fox, Fulke, etc."[141] Hooker's prefaces and discourses before he comes to the treatment of specific questions seem particularly troublesome to his critic, who likens himself to a man who, "afar off beholding a briar tree all blown over with his flowers," approaches near only to find himself deceived, and the book "far unlike the goodly show and appearance." Much more to the taste of the times was the cruder method in controversy after which the opinions of one's adversary were "judicially set down" and answers to them found, "either from holy Scripture, from Fathers, or new writers, without all circumference and crooked windings, directly applied."[142] The very largeness of Hooker's mind made him seem unintelligible to many of his contemporaries, who found in the ample sweep of his reasoning merely an evidence of pride of intellect. But with Hooker controversy becomes something more than an ephemeral and personal interchange of opinion. The right of private judgment enounced by Wiclif and many a seeker after freedom of thought following him, is also defended by Hooker, who goes even further than Wiclif in the vindication of natural reason. But Puritanism, as it narrowed its field of vision, came to be more and more dogmatic, and in the conviction of its own righteousness, to exert more and more the right of personal

[141] Bayne, p. 630.

[142] Ibid., p. 630.

criticism. The "snibbing" of Wiclif's day results ultimately in the impudence and violence of Martin Marprelate. It was Hooker who saved English controversy from smothering itself in a wallow of personal abuse, and who showed how really great subjects could be treated in a reasonable and philosophical way. His service was not merely to the Established Church of England, but to the English people, and Puritanism itself in the succeeding generation took on an added dignity by following the example and standards which Hooker had provided.

The greatness of mind which appears in Hooker's feeling for the structure of his subject as a whole, is manifest also in the minuter details of the technic of style. He is above all an artist in the grand style, which he employs not as a rhetorical garment, but because it is the only appropriate expression of his grave and lofty mind. Censured by the author of the *Christian Letter* because his manner of writing was not like other men's, Hooker answers: "You might with as great discretion find fault that I look not like Calvin, Beza, Paulus Fagius, P. Martyr, M. Luther. For I hold it as possible to be like all those in countenance as them in style whom you have mentioned. . . . I must look as nature, speak as custom, and think as God's good Spirit hath taught me, judge you howsoever of my mind, or of my style, or if you will of my look also."[143] The same feeling for order and dignity which led Hooker to defend what he conceived to be the most orderly and dignified form of church government and to advocate the maintenance in the church of certain becoming rites and ceremonies which the Puritans would have swept aside in the interests of a barren simplicity, governed him in the formation of his literary style. By his day it had been established once and for all that English controversy must be carried on in the

[143] Bayne, p. 630, note 219.

English tongue. Latin therefore was not permitted him, nor could he write, as Pecock had mistakenly done, in a technical language of philosophical and theological discussion. His problem was to write in such a way as to be intelligible to the average English mind without, if possible, sacrificing any of the inherent dignity of his subject. How well he solved this problem, many succeeding generations of readers have borne evidence. The *Ecclesiastical Polity* is the one book in the English controversies of the fifteenth and sixteenth centuries which still has a permanent and general interest, and it has this interest not merely for the significance of its thought, but in large measure for the spirit and manner in which Hooker treated his subject. In the words recorded by Walton, the book has got " reverence with age."

Hooker was consciously and intentionally literary. He made no attempt to meet Martin and his crew on their own ground, to make his writing popular by making it amusing. Nor did he cheapen his phrase by yielding to contemporary fashionable notions of wit and eloquence. His standard of dignity he found in Aristotle, in Cicero, Chrysostom, St. Augustine, and Thomas Aquinas. At times he writes with the epigrammatic and aphoristic brevity of Bacon, and very rarely he descends to the simple picturesque style of native colloquial origin which was the almost universal possession of English writers of the Elizabethan age. But in the main Hooker seldom falls below the lofty mark he set for himself. What one misses most of all, though not with surprise, is the power of expressing concrete detail vividly which so many Elizabethan writers possessed. But Hooker's life was mainly the life of the intellect and his writing could not be picturesque. He thought in concepts, not in images. Nor, aside from occasional passages of grave irony, does one find in Hooker much sense of humor. His eyes were turned too intently inward in serene contemplation of the activities of his own mind to permit him to see the rich contrasts of the life about him, the heroic jostling the grotesque, which other English writers found so fascinating. Echoes from neither court nor town find their way to Hooker's secluded retreat, and even the beauties of nature, those blessings of God which he rejoiced to see spring out of the earth and by which throughout his life he was surrounded, all belong to another order of things from that in which Hooker most truly lived. The individual in his experience is always transmuted into the general, and though the vision of natural objects and forces often moves him to expression of great power and majesty, this vision is always an inward one, like that of Lucretius whom he in many respects resembles, not the vision of immediate, tangible realities in a circumjacent world.

Order and dignity, the two great passions of Hooker's life, are the principles which govern his feeling for the structure of the sentence as well as for the structure of the whole. The loose shambling sentence of the naïve English style he never employs. Usually long, sometimes involved, and not always at the first reading clear, Hooker's sentences generally fall into the long rolling cadences of the periodic structure. They are not unvaried, however, and the ground tone of the harmony is now and then interrupted by short quick sentences, the 'little daggers'[144] recommended by Cicero for variety. Another device which he occasionally employs to hasten the action is of Latin origin and consists in the omission of the verb entirely, or of all except the past participle.[145] The antithetic sentence of Lyly and his

[144] *pugiunculis, Orator,* § 224.

[145] As in the following instances from the opening of Bk. I: Many times no reason known to us (Church, p. 9); Who the guide of nature but only the God of nature? (ibid., p. 15); Therefore Christianity to be embraced, whatsoever calamities in those times it

Euphuistic imitators did not extend its influence so far as Hooker, nor was he affected by the complicated and manneristic style of Sidney. In general the surface ornamentation of style, such as verbal antithesis and balance, alliteration, heaping of synonymous words, plays upon words, and learned or picturesque allusions, appears scarcely at all in Hooker's writing.

At first acquaintance certain passages in the *Ecclesiastical Polity* impress the modern reader as being heavy and obscure. This is partly due to the comprehensiveness of the thought to be expressed, and partly also to Hooker's desire to do justice to as many aspects of an idea as possible within the compass of a single sentence. It thus happens that occasionally sentences must be read twice before they yield their full meaning. Yet Hooker's philosophical style is much easier reading than Bacon's, and the difficulty the reader may find in getting Hooker's meaning is not due to inexperience or lack of technical skill on the part of the writer. Hooker completely mastered his form of expression, and the reader having once attuned himself to the author's rhythms, has little difficulty in following the flow of his thought. Unconsciously his familiarity with Latin occasionally affected his English word order, making it slightly unidiomatic, but not misleading. One instance has already been mentioned in the omission of the verb. Similar Latinisms are the separation of verb and past participle and the placing of the latter at the end of the sentence or clause, as in "that root . . . is in the bosom of the earth concealed," [146] or, "such as are not for any other cause than for knowledge itself desired." [147] Sometimes the object or

was accompanied withal (ibid., p. 38); All this endless and everlasting (ibid., p. 72).

[146] Church, Bk. I, 3.

[147] Ibid., p. 23.

predicate nominative precedes the governing word, the aim being either to place the logically important words in the emphatic position, or quite as often merely to vary the normal fixed order of words in the English sentence, as in, "Expedient it will be that we sever the law of nature," etc.; [148] or, "Impossible it was that ever their will should change"; [149] or, "In like manner, the use and benefit of good laws all that live under them may enjoy with delight and comfort, albeit the grounds and first original causes from whence they have sprung be unknown, as to the greatest part of men they are." [150] On the other hand, sometimes an adjective or substantive is suspended until the end of the sentence, as in the following, "every man is towards himself and them whom he greatly affecteth partial." [151] Not infrequently the adjective follows the noun it modifies, as in "a Trinity personal," "sundry arts mechanical," "some kind of government public," "any man's deed past," "of laws human." These are exceptions, however, and the order of words, though varied in many ways for the sake of cadence and logical emphasis or precision, follows in the main the normal customs of English speech. The few instances to the contrary may readily be pardoned in a writer who was not following a model of English style, but constructing one.

In his use of words, Hooker is more simple and idiomatic than in his feeling for phrasing. Though he writes learnedly on philosophic and theological questions, he practically never yields to the natural desire, and in that day the almost universal practice, of the scholar to coin new words. In this respect he again compares favorably with Bacon, who often cannot rest content with an adequate English or naturalized foreign word, when a new Latin coinage suggests itself

[148] Church, p. 12.
[149] Ibid., p. 21.
[150] Ibid., p. 3.
[151] Ibid., p. 54.

to him. " We see that assuetude of things hurtful doth make them lose their force to hurt," writes Bacon, where Hooker would certainly have said " customary " or " habitual use." This contrast is fundamental, and means that Hooker had frankly accepted the English language of his day on its own plane, that, in accordance with his general principles, his duty was to employ the resources which the traditions of the language placed at his disposal and to make the best possible use of them, shunning both extremes of too great respect for the past and too great love of the merely learned or striking and novel. The wisdom of this course time has shown, for those uses which general custom had sanctioned in Hooker's day have remained in most instances the permanent possessions of the language.

The publication of the fifth book of Hooker's *Ecclesiastical Polity* may be taken as marking the close of the first great controversial struggle in English thought and literature, not because of the persuasive power of the work itself, which at the best could have had no such immediate effect, but because the general tendency of the later years of the reign of Elizabeth made for peace and quietness. The compromise in theological doctrine and church discipline which by degrees had been effected in the Elizabethan establishment had proved itself to be both practicable and to the great majority of Englishmen, reasonably satisfactory. The elements of unrest were not completely silenced, and beneath the surface of apparent uniformity both the forces of a Catholic reaction and of a protesting Puritan nonconformity were quietly biding the opportunity when they might again fight in the open. For the time being, however, episcopalianism seemed finally to have triumphed, and the closing years of the sixteenth century were years of comparative peace.

In the retrospect of the two centuries of controversy thus brought to a temporary conclusion, several results stand out prominently. Under the circumstances controversy must necessarily have centered about questions of theology. These theological questions embraced a much wider range of thought, however, than do similar questions in later generations. All change, whether in the political, the intellectual, or the social world, connected itself immediately with questions of theological doctrine. Even a mind as liberal and rational as that of Hooker could hardly have expressed itself except in terms of some kind of theocratic system. Hooker generalized as naturally in such terms as a thinker of to-day would in the terms of evolutionary science. The controversies with respect to theological doctrine meant much more, consequently, than hair-splitting argumentation on points of metaphysical belief or mere personal quarreling over differences of practice in church discipline. At bottom the real question was how men could live together and commune with each other in social concord without the sacrificing of too much of personal liberty on the part of the individual, or on the other hand, without the inconsiderate exploitation of individuality at the expense of social harmony. That this problem was ultimately solved by the controversies of the two centuries from Wiclif to Hooker it would be rash to maintain; it was fairly posed, however, and the history of succeeding generations shows that it did not then and, under human conditions, probably never will reach a final solution. The achievement of this first period of English controversy consists in the fact that it made the first great step in the direction of the solving of social complications by evolving the only effective means to that end, free and reasonable discussion of the questions concerned. Denying the authority of pope or church council to govern and regulate the activities of his mind, the seeker after liberty of thought was logically compelled to deny also all other formal and absolute authority, for example the single authority of the Bible which the narrower Puritanism sought to establish. In the lack of any fixed and absolute authority, the only guide left was that common sense of mankind as to what was true and good and reasonable, which can be arrived at only by attaining some degree of common understanding. English controversy, therefore, did not seek to fight its battles on the limited field of special and technical scholarship. Since the questions under discussion were such as concerned the welfare of mankind in general, the validity and sanity of all arguments adduced must be tested by the degree of their consonance with the general sense of truth. Submission to an intellectual aristocracy, it was felt, would be but little better than submission to a formal or mechanical authority.

And since the appeal was to the common understanding, it followed necessarily that controversy must be carried on in a language commonly intelligible. This language must be the English of commonly accepted tradition, the language in which words have values immediately appreciable without definition, and in which not only intellectual concepts but also feeling and mood can be expressed. Moreover, although controversy must be personal and the right of individual judgment was to be respected, a further compromise was necessary. The liberty of judgment and the liberty of reproof must be tempered by a humane respect for an adversary's right to his own opinions. Intellectual property must receive the same degree of protection from abuse as that afforded to physical possessions in civilized communities. These, in brief, were some of the ends towards which English controversy in the period under discussion, sometimes unconsciously, but none the less certainly, was tending. Its main result, so far as the development of English prose is concerned, was not the production of great masterpieces of art, but rather the invention of a form of English expression, dignified yet intimately idiomatic and many-colored, capable not only of the language of reason, but also of moving the hearts of men, in the profoundest as well as in the simplest of their daily experiences.

IV

THE PULPIT

MEDIEVAL PREACHING—JOHN MIRC—BOY-BISHOPS—LOLLARD PREACHING—COLET—BISHOP FISHER—SENSATIONAL PREACHING—BRADFORD, LEVER, LATIMER—PAUL'S CROSS—NON-CONFORMIST PREACHING—HENRY SMITH—BISHOP ANDREWES—JOHN DONNE—CONCLUSIONS

THE medieval church in England produced no great preachers, nor did it develop a very animated art of preaching. It was Wiclif who first utilized the sermon, in any extensive way, for the popular discussion of matters of intimate concern to his audiences. The time was ripe for a change. By constant repetition both preacher and audience had become weary of the seven deadly sins, the seven works of mercy, the five joys of the Virgin, the fifteen signs of the doom, and the other numerical and summary topics of conventional preaching. The popular preachers had degraded the sermon by the extravagant use of certain entertaining devices which Wiclif sternly reprehended as opposed to the high purpose towards which preaching should aspire. They made use of meter or of highly alliterative prose in order to produce an impression of eloquence. They filled their sermons with stories and examples which were supposedly of an edifying character, but which frequently used the moral merely as a specious excuse for telling the tale.[1] Among the more scholarly and by

[1] For a good summary of the lighter side of English preaching at this time, see Miss Lucy Toulmin Smith's essay on "English

the dignitaries of the church, sermons were preached only on rare and important occasions. They were then heavy and learned, filled with allegorical and tropological interpretations of the scriptures and with abundant scriptural and patristic quotations. But the methods by which interest in the sermon might most easily have been aroused, both popular and learned preachers cautiously avoided. They preached zealously against greed and luxury and sloth and false belief in general, but they were careful not to turn the pulpit into anything like a debating platform from which the popular side of specific social, political, and moral reforms could be discussed.

As illustrative of the character of popular parish preaching at the time of transition from medieval to modern England the *Festial* of John Mirc will serve. This work, a kind of model sermon-book, was probably written in the first decade of the fifteenth century, but its continuous popularity is evidenced by numerous manuscript copies, and at the end of the century, by printed editions.[2] Mirc also wrote a *Manuale Sacerdotum,* and an English poem, *Instructions for Parish Priests*. But his most popular work was his *Festial,* containing seventy-four sermons written in simple and easy prose. These sermons were intended to constitute a complete cycle for the year. They contain brief expositions of the meaning of the feast-day for which they were respectively intended, with exhortations to observe the simple duties of confession, alms-giving, continence, pen-

Popular Preaching in the Fourteenth Century," in *English Historical Review,* VII (1892), 25-36. See also Petit-Dutaillis, "Les Prédications Populaires, Les Lollards et le Soulèvement des Travailleurs en 1381," in *Études d'Histoire dédiées à Gabriel Monod* (1896), pp. 373-388.

[2] According to Schofield, *English Literature from the Norman Conquest to Chaucer,* p. 395, no less than eighteen editions appeared between 1483 and 1532.

ance, and similar generalized virtues. Edification, however, is always sauced with entertainment in the shape of illustrative anecdotes and stories. The bulk of these stories is on the whole considerably greater than that of the expository or hortatory parts of the discourses. From one to four anecdotes are added at the end of each sermon, derived mainly from the well-known sources of medieval exempla. The stories are of the mildest character, and Mirc expressly declares that he has no interest in "a tale of rybawdy." [3] His appeal is always to the naïve and credulous side of human nature, and it is easy to see how, by a slight shifting of the point of view, Mirc's simple and crude conception of the spiritual life might move not to devotion, but to scorn and laughter. To the modern reader Mirc would be more interesting if the popular life of his own times had been more fully pictured in his pages. He had, however, as little sense for the reality of men and women passing up and down before his eyes as he had for the inner life of the spirit. His themes and his characters are few and conventional; and they are repeated again and again with a persistency and simple belief in their sufficiency which leaves the mind of the reader utterly vacant.

The sixteenth sermon, for Sexagesima Sunday, is typical of the whole collection. It begins with the usual address to "Goode men and woymen," and then passes on to comment on the meaning of sexagesima. Mirc points out that nowadays a man who lives sixty years "was taken for a long lyving man," but that formerly men lived nine hundred years and more. Such is the goodness of God, however, that if we conduct our short lives wisely, he will give us as great reward as to those who lived so much longer. Now in order to live wisely we must do three things, suffer tribulation meekly, do alms-deeds discreetly, and hate sin espe-

[3] Erbe's ed., p. 156.

cially. Then follows the exposition of these three points, the second being illustrated by a familiar story of the return of a rich man from purgatory who tells how his alms-deeds in life have been blown away by the wind of "vayn glorie." The third point is illustrated by the story of the way in which St. Dominic was commissioned by Our Lady to go forth and preach in order to turn the people from their wickedness; and the whole concludes with a brief application to the preacher's own contemporaries, who though they hear preaching and teaching will not amend them nor leave their sin. The sermon is neatly put together, as are all the sermons in the collection, the points are few and clearly made, and as the applications are sufficiently general and remote, no doubt the audiences of the time were able to listen patiently. They could always be sure, at any rate, of a pleasant ending, when the preacher came to the narration of his illustrative stories.

For another glimpse of conventional fifteenth-century preaching of a somewhat more learned character, we may turn to a sermon preached by a boy-bishop, in the last quarter of the century. This picturesque custom of appointing annually a mock bishop from among the boys of the choir school who should wear the vestments and perform the services of a real bishop, was of ancient standing in the church. It continued actively until by royal proclamation in 1541 it was forbidden that boy-bishops should "singe masse and preache in the pulpitt, with such other unfittinge and inconvenyent usages."[4] The sermon in question was delivered at St. Paul's in London, on the text *Laudate pueri Dominum.*[5] Whether or not it was actually composed by

[4] For a fuller account of the boy-bishops in England and on the Continent, see Chambers, *The Medieval Stage,* I, 336-371.

[5] Printed by Nichols, *Two Sermons preached by the Boy Bishop,* Camden Society, 1875. The second of the two sermons here printed

a choir-boy, there is no way of telling. There is no reason, however, why a clever boy who had listened to many sermons might not have written this one. It is not altogether a parody, but rather an imitation. It opens with a supposedly subtle discussion of the methods of "cognition," that is, the way by which men come to knowledge. First of all children are sent to school where they learn their A B C, and this leads the preacher into an extended allegorical interpretation of the next to the last letter of the alphabet, "the whyche as Ysider[6] sayth *Ethimologis* is formyd and made after the symylytude of mannes lyfe." After a long prayer for the pope, the archbishop, and for "the ryghte reverende fader and worshypfull lorde my broder Bysshop of London," the preacher turns his attention to his audience. He is struck with fear, however, at sight of his schoolmaster, for whom he wishes the same fate that Nero the Emperor wished for his master Seneca. And for all his masters, he hopes they may be promoted "to be perpetuall felowes and collegeners of that famouse college of the Kynges foundacyon in Southwarke that men call the Kynges Benche." In charity he petitions that they may end their lives "in that holy waye the whyche often tymes I radde whan that I was Querester, in the Marteloge of Poules, where many holy bodyes deyed, callyd in Latin *Via Tiburtina:* in Englysshe asmoche to saye as the highe waye to Tyburne." After this burlesque passage, he continues seriously with his sermon. He divides life into three ages, "infant age," "growynge age," and "mannes age," on the basis of which he amplifies his general theme of cognition. Because of the lack of good masters and guiders, Truth,

was "Pronounsyd by John Stubs, Querester, on Childermas Day at Gloceter, 1558," and was the result of an attempt to revive the ancient custom in the time of Queen Mary.

[6] Isidore of Seville.

which formerly stood upright, he declares has now fallen. " Goode men have inserchyd the strete where he felle; some sayde he fell in Lombarde strete, some sayde in Buklarsbury"; but the fact was that he was fallen in every street (*Veritas corruit in plateis*). The appropriate ways of worshiping God in these three ages the boy-bishop then works out "by a prety conceyte of oure comyn Kalendar," with its divisions of Kalends, Nones, and Ides, in which he displays both his learning and his ingenuity. He digresses here for a moment to inveigh against extravagance of manner and dress in young men, a well-worn preacher's theme, to which he gives a new turn by declaring that "boyes of fyfty yere of age are as newe fangled as ony yonge men be." The sermon is altogether an amusing mixture of boyish fun, of popular satire, of conventional exhortation, elaborate allegorizing, and commonplace scriptural and classical learning. If it is not quite a typical sermon, it is all the more instructive as being a composite made up from the accepted receipts for sermons.

It is unfortunate that no collections survive of the sermons of those "poor priests" who went out from under Wiclif's instructions to carry his message to the simple folk of England. Wiclif's own sermons were addressed to this special class of his followers who were themselves to be the real popular preachers. Perhaps this accounts for the lack of warmth and eloquence which the student of Wiclif's life is surprised to observe in the sermons. His method was that of exposition, and though he spared no pains to make matters clear to the simplest intelligence, Wiclif apparently felt little interest in the arts of persuasion. The title *doctor evangelicus,* given to him because he based everything on the scriptures, should not be interpreted, therefore, as meaning that he was given to evangelical preaching in the modern sense, for nothing was further removed from his method.

No great masters of popular eloquence seem to have arisen from the Wiclifite movement in England, partly because the impulse which Wiclif gave to it was so largely intellectual, and partly also because the movement itself was not permitted to develop sufficiently long or freely to acquire any great momentum. Wiclif had prepared the way for a new school of English preaching, but the circumstances were not auspicious for its development. After his death and throughout the fifteenth century, popular preaching of the new kind was held in check by the repressive measures adopted to combat Lollardy. That the poor priests were completely silenced we cannot suppose, since if that had been so, there would have been no occasion for the frequent complaints made of their activities and for the official efforts made to quiet them. Indeed the caution and the fear which Lollard preaching inspired infected all preaching. Preachers at Paul's Cross were required to have their sermons censored, no matter who they were, and if they failed to follow directions, they received no pay or entertainment. One William Ive in 1458 was "commaunded to leve owte and put a way many troughtys." He disobeyed and said before the king that the censors made the sermons and not those who preached, which brought it to pass that the men who preached had but "sympylle sarmons," because their purpose was "alle turnyde upsodowne." For this boldness he was sent back home unrewarded, "and alle hys frendys fulle sory for hym." [7]

The preaching of the reformers thus came to be regarded more and more as irregular and unauthorized. The lack of a great leader who could gather together the scattered forces of the popular party was keenly felt. The movement towards reform was never extinguished, but its most im-

[7] *Historical Collections of a Citizen of London in the 15th Century,* ed. Gairdner, p. 203.

portant expression under the abortive leadership of Sir John Oldcastle was not of a kind to secure friends and supporters for it among the more influential members of English society. The voice of the popular orator was therefore silenced, and the preaching of this period between the Wiclifite movement and the Reformation of the early sixteenth century was merely a weak continuation of the medieval traditions. Such as it was, it was limited almost exclusively to the preaching of parish priests for whom Mirc and others like him provided materials. The higher church dignitaries, occupied either with secular matters or with the business of their offices, sought no opportunity to instruct or exhort the people from their pulpits. This was the time of the "unpreaching prelates," of those powerful churchmen who by their zeal in gathering worldly riches and by the neglect of their spiritual duties helped to bring upon the church the spoliations of the succeeding century. Colet in his sermon before Convocation in February, 1511-12, shows how little bishops had to do with the people when he declares that they should "personally appear in their churches at least on great festivals."[8] The disinclination of the bishops to preach was not entirely due, however, to sloth or to incompetence. They were not without a certain theoretical justification of their silence, and it will be recalled that all through the century of the Reformation the question of the relative importance of preaching and of the service in divine worship remained unsettled. The constant tendency of the reformers was to exalt preaching at the expense of prayer and the liturgy, perhaps we may say to exalt the reasonable side of religion at the expense of the spiritual apprehension of truth without proof. If the reformers had all been reasonable men themselves, there might have been less objection to their methods. They

[8] Seebohm, *The Oxford Reformers*, p. 242.

were, however, but recently come to a sense of religious liberty. They were untrained in theology, undisciplined in any kind of close thinking. Little wonder, therefore, that they were content "to babble the Bible," and that they aroused nothing but a feeling of scorn on the part of the conservative members of the church.

The point of view of the non-preaching clergy is fully explained by Pecock. He states the dilemma in this fashion: if you preach so as to interest the people, you must make use of all manner of unworthy tricks in order to amuse and entertain them; if, on the other hand, you preach in such a way as adequately to set forth the ideas appropriate to a serious theme, you shoot above their heads. They understand nothing of what you are saying and your preaching is in vain. Pecock's conclusion is, therefore, that there is no place for preaching which is both serious and thorough, and that the sermon is a less effective means of feeding the flock than the worship of images, going on pilgrimages, and the observance of formal traditions. A greater mind than Pecock's might have seen that any truth which affects common human experience is all the truer for being simply stated, but the fact remains that no such mind appeared among the accredited intellectual leaders of the time to illuminate for the people the new ideas in the midst of which they were blindly wandering.

By the beginning of the reign of Henry VIII several new forces were making themselves felt in English life which tended to raise the general level of pulpit discourse. The humanistic ideals of the Renascence were by this time becoming familiar to Englishmen and were demanding a more dignified and broader treatment of matters of intellectual interest than the orthodox and scholastic learning of the medieval tradition had required. New theological ideas were also beginning to enter England from Germany, confirming tendencies already present but greatly in need of outside support. And as the years went by, Henry's own attitude of independence naturally encouraged a similar spirit among the clergy and all interested in theological questions. In general one may discern several clearly marked stages in the development of sixteenth-century preaching, corresponding to and reflecting the general changes in thought and temper of the times. In the early part of the century, before the complete break with Rome, such preachers as Colet and Bishop Fisher are representative of a kind of vernacular preaching which exhibits some of the liberalizing effects of humanism, but which has not yet been caught in the full tide of the Reformation. This moderate kind of preaching, however, had but a short period in which to develop. The mild beginnings of the Reformation soon swelled into a tempest, and Henry found that he had raised more spirits than he could quell. During this time of heated discussion and violent differences of opinion, the tone of preaching naturally became more vehement, more personal, and much more contemporary than English preaching had ever been before. Especially in the reign of Edward the pulpits rang with the fervid oratory of the apostles of the new cause. In the third quarter of the century, under Elizabeth, order begins to appear out of the theological chaos of the several preceding generations, and though feeling continued to run high, and though the battle between episcopacy and presbyterianism was as bitter as that between catholicism and protestantism, on the whole a new sense of decorum was beginning to prevail. The sermon again becomes more restrained, more scholarly, and towards the end of the century, in the peace of the Establishment, more literary.

Of the first stage, John Colet is the typical representative. He began his career as a lecturer on the New Testament before the university students of Oxford. Colet was inspired by the zeal of the reformer who desired to free the church from the corruptions of later ages and to bring it back to the purity of its primitive doctrines. He was not a Wiclifite, not a Lollard, yet in harmony with these he recognized the necessity of making religion of more vital concern in the personal experience of individuals than it seemed possible for the church with its traditional methods to do. It was not, however, merely the poor, the simple, and the oppressed that Colet wanted to help. Reform as he understood it must begin at the top, with the bishops and the higher authorities, and proceed thence gradually through the whole ecclesiastical fabric. He began his share in the work consequently not as a popular preacher but in lectures which made their appeal to the most intelligent and the most thoughtful element in the church.

The second period in Colet's career came with his appointment as dean of St. Paul's cathedral in 1504. His lectures at Oxford had been voluntary and gratuitous, and now as dean he continued freely to serve the cause of enlightenment in ways not called for by the duties of his office. Among other things, he delivered regularly sermons from the pulpit. As Erasmus points out, this was a novelty at St. Paul's, for it was then neither the duty of the dean nor of any other regular officer of the cathedral to provide pulpit instruction for the people. Besides delivering these voluntary cathedral sermons, Colet was also called upon at various occasions to address special audiences of ecclesiastics or courtiers. One of these formal sermons, delivered in Latin at a meeting of Convocation in 1511-12, the chief business of which was to consider methods of repressing the growing heresy of the Lollards, is still extant. It reveals Colet as a fearless diagnostician of the contemporary evils of the church and as a friend of reforms which within a generation were to lead the church much further in the direction of protestantism than Colet would have been willing to go.[9] Of Colet's English sermons, those that were delivered in St. Paul's before audiences of citizens and such others as cared to come, unfortunately no examples survive. They were probably never written out, for Colet was in agreement with most of the later reformed preachers in his express disapproval of reading written sermons.[10] His method in preaching was like that he had followed in lecturing. He took a general subject, such as the life of the Savior, the Creed, or the Lord's Prayer, and considered it thoroughly in a group of sermons.[11] The Bible and the Apostles' Creed were to him sufficient foundation for the Christian faith, and the simplicity of his doctrine and of his presentation drew to him large numbers of those who were earnestly seeking for more light. The Lollards themselves were accustomed to go to hear him, probably finding in his preaching an earnestness and sincerity in harmony with their own serious purposes. At one time charges of heresy and of favoring the teachings of heretics were even brought against Colet, but they were not sustained.

As to Colet's manner of preaching not much information is available. It is certain that he cultivated none of the tricks of the conventional sermonizers of his day. His sermon before Convocation reveals him as an impassioned but not highly rhetorical speaker. The effect of his preaching probably depended more upon his own personal seriousness of conviction and upon an apparent desire to help

[9] See Seebohm, *The Oxford Reformers,* pp. 230-247, for a modern English translation of the Latin. A contemporary English version is printed by Lupton, *Life of Dean Colet,* pp. 293-304, but there is no evidence to show that Colet himself made the translation.

[10] See Lupton, ibid., p. 203.

[11] Erasmus is again the authority for this statement; see the passage quoted in Seebohm, p. 141.

others than upon any formal devices of style. Erasmus describes his method of preaching as ardent but not extravagant. He declares also that even in his early years Colet zealously studied books of history and those poets who occupy among the English the position which Dante and Petrarch occupy among the Italians in order that he might polish his language and that he might prepare himself for the work of preaching.[12] But the New Learning with Colet had not yet degenerated into a cultivation of the artifices of expression as it did with many later writers who came under its influence. His message had to do not merely with the external form but with the spirit of sacred literature.

Colet did not stand entirely alone among orthodox churchmen of the early sixteenth century in his realization of the importance of preaching. An honorable place at his side should be given to John Fisher, bishop of Rochester, who, in 1535, shared the fate of his friend Sir Thomas More. A learned man himself and a patron of scholars, Fisher may be taken as representative of the best among the great prelates of the church in his day. His influence was especially felt at Cambridge, and when in 1502, Margaret, Countess of Richmond, the mother of Henry VII, founded professorships of divinity at Oxford and at Cambridge, Fisher was the first to hold the office in the latter university. A short time afterwards and probably at the suggestion of Fisher, the Lady Margaret founded a preachership for preaching in English. The preacher was to be a fellow of Cambridge, but was to have no parish. He was to preach once every

[12] Denique nullus erat liber historiam, aut constitutiones continens majorum, quem ille non evolverat. Habet gens Britannica qui hoc praestiterunt apud suos, quod Dantes ac Petrarcha apud Italos. Et horum evolvendis scriptis linguam expolivit, jam tum se praeparans ad praeconium sermonis Evangelici. *Epistolarum D. Erasmi Libri XXXI,* London, 1642, Col. 703.

two years in each of twelve different parishes in the dioceses of London, Ely, and Lincoln.

Fisher himself was a zealous preacher, and was famous in his day for his eloquence. He was frequently in request on formal occasions. Among his surviving works are a funeral oration or sermon delivered at the death of Henry VII, a "mornynge remembraunce" for the "moneth mynde" of Margaret, Countess of Richmond, seven sermons on the penitential Psalms, "made and compyled by the ryght reverente fader in God Iohan Fyssher doctour of dyvynyte and bysshop of Rochester at the exortacion and sterynge of the moost excellent princesse Margarete countesse of Rychemount and Derby," a Good Friday sermon on the passion, a sermon against Luther, another "concernynge certayne hereticks," and several devotional treatises which do not greatly differ from the sermons. In these various writings, Fisher appears as a man of devout and sincere religious feeling. He lacks, however, both the freshness and earnestness of conviction of Colet, and on the intellectual side, for example, when he endeavors to answer the teachings of Luther and the reformers, what he says seems inadequate and feeble. Perhaps Fisher, like Sir Thomas More, did not fully realize the passionate earnestness of the opponents whom he was trying to convict of heresy. His eloquence, therefore, which made him the proper official spokesman of the church on formal public occasions, seems somewhat beside the mark in discussions involving the new point of view in religious matters. Tindale speaks scornfully of him as an "orator,"[13] as he spoke of Sir Thomas More as a "poet," and the charge, if so it be construed, is one of which Fisher cannot be acquitted.

Of the several general types of discourse, Fisher cultivated the one most conveniently described as Ciceronian.

[13] *Obedience of a Christian Man,* pp. 221, 341.

Very little evidence of direct imitation of Cicero can be found in his sermons, but it was the general effect of the ceremonial, rotund Latin style which he endeavored to reproduce in English.[14] This is especially apparent in his two funeral orations, in which he followed what he accepted as the standard formula of structure. The first psalm of the dirige he declares may rightly be read at the funeral obsequies of a Christian person, "for in it is comprysed all that is to be sayd in this mater. And in the same ordre that the secular oratours have in theyr funerall oracyons moost dylygently observed whiche resteth in · IIJ · poyntes. Fyrst in the commendacyon of hym that deed is. Seconde in a styrynge of the herers to have compassyon upon hym. And thyrde in a comfortynge of them agayne."[15] In spite of his learned tendencies in style, however, Fisher's longer sentences are usually chaotic and labored, mere size being substituted for the Ciceronian intricate pattern. Doubtless in their spoken forms the sermons were more successful than in the printed versions. In the pulpit, Fisher probably allowed himself to be directed by that natural gift of oratorical expression which he undoubtedly possessed, and which is sufficiently apparent, in spite of their crudities, in the written forms of his sermons.

Though an admirer of the high style, Fisher does not use an extravagantly Latinistic vocabulary. His words are learned, but not ingenious or pedantic, except perhaps in the consistent use of the Latin form of the past participle instead of the English in words of Latin origin.[16] He makes frequent use of word-pairs, such as "warned, instructe

[14] He quotes Cicero, "in his thyrde boke de oratore," *English Works,* ed. Mayor, p. 285.

[15] Ibid., p. 269. At the end, pp. 287-288, he recapitulates in formal style under these three points.

[16] Examples are "alyenate," p. 142, "assumpt," p. 134, "compuncte," p. 133, etc. See Mayor, p. xxix, for a full list.

and monysshed," "searche and inquisition," a device which seems naturally to inhere in the oratorical style. The most notable characteristics of his oratorical vein are his passages of set eloquence and of figurative ingenuity. "Where is now," begins one such passage cast in the familiar *Ubi sunt* formula, "the innumerable company & puyssaunce of Xerses & Cesar, where are the grete victoryes of Alexander and Pompey, where is now the grete rychesse of Cresus & Crassus," and so through the catalogue for a full page.[17] A similar theme in "A Spirituall Consolation" is developed at great length by means of the medieval device of an address of the soul to the body. The form, as Fisher employs it, is one-sided, the body not being permitted to answer:

"What avayleth my vanitie or pryde that I had in my selfe eyther of apparel or of any other thing belonging unto me? what avayleth the filthie and uncleane delightes and lustes of the stincking flesh, wherein was appearance of much pleasure, but in very deede none other than the Sowe hath, waultering hir self in the myerie puddle?"[18]

But for the grace of God, there goes John Mirc. Medieval and scholastic are likewise Fisher's ingenious figures of speech, which are sometimes worked out with extreme elaborateness. As iron is made bright by rubbing, so the soul is made fair and white by weeping.[19] The right directing of a man's soul and life is minutely compared with mending a clock.[19a] Another long-drawn-out figure makes a comparison "betweene the lyfe of Hunters and the lyfe of religious persons."[20] But the most elaborate of all is the figure of the crucifix as a book:

"A booke hath boardes, leaves, lynes, wrytinges, letters booth small and great. First I saye that a booke hath two

[17] Mayor, p. 145.
[18] Ibid., p. 358.
[19] Pp. 16-17.
[19a] Pp. 117-118.
[20] Pp. 365 ff.

boardes: the two boardes of this booke is the two partes of the crosse, for when the boke is opened & spread, the leaves be cowched upon the boardes. And so the blessid body of Christ was spred upon the crosse."

The leaves of the book are the members of Christ's body; as there are many lines drawn upon the pages of the parchment and letters red, black, and blue, so in Christ's body were many lines, for it was scourged with whips, and his wounds were engraved with sharp pens (i.e. the nails and the spear).[21] The figure, tortured through more than three pages, is a striking example of metaphysical ingenuity, scarcely to be surpassed by any of Sidney's achievements in the *Arcadia*. One can imagine the scorn with which Tindale and the other advocates of plainness of speech regarded such attempts at eloquence. The people were asking for bread, they might have said, and Fisher thought to satisfy them with fine phrases. And yet despite a certain element of truth, this criticism would not have been a just one. Beneath all of Fisher's medieval ingenuity and literary artifice, there lay a foundation of genuine feeling. He describes the poor of London and the sick people lying in the street,[22] with as much vividness and sympathy as any of the later popular preachers could have done. At times he can be simple and direct. The story of the Prodigal Son, for example, is admirably told and with full realization of its human implications.[23] Nevertheless it is true that religious feeling was beginning to learn a new language in his day, which Fisher only partially apprehended. Traditional methods in preaching, no matter how they were dignified by learning and literary ingenuity, no longer sufficed for all needs. Though he was the most distinguished public preacher of his day, Fisher was not the

[21] Pp. 393 ff. [22] P. 240. [23] P. 234.

model upon which the popular preaching of the succeeding generation formed itself.

To the average auditor of the times, perhaps the most striking characteristic of the preaching of the early years of the Reformation was its audacity. It was audacious not only in the doctrines which it attacked and defended, but also in its personalities, in its homely picturesqueness, and in the character of the preachers who were now heard from the pulpit. This was the day of the railing preachers. Any person apparently, tailor, cobbler, or parson, with a gift of speech and an abundant vocabulary of abuse, was sure of an audience. For this state of affairs the ecclesiastical authorities themselves were not without blame. After it had been established that the scriptures were to be in English and freely accessible to all, it followed necessarily, as Tindale had foreseen, that from the study of them there must arise much discussion and violent difference of opinion. About the year 1541 Cranmer commissioned six preachers at Canterbury, three being of the new learning and three of the old, "to the intent that they might between them try out the truth of doctrine."[24] This plan, which by no means met with universal approval, was distinctly in the spirit of the new theology, according to which it was the preacher's function not merely to state truth dogmatically but also to find truth. A few years later, in 1545, Henry VIII found it necessary publicly to reprimand the violent methods of the popular preachers. In an address before the House of Lords, he requested his subjects to behave more charitably towards each other, declaring that the clergy "preach one against another, teach one contrary to another, inveigh one against another, without charity or discretion." The people have the privilege of reading the scriptures in English, he

[24] Gairdner, *Lollardy,* II, 368.

adds, only to instruct themselves, "and not to make Scripture a railing and a taunting stock against priests and preachers, as many light persons do."[25]

Preaching at this time was no longer exclusively in the hands of persons authorized to perform that function, but now the "lay exhorter" begins to appear. John Harridaunce was apparently one of this sort. In an examination before the Lord Mayor, he acknowledged that he could neither read nor write, but declared that for thirty years he had been endeavoring to learn the scriptures and always carried a New Testament with him. Like Chaucer's manciple he had heard enough Latin to remember a few phrases, and was accustomed to begin his sermons *In nomine Patris et Filius et Spiritus Sanctus.*[26] Edward Underhill, "the hot gospeller" who in the reign of Edward VI won notoriety for himself by his fervid addresses to the children of this world, was never in orders. And throughout the pages of Foxe we catch glimpses of irregular exhorters with occasional picturesque phrases from their sermons which show the sensational character of popular preaching.

Sensationalism, however, was by no means limited to the lay preachers. The spirit of the times shows itself in the sermons of both orthodox and reformed preachers, often in a way which makes the most highly colored preaching of modern times seem modest. Among orthodox preachers, a certain Parson Hyberdyne or Hubberdin seems to have been contemporarily famous. A mock sermon is preserved in two manuscripts,[27] which purports to have been delivered by Parson Hyberdyne at the command of certain thieves

[25] Gairdner, ibid., pp. 425, 426.

[26] Ibid., pp. 208-209.

[27] See Viles and Furnivall, *The Fraternitye of Vacabondes,* E.E.T.S., Extra Series No. IX, 92-95. In one MS. (Lansdowne) the preacher is called Parson Haben, in the other (Cott. Vesp.), Parson Hyberdyne.

after they had robbed him "besydes hartlerowe, in hamshyer." The theme of the sermon is the praise of thieves and thievery; biblical example is found in defense of thievery, and thieves are likened to Christ in that neither have a dwelling place, nowhere to lay their heads, but wander from town to town, and are hated of all men. The hero and victim of this parody was evidently no other than the Hubberdin, "an old divine of Oxford, a right painted pharisee, and a great strayer abroad in all quarters of the realm," about whom Foxe has much to say.[28] This man's "doings and pageants," if they might be described at large, Foxe declares, "were as good as any interlude for the reader to behold." He passes over his "hoppings and leapings, with other like histrionical toys and gestures used in the pulpit" to tell of a famous dancing sermon delivered by Hubberdin. Passing by a churchyard where the youth of the parish were dancing, Hubberdin took this occasion to call the people into the church and to give them a "sermon of dancing." First he collected, says Foxe, certain common texts out of the scriptures, and then passed to the doctors, to Augustine, Ambrose, Jerome, Chrysostom, and other doctors, all called forth "for the probation of the sacrament of the altar" against the views of the reformers.

"At last, to show a perfect harmony of these doctors together—as he made them before to sing after his tune, so now to make them dance after his pipe—first he calleth out Christ and his apostles; then the doctors and ancient seniors of the church, as in a round ring all to dance together, with 'pipe up Hubberdin.' Now dance Christ; now dance Peter, Paul; now dance Augustine, Ambrose, Jerome. And thus old Hubberdin, as he was dancing with his doctors lustily in the pulpit against the heretics how he stampt and took on I cannot tell, but 'crash,' quoth the pulpit, down

[28] *Acts and Monuments,* VII, 477 ff.

cometh the dancer, and there lay Hubberdin, not dancing but sprawling in the midst of his audience, where altogether he brake not his neck, yet he so brake his leg the same time and bruised his old bones, that he never came in pulpit more, and died not long after the same. Whereupon when the churchwardens were called, and charged for the pulpit being no stronger, they made answer again, excusing themselves, that they had made their pulpit for preaching and not for dancing."

Another "railing friar" mentioned by Foxe was Dr. Venetus, "an outlandish man," or foreigner, who in his "brawling sermons" railed and raged against Latimer, "calling him a mad and brainless man and willing the people not to believe him." This man Latimer answered out of the fifth chapter of Matthew. Latimer's famous sermon "On the Card," with its text "Hearts is trumps," itself a daring experiment in picturesque metaphor, called forth an answer from a certain Black Friar, called Buckenham, "otherwise surnamed 'Domine Labia.'" Buckenham answered Latimer's cards with his dice, "casting there to his audience *cinque* and *quatre;* meaning by the *cinque* five places in the New Testament, and the four doctors by the *quatre;* by which his *cinque quatre* he would prove that it was not expedient the Scripture to be in English." On the afternoon of the day of this sermon, Latimer preached an answer, explaining the nature of figurative and metaphorical language, by which friar Buckenham "was so dashed that never after he durst peep out of the pulpit against master Latimer." [29]

Though such extravagances as Foxe has here recorded are not universally characteristic of the preaching of the middle years of the century, nevertheless a similar spirit and tone is to be found in many of the most successful

[29] Foxe, VII, 450.

preachers of the times. Little is known of Tindale's method of preaching, though we cannot doubt that it was always vigorous and to the point. Coverdale, who had a natural gift of oratorical expression, was among the famous preachers of his day; no body of his sermons has survived, however, and it is impossible to tell how far his gentle and kindly spirit was influenced in public preaching by the atmosphere in which he lived. Though not many of John Bradford's sermons are extant, enough remain to show how different in tone they were from his meditations, prayers, paraphrases, and letters. In these latter writings, Bradford is seen at his best. Here his self-searching temper, his piety and mysticism are uppermost. His most persistent strain in these writings is one of self-accusation, of self-abasement. The meditative lyric mood of these confessions is in complete contrast to the violence of the contemporary polemical spirit and to the abusive style of preaching in which the times delighted. Bradford's own sermons exhibit neither so great restraint in feeling, nor is his literary taste as fine in them as it is in his meditative writings. His contemporaries spoke of his preaching with admiration. "Sharply he opened and reproved sin," writes Foxe;[30] "sweetly he preached Christ crucified; pithily he impugned heresies and errors; earnestly he persuaded to godly life." John Knox, in his *Godly Letter,* notes Bradford's tendency to fall into an ejaculatory style of preaching. "Master Bradford," says Knox, "spared not the proudest; but boldly declared that God's vengeance shortly should strike those that then were in authority, because they loathed and abhorred the true word of everlasting God . . . 'Will ye or will ye not, ye shall drink the cup of the Lord's wrath. Judicium Domini, judicium Domini! The judgment of the Lord, the judgment of the Lord!' lamentably cried he with

[30] *Acts and Monuments,* VII, 144.

a lamentable voice and weeping tears." [31] These exclamatory passages are not always given at length in the surviving form of the sermons, but the theme is merely indicated to be developed at will. "God's anger," runs one such passage, "at length hath taken him away by death; death! cruel death! fearful death, death! etc." [32] Another device of the popular oratorical style which Bradford often employed is that of long lists or catalogues of words of the same general meaning—"swearers, blasphemers, liars, flatterers, idle talkers, jesters, bribers, covetous, drunkards, gluttons," and so on as long as breath lasts. Alliteration is likewise used with an abandon which one may hope resulted from the heat and inspiration of the moment in the pulpit rather than from set intention. The negligence of Eli, he says, in correcting his sons, "nipped his neck in two." "But ours, which pamper up our children like puppets, will put us to no plunge." [33] We see God's anger directed against those guilty of lying "so plainly that we cannot but groan and grunt again, in that we a little more have gushed out this gear gorgeously [34] in word and deed." [35] Again he hopes that "the tossing to and fro of these examples, and specially of our late king and this troublesome time, will tumble some tears out of thine heart." [36] The dignity of preaching may be supposed to have suffered from the use of such trivial artifices, perhaps more than it gained in vivacity.

In his *Piteous Lamentation on the state of the Church of England*,[37] Bishop Ridley groups together four preachers,

[31] *Writings of John Bradford*, ed. Townsend, I, 111.
[32] Ibid., I, 62.
[33] Ibid., I, 60.
[34] I.e., from the gorge or throat.
[35] Ibid., I, 61.
[36] Ibid., I, 62.
[37] See Arber, *Reprints*, XII, 5.

Latimer, Lever, Bradford, and Knox, as pre-eminent for their sharp tongues in reprehending the abuses of the times. On his tombstone when he died in 1577, Thomas Lever was described as "Preacher to King Edward the Sixte." To this dignity, which he shared with various others, Lever was called in 1550, and from this year date his three extant sermons. Though not without occasional alliterative and punning passages, Lever's sermons are in the main straightforward and simple, depending for their effect on plain and direct dealing with the specific abuses of the day. He has much to say concerning economic conditions, about what in modern phrase we call 'social service,' and he declares that Christ, though he often "disputed learnedly and preached plainly," accomplished not so much by his preaching as he did "in feeding and cherishing the people" by means of the miracle of the loaves and fishes. So, says Lever, "a meane learned person," who keeps a good house in his parish, will accomplish more good than "the best lerned doctor of divinitie kepyng no house, can perswade or teache in his parish by preaching a dosen solemne sermons." And a gentleman who keeps a good house shall stand in better credit with his people "than the best oratour or lawyer in England, for all his eloquence." [38] This practical piety, this 'institutional Christianity,' of Lever is characteristic of the popular preachers, who became now not only the instructors of the people in a new theology, but also the defenders of their rights and the advocates of a new feeling for humanity. Lever's sermons point out various public abuses, the thieving of prelates and magistrates, the buying of office, the evils of pluralities, peculation in public transactions, the covetousness of all both high and low. The contemporary popular theory of common property, strangely like certain socialist doctrines of to-day, is carefully considered, and though

[38] Arber's ed., p. 88.

Lever is in sympathy with the people, he points out the necessity and the methods of correcting the evils of poverty by law. His constant cry of robbery in high places was not one calculated to quiet the dissatisfaction of the people, but Lever explains that such plain speaking he would employ in London before an audience of courtiers and magistrates, but " an other trade of preachynge " he would follow before a different audience.[39] One is continually impressed in reading these few sermons of Lever preserved in writing and print, by their similarity in tone to much modern public discussion, not specifically to pulpit oratory, but to that wider range of platform speaking which deals with the reform of social theory and with those evils of injustice which become apparent only when a new social theory is accepted. It was a necessary result of the increased liberty of thought in intellectual and religious matters granted to the individual in the early years of the Reformation that he should soon demand also broader economic rights and liberties.

But the place of pre-eminence among the popular preachers of the Reformation must be accorded to the first of Bishop Ridley's quartet, to Hugh Latimer. In him the virtues and the defects of the popular manner are strikingly exhibited, and by a happy accident, a sufficient body of his sermons has been preserved to enable us to discover fully his methods. It was not Latimer's custom to write out his discourses. As was generally true of the popular sermons of the time, they were delivered first freely and colloquially, not without premeditation, but with much dependence on the inspiration of the moment; and afterwards, as we learn from constant statements to this effect, they were sometimes put into writing and print either from the preacher's own recollection or from the notes of some person in the audi-

[39] Arber's ed., p. 67. Latimer makes a similar statement, that he preaches one way to courtiers and in a different way to countrymen.

ence. It was in this latter way that Latimer's sermons were placed on record. To Thomas Some, "humble and faithful orator" of the Duchess of Suffolk, and to Augustine Bernher, a personal servant and follower of Latimer, we are indebted for the greater part of the considerable number of Latimer's extant sermons. It is not probable that Latimer himself had anything to do with seeing them through the press, or that he even revised the manuscript copy of them. Most likely the sermons were taken down in shorthand as they were delivered, and these notes were afterwards amplified for publication. The words of the sermons are consequently not in every respect exactly as Latimer spoke them, for so Thomas Some acknowledges, but one cannot read far without realizing that in the main the recorders have done their work faithfully. The flavor of a personality is in the sermons, and the words ring too true to be any other in the main than the very words which Latimer's faithful friends heard him speak from the pulpit.

Latimer began his career as a preacher at Cambridge, whither he had gone an ardent defender of orthodox principles, and where, under the influence of Thomas Bilney, "Master Bilney or rather Saint Bilney," as Latimer describes him,[40] he had embraced the doctrines of the reformers. From that time Latimer declares he "began to smell the word of God, and forsook forsooth the school-doctors and such fooleries." He preached before the king at Windsor, on March 16, 1530, and soon after was appointed one of the royal chaplains. Five years later he was made bishop of Worcester, and continued preaching and in the performance of the duties of his office until the passing of the Six Articles in 1539, when rather than subscribe to them, he resigned his bishopric. On the accession of

[40] *Sermons,* ed. Corrie, p. 334.

Edward VI he was offered his bishopric again, but he refused in order that he might devote his whole time to preaching and to defending the rights of the people. He would be none of those strawberry-preachers, those unpreaching prelates who made a luxury of the sermon, "ministering it but once a year," but in his own practice he exemplified his conviction that the people must have spiritual food "daily given unto them to feed upon." In the troublous days of Mary he was cast into prison, and together with Cranmer and Ridley was condemned of heresy. He was retried and again condemned in the year following, and sharing the fate of his two associates, was burned at Oxford, October 16, 1555.

In general tone, Latimer's preaching was always simple and direct, even colloquial. He appeared before his audiences as a fellow-citizen, discussing with them matters of conduct in a familiar, humorous way, but as no one could fail to see, in a spirit of profound seriousness. His sermons are never learned in the usual sense of the term, nor are they ever scholastic and ingenious in the old fashion. He quotes occasionally from Terence, from Valerius Maximus, sometimes from the church fathers, but in general Latin is very sparingly used. He made his appeal direct to human nature and rarely sought to bolster up his teachings by the authority of learned doctors. Indeed few subtleties of doctrine are discussed, and there is no logical quibbling. With characteristic common sense, he answers as follows his own question as to where the soul of Jairus' daughter was during the time that she was dead:

"Now I will make a clerkly answer unto my question, and such an answer that, if the bishop of Rome would have gone no further, we should have been well enough; there would not have been such errors and fooleries in religion as there hath been. Now my answer is this: 'I cannot tell;

but where it pleased God it should be, there it was.' Is not this a good answer to such a clerkly question?" [41]

He was perhaps not a notably deep or original thinker as compared with some of his contemporaries, but he held the current ideas of the Reformation with a steadiness of conviction that few could equal. His directness and concreteness, his simplicity and his sympathy are his most admirable characteristics. He is Chaucerian in his broad humanity, but he had something which Chaucer seems to have lacked, an assurance of the sanctity of popular rights. His mission he felt to be not merely to feed the people with the right interpretation of the word, but to defend them also against civil and ecclesiastical oppression. And in this he was moved not by the centrifugal medieval conception of charity, but by a sense of social responsibility, of the new meaning of good works which was one of the lost inheritances from primitive Christianity that the reformers of the sixteenth century were endeavoring to restore to its proper place as a living element in personal character. Dishonesty and greed in high places as in low are constant themes with him and his endeavor is to awaken in men a fresh sense of fidelity and honesty.

As one expects from the temper of the man, Latimer's style in preaching was not finically artful. He used few learned words, after the fashion of the aureate writers, and on the other hand, he used few archaic words. In vocabulary he was neither an innovator nor a purist, was not a theorist at all. His vocabulary was that of normal colloquial use in his day, simple and popular, and at times to modern ears, coarse. Though he antedates Shakspere by two generations, his language, like Tindale's, is more modern than Shakspere's because he was not affected by the extravagances of sixteenth-century courtly experiment and theory.

[41] *Sermons,* p. 550.

His sentences are prevailingly short, and always clear. Perhaps they have been somewhat abbreviated in the process of writing down, but the elements of the structure cannot have been altered. They are the typical short sentences of colloquial discourse, and show none of Bishop Fisher's striving after Ciceronian amplitude of form. He defends the use of English, necessarily so, since his interests are mainly popular. But he was not hostile to learning, and he also defends the universities and scholarship, as safeguards against narrowness and provincialism in learning. "If ye will not maintain schools and universities," he declares, "ye shall have a brutality." [42]

Yet Latimer's style, if it is not highly literary, is by no means colorless and lacking in rhetorical artifice. Word pairs after the conventional fashion, "search and inquiry," "fused and shed," "behold and see," "sleights and subtle means," he employs frequently, though not extravagantly. Alliteration is found, but again not as obtrusively as in some other contemporary popular styles. The heaping of words of similar meaning or of phrases of similar construction, a common device of tumbling style in popular oratory, is usually combined with alliteration:

"But now for the fault of unpreaching prelates, methinks I could guess what might be said for excusing of them. They are so troubled with their lordly living, they be so placed in palaces, couched in courts, ruffling in their rents, dancing in their dominions, burdened with ambassages, pampering of their paunches, like a monk that maketh his jubilee; munching in their mangers, and moiling in their gay manors and mansions, and so troubled with loitering in their lordships, that they cannot attend it." [43]

Though there are numerous passages of this kind of alliterative volubility in Latimer, there are few places that

[42] *Sermons*, p. 269. See also p. 179.

[43] Ibid., p. 67.

could be called eloquent. He rarely spoke at a white heat, as Tindale often wrote, but even when the words flow forth most abundantly, they are vigorous, as in Langland, only in a homely, half-humorous way. It was not the admiration but the sympathetic attention of his audiences that Latimer was striving to secure.

At times Latimer indulges in the habit, only too common in his day, of punning and similar trivial plays on words. The king's chaplains, he says, are "of the closet and keep close such matters";[44] and at another place, "he would not walk in by-walks where are many balks";[45] or again, "watching and prying what they might hear or see against the see of Rome."[46] The old word "cough" or "coff" in the sense of "procure," "secure,"—"if every man that hath beguiled the king should make restitution after this sort, it would cough the king twenty thousand pounds, I think"[47]—offers an obvious opportunity of which Latimer does not hesitate to avail himself. Latimer's epithets are also often more picturesque than dignified. The answer of the Pharisees, *Num et vos seducti estis?* he translates, "What, ye brainsick fools, ye hoddy-pecks, ye doddy-pouls, ye huddes, do you believe him? are you seduced also?"[48] And 'dodipole' is a favorite term of reproach with him. Like all persons who have accustomed themselves to the use of strong language, Latimer probably felt his picturesque phrases less keenly than his auditors and may thus have come to seem more familiar than he intended to be. But it was in his nature to be picturesque, and even if he had tried, he probably could not have done otherwise. He saw things concretely and dramatically, and religious or theological ideas so presented necessarily afforded strong contrasts. His imagery is thus at times almost grotesque,

[44] P. 98.
[45] P. 96.
[46] P. 287.
[47] P. 262.
[48] P. 136.

as in the famous card sermon, with its "Hearts is trump" and other figurative applications of the game of cards; or the sermon on the Lord's Supper described as a great feast, with all the parts of a dinner specified, from the beginning down to the sweetmeats, "*bellaria,* certain subtleties, custards, sweet and delicate things." "What is that? Marry, remission of sins and everlasting life."[49] Elsewhere the beatitudes are discussed under the figure of a pilgrimage, eight days or eight miles, as you wish to take it.[50] Faith is a noble duchess with her gentleman-usher, repentance, going before her.[51]

Latimer's illustrative stories are usually fresh and contemporary. The old story of Cambyses, who slew the unjust judge and hung up his skin, he uses several times, following Bishop Fisher[52] and various others. But the characteristic illustrative story in Latimer is not the exemplum but the short anecdote of real life. A powerful appeal *ad hominem* is made when Latimer declares that the person who "took the silver basin and ewer for a bribe, thinketh that it will not come out; but he may now know that I know it." And again, still on this same theme of bribery, he catches the ear of the people with a bit of familiar narrative:

"A good fellow on a time bode another of his friends to breakfast, and said, 'If you will come, you will be welcome; but I tell ye aforehand, you shall have slender fare: one dish and that is all.' 'What is that?' said he. 'A pudding and nothing else.' 'Marry,' said he, 'you cannot please me better; that is for mine own tooth; you may draw me round

[49] P. 467.
[50] P. 474.
[51] P. 237. Bradford has the same figure: "This faith is not without repentance, as her gentleman usher before her: before her, I say, in discerning true faith from false faith, lip faith, Englishmen's faith." *Writings of John Bradford,* ed. Townsend, I, 40.
[52] *English Works,* pp. 397-398.

about the town with a pudding.' These bribing magistrates and judges follow gifts faster than that fellow would follow a pudding." [53]

If modern taste is at times offended by Latimer's colloquial ease and broadness, there are certain considerations pertinent to the preaching of his day which should soften judgment. It should be remembered that the sermon was the one place in the service of the church which could make a direct appeal to the interest of the people. The language of the Latin liturgy was not intelligible to them, and its symbolism was often too remote and subtle for the average worshiper to grasp. In the sermon the service descended to the human level of the congregation. Moreover it should be remembered that Latimer, though he belongs to the protestant Reformation, preached before the stern and arid tendencies of Puritanism had imposed upon the church in all its branches that serious and somewhat melancholy sense of decorum which impresses one as still characteristic of English churches as contrasted with those of the Continent. It is a curious fact that the reformed church in granting a fuller and more liberal share to the people in the control and in the services of the church, tended to crowd out the lighter and more familiar sides of popular interest. Then again, the church of the early sixteenth century was still connected vitally with the political life of the times. The king, by his very assumption of supremacy, exposed his own actions, and those of his lawgivers, to the inspection and criticism of the preachers. Thus the sermon often became a direct address to the people in which matters of concern in the practical moral and public affairs of the day were discussed.

Paul's Cross in London, as the best known of many similar meeting places throughout the country, may stand as

[53] P. 141.

representative of this combination of popular theological, moral, and political interests. From a period antedating the Conquest, the citizens of London had been accustomed to come together in their folk-moots under the shadow of the cathedral. At first these meetings were probably civil rather than religious, and just when the Cross itself was erected and a covered rostrum for the speaker built, has not been determined. Early in the fourteenth century, however, the Cross and the meeting place seem to have become distinctly the possession of the cathedral, and although civil proclamations and enouncements continued to be made from it, the church used it primarily as its own instrument, gradually making of it a forum of religious discussion. The civil side in this discussion was always prominent, however, and Paul's Cross was often the place of publication of "inspired" utterances which owed nothing to divine inspiration. Thus Archbishop Grindal, in one of his extant letters, asks Sir William Cecil if there are any matters of state which he wishes Grindal to mention in his sermon at Paul's Cross the next Sunday.[54] As Carlyle has said, Paul's Cross became "a kind of *Times Newspaper,* but edited partly by Heaven itself." [55] The active history of the Cross continues to the middle of the seventeenth century, but it was never as popular with the Puritans as it had been in earlier times.

In its days of prosperity the audiences at the Cross were made up not only of citizens, but also of courtiers and nobles, even royalty itself being often present. The earliest sermon preached at Paul's Cross still extant dates from 1388 or 1389, and is preserved by Foxe.[56] Records of activities at the Cross after this time are abundant. In 1457 Reginald Pecock recanted his heresies at the Cross, and here many a

[54] Grindal, *Remains,* ed. Nicholson, p. 253.
[55] *Cromwell,* Introduction, Chapter IV, under 1629.
[56] *Acts and Monuments,* III, 292-307.

Lollard bore fagots and watched the burning of his heretical books. In 1482 Dr. Shaw delivered here that unhappy sermon which was to have turned the people's hearts to Richard. In 1521 Cardinal Wolsey was present at the Cross when the pope's sentence against Luther was read. Nine years after this, Tunstall here burned all those copies of Tindale's New Testament that he could secure. Only a few years later, however, these same persecuted reformers were denouncing their enemies from this very pulpit. All through the sixteenth century the Cross reflected the many changes of religious feeling and opinion which took place, and one need only read in the old chronicles and histories to see how large a part it played in the life of the city. The stream of pulpit eloquence flowed forth most abundantly in the days of Edward. The old rule had been to have preaching at the Cross only on Sunday in the afternoon, but now there were sermons four or five times a week, and sometimes two on one day. The voices of Ridley, Lever, and Latimer were often heard from this pulpit. When Ridley preached on the new Prayer Book, he spoke so long and earnestly that the audience remained until five o'clock of a November evening and was then constrained to go home by torchlight.[57] The historians have preserved many picturesque details with reference to these citizens' meetings, which were not always peaceful and well behaved, and by means of their accounts one arrives, perhaps better than in any other way, at an intimate realization of the popular temper of the times in matters of politics and religion.

Though the opponents of the episcopalianism of the Established Church continued their attacks upon "unpreaching prelates" late into the century, and Martin Marprelate spares not "Lord dumb John of London," it would

[57] Strype, *Ecclesiastical Memorials,* II, I, 108.

seem, from the number of surviving examples, that any reasonable appetite for sermons must have been satisfied by the supply. The bishops of the Elizabethan church whether conservative or radical in their tendencies, quite generally accepted the duty of public preaching and many of them preached with great vigor. Among the minor clergy, although the number of preachers was small in comparison with the whole body of the clergy,[58] the habit of preaching was spreading. It was Elizabeth's policy to encourage preaching, though only of a zealously guarded kind. Having cared for the revision of the service book, Elizabeth began to "tune her pulpits." Preaching at Paul's Cross had been inhibited for some time, after her accession, and when it was resumed, it was provided that "none but men of good wisdom and learning should come up at the Cross." [59] To be sure some of the survivors of the earlier period of the Reformation were still heard. John Foxe preached from the Cross in 1578, and old Miles Coverdale is frequently mentioned in the records. In the main, however, authorized preaching was now of a new type. It was more restrained, more learned, and more doctrinal than the preaching of the early reformers had been. The first enthusiasm of the popular movement had given place to a less exalted, if not more peaceful mood. This was pre-eminently a period of learned controversy, and the controversial pamphlet was a better form of expression for the religious thought of the formative period of the Estab-

[58] See Frere, *A History of the English Church in the Reigns of Elizabeth and James I,* pp. 107-109, for the figures. Dibdin, *Library Companion,* I, 66-85, has a section on "Old Sermons" in which he gives extracts from Latimer, Fox, Drant, and Roger Edgworth, the last a Roman Catholic preacher of the eve of the Reformation. A complete study of early Reformation preaching is much to be desired.

[59] Strype, *Annals of the Reformation,* I, Pt. I, 198 (Oxford, 1824).

lishment than the sermon. In consequence, though there are many Anglican preachers in the third quarter of the century, there are none who are principally distinguished for their preaching.

Interest in preaching at this time being largely doctrinal, efforts were made to provide a body of authorized pulpit discourses which might serve as models for preachers, or which might be read in the place of original sermons by such as had not the skill or the authority to write sermons of their own. The first book of *Homilies,* in part written by Cranmer and as a whole supervised by him, appeared in 1547, and a second and enlarged edition early in Elizabeth's reign. The doctrinal discourses of certain foreigners were also held in high esteem. Anne Cooke, afterwards the wife of Sir Nicholas Bacon, probably in 1549, published a collection of the sermons of Bernardino Ochino, an Italian who came to England with Peter Martyr in 1548, on the invitation of Cranmer. Two collections of Ochino's sermons in English had already appeared in 1548, another, Englished by John Ponet, was published in 1549, and still another by William Phiston in 1580. Various collections of the sermons of Henry Bullinger, the Swiss reformer, were published in English, one by John Daus in 1561, another in 1573, and three editions of a translation of Bullinger's *Decades* (in 1577, 1584, 1587), made, according to Strype, by a " person of eminency in the church." Among the orders issued by Archbishop Whitgift in 1586, " for the better increase of learning in the inferior ministers and for more diligent preaching and catechizing," was one that every member of the inferior clergy " shall before the second day of February next provide a Bible and Bullinger's Decads in Latin or English, and a paper book, and shall every day read over one chapter of the holy scriptures, and note the principal contents thereof briefly in his paper booke, and shall every week read over one sermon in the said Decads, and note likewise the chief matters therein contained in the said paper." [60] These sermons of Bullinger are dignified scholarly expositions, but colorless, as compared with the sermons of the early preachers of the English Reformation. Numerous translations of Calvin's and of Beza's sermons also appeared, and though they were not made doctrinally authoritative for the Established Church as were Bullinger's *Decades,* there can be no doubt that they were generally and diligently studied and often imitated.

In non-conforming and dissenting circles, among Puritans, Brownists, and Barrowists, the sermon occupied a more important place than it did in the churches of the Establishment. Indeed its place was so important that the Puritans were often criticised for permitting the sermon to crowd out prayer and other aspects of religious worship. Most of this sermonizing, being of an extempore and hortatory character, was never reduced to writing. On the basis of a narrow scriptural outlook, it seems to have developed mainly in the direction of apocalyptic eloquence. It affords further evidence that the apostolic age of reform was past, and that what the church now needed was scholarship and discretion, not merely fervor, to guide it safely. Bacon calls attention to the fact that "if a preacher preach with care and meditation," the non-conformists censure it as a form of speaking "not becoming the simplicity of the Gospel, and refer it to the reprehension of St. Paul, speaking of the *enticing speech of man's wisdom.*" [61] Improvised preaching naturally encouraged a free expression of feeling which was

[60] *The Decades of Henry Bullinger, translated by H. I.,* ed. Harding, Parker Society, IV, xxix.

[61] *On the Controversies of the Church,* 1589, *Letters and Life,* I, 91.

only too often violent and bitter. The non-conformists were now the under dogs, as the reformers once had been, and little difference is to be observed in the spirit of dissent as manifested in 1530 and 1580. Yet with all the liberty of speech which the radicals and non-conformists permitted in preaching, they failed to develop a preacher of great power. The reason for this was partly that their opinions were still in a formative stage of development, partly also that they themselves were subject to constraint from ecclesiastical and civil authority which in general prevented men of ability and training from openly espousing their cause. The typical separatist congregation of the Elizabethan period was composed of people from the humbler walks of life who made no great demand except that of earnestness, on the part of their preachers, and who met in obscure places, gravel pits, the open fields, any place where they hoped to escape observation. Nashe speaks scornfully of popular preachers, such as "preach in ditches and other conventicles, when they leape from the Coblers stal to their pulpits."[62] Such preachers felt and expressed a great contempt for literary form. They preached as the spirit gave them utterance, and extemporary preaching of this kind is not likely to be lasting. The more extreme of the non-conformists refused to listen to the sermons delivered from the pulpits of the Established Church, regarding the preachers altogether as wicked and false prophets. Robert Browne, the founder of the sect of Brownists, denied the authority of the church officially to license preachers for preaching. He characterized the licensed preachers as "hired Lecturers" and "wicked Preachers and hirelings." The words they spoke were not their own, but came from those by whom they held their authority. For their learning Browne had the greatest contempt, declaring that you "may smell out their

[62] *Works,* ed. McKerrow, I, 192.

spirites by the sent of their Greeke or Ebrewe sentences."[63] And for their literary style, his scorn was equally great:

"These Maidens of the Bishoppes, are called to the Pulpit, and there everie Maiden must hurle to them her dressing out of a hoode. If John London do not sauce it with a Methode of preachinge, if they have not his Rhetoricke to make the hearers heedful, wel-willers, and teacheable (o pure divinitie), or if their cookerie be not welcomed with the Beadle & the typstaffe, to bring it to the pulpit, then may it go for no servis. Their Latin is phisik to make hole the sicke, and their greeke and hebrewe wiil blesse you from evill spirits. By these and by their booke of the order of preaching, they may stand before the Queene, as did Daniel before the king. For so soone as they have stood up in famouse places, & shewed their universitie degrees, and how wel they become their hoodes, or their skarlett gownes, and of what standing in Cambridg, and reading they are of in the tongues and Doctors; There may then be none like them: then must you needes call them Rabbie, Master Doctor, My Lords Chaplain, Maister Preacher, and our Divinitie lecturer. This Phisicke will heale all at Paules Crosse in one day. For as soone as they have shewed it and receyved a Dinner, and their honour and the hope of some preferrement, all is made whole, and they goe away as if no bodie were sicke."[64]

Browne would have the preacher's authority come only from Christ himself, and though he permitted the ordaining of preachers by the laying on of the hands of elders, this was in no sense to imply the transmission of a special power to preachers thus ordained. Anyone was to preach who had "the gift," without examination in Latin or the catechism, or in any of those matters of doctrine which the Established Church taught its preachers, to be spit out upon others, in Browne's words, that men might feed upon their graceless

[63] Burrage, *The True Story of Robert Browne,* p. 21.
[64] Ibid., pp. 21-22.

spewings.[65] In the Barrowist congregations likewise it was held that public ministers were no longer needed now that the office of the apostles had ceased, and that any layman who was a brother, that is a member of the congregation, whatever his calling, might preach. He must be able "to divide the word of God aright," and must be careful "to deliver his doctrine pure, sound & plaine, not with curiositie or affectation, but so that it may edifie the most simple, approving it to every mans conscience." [66] The Barrowists also practiced extemporary prayer, and refused to use any form of read or "stynted" prayer. When they pray, says a contemporary description, "one speketh and the rest do grone, or sob, or sigh, as if they wold wringe out teares." [67] All this sounds very familiar to modern ears, but the note was a new one in the sixteenth century, and to many minds extremely disturbing. Bishop Cox, writing in 1571, speaks sadly of these separatist preachers who "by the vehemence of their harangues have so maddened the wretched multitude, and driven some of them to that pitch of frenzy, that they now obstinately refuse to enter our churches, either to baptize their children, or to partake of the Lord's supper, or to hear sermons." [68] And the violence of the sermons of dissenting preachers and of their opinions expressed in writing was such as to call forth protest even from friends of their cause. The elements of right and justice in the principles of the dissenters at this day call neither for defense nor elucidation. Bitterness and narrowness and discord were perhaps in no greater degree the first fruits of nonconformity than they were those of the Reformation. For the time being non-conformist principles were struggling,

[65] Burrage, ibid., p. 24.
[66] Barrowe, *A True Description,* in Walker, *Creeds and Platforms of Congregationalism,* p. 35.
[67] Burrage, *Early English Dissenters,* I, 126.
[68] Ibid., p. 90.

like those of the Lollards a century and more before, amid all the confusion and error of truth in the making, and their expression in consequence was correspondingly imperfect.

It would be unfair to the early history of non-conformity, however, to take men like Browne and Barrowe as representative of the whole movement. Between the extremes of full conformity and of separatism, there stood a body of moderate Puritans who acknowledged the authority of the state church but who refused to accept the ceremonies and practices which the church was endeavoring to impose upon all its members. The most admired spokesman from the pulpit of these non-conformists of the center was one whose name must have been extremely familiar to Londoners of the later eighties in the sixteenth century, but whose fame in after days has been eclipsed by that of his more orthodox contemporaries. This was Henry Smith, who having already won much favor as a popular preacher, in 1587 was appointed lecturer at St. Clement Danes. He continued to address the citizens of London at this place, until ill-health compelled his retirement in 1590. Though he had received university training, from conscientious scruples Smith refused ordination, and being a man of large private means, he was enabled to devote himself to the service of the ministry in the unremunerated position of lecturer. On doctrinal points he accepted the teachings of the established church, in his sermons frequently preaching against separatists, but he reserved the right of non-conformity in certain details of practice. It is an evidence of the extent to which this right was recognized in Smith's day that with the consent of the rector and all concerned, he could be appointed to a dignified lectureship in an important church like St. Clement Danes, and that in the exercise of his office he was permitted to overshadow the regular preaching of the church.[69] He died early, at about the age of forty, in 1591, and during the last year of his life, in the leisure enforced by illness, he prepared for printing an edition of his sermons, some of which had already been printed from shorthand notes taken at the time of their delivery. Smith did not live to see his works through the press, though the first collected edition of the sermons, which appeared in 1592, was said to have been "perused by the author before his death." [70] Frequent later editions attest the great popularity of the sermons, which even to-day are not without their faithful readers.

All accounts go to show that Smith possessed an extraordinary following in the middle class of English society in his day. He addressed himself primarily to the sober, well-regulated citizens of London, and among them he found his chief supporters. He exhibits unfailingly a strong commonsense which leads him to treat with scorn the dreamings of the religious visionaries in which the age abounded, and which perhaps also accounts for his dislike of the ceremonial of the Roman and of the Established Church. The character of his audience determined both the themes and the method of his preaching. He has much to say against city vices, against the sin of usury, as it was then regarded, against lawyers, against sleeping in church, physical and spiritual, gambling, extravagance in dress and fashion, drunkenness and other crudities of conduct, though it should be said that these topics are only introduced by the way as practical applications of spiritual truths which are more broadly apprehended. His treatment of morals is serious, never colloquial and familiar as it is with Latimer.

[69] He was suspended from preaching for a short time in 1588, by Aylmer, the tyrannical bishop of London, but was soon restored through the influence of Burghley. See Cooper, *Athen. Cantab.*, II, 104.

[70] *Works,* ed. Miller, I, xvii.

On the whole he has relatively little to say about controversial matters. Though he defends the preacher's right and duty to reprove,[71] he is not given to railing, whether against Papist, Anglican, or separatist. He laments the fact that zeal, commended in others, is held in derision in the protestant,[72] and in another striking passage he shows the danger to which the social reformer is exposed of being regarded as a disturber of peace:

"If ye ask the atheist, or epicure, or those roguish players, what is a disturber? you shall see that they will make Solomon one, because he spoke against vanity, for this is their definition. He which will not allow men to profane the Sabbath, but saith, that cards, and dice, and stage-players, and May-games, and May-poles, and May-fools, and morris dancers are vanity, is a prattler, disturber, and an arch-puritan, by the law, which the Jews had to kill Christ, John xix, 7. The reason is, because men cannot abide to be controlled of their pleasures, Prov. xiii, 1. Therefore they hold it as an offence to speak against their sports, or their customs, or their follies, or their pleasures, or their titles, or their toys; and they which would not be counted precise in these times, must take heed that they go not so far as Solomon, to term all vanity. But they must say, that the vanities of great men are necessary recreations,[73] and the vanities of the people are means to make unity." [74]

The similarity of these arguments of Smith's opponents to those of the modern defenders of 'personal liberty,' will be apparent. It is characteristic, however, of Smith's moderate treatment of morals that he attempts to answer such arguments not with bitterness, or taunting, or self-right-

[71] *Works,* II, 213.
[72] Ibid., I, 131.
[73] Perhaps referring to the Bishop of London's known fondness for playing bowls on Sunday.
[74] Ibid., I, 383-384.

eousness, but with reasons that must have appealed strongly to the sense of order and propriety of the decent London citizens whom he was addressing.

Though commonsense and good order in morals and religion were the foundation of Smith's character as a preacher, they were not the sole grounds of his popularity with the audiences that gathered to hear him. He was the most eloquent preacher in London, and according to the contemporary evidence, awakened in his hearers not only admiration but warm feelings of personal respect and affection. If not Smith, it must have been some preacher like him that Lady Bacon, the mother of Sir Francis, had in mind, when she wrote to Lord Burghley in 1584 that she had profited more by the " sincere and sound opening of the Scriptures by an ordinary preaching within these seven or eight years " than she had by hearing " odd sermons at Paul's well-nigh twenty years together."[75] Another of Smith's contemporaries, Thomas Nashe, preserves the title of " silver tongu'd Smith " by which he was most frequently described. Nashe groups Smith with those divines who shine " above the common mediocritie," and declares that he was such a " plausible pulpit man " because he refined, prepared, and purified his mind with " sweete Poetrie " before he entered upon the rough ways of theology. " If a simple mans censure may be admitted to speake in such an open Theater of opinions, I never saw aboundant reading better mixt with delight, or sentences which no man can challenge of prophane affectation sounding more melodious to the eare or piercing more deepe to the heart."[76] In the short life which he prefixed to his edition of the sermons of Smith, Fuller says that Smith was " commonly called the *Silver-tongued preacher,* and that was but one metal below St.

[75] Bacon, *Letters and Life,* I, 41.
[76] *Pierce Penilesse,* ed. McKerrow, *Works,* I, 192-193.

Chrysostom." He adds that his church was so crowded with auditors that "persons of good quality brought their own pews with them, I mean their legs, to stand thereupon in the alleys," and that he "held the rudder of their affections in his hands, so that he could steer them whither he was pleased."[77] Gabriel Harvey, who had himself heard Smith from the pulpit, gives his "slender opinion" of sundry contemporary preachers, providing each with an appropriate epithet. Among others, he describes Whitgift as "pithy," Andrewes as "learned," but Smith's vein he declares was "patheticall."[78]

The epithet pathetical was well chosen, for it touches the source of Smith's oratorical power. Circumstances probably aided in heightening the emotional appeal of his sermons. The preacher himself was young, he lived in the lonely state of bachelorhood, he had the support of neither court nor church, and the disease, probably consumption, which carried him off in about his fortieth year, had already plainly laid its hand upon him. One of his most frequent themes is death, not painted in the ghastly lights and shadows of the familiar Puritan accounts of hell-fire and judgment but with a sense of human helplessness and stupefaction in the face of this most dreadful of all realities:

"Our fathers have summoned us, and we must summon our children to the grave. Every thing every day suffers some eclipse, nothing standing at a stay; but one creature calls to another, Let us leave this world. While we play our pageants upon this stage of short continuance, every man hath a part, some longer, and some shorter; and while the actors are at it, suddenly death steps upon the stage, like a hawk which separates one of the doves from the flight; he shoots his dart; where it lights, there falls one

[77] *Works of Henry Smith,* ed. Miller, I, ix.

[78] *Works,* ed. Grosart, II, 292; *Elizabethan Critical Essays,* ed. Gregory Smith, II, 281.

of the actors dead before them, and makes all the rest aghast; they muse, and mourn, and bury him, and then to the sport again! While they sing, play and dance, death comes again and strikes another; there he lies, they mourn for him, and bury him as they did the former, and play again. So one after another till the players be vanished, like the accusers which came before Christ, John viii, 9; and death is the last upon the stage, so 'the figure of this world passeth away.'"[79]

The simplicity of this passage is characteristic of Smith's method throughout. If he was eloquent, he succeeded in being so without straining. He consistently avoided ingenuity and rhetorical artifice of all kinds. His text is generally a brief sentence, of broad and obvious significance, and he proceeds to develop it, without minute analysis, in its general moral and spiritual applications. Except for an occasional pun, tricks of style are consistently avoided. His figures are sometimes homely, as when he speaks of washing the soul clean with the "soap of the gospel," or of the people of this world who are never without excuses, they can "very easily find a staff to beat a dog," but they are never coarse or used merely to raise a laugh. He employs neither alliteration, balance, ingenious metaphor, high-sounding lists of words, nor any other of the common devices of popular preaching. His vocabulary is so extremely simple that scarcely a word of it requires explanation to-day. His sentences are as simple as his vocabulary, short, compact, and crisp in an astonishingly modern degree. In his own mind he had evidently worked out a clear conception, not only of the spirit and content, but also of the style, appropriate to popular preaching. "But indeed," he declares, "to preach simply is not to preach rudely, nor unlearnedly, nor confusedly, but to preach plainly and perspicuously, that the simplest man may

[79] *Sermons,* I, 367.

understand what is taught, as if he did hear his name." He reprehends that kind of preachers "risen up but of late, which shroud and cover every rustical and unsavoury and childish and absurd sermon, under the name of the simple kind of teaching." "As every sound is not music, so every sermon is not preaching, but worse than if we should read a homily." [80] The kind of preaching which Smith defended, and which in his own sermons he exemplified, stood midway between the excessive refinement of scholarly preaching, then becoming fashionable, and the rude and ill-considered outpourings of those zealots whose fervor exceeded their discretion. He may be regarded as London's first great city preacher, and in his character of representative of the better and more thoughtful side of Puritanism in his day and in his community, as spokesman for certain standards of propriety in conduct and expression which the English people have frequently seen exemplified in their pulpits.

The simple, direct methods of Henry Smith contrast strikingly with those of Launcelot Andrewes, courtier, scholar, controversialist, and ingenious analyst of the letter of the spiritual life. If Smith was the most popular London preacher in his short day, Andrewes by common consent is regarded as the greatest of the preachers in the period of the Establishment.

After a distinguished career at Cambridge, in 1589 when he was thirty-four years old, Andrewes received the London living of St. Giles, Cripplegate. Soon after he became prebend residentiary of St. Paul's, where he lectured three times a week during term time, besides preaching at St. Giles. He became chaplain to Archbishop Whitgift, and also chaplain in ordinary to Queen Elizabeth. He was successively bishop of Chichester, Ely, and finally of Winchester. In the list of divines appointed in 1607 to

[80] *Sermons,* I, 139-140; see also I, 337; II, 213.

prepare what is known as the Authorized Version of the Bible, his name stands first. In the reign of James he took an important part in the Bellarminian controversies concerning the nature of royal and episcopal authority. He died in the second year of Charles I, after a life of unceasing and splendid activity. His gifts were remarkably varied. With a sense for order in secular and ecclesiastical affairs and a deep feeling for the significance of ritual and ceremony he combined a sincere personal piety, scholarship which was the wonder of his age, and a tolerant appreciation of spiritual values which make of him not indeed a typical prelate, but the very flower of the English Establishment.

Throughout his career, Andrewes preached incessantly. In the latter half of the reign of Elizabeth and during the whole of the reign of King James, he was the leading preacher at the English court. At St. Giles' and in various pulpits of the city, he addressed audiences of a more composite character. He was always, however, the spokesman for the great, for the higher official life of the country, for the learned, and for the rich merchants of the city. "Christ is not only," he declares in one of his sermons on the Nativity, "for russet cloaks, shepherds and such: shows himself to none but such. But even the grandees, great states such as these, *venerunt,* 'they came' too; and when they came were welcome to Him. For they were sent for and invited by this star [of Bethlehem], their star properly." [81] The people, whom Andrewes regards with compassion rather than respect, in his conception were always to be held in check and under control. "Therefore guiding they need—both the staff of unity, 'Bands,' to reduce them from straying, and the staff of order, 'Beauty,' to lead them so reduced. And would God they would see their own

[81] *Ninety-six Sermons,* I, 243.

feebleness and shallowness, and learn to acknowledge the absolute necessity of this benefit; in all duty receiving it, in all humility praying for the continuance of it, that God break not the fold, and smite not the shepherd for the flock's unthankfulness!"[82] His theories with respect to authority and law are very fully presented in sermons which consider the nature of kingly power and the right of the people to oppose their constituted rulers. He accepted the doctrine, much debated in the reign of James, of the divine right of kings. Being anointed, kings become parts of God himself; anointing has a holy power "not only to make their persons sacred, and so free from touch or violating (all agree to that) but even their calling also. For holy unction, holy function."[83] The right of revolt is thus completely withdrawn from all private persons; they are not to do so much as "rise or stir the foot, but keep every joint quiet."[84] For to go about to oppose the king is as much as to do it. The people must be controlled by law, not merely such law as they are willing to accept, the mild options of the Gospel, but also by stern precept and command. "Gospel it how we will, if the Gospel hath not the *legalia* of it acknowledged, allowed, and preserved to it; if once it lose the force and vigour of a law, it is a sign it declines, it grows weak and unprofitable, and that is a sign it will not long last."[85] It is in such utterances of an almost Old Testament severity, that Andrewes reveals his deep-seated sense of authority, his hatred of all that approaches sacrilege, of all tendencies towards disorder and violence in the political and spiritual conduct of men. As one might expect, he has little sympathy with that genial inspiration of the natural man, powerful but ill-regulated, upon which the advocates of a naïve religion placed so great dependence, and in general he

[82] *Ninety-six Sermons,* II, 29.
[83] Ibid., IV, 84.
[84] Ibid., IV, 32.
[85] Ibid., I, 289.

made little effort to appeal to the simpler emotions of his auditors. His themes are usually somewhat remote. If he alludes to contemporary events, he does not do so explicitly, but merely remarks that his hearers know what he has in mind. It may be that in sermons which have not been preserved, he preached more personally and directly, but it was the temper of his mind to dwell upon intellectual refinements and principles rather than on immediate, concrete details. He trusted to the discretion of his hearers to make the applications, which indeed, for one who takes the trouble to follow his exposition, are never left in doubt.

Eloquence in the sense of impassioned oratory is entirely foreign to Andrewes's nature. He writes at times with a refined and delicate fancy which approaches poetic imagination of a rarefied kind. Nashe describes him as "the absolutest Oracle of all sound Devinitie heere amongst us," and declares that he mixes the "two severall properties of an Orator and a Poet, both in one, which is not only to perswade but to win admiration." [86] But Andrewes's poetry was not the poetry of strong and simple feeling. He never thunders from the pulpit, but as his destructive weapon, employs occasionally a gentle scholarly irony. Limitations as they may seem from one point of view, these traits were indeed Andrewes's gifts. Vague enthusiasm, often growing into passion and violence, were frequent enough in English religious life during the fifteenth and sixteenth centuries, as was also the arid disputatiousness which spent itself in the discussion of mere subtleties of practice and doctrine. The finer balance of Andrewes was more difficult to maintain. He was not a theorist or system builder, nor did he belong to that class of rhapsodists who often degraded religious feeling by not setting to it proper metes and bounds.

[86] *Works,* ed. McKerrow, III, 105.

He preached to select audiences, not to those who flock to hear sermons as they would to an entertainment, but to people capable of appreciating nice distinctions of thought and feeling.

The published sermons of Andrewes all show evidence of careful preparation. He himself expresses his scorn both for the facile listener and facile preacher. In the funeral sermon preached by the bishop of Ely at his death, he is described as "a diligent and painful preacher." He is said to have been exacting in the preparation of his sermons. "I dare say few of them but they passed his hand, and were thrice revised, before they were preached; and he ever misliked often and loose preaching without study of antiquity, and he would be bold with himself and say, when he preached twice a day at St. Giles', he prated once." [87] His study of antiquity indeed begets wonder. He was at ease in the theological literature of his own day, in the church fathers, in the schoolmen, and in classical literature. He knew the Old Testament at first hand in the Hebrew, and his command of details was such as to enable him to draw upon the most obscure characters or incidents for analysis or illustration. He had little need to go to the world immediately about him for the material of life when he had the whole world of the Bible at his fingers' ends. His scholarship is to be sure often obtruded in a way long since gone out of fashion. He not only quotes Latin and Greek freely, but he often uses Latin words or phrases in English context and co-ordinate in syntax with English words. This is not always mere pedantry. The Latin words often serve as a kind of abbreviation, repeating and summing up a general idea which appears again and again and which can thus be conveniently and briefly indicated. Commenting on the twelfth verse of the second chapter of

[87] *Ninety-six Sermons,* V, 295.

Luke,[88] he catches up the various words of the text as follows:

"*Invenietis* leads us to *Hoc erit signum.* For how shall they find Him without a sign? So come we from *Christus natus* to *Christus signatus. Natus,* 'born,' to be found; *Signatus,* 'signed or marked,' that He may be found. Born He is, that they know: and when, they know;—*hodie.* And where, they know—in Bethlehem. To Bethlehem they will; but when they come there, how then? In such resort, the town so full of strangers, as 'no room in the inns,' whither should they turn them? What could they wish, but *O quod erit signum! Natus est;* O that He were *signatus!* O that we had a sign to find Him by!"[89]

His method of treating the text was minutely and rigorously logical. No one could have been more exhaustive than he in dividing the text. The very words are analyzed, often one by one, their meanings are determined by careful study of the language in which they were originally written or into which they have been translated, their cases, moods, tenses are often specifically dwelt upon, and the possible logical connotations of the words in their context are all fully developed. The sermons usually begin with a formal statement of the 'points' to be considered in the text, and from this preliminary outline, no excursions are made.[90]

In the details of Andrewes's style, the same scholarly refinement is exhibited as appears in his thought. His vocabulary is on the whole extremely simple, though it is also carefully selected. None realized more clearly than the preachers how fantastic were the fashionable mannerisms

[88] *Et hoc erit vobis signum: invenietis Infantem,* etc.
[89] *Ninety-six Sermons,* I, 197.
[90] This method of "crumbling a text into small parts," to use George Herbert's phrase, persisted well into the seventeenth century in England and died a natural death in the arid deserts of Scotch Presbyterianism.

of the fine literary styles of the day. Extravagances of expression which might be written were immediately felt to be false coin as soon as the touch of public delivery was applied to them. Yet Andrewes's style is very far from being colorless. Minor ornaments of style he uses sparingly; alliteration, verbal antithesis, balance, ingenious metaphor, all these are entirely wanting. The universal Elizabethan infection of punning, however, both in Latin and in English, he suffers from; but obviously these puns were not intended to be flippant or amusing. They are either mere verbal echoes, and as such not reprehensible according to the standards of taste of the time, or they suggest a collocation of ideas which are really related to each other. But the most characteristic element in Andrewes's style is the rhythm or cadence of his phrasing. The sentences are often extremely compact and even elliptical. "These words then," to choose a passage from a sermon delivered before Queen Elizabeth in 1598, "are a report. A report; but such an one as when St. Paul heard of the Corinthians, he could not commend it. 'What shall I say? Shall I praise you in this? No; I praise you not.' Neither he them for that, nor I these for this."[91] Even when the expression is most free, it never develops into a flowing oratorical style. The rhythm is always somewhat angular, not harsh, but clipped and restrained. Occasional passages of colloquial ease, popular proverbs, and bits of sententious wisdom stand out in contrast to the generally formal tone of the expression. The style is restrained, even when it is most popular:

"Our fashion is to see and see again before we stir a foot," he says, commenting on the coming of the wise men to Jerusalem, "specially if it be to the worship of Christ. Come such a journey at such a time? No; but fairly have put it off to the spring of the year, till the days longer,

[91] *Ninety-six Sermons,* I, 306.

and the ways fairer, and the weather warmer, till better travelling to Christ. Our Epiphany would sure have fallen in Easter-week at the soonest . . . But when we do it, we must be allowed leisure. Ever *veniemus,* never *venimus;* ever coming, never come. We love to make no very great haste. To other things perhaps, not to *adorare,* the place of the worship of God. Why should we? Christ is no wild-cat. What talk ye of twelve days? And if it be forty days hence, ye shall be sure to find His Mother and Him; She cannot be churched till then. What needs such haste? The truth is we conceit Him and His birth but slenderly, and our haste is even thereafter. But if we be at that point, we must be out of this *venimus;* they like enough to leave us behind. Best get us a new Christmas in September; we are not like to come to Christ at this feast. Enough for *venimus.*" [92]

The preaching of Bishop Andrewes was distinctly of his day and generation. His scholarship, his fancy, his minute analyses of texts, even his thought on broader themes, now all have the flavor of antiquity. He seems indeed much less modern than a popular and simpler preacher like his contemporary, Henry Smith, a man of far less intellectual power. Modernity, however, is not necessarily a test of ability. Preaching with Andrewes became a finer art than it had ever before been in England. He raised it to a new level, in harmony with the dignified services and aristocratic tendencies of the newly established church. One cannot but admire the fine sense for form in Andrewes which saves ease from descending to vulgarity, the learning which is vast but not often labored or wearisome, the subtle irony of the scholar which enables him without rant or bluster to prick many a bubble of vain belief in his day. Yet the sermons of Bishop Andrewes already give some hint that the church of Elizabeth and James had its limitations as truly as that of Calvin. The sermons were intended for a class, and they

[92] *Ninety-six Sermons,* I, 258.

have remained permanently interesting only to a class. The church of the Establishment was not a church for all time, and it was perhaps Andrewes's misfortune that his sermons satisfied so perfectly the conditions under which they were preached.

By the side of Bishop Andrewes must be placed his great companion figure in the history of the English pulpit, John Donne. Modern readers think of Donne chiefly as a poet; in his own time, especially during the latter years of his life, he was more highly regarded as divine and preacher. Having been educated in his youth as a Roman Catholic, Donne accepted the Anglican position only after careful and independent investigation. The strong logical bent of his mind and his power of reasoning, evidenced thus early, were again called into service when, at the request of James I, he wrote his *Pseudo-Martyr* (1610), in answer to those recusants who preferred persecution to taking the oath of allegiance. For a number of years, Donne endeavored to make a career for himself at the court, but found his way blocked, at least so far as James was concerned, by the latter's determination that Donne should receive preferment as a divine or none at all. After a long period of hesitation, Donne finally was ordained in 1615, being then forty-two years old. He was immediately made one of James's chaplains, and in a short time received various preferments. One of his most important appointments was that of divinity reader to the benchers of Lincoln's Inn, an honorable position which he occupied for six years, from 1616 to 1622. In 1621 the highest honor of his life came to him in his appointment as dean of St. Paul's. Three years later he received the vicarage of St. Dunstan's-in-the-West, where many of his sermons were delivered. Donne's activity as a preacher was not limited, however, to the delivery of sermons at these three places. He preached often at the court before James I and afterwards before Charles I. He preached at Paul's Cross, before the Virginia Company, before special congregations of noblemen or ecclesiastics, or citizens of London, and on various memorial and other occasions. The number of his extant sermons is at least one hundred and eighty; these were carefully prepared by himself for printing, though they probably represent but a small portion of the number he actually delivered. Donne continued to preach to the last days of his life, which fell in the year 1631, five years after the death of Bishop Andrewes.

Learning is the framework by which all of Donne's sermons are held together. Like Andrewes, he uses Latin freely and makes much of the precedents of antiquity. The church fathers are his constant supports, especially St. Augustine, to whom he appears to have been especially drawn. Among the moderns, Calvin with his sense for order and logic seems to have appealed to him most strongly. Donne does not make the mistake, however, of resting his message merely upon learning and formal logic. Though he has little confidence in "immediate and continuall infusions and inspirations from God himselfe," [93] such as the teachers of certain doctrines of the time claimed for themselves, and though he glorifies reason as man's highest faculty, his appeal to reason is always tempered by a gentle persuasiveness and much kindly feeling. The reader of the sermons is constantly reminded not merely of the methods and ideas, but also of the broad and charitable spirit of Hooker. Passages directed against the Roman church, especially the Jesuits and their contemporary activity in England, are not lacking, but they are rarely bitter or violent in tone. The separatist congregations of the time are treated in a similar spirit, not indeed of toler-

[93] *Eighty Sermons,* London, 1640, p. 494.

ance, but of reasonable argumentation. Donne always endeavors to see the good in everything; even the devil has some good in him, and the Roman church has profited by the Reformation. Man, he declares in a third passage which recalls the thought of Browning, the modern poet with whom he has often been compared, is all the better for not being perfect, for having some sin.[94] Controversial topics and the more refined subtleties of theological opinion he refrains from discussing, following in this the expressed wish of James, who desired "to have slumbered all Pulpit-drums."[95]

The learned and logical superstructure of Donne's sermons rests upon a profound conviction of spiritual truths. A moral idea apprehended as true does not become any less true to him because it is supported by authority. Perhaps it does not become any more true for this reason, either, but the ideal which Donne and the conservative thinkers of his time were striving to realize was to enunciate truth in such terms as appealed to the common judgment of reasonable men and as would save the quest for truth from sinking into the expression of personal and individual extravagances of opinion. The principle which comes out most clearly in Donne's preaching is that the religious life of men should be a part of their general social experience. Going to church, liturgy, sermons, all have this one purpose of enabling men to participate intelligently in the religious life. The wisdom of the whole is greater than the wisdom of the one; Christ himself praised unity, not singularity, and "conventicle purity," Donne is convinced, is

[94] *Works,* ed. Alford, IV, 286.

[95] *Eighty Sermons,* p. 778. See also the sermon preached at Paul's Cross, Sept. 15, 1622, which was published at the command of James I, *Works,* ed. Alford, VI, 189-222. The purpose of James, says Donne, was "to put a difference between grave and solid from light and humorous preaching."

but a snare and a delusion. "To be pure and not peaceable," so he writes with broad charity, "to determine this purity in ourselves and condemn others, this is but an imaginary, but an illusory purity." [96]

The style of Donne's sermons is a dignified and carefully chosen literary style, not merely applied in the revision for printing, but inherent in the original conception of them. Though one is not allowed entirely to forget the audience, the tone of the sermons is rarely colloquial or familiar. The scriptures, according to Donne, are the most eloquent books in the world, and man should not come to the handling of them "with an extemporall and irreverent, or over-homely and vulgar language." [97] On the other hand, that preacher is equally reprehensible who, having made "a Pye of Plums, without meat, offers it to sale in every Market, and having made an Oration of Flowres and Figures and Phrases without strength, sings it over in every Pulpit." [98] In conformity with these opinions, shallow ornament of no kind finds a place in Donne's preaching. He occasionally uses learned words—e.g. colluctation, exinanition, conculcation, collineate, luxation—but this does not become a painful habit with him; and one is grateful to find no puns or other verbal ingenuities. "If your curiosity extort more than convenient ornament in delivery of the word of God," declares Donne, "you may have a good oration, a good panegyric, a good encomiastic, but not so good a sermon." He does not altogether forbid "secular ornament" or "witty preaching" before learned audiences, but he urges the necessity of avoiding "excess in the manner of doing it." [99]

[96] *Works,* ed. Alford, V, 243.
[97] *Eighty Sermons* (1640), p. 47; Alford's ed., I, 96.
[98] Ibid., p. 114; Alford's ed., I, 194.
[99] *Works,* ed. Alford, IV, 415.

Like Andrewes, Donne probably never felt the desire to spread his wings in any extended flight of eloquence. The learned and analytical method he employed must have prevented any such free ranging of the emotions; he is carried along by the chain of reasoning, not by the tide of feeling. In consequence the sermons are less interesting from the rhetorical point of view as wholes than for detached passages and paragraphs. But the close-knit logical structure of the sermons of the great divines of the seventeenth century, for example Tillotson, is not to be looked for in Donne. And on the other hand there is present a frequent efflorescence of rich imagery, often verging on fantasy, which the advocates of a simpler style in preaching were soon scornfully to reject. Donne, like Andrewes, belongs distinctly to the Elizabethan age of opulent expression. The somber, sometimes grewsome strain of his poetry also appears now and then in the sermons. But the ruggedness of metrical form which Donne seems to have cultivated in his verse is not paralleled by any corresponding roughness of manner in the prose of the sermons. In his poems Donne seems to have found difficulty in making language, "with her tough thick-ribb'd hoops"[100] supple enough to gird about his giant fancy. No such difficulty appears in the sermons. They are written, not in a swift or facile style, but in a long, full rhythm, often complicated but perfectly mastered. Commenting on the idea that the excellence of Christ inheres mainly in his divinity, Donne proceeds as follows:

"Now this leads us into two rich and fragant fields; this sets us upon the two Hemispheares of the world; the Western Hemispheare, the land of Gold and Treasure, and the

[100] Carew, *An Elegy on the Death of Dr. Donne,* in *Poems,* ed. Ebsworth, p. 112.

Eastern Hemispheare, the land of Spices and Perfumes; for this puts us upon both these considerations, first, That nothing is Essentially good but God (and there is the land of Gold, centricall Gold, viscerall Gold, gremiall Gold, Gold in the Matrice and womb of God, that is Essentiall goodnesse in God himself) and then upon this consideration, too, That this Essentiall goodnesse of God is so diffusive, so spreading, as that there is nothing in the world that doth not participate of that goodnesse; and there is the land of Spices and Perfumes, the dilatation of Gods goodnesse."[101]

The call to become fishers of men suggests many ideas and associations in the preacher's mind:

"The world is a Sea in many respects and assimilations. It is a Sea as it is subject to stormes and tempests; Every man (and every man is a world) feels that. And then, it is never the shallower for the calmnesse. The Sea is as deepe, there is as much water in the Sea in a calme as in a storme; we may be drowned in a calme and flattering fortune, in prosperity, as irrecoverably as in a wrought Sea, in adversity; So the world is a Sea. It is a Sea, as it is bottomlesse to any line, which we can sound it with, and endlesse to any discovery that we can make of it. The purposes of the world, the wayes of the world, exceed our consideration; But yet we are sure the Sea hath a bottome, and sure that it hath limits that it cannot overpasse; The power of the greatest in the world, the life of the happiest in the world, cannot exceed those bounds which God hath placed for them; So the world is a Sea. It is a Sea as it hath ebbs and floods, and no man knows the true reason of those floods and those ebbs. All men have changes and vicissitudes in their bodies (they fall sick), And in their estates (they grow poore), And in their minds (they become sad), at which changes (sicknesse, poverty, sadnesse) themselves wonder, and the cause is wrapped up in the purpose and judgement of God onely, and hid even from them that have them; and so the world is a Sea. It is a Sea, as the Sea affords water enough for all the world to

[101] *Eighty Sermons,* p. 167.

drinke, but such water as will not quench the thirst. The world affords conveniences enow to satisfie Nature, but these encrease our thirst with drinking, and our desire growes and enlarges it self with our abundance, and though we sayle in a full Sea, yet we lack water; So the world is a Sea."[102]

This almost strophic passage does not end here, but continues in a chain of varying figure and allusion combining poetic imagery with profound moral reflection. The "plain and sober Christian precepts" are thus ever colored by the poet's fancy, sometimes gracefully, sometimes with an intellectual ingenuity that verges on the fantastic and grotesque. Donne's message was not to simple folk who looked for instruction in the alphabet of the religious life. His was an "imperious wit," and he calls upon all the resources of his hearers to follow him in his progress often through remote, dark, and unexpected parts of the realm of human experience. But he was the last of the Elizabethan preachers. Taste in pulpit discourse was changing, and the poetry and fancy of the older divines was soon to give way to the cool and commonsense discourse of the preachers of simplicity and reason.

The English sermon, taking its beginnings in the crude didacticism of medieval preaching at the end of the fourteenth century, reached its first culminating point in the highly analytic, scholarly, and intellectual productions of the end of the sixteenth and the first quarter of the seventeenth centuries. In the interval between these two extremes, the trend of development was in general in a single direction. The pioneers of the Reformation started with a simple and primitive conception of the religious life in which the plain people were to be the final court of appeal. Re-

[102] *Eighty Sermons*, p. 735.

ligious experience was to be intelligible to simple minds and was to take account of the elementary, natural emotions. The plowman, the artisan, the untutored folk of field and village, as in the days when the founder of Christianity walked among men, these were to be the special charge of the ministers of religion. For them Tindale translated the New Testament, for them, and for the great only as they could become like these, as little children, the first preachers of the Reformation spoke from the pulpit. They put their faith in "continual infusions" of divine inspiration, in the powerful, direct, even if undisciplined, impulses of those who felt themselves to be in immediate contact with truth.

Very soon, however, one notes signs of distrust of this newly discovered and suddenly esteemed populace. As in the days of Lollardy, so in the days of the Reformation, the aroused people became disturbers of the peace. They claimed their new rights not in a moderate and limited way, but passionately, arrogantly, universally. The inevitable conflict arose between undisciplined feeling and the conservative sense for law or order which is based on a knowledge of the past, upon a philosophical consideration of a great variety of circumstances, and upon the desire to retain the tried and the familiar. The development of preaching in the sixteenth century reveals the various steps of an increasing disinclination to trust to the impulses of the natural man. Old organizations were replaced by new, and new orders of priesthood were authorized with power to enforce new standards of observance and conduct. The purely popular side of the movement in preaching sank more and more to the lower levels, where it maintained an existence unhonored and even forbidden. Civil statutes were passed to aid in the task of bridling the tongues of the people. The first of these fell even within the days of Henry

VIII. An act of the year 1547, in the reign of Edward VI, provided penalties for those who spoke violently against the sacrament in sermons, preachings, readings, lectures, etc.[103] In the first year of her reign, Elizabeth forbade preaching because thereby arose "among the common sort not only unfruitful dispute in matters of religion, but also contention and occasion to break common quiet."[104] And when, the next year, the right to preach was restored, the place of sermons, homilies, and readings was narrowly specified. When Whitgift became archbishop of Canterbury in 1583, one of his earliest acts was the promulgation of a set of elaborate regulations with respect to preaching, to the ordaining of preachers, their preparation and training, and various other limitations of their calling. James I also reflected, and in part directed the tendency of the times in his regulations governing preaching. We may respect him for his rule that no preacher shall "fall into bitter invectives and indecent railing speeches against the persons of either papists or puritans." But his restrictions did not stop here. The subject-matter of preaching was carefully restricted; the mysteries and subtleties of religion were not to be discussed, but were to be kept, as of old, in the hands of the specially constituted conservers of such matters; political references were likewise to be avoided, and the preachers were generally "to confine themselves wholly to those two heads of faith and good life, which are all the subject of ancient sermons and homilies."[105] In brief the Reformation aroused a power it soon began to fear. The ideal which Milton later so hopefully and eloquently set forth, of a free nation arriving by means of an entirely un-

[103] Gee and Hardy, *Documents Illustrative of English Church History,* pp. 322-328.
[104] Ibid., p. 416.
[105] Ibid., pp. 516-520.

trammeled interchange of opinion at a complete and a mutually charitable understanding of itself in all its members, was not an ideal that commended itself to the leaders of thought either in the days of Elizabeth or of James. The expressions of scorn and reproof of the many-headed multitude which one meets so frequently in Elizabethan literature, in plays, poems, sermons, and controversial treatises, may in part be conventional and traditional, but at bottom it reveals also a deep distrust of primary natural instincts uncontrolled by reason and law and order.

The Elizabethan establishment was a compromise, and the sermons of the Established Church breathe the spirit of compromise. The rough and ready eloquence of Latimer, Bradford, Lever, and the early popular preachers, the familiar colloquialism of the direct appeal to everyday life, and the effort to plumb the deepest mysteries by the measure of universal experience, these were in large measure replaced by formalized standards of propriety, by minute logical analyses of the text of the scripture, and by a stylistic ingenuity which often passed into the mere exercise of wit. The plain commonsense of the rationalistic method of preaching so admirably exemplified a little later in Tillotson had not yet come into being. Enthusiasm, that bugbear of mid- and late-seventeenth century moralists, was still too much in the air for preachers like Andrewes and Donne altogether to escape it. And yet they could not abandon themselves to the full flow of natural feeling, which, when all is said, must ever be the source from which oratory derives its power. On the whole the learned sides of preaching continually tended to overshadow the more broadly human and emotional. No one will deny that this learned preaching has its merits. It helped to bring order and dignity into public expression, to prepare the way for the clarity and simplicity of statement which are the peculiar virtues of later seventeenth and of eighteenth century pulpit discourse. The reader's progress through the sermons of the time is also gladdened now and then by passages of vigorous feeling, of picturesque figure or description, even of impassioned eloquence. But passages of this latter kind, even in the sermons of the greatest preachers, are only episodes. The preachers have strength only for short flights, and soon return to their Greek and Latin, to their precedents of antiquity, to their intellectual game of minute exposition and argument. Their message on its human side seems to have dwindled in significance, and in spite of a certain respect for the learning, the earnestness, even for the highly colored style of the great preachers of the Establishment, one leaves them with the conviction that the new task which the church had set for itself in the reform of popular preaching had not been completed, had not even been squarely faced.

V

BIBLE AND PRAYER BOOK

Early Translations—The Wiclifite Bible—Tindale and His Translations—Other Experiments—Roman Catholic Versions—Growth of the Accepted Version—English Service Books—Origin of the Prayer Book—Its Literary Style

I

Most Englishmen were doubtless aware of the existence of such a book as the Bible before Wiclif's English version was made, but very few could have known any practical use of it. As an English book, the history of the Bible begins with the third quarter of the fourteenth century. But even this beginning was abortive, and not until Tindale published his New Testament in the first quarter of the sixteenth century did the Bible speak the language which ever since has been familiar to all whose native tongue was English. The Bible is the oldest and has always been the most widely distributed of popular English books. By its side, a little younger and less general in its interest, stands the English Prayer Book. Both are to be regarded as monuments of English literature, for whatever their origins, generation after generation of Englishmen has accepted them as possessions of the English people in no less degree than the plays of Shakspere or the allegories of Bunyan. Only the learned pause to think that these books have a history which passes beyond specifically English bounds.

But though Bible and Prayer Book are popular possessions of the race, they were at the beginning and have remained so in different degrees. The English Bible of the sixteenth century was really the growth of centuries. Its preliminary forms were many, and its adaptation to the English mind was gradual. Around it in time were gathered many popular aspirations and enthusiasms. It was fought for because it was wanted. In this slow process of development, the Bible became one of the ineradicable traditions of the English people. They appropriated it and incorporated it into the very structure of their being. It became the common law of a large part of their moral and social life. On the other hand, the Prayer Book from the beginning satisfied the thought and feeling of a more limited section of the English people. It came not in answer to a general popular demand, but to a large extent it was imposed upon the public by the organized authority of the Elizabethan establishment. English churches have seldom raised the question whether or not there should be an English Bible, but they have continually raised the question whether or not there should be a service-book, and nonconformist churches have usually answered this question in the negative. The Prayer Book expressed with dignity and elevation one mood or temper of the spirit of reverence, but it has never been adequate to satisfy all shades and degrees of religious feeling. Though second only to the Bible in the familiar knowledge of the English people, it has always been more or less tinged by the narrowing prejudices of sect and class in such a way as to deprive it of that universality of appeal which of all English books the Bible alone possesses. The Prayer Book was the child of the Established Church, but the English Bible sprang from that common ground of English character where sects and creeds disappear and where the literary and the artless, the learned and the unlearned, freely meet.

The story of the vernacular translation of the scriptures runs back almost to the beginnings of the English race in England. Even before any attempt at specific translation was made, the text of the scriptures was freely drawn upon by the poets who sang in the native tongue. According to Bede,[1] Cædmon composed a versified narrative of practically the whole Bible. Some of the poems of Cynewulf are based, directly and indirectly, upon the story of the New Testament. Besides these two, doubtless there were many other poets of the Old English period, not now known to us by name, who followed a general custom of paraphrasing Biblical narrative in the terms of native heroic poetry.

All this, however, was very different from translation in the specific sense. The purpose of Old English Christian poetry was literary and devotional, to a very slight extent doctrinal. There was no attempt in these poems to reproduce the text of the scriptures with any verbal exactness. Experiments in more exact translation were made, however, by a number of scholars. Bede, according to the well-known story, completed a translation into English of the Gospel of St. John upon his death-bed, of which unfortunately no manuscript has survived. An Old English translation of the Psalms, however, is still extant, and a number of Biblical manuscripts with glosses in the vernacular are further evidence of early attempts at translation. Towards the end of the Old English period came Ælfric's translation of parts of the Old Testament, and the more important translation of the Gospels into West Saxon by one, or perhaps several, unknown scholars. But there is

[1] *Historia Ecclesiastica,* Lib. IV, Cap. 24.

no evidence of any attempt to translate the whole of the Bible in the Old English period, nor is there any evidence that such translations as were made were intended for popular use. Ælfric expresses his unwillingness to continue with his work of translation for fear that the English version of the text might be put to improper uses by the ignorant of both clergy and laity. And the numerous interlinear versions of and glosses on Latin texts were obviously intended as aids in the reading of Latin, not as a means by which those ignorant of Latin could dispense with the Latin originals.

In the years which immediately followed the readjustment of English life and affairs after the Conquest, no great change appears in the English attitude towards the scriptures. Popular interest continued to be satisfied by versified paraphrases of portions of the Old and New Testaments, which were hardly distinguishable from the general body of current legendary and hagiological literature. Bible paraphrases on a large scale after the manner of the *Historia Scholastica* of Peter Comestor, were written in French, but the nearest parallel to these works in English is the long poem entitled *Cursor Mundi,* to a great extent based upon the *Historia Scholastica,* but including much miscellaneous historical and legendary material. A century earlier, about the year 1200, was written another long poem known from the name of its author as the *Ormulum,* in which Orm intended to translate all the Gospels for the year, adding expositions on them. The book was designed for the instruction of the people in 'holy Gospel's lore,' but the poem, although it reaches ten thousand lines in length, does not carry the plan to completion. As it is, the pearls of the Gospel are almost completely lost in Orm's ocean of commentary.

Paraphrases of Genesis and of Exodus were also made in

a popular metrical form, and at the beginning of the fourteenth century an English prose Psalter, the work of a not unskillful translator, appeared in the West Midland dialect. Biblical texts were of course freely inserted in homilies and sermons, many sermons being, as Wiclif complained, nothing more than a string of scriptural quotations with just enough connecting commentary to make it impossible for the hearer to tell where the scripture left off and the commentary began. Indeed the average layman down to the time when printed texts of the Bible began to be circulated must have had a very confused sense of what was scripture and what was not. He knew perhaps his Pater Noster and a certain number of texts, and undoubtedly he was familiar with a great number of Biblical stories, especially those of the more picturesque and dramatic kind. But he must have found it difficult, if the thought ever occurred to him, to distinguish the exempla of profane origin with which the preacher adorned his sermon from the authentic narratives of the scriptures. The seven deadly sins, the marvels of the Physiologus, in short all the store of pious legend and doctrine which he heard from the pulpit must have seemed to him of equal authority with the narrative of the creation or of the atonement and resurrection. For the scriptures as a book with a definitely limited content he could have had scarcely any appreciation until such time as the actual pages of the volume could be held in hand. Only then was it possible to make the Bible the single and all-sufficient rule of conduct for this life and the next which it was soon to become.

For the first attempt to construct an English version of the scriptures with a view to presenting the Bible as a whole, we must turn to the age of Wiclif. The conception of a complete popular translation of the scriptures probably originated with Wiclif himself, but before the Wiclifite version was finished, orthodox tendencies in the same direction had already manifested themselves. These orthodox experiments, however, differed from Wiclif's in that the translations were intended only for the use of members of religious orders and others who occupied some more or less officially recognized position in the church, and who found difficulty in reading the Latin and French versions already extant. They were not intended for the use of the common people. An interesting example of this more limited kind of translation is the version made in the latter part of the fourteenth century at the request of the members of some unknown religious house.[2] This book opens with a prologue giving a brief narrative account of the creation, of the fall of Lucifer, and of the story of Adam and Eve. It then takes the form of a dialogue between a " lewed and unkunnynge " brother and sister, that is, monk and nun, on the one hand, and their brother superior on the other. The brother superior acts as instructor and gives a running account of the Old Testament, and more briefly, of the teachings of the New Testament. Then follow translations of the Epistles, Acts, and the first chapter of Matthew. Perhaps the intention was to translate all the Gospels, and indeed this may have been done, although no such complete manuscript has survived. The significance of this translation lies in the fact that it was frankly intended for the orthodox unlearned in the church. The main purpose of the translator was to make the meaning of the text clear, and his English is in general simple and idiomatic. It is not an unreasonable supposition that if the Wiclifite version had not appeared under Lollard auspices and had not consequently brought to a focus and intensified the hostility of ecclesiastical authorities towards vernacular versions of the scripture, the church itself might soon have

[2] Paues, *A Fourteenth Century English Biblical Version,* p. xxiv.

put forth, as it constantly maintained its intention of doing, an authorized and complete English Bible.

The exact extent of Wiclif's share in the translation which is usually known by his name, cannot now be determined. That the project was inspired by Wiclif was the common opinion of his day and likewise of his successors in the task of making an English Bible. It seems probable that the New Testament was taken up first, and this translation may have been made by Wiclif himself. The Old Testament was in part the work of Nicholas de Hereford, who translated as far as the book of Baruch, where the translation breaks off in the middle of a sentence. The probable date at which Hereford was interrupted in his work was the year 1382.[3] The Old Testament was then completed by a different translator, who again may have been Wiclif himself. Shortly after Wiclif's death the whole translation underwent a revision, probably at the hands of John Purvey, Wiclif's successor in the leadership of the Lollard party. The extraordinary popularity of these translations, all made from the Latin of the Vulgate, is attested by the large number of manuscripts scattered throughout England which are still extant in various degrees of completeness;[4] and these, it should be remembered, are probably but a relatively small number which survived the wear and tear to which popular books are always subject and the no less destructive zeal of the orthodox party in the early part of the fifteenth century.

Of the many hampering considerations which attended the translation of the scriptures in the fourteenth century, perhaps the most disturbing was the uncertainty which prevailed as to the proper balance to be maintained between literal translation and paraphrase. No such feeling existed

[3] Forshall and Madden, *The Holy Bible*, p. xvii.

[4] Forshall and Madden, I, xxxix-lxiv, give a list of 170.

when the question was one of the translation of monuments of profane literature into English. In such cases the universal method was that of paraphrase, the purpose of translation being assumed to be the transference of the sense of the original to the forms of English speech. The scriptures themselves had indeed often been paraphrased in this manner. But when it came to the question of translating the Bible as a book, a paraphrastic version of any man's conception of the content or sense of the book could not be regarded as satisfactory. The task before the translator was not that of interpreting the book, but of transferring it literally in body to another language. Two great opposing necessities therefore confronted him. On the one side he must take heed not to do violence to the almost sacred forms of speech in which the original was written, and on the other lay the necessity of making his translation at least intelligible, and if possible, natural and idiomatic. Deficiencies of vocabulary in the native speech and lack of parallelism in grammatical structure and word-order between English and Latin were the main obstacles in the way of the translator who should attempt to produce in English an exact equivalent of the Latin version. At a later period the task of translation was further complicated by questions of the doctrinal coloring of English words, but at the time the Wiclif versions were made, theological discussion had not advanced so far as to make these questions seriously felt. Wiclif's problem was the relatively simple one of finding the safe mean between the extremes of literal translation and of free adaptation of the Latin originals.

Three differing conceptions of the art of translation, which for convenience' sake we may ascribe to Wiclif, Hereford, and Purvey, with passing acknowledgment that the exact share of each in the specific work of translation is not altogether certain, may be distinguished in this first English Bible. Of these three, Hereford was the most literal, Purvey was the most idiomatic and free, and Wiclif occupied a middle ground between the two extremes. Hereford's version of the Old Testament is often extremely literal, in this respect going even farther than Wiclif, who not infrequently sacrifices English idiom for the sake of close correspondence between the English and Latin. The principles which Purvey followed in his revision of the whole "were designed to render the version more correct, intelligible and popular; and it manifestly becomes more easy and familiar as the translator advances."[5] In the Prologue to his revision, Purvey has set down some of the rules which governed him in his work. He tells how he first collated many "elde biblis," taking into consideration the statements of the doctors and the glosses in the text in order to make "oo Latyn bible sumdel trewe." Having collected his materials, he then studied them and took counsel of "elde gramariens and elde dyvynis of harde wordis and harde sentencis, hou tho miȝten best be undurstonden and translatid." And finally he translated the text as clearly as he could, according to the significance, taking care to have "manie gode felawis and kunnynge at the correcting of the translacioun." Purvey insists strongly upon the necessity of translating not too literally, but according to the thought of the original. The best translation from Latin into English, he says, is to translate "aftir the sentence, and not oneli aftir the wordis, so that the sentence be as opin, either [or] openere, in English as in Latyn"—but he adds the saving clause, "and go not fer fro the lettre." If the letter may not be followed in translating, then let the thought be ever whole and open, for the purpose of words is to express thought and meaning, and if

[5] Forshall and Madden, I, xxix.

they do not serve this purpose, they are superfluous or false. Specific instances are then cited by Purvey of ways in which the English translation may legitimately vary from the Latin original in order to make the thought more clear. Ablative absolutes may be translated as finite clauses, "the maistir redinge, I stonde" being rendered "while the maistir redith, I stonde," or "if the maistir redith," etc., or "for the maistir," etc. Sometimes the construction may be rendered by *whanne* or *aftirward,* as in "whanne the maistir red, I stood," or "aftir the maistir red, I stood," or it may even be rendered by an independent clause, *arescentibus hominibus prae timore* being translated, "and men shulen wexe drie for drede." In a similar way, a participle, present or past, active or passive, may be resolved into a verb of the same tense, *dicens* being translated "and seith" or "that seith." Or a relative may be resolved into a phrase containing a conjunction and the antecedent of the relative, "which renneth," for example, being equivalent to "and he renneth." When the Latin order of words would be obscure in English, the English order is to be preferred; thus the Latin sentence *Dominum formidabunt adversarii ejus,* would read literally in English, "the Lord hise adversaries shulen drede," but, continues Purvey, "I Englishe it thus bi resolucion, 'the adversaries of the Lord shulen drede him.'" In translating words which may have several meanings in Latin, care should be used to choose the English word which accords with the thought of the sentence in which the Latin word occurs. The Prologue insists a number of times that an English translation may be as clear, or even clearer than the Latin original. It also comments on the necessity of taking figurative speech figuratively, adding the caution that "autouris of hooly scripture usiden moo figuris, that is, mo fyguratif spechis, than gramariens moun gesse, that reden not tho figuris in holy scripture." Purvey then announces the less tenable position, that whatever thing in God's word may not be referred properly to honesty of virtues or to the truth of faith, " it is figuratyf speche." [6] Spiritual interpretations, finally, are commended, but it is pointed out that the literal understanding of the scriptures is the foundation of all spiritual interpretation.

Such were some of the problems to be considered by a fourteenth-century translator of the scriptures who would realize the proper mean between an exact literal translation and the more familiar medieval method of paraphrase. In the light of the later development of the translation of the scriptures into English, the modern reader will feel that neither Wiclif nor Purvey went far enough in accommodating their versions of the Latin to the English idiom. In many instances the later revision improves greatly upon the earlier text, as, for example, in the translation of Mark i, 31-33, where the earlier version reads:

" And he cummynge to [Vulgate *accedens*], reride hir up, the hond of hir taken [*apprehensa manu ejus*], and anoon the fevere left hire and she mynystride to hem. Forsothe the evenynge maad [*vespere autem facto*], whenne the sone wente doun, thei brouȝten to hym alle havynge yvel and havynge develis."

This is more idiomatically, and indeed quite adequately, expressed in the revised version:

" And he cam nyȝ, and areride hir, and whanne he hadde take hir hoond, anoon the fever left hir, and sche servede hem. But whanne the eventid was come, and the sonne was gon doun, thei brouȝten to hym alle that weren of male ese, and hem that hadden fendis."

[6] St. Augustine expressed the same principle, *De Doctrina Christiana,* Lib. 3, tom. 3, p. 53; Tillotson, *Works,* II, 424.

Often, however, even Purvey's revision is not carried far enough, especially in the books of the Old Testament. Translating Genesis i, 11, the earlier version reads:

"Burion [burgeon] the erthe grene erbe and makynge seed [*facientem semen*], and appletre makynge fruyt [*faciens fructum*] after his kynd, whos seed ben in hym silf, upon the erthe; and maad it so [*et factum est ita*]."

Purvey's translation is only slightly better:

"The erthe brynge forth greene eerbe and makynge seed, and appil tre makynge fruyt bi his kynde, whos seed be in it silf on erthe; and it was doon so."

The inadequacies of the revised translation arise less from the difficulties attaching to words in themselves, for the words of the Vulgate usually find a fairly satisfactory English or Latinized English equivalent, but rather from a disregard of the native idiom. Thus the definite article is often omitted, as in Matt. v, 13, "Ye ben salt of the erthe" [*Vos estis sal terrae*]. In verse 11 of the same chapter the English revision reads, "whanne men schulen curse ȝou . . . for me," where "for me" renders the Vulgate *propter me*. In Matt. v, 25, "Be thou consentynge to thin adversarie soone," the English is a literal translation of the Vulgate, *Esto consentiens adversario tuo cito*. The unidiomatic "Nyle ȝe" is frequently used as an imperative, translating Latin *nolite*, e.g. Matt. vi, 19, "Nile ȝe tresoure to ȝou tresouris in erthe, where ruste and mouȝte destrieth." Such passages as these are not sporadic, but are so persistent as to give the general tone to the translation. As a work of literary art the Wiclifite Bible cannot be said to have established a new and high standard of English style, nor does it seem probable that it could ever have become a genuinely popular Bible. Nevertheless the work was nobly conceived, and it was carried out with respect for the highest standards of scholarship and of dignity in expression which were possible in its time. Its errors were all on the safe side of caution, and when one considers the difficulties and constraints which must have attended any attempt to translate the scriptures in Wiclif's day, the wonder is not that it failed to be a permanently satisfactory translation, but that it should be as good as it is.

Further growth in the form of this first English version of the Bible was checked shortly after its completion by the hostility which it aroused on the part of the clerical and anti-Lollard authorities in church and state. The attitude of the conservative element in English society towards the vernacular translation of the scriptures is well illustrated by the frequently quoted remarks of the contemporary chronicler, Henry Knighton. Wiclif, he says, has translated the Bible, which Christ gave to clerks and teachers of the church, so that now it is better known to lay men and women who can read than formerly it was to learned clerks. "In this way the pearl of the Gospel is scattered broadcast and trodden under foot by swine. And thus, what is wont to be esteemed by clerks and laity as precious is now become as it were the common joke of both; the jewel of the clerics is turned to the sport of the lay people."[7] Wiclif himself frequently commented on the hostility of the friars towards English versions of the Bible and explicitly defended their use.[8] He often insisted also on the necessity of presenting the Gospel to humble people and dwellers in "litil touns," following the example of Christ who himself "wente to smale uplondishe touns, as to Bethfage and to

[7] *Chronicon Henrici Knighton,* ed. Lumby, II, 151-152; quoted by Paues, p. xxxi, whose translation of Knighton's Latin is here followed.

[8] See above, pp. 47-48.

Cana in Galile."[9] Rich men might possess copies of the English scriptures for themselves, but the inhabitants of the villages and of country communities were dependent upon the poor priests, many of whom doubtless carried with them in their wanderings more or less complete copies of the Wiclifite Bible. In this way the laity not only became acquainted with the idea of an English Bible, but also with a considerable body of the text itself. A movement was thus set on foot which, if it had not been checked, must soon have resulted in further revisions of the English scriptures, and perhaps in the production of a version more completely in accord with the popular feeling for idiomatic expression than was possible in the first experiments of Wiclif, Hereford, and Purvey. Powerful influences were brought to bear, however, to obstruct the popular movement thus begun. In the year 1408 were issued the famous Constitutions of Archbishop Arundel, in which the use of vernacular translations was forbidden, *sub majoris excommunicationis poena,*[10] unless the translation had been approved by a provincial council of the church. More specifically this prohibition was directed against Wiclif, who is mentioned by name.

There is no reason for supposing that at this early period the use of vernacular translations of the scriptures was absolutely forbidden by the authorities of the church. Men of high position and members of religious orders probably met with little difficulty in obtaining approved copies of translations of at least parts of the Bible, if they wanted them. But the evidence is conclusive that the orthodox party did not itself father an English translation of the Bible, and that it powerfully discouraged the use of any such translation by common folk and the laity. Sufficient

[9] Arnold, *Select English Works,* I, 197.
[10] Wilkins, *Concilia,* III, 317.

confirmation of this is found in the fact that in the many trials of Lollards for heresy which were held in the early fifteenth century, the possession of a copy of the English Bible, or even attendance upon readings of it, was regarded as damnatory evidence. In 1431, John Stafford, the bishop of Bath and Wells, "threatened with excommunication any who translated the scriptures or copied such translations."[11] In the face of such opposition, the use of the Wiclifite Bible necessarily became more and more limited, and, at least so far as the common people were concerned, more and more furtive. With the gradual changes in English speech which took place in the fifteenth century, important changes in vocabulary, in inflections and in syntax, the language of the Wiclifite Bible must also soon have needed revision in order to make it intelligible to readers of later times. This lack of authoritative support and of revision are in themselves causes sufficient to account for the fact that the Wiclifite Bible did not become the foundation of the English Bible of the Reformation, that by the end of the fifteenth century it was remembered mainly as having established the tradition of an English Bible, and that when Tindale set about the task of creating a new popular version, he carried on his work in almost complete disregard of what Wiclif and his assistants had already done. The influence of Wiclif's English Bible must be sought not by the way of any immediate literary successors, but in the hidden current of popular thought and feeling which it set in motion and which for many years it secretly fed. In a later generation the popular tradition thus established exerted a powerful influence upon the minds of the public leaders of men in politics and religion and upon the forms of English literary art.

[11] Capes, *The English Church in the Fourteenth and Fifteenth Centuries,* p. 129.

Over a hundred years were to pass after the completion of the Wiclifite Bible before another successful attempt could be made to translate any considerable portion of the scriptures into English. The story of the translation and the publication of Tindale's New Testament, obscure in some minor details, is on the whole clearly known. Tindale submitted himself to a long period of preparatory discipline before he undertook the task which was to be the chief labor of his short life. After a residence at Oxford and Cambridge which covered a period of at least ten years, he removed in 1521 to the country, where he became tutor in the family of a Gloucestershire gentleman. It was not long before his advanced opinions with respect to the use of the scriptures led him into conflict with some of the local clergy, and it was at this time that he is reported to have made his famous answer to one who declared that it were better to be without God's law than the pope's: "If God spare my life, ere many years I will cause a boy that driveth the plow shall know more of the scripture than thou doest."

In pursuance of this purpose, two years later Tindale journeyed to London with the expectation of finding support from Tunstall, the bishop of London, as a scholar and one interested in the translation of the New Testament. As testimony of his ability, he bore with him a translation into English from the Greek of Isocrates. But Tunstall received him coldly and could find no place for him in his household. His hope of episcopal support having proved vain, Tindale soon realized the impossibility of completing in England the work which he had undertaken. "I . . . understode at the laste," he wrote later, "that there was no rowme in my lorde of londons palace to translate the new testament, but also that there was no place to do it in all englande." [12]

In 1524 he sailed for Hamburg, and soon after passed

[12] *Preface to Genesis,* Parker Society, p. 396.

on to Wittenberg, where he almost certainly saw Luther.[13] The work of translation advanced apace, and in 1525 a part of the New Testament was printed at Cologne. Forbidden to continue the printing of the text by the civil authorities of Cologne, Tindale escaped to Worms, where the printer Schoeffer was successful in carrying the work of printing to completion before the end of the year. With the aid of certain of those liberal-minded merchants who throughout were Tindale's chief supporters and patrons, copies were straightway sent over to England and distributed. Tunstall, in a sermon preached at Paul's Cross, October 24, 1526, bitterly denounced the translation, declaring that he had found three thousand errors in it. The translation was condemned to be burned by a conclave of bishops, and this sentence was executed upon as many copies as could be discovered. In this, says Tindale, the bishops did not otherwise than he expected. Having completed his New Testament, Tindale turned his attention to the other parts of the scriptures, publishing a translation of the Pentateuch in 1530, and one of the Book of Jonah in 1531. He also added to a revised edition of his New Testament in 1534, the Epistles from the Old Testament, which included passages from the historical books of the Old Testament as well as from the Pentateuch. No more of Tindale's Old Testament was printed during his life, but his manuscript translation of the books from Joshua to 2

[13] Tindale's name, however, is not found in the *Table-Talk* and *Letters* of Luther. A year before the printing of Tindale's first fragmentary New Testament at Cologne, Luther had "opened his hospitable house at Wittenberg to the English and Scottish refugees." "Dr. Edward Lee writes to Henry VIII from Bordeaux, December 2, 1525: 'An Englishman . . . at the solicitation of Luther with whome he is hathe the New Testament into English.'" This may have been Tindale. Cf. Flügel, *Neuenglisches Lesebuch,* I, 489, and *References to the English Language in the German Literature of the First Half of the Sixteenth Century, Modern Philology,* I, 19.

Chronicles was probably used by his friend Rogers in the preparation of the so-called Matthew Bible. A second slighter revision of the New Testament appeared in 1535, and this brought to an end Tindale's work in the English version of the scriptures. He died at Antwerp, at the martyr's stake, in October, 1536, young in years but with the realization of a great task carried nearly to completion.

Two endeavors, not easily combined, were constantly before Tindale in the preparation of his English Bible. On the one side, the ideal of scholarly exactness demanded a truthful, though not a literal, reproduction of the original, and on the other, the translation could be effective, as Tindale meant it to be, only by being intelligible and, still more, by being interesting to the simple folk in whom Tindale was mainly interested. Tindale was convinced that it was impossible "to stablysh the laye people in any truth, excepte the scripture were playnly layde before their eyes in their mother tonge, that they might se the processe, ordre and meaninge of the texte." [14] And this thing only, he declares, moved him to translate the New Testament. At another place he sets forth in greater detail the reasons which justify an English translation of the scriptures.[15] His main points are as follows:

(1) The Old Testament was written in Hebrew, not a learned tongue but the speech of the people: why then may we not have both the Old and the New in our tongue?

(2) "They will say haply, the scripture requireth a pure mind and a quiet mind: and therefore the lay-man, because he is altogether cumbered with worldly business, cannot understand them. If that be the case, then it is a plain case that our prelates understand not the scriptures themselves: for no lay-man is so tangled with worldly business as they are."

[14] *Preface,* p. 394.

[15] *Obedience of a Christian Man,* in *Doctrinal Treatises,* pp. 144 ff.

(3) Another objection was that if the scriptures were in the mother tongue, every man would understand them after his own way. "Wherefore serveth the curate," answers Tindale, "but to teach him the right way? Wherefore were the holy days made, but that people should come and learn? Are ye not abhominable schoolmasters, in that ye take so great wages, if ye will not teach?"

(4) The apostles preached in their mother tongue, and if one preach a good sermon, why may it not as well be written?

(5) St. Jerome translated the Bible into his mother tongue, and why may we not do the same?

(6) "They will say it cannot be translated into our tongue, it is so rude. It is not so rude as they are false liars. For the Greek tongue agreeth more with the English than with the Latin. And the properties of the Hebrew tongue agreeth a thousand times more with the English than with the Latin."

(7) People are wont to follow different authorities, i.e. the various doctors of the church. "Whereby shall I try and judge them [the doctors]? Verily, by God's word, which only is true. But how shall I that do, when thou wilt not let me see the scripture? . . . Nay, say they, the scripture is so hard, that thou couldst never understand it but by the doctors. That is, I must measure the mete-yard by the cloth. Here be twenty cloths [i.e. doctors] of divers lengths and of divers breadths: how shall I be sure of the length of the mete-yard by them?"

(8) They will say that you cannot understand the scriptures without philosophy, without a knowledge of Aristotle. "Aristotle saith, 'Give a man a law, and he becometh righteous with working righteously.' But Paul and all the scripture saith, 'That the law doth but utter sin only, and helpeth not: neither hath any man power to do the law, till the Spirit of God be given him through faith in Christ.'" Teaching of the scriptures, says Tindale, should be the teaching of God's law, and not the philosophies of nominalists and realists, with their "predicaments, universals, second intentions, quiddities, haecceities, and relatives." Diversity of teaching among the doctors is to be corrected

by return to the pure word of the scriptures. "Now whatsoever opinions every man findeth with his doctor, that is his gospel, and that only is true with him, and that holdeth he all his life long; and every man, to maintain his doctor withal, corrupteth the scripture, and fashioneth it after his own imagination, as a potter doth his clay. Of what text thou provest hell, will another prove purgatory; another limbo patrum; and another the assumption of our lady; and another shall prove of the same text that an ape hath a tail."

(9) "Finally that this threatening and forbidding of the lay people to read the scripture is not for the love of your souls (which they care for as the fox doth for the geese) is evident, and clearer than the sun; inasmuch as they permit and suffer you to read Robin Hood, and Bevis of Hampton, Hercules, Hector and Troilus, with a thousand histories and fables of love and wantonness and of ribaldry, as filthy as heart can think, to corrupt the mind of youth withal, clean contrary to the doctrine of Christ and of his apostles."

(10) "A thousand reasons more might be made, as thou mayest see in *Paracelsi Erasmi,* and in his preface to the *Paraphrase of Matthew,* unto which they should be compelled to hold their peace or to give shameful answers."

The form and manner of expression which Tindale settled upon as adequate to realize his conception of an English Bible for lay readers were of his own invention. He had no predecessors in English who served him as models. In the Epistle to the Reader at the end of the Worms edition of his New Testament, he begs that his readers be not offended at the rudeness of the work and he asks them to consider that he "had no man to counterfeit, neither was helped with English of any that had interpreted the same or such like thing in the scripture before time. . . . Count it as a thing not having his full shape, but as it were born before his time, even as a thing begun rather than finished." [16]

[16] *Doctrinal Treatises,* p. 390.

Comparison of Tindale's translation with earlier English versions of the Bible, or parts of it, bears out Tindale's claim to independence. The style of his first New Testament is altogether new in the development of English translations of the Bible; but it was not rudely or imperfectly conceived. By the time Tindale began the actual task of translation he had definitely established the principles of his work, and from these he never greatly departed. The style which he accepted was above all simple and popular. He avoided, not altogether, but with rare exceptions, the use of unidiomatic Latinisms in syntax, and also the use of unfamiliar Anglicized Latin words. Long words were not cultivated as a means of elevating the style, nor were the rolling cadences of liturgical prose imitated. Obvious ornaments of style, such as alliteration, the heaping of synonyms, puns, antitheses, and similar mechanical devices of wordplay, were not called for by the original and were not added by Tindale. More striking is his avoidance of the quaint and pointed picturesque style of familiar colloquial origin which was the almost universal possession of writers and translators in sixteenth-century England and which Tindale himself frequently employed in his freer and easier prose writings. He made no effort to reach his readers by bringing his translation down to a low level, to color it, as Sir Thomas North did his Plutarch, by broad suggestions of the familiar realistic sides of English life. Striking a happy balance between simplicity and dignity, between the artful structure of a learned style and the easy informality of colloquial speech, Tindale attained a form of expression, *simplex munditiis,* unsurpassed for his purposes. The limits of faithful translation to be sure imposed certain restrictions upon any tendencies towards stylistic exuberance which he may have had, and the quiet tone of the originals from which he translated provided useful models of restraint and propriety in expression. It was no small merit in Tindale, however, that he was content to work within the bounds which his originals and his own purpose established for him. So completely did he realize these limits that he produced a translation which has all the idiomatic propriety and the vitality of original composition. Translation with him became a creative process.

Although Tindale in his first translations of the New Testament had already struck the note which was to become ever afterward the form of expression peculiar to the English scriptures, he did not cease to alter and improve. Many changes were made in the edition of 1534, some for the sake of more exact correspondence in meaning between the English and the originals, some for the sake of brevity, and a multitude of minute corrections for the sake of " more proper English." The great majority of the changes of this latter sort were made in order to avoid a certain meagerness of phrasing, and also to correct rapid and awkward transition from one thought to another. The style which lay at the base of Tindale's translation was the easy, polysyndetic, and naïve style of simple narrative. In his revisions he carefully corrected locutions which interrupted this simple rhythm, and he very often added connectives which improved it. Very frequently he merely added an *and* to a sentence to soften an abrupt beginning, or the simpler logical relations were indicated by other conjunctions, such as *but, or, if,* and *though.* Sometimes also he changed the order of words, as, for example, John viii, 45, *beleve ye nott me* (1525), which becomes the more idiomatic, *ye beleve me not* (1534); or again he simplified by omission, as in Luke xiv, 28, *which of you is he that is desposed to bilde a toure* (1525), which reads in the revision, *which of you disposed to bilde a toure* (1534). Numerous changes were made for grammatical reasons, and words more appropriate to the meaning were substituted for others. Nowhere is there any indication that Tindale translated with the desire to interpret the scriptures by paraphrase in favor of any particular set of doctrines. His purpose was above all to make the meaning clear as he understood it, and he translated always "of a pure intent, singly and faithfully."[17] As to vocabulary, he used in the main words which had established themselves in the language and which were in general use. He avoided learned Greek and Latin coinages. His attempts to replace conventionalized ecclesiastical terms by words of familiar and fresher value, such as *seniors* or *elders* for *priests, congregation* for *church* in the sense of the membership, not the physical structure, of the church, *love* for *charity,* are few in number and by no means violent. Sir Thomas More declared that Tindale's New Testament was full of heretical translations, maliciously inserted. But though he charges that over a thousand texts are mistranslated, More limits his illustrations to a very few examples of the kind just mentioned. The truth is that Tindale was not doctrinaire in his translation, and seldom or never forced unusual meanings into words. The differences of opinion between Tindale and More were such as affected ideas and institutions, not merely words, and these differences would have been the same whether the institutions were called by one name or another. In fairness to himself Tindale could not have done otherwise than use the terms which expressed most clearly his understanding of the ideas which the words were supposed to designate. The proof of the essential justice and sanity of Tindale's translation is to be found in the fact that, both in general tone and very largely in detail, it was followed in all important later English versions of the Bible. The Authorized Version derives not merely phrases from Tindale's translation,

[17] *Doctrinal Treatises,* p. 390.

but whole connected passages. In the history of English prose the origin of the English Bible is consequently to be dated not from the early years of the seventeenth century, but from the second quarter of the sixteenth century when the work in its essentials was both conceived and executed.

The question was formerly much discussed whether Tindale's scholarship was adequate for translation from the Greek of the New Testament and the Hebrew of the Old Testament, and it was often assumed that he translated only from the Vulgate or from Luther's Bible. But this question is now happily and finally settled. It is certain that Tindale was a competent Greek scholar before he began the work of translation, and certain also that he acquired sufficient command over Hebrew to undertake independent translations from that language. His main sources were the original Greek and Hebrew texts. In the mechanical arrangement and in the marginal glosses which accompanied the first fragmentary edition of the New Testament, Tindale followed the model of Luther's Bible. "Tyndale's New Testament is Luther's in miniature; the general appearance of the page is the same; the arrangement of the text is the same; and the appropriation of the margins, the inner one for parallel passages, and the outer for glosses, is also the same." [18] But this statement of the dependence of Tindale upon Luther does not apply to his text. Tindale's New Testament is primarily based on the Greek text of Erasmus, the third edition of which appeared in 1522, accompanied by a Latin translation, occasionally followed by Tindale in preference to the Greek. After Erasmus, Luther seems most to have influenced Tindale's translation, and after Luther the Vulgate. His method in translation was more or less eclectic, but on the whole he followed the most authoritative source for the text, which was

[18] Demaus, *William Tyndale,* pp. 129-130.

the Greek of Erasmus. In the Old Testament as well, comparison of Tindale's translation with the Hebrew, with the Vulgate, and with Luther shows that the Hebrew original was not only consulted, but was carefully studied and followed as the final authority. Tindale's translations have, therefore, not only the distinction of being the first acceptable version in the English idiom, but also of being the first to rest upon an adequate scholarly understanding of the originals.[19]

After the publication of Tindale's translations, the further history of the English Bible must be followed in several directions. In the immediate line of succession come the various adaptations and modifications of Tindale which resulted finally in the Authorized Version of 1611. Before these are discussed, however, it will be convenient to consider several efforts that were made to produce a different kind of English Bible from Tindale's. It was Tindale's desire that every reader, no matter how simple, should understand the text of the scripture without the aid of special knowledge of any kind. So far as possible, therefore, he made his translation speak the language of the normal daily life of English men and women. At heart in sympathy with this theory of translation, Sir Thomas More was in some instances unable to reconcile his feeling for the special and traditional value of the scripture with Tindale's practice. For this reason he protested when Tindale translated the traditional words *church, priest, grace, confession, charity, penance* by *congregation, elder, favor, knowledge, love, repentance,* words in Tindale's mind of a fresher and clearer significance to English people than the ecclesiastical

[19] Tindale's independence as a translator is amply demonstrated, with the aid of comparative tables of illustrations, by Cheney, *The Sources of Tindale's New Testament,* Halle, 1883, and by Westcott, *The History of the English Bible,* 3rd ed., edited by Wright, London, 1905, pp. 131 ff., 152 ff.

traditional terms, which to the pious implied many irrelevant connotations, and to the thoughtless had lost almost all significance because they were so familiar. This feeling of Sir Thomas More that the Bible by reason of its special distinction among books demanded a form peculiar to itself was shared by many others, and all through the sixteenth century was cherished by the advocates of a more learned and exclusive Bible than the popular English Bible of Tindale. Naturally the higher dignitaries of the church, and in general the conservative theorists in matters of church polity, were the chief opponents of the popular English Bible. Frequent protests were uttered by the bishops against the various popular translations as they were made, and promises of a version of their own were given. In the year 1534 the bishops presented a petition to the king for an English Bible to be made "by certain upright and learned men," closing their petition with a request that no layman for the future be permitted to discuss the articles of faith publicly or the scripture and its meaning.[20] What such a Bible would have been if it had ever been made in the spirit of the more conservative scholarship of the time may be inferred from Gardiner, the bishop of Winchester's proposals for the revision of the Great Bible in 1542. At a meeting of Convocation held in that year, Gardiner presented a list of a hundred Latin words which "for their genuine and native meaning, and for the majesty of the matter in them contained" ought to be retained either in their original form, or "fitly Englished with the least alteration." [21] Some of these words were already in general

[20] Pollard, *Records of the English Bible,* pp. 175-177, reprints the petition.

[21] Moore, *Tudor-Stuart Views on the Growth, Status and Destiny of the English Language,* pp. 89-90. This list of words has been frequently printed, e.g. by Mr. Moore, and conveniently and better in Gairdner, *Lollardy and the Reformation,* II, 296.

use in slightly Anglicized forms, such as *justice, glory, mystery, communion, prudence, society, apostle,* and others. But apparently Gardiner would have had the Latin origin of even these words show more plainly, perhaps to distinguish the ecclesiastical from other uses of the words. Many of the words in the list, however, whether in a Latin or in an Anglicized form, would have been unintelligible to most English readers, and a translation of the Bible made in accordance with the principle Gardiner announces would have been in almost as great need of official interpretation as the Greek or Latin originals.

The fullest exemplification of this theory of an ecclesiastical English Bible was to appear a generation later, not under Anglican but under Roman auspices. The Rhemish New Testament, first published in 1582, and the Douai Old Testament, finished earlier but not published until 1609-10, were prepared under the same general direction in order to supply English Roman Catholics with an approved text of the Bible in their native tongue. The translation was published not "upon erroneous opinion of necessitie, that the holy Scriptures should alwaies be in our mother tonge, or that they ought, or were ordained by God, to be read indifferently of all, or could be easily understood of every one that readeth or heareth them in a knowen language," or for any of a number of similar reasons which are specified, but merely as a practical and expedient measure, "profitable and medicinable now, that otherwise in the peace of the Church were neither much requisite, nor perchance wholy tolerable." [22] For reasons which are given in detail, the translation was made from "the old vulgar Latin text, not the common Greeke text." The method of the translation was carefully considered and it is specifically

[22] Preface to the Rheims New Testament, in Pollard, *Records,* pp. 301-302.

defended. The translators declare that they are very precise and religious in following their copy, not only in sense, but also in the very words and phrases, which may seem at first "to the vulgar Reader & to common English eares not yet acquainted therewith, rudenesse or ignorance," but which in time will become familiar and then will be more highly esteemed than if the words were "the common knowen English." From this feeling of the sacredness of the text, the retention of many words in untranslated form is defended. If the older English Bibles retain *Hosanna, Raca,* and *Belial* untranslated, why may not the same be done with *Corbana* and *Parasceve?* "But if *Pentecost,* Act. 2. be yet untranslated in their bibles, and seemeth not strange: why should not *Pasche* and *Azymes* so remaine also, being solemne feastes, as Pentecost was?"[23] And if *proselyte* remain, why not also *neophyte,* if *phylacteries* be allowed, why not *prepuce, paraclete,* and such like? The verb *evangelizo* must be translated *evangelize,* not "as the English Bibles do, *I bring you good tydings,* Luc. 2. 10." "Therefore we say *Depositum,* 1 Tim. 6. and, He *exinanited* him self, Philip. 2. and, You have *reflorished,* Philip. 4. and, *to exhaust,* Hebr. 9. 28. because we can not possibly attaine to expresse these words fully in English, and we thinke much better, that the reader staying at the difficultie of them, should take an occasion to looke in the table folowing, or otherwise to aske the ful meaning of them, then by putting some usual English wordes that expresse them not, so to deceive the reader."[24] Moreover, continue the translators, we presume not in hard places to mollify the speeches or phrases, but religiously keep them word for word, and point for point, "for feare of missing or restraining the sense of the holy Ghost to our phantasie." If the meaning is not transparent in the Latin or Greek

[23] Pollard, *Records,* p. 306. [24] Ibid., pp. 307-308.

original, according to the logic of the translators, there is no reason why it should be made clear in an English translation. The extreme learned bias of the translators is emphatically expressed in this concluding remark: "And why should we be squamish at new wordes or phrases in the Scripture, which are necessarie, when we do easily admit and folow new wordes coyned in court and in courtly or other secular writings?" [25]

If the translation were to be used only by learned and courtly readers there was indeed little reason why the translators should not invent as many learned words as they pleased. And in fact the authors of the Rhemish Bible are much less extreme in their treatment of vocabulary than many a contemporary secular writer with a passion for aureate diction. The important question in this instance was not whether this or that new word should be accepted, but whether the whole project of a learned English Bible should be approved. In answering this question, by the end of the sixteenth century theoretical considerations carried little weight. By that time it had been determined once and for all that the accepted English Bible for protestant readers was to be a popular and not a learned book, that the text was to be as frank and open as possible, not recondite and cryptic. In justice to the Rhemish translation it should be said, however, that the effect of the whole is not as grotesque as might be inferred from the more extreme examples of learned locutions just cited. Consecutive passages of some length are frequently found which differ but slightly from the earlier English translations based on Tindale, and many readings which differ in the Rhemish translation from the earlier translations are familiar to us now because they were incorporated in the Authorized Version of 1611. The Rhemish Bible was an unsuccessful, but not

[25] Pollard, *Records,* p. 310.

an uninfluential experiment. In a revised form it remains to this day one of the standard English Bibles for Roman Catholic readers, but it has never been regarded as a fountain of pure English in the same degree as Tindale's popular English Bible.

Several other translations which fall outside the main line of descent of the English Bible must be noticed. In general the tendency in the development of English translations was in the direction which the Rhemish translation followed to the extreme, that is, in the direction of more exact and scholarly translation. Several efforts were made, however, to develop an English biblical style which should be more popular, or at least less learned, even than Tindale's. The first of these found expression in the English Bible of R. Taverner, published in 1539, the year of the Great Bible. A lawyer by profession and a not incompetent Greek scholar, Taverner makes no pretension to being an original translator. His work is based upon the so-called Matthew Bible, and his alterations are mainly made for the purpose of securing what he regarded as a more idiomatic English phrasing and vocabulary. Thus in I John ii, 1, where the other versions read *advocate,* Taverner uses the native word *spokesman;* and in the following verse, where the earlier versions follow Tindale in translating ἱλασμὸς by *he it is that obtaineth grace for our sins* (the Rhemish version followed by the Authorized Version reading, *he is the propitiation for our sins*), Taverner invents an entirely new native word, *he is a mercystock for our sins.* Similar changes are the substitution of *wickedness* for *iniquity* (Matt. xiii, 41); *ended* for *finished,* (Matt. xiii, 53); *break* for *transgress* (Matt. xv, 2); *lodged* for *had his abiding* (Matt. xxi, 17); *and because of the abundance of wickedness, the charity of many shall wax cold* for Tindale's *and because iniquity shall have the upper hand, the love of many shall abate* (Matt. xxiv, 12); *age* for *generation* (Matt. xxiv, 34); *nailed to the cross* for *crucified* (Matt. xxvi, 2); *to the forgiveness* for *for the remission* (Matt. xxvi, 28). Taverner's Bible, however, is interesting merely as an experiment; it was crowded out of use by the Great Bible and it seems not to have exerted any influence upon later revisions of the text.[26] Another experiment similar to that of Taverner, though much more extreme, was the English translation of St. Matthew and the beginning of St. Mark, made by Sir John Cheke, in his own day regarded as the chief defender of the purity of the English language as opposed to those who would enrich, or according to the purists, corrupt, the language by freely borrowing words of foreign origin. This translation was never published in Cheke's lifetime,[27] and it is interesting mainly as an illustration of the form which extreme respect for the native idiom took in the time when it was made. Cheke's endeavor was to use only such words as had an immediately intelligible meaning in the English language. The older ecclesiastical words he consequently translates by means either of popular native words, or frequently by means of new coinages made up from native elements. Thus he translates *apostle* by *fro-sent, parable* by *by-word, regeneration* by *gain-birth, resurrection* by *uprising* or *gainrising, money-changers* by *tablers, publicans* by *tollers, proselyte* by *freshman, crucified* by *crossed, centurion* by *hundreder, founded* by *groundwrought,* etc. Though Cheke's strange vocabulary is for the most part readily intelligible, the general effect produced by it is of an artificial and unidiomatic language, in its way quite as pedantic as the English of the extreme Latinists. Cheke

[26] The above illustrations are taken from Westcott, *History of the English Bible,* pp. 208-211.

[27] First printed and published by Goodwin, Cambridge, 1843.

was the victim of a theory in the making of his translation, and his fantastic English brings out the more clearly the effectiveness of Tindale's simple and natural Biblical style.

After Tindale the next important figure in the development of the English Bible from the point of view of its literary form was Miles Coverdale. In his own Bible, published in 1535, Coverdale for the first time presented to the English people a complete Bible in their native tongue between two covers. This translation Coverdale declares to have been made with the help of "sondrye translacions, not onely in latyn, but also of the Douche interpreters." [28] At another place he states that he has "with a cleare conscience purely & faythfully translated this out of fyve sundry interpreters, having onely the manyfest trueth of the scriptures before myne eyes." [29] The Latin version which Coverdale followed was the translation of Pagninus, 1528, though he used also the Vulgate; and his German interpreters were first of all the Swiss-German version of Zwingli, known as the Zurich Version, completed in 1529, and secondarily, Luther's Bible. The Zurich version provided the basis for Coverdale's Old Testament, and Tindale, who was probably the fifth of the interpreters mentioned by Coverdale, is closely followed in the New Testament. Coverdale also used such parts of the Old Testament as Tindale had already published, that is, the Pentateuch and the Book of Jonah. Coverdale's Bible can consequently lay claim to no distinction from the point of view of original translation. Its merit consists first of all in assembling the different parts of the Bible into one complete volume, and secondly in the addition of a multitude of minute changes which do not indeed replace Tindale's Biblical style with a new one, but which in many instances

[28] Pollard, *Records*, p. 203. [29] Ibid., p. 201.

result in a freer and ampler manner of expression than Tindale, severe because of his earnestness, permitted himself.

But Coverdale's influence upon the text of the English scriptures was exerted also through another channel. Following the publication of the Matthew Bible in 1537, a compilation made by Tindale's friend, John Rogers, from the translations of Coverdale and Tindale, the next important Bible was the Great Bible of 1539, the second edition of which, appearing the following year with a preface by Cranmer, is often referred to as Cranmer's Bible. It was the first authorized English Bible, and is thus often known as the Bishops' Bible. The work of revision in the Great Bible was intrusted to Coverdale, who returned more or less to the originals in the formation of his text, but who in the main revised on the basis of his own earlier translations and of Tindale's.

This list of the important revisions of the text is completed by the two later versions, the Genevan version of 1560 and the Authorized Version of 1611. The Genevan Bible was the joint work of a number of Puritan exiles temporarily resident at Geneva during the reign of Queen Mary. The revision was thorough, both for details of scholarship and for style, but the basis of it was the Great Bible and the effort in the preparation of it was distinctly not to make a new translation, but to revise the old one. Like the Genevan version, the Authorized Version was the work of a number of different scholars, "to the number of four and fifty," according to King James' letter of instructions,[30] who carried on the task of revision more or less independently but following a set of principles agreed upon beforehand. First of all they agreed that "an entirely new version was not to be furnished, but an old version, long

[30] Pollard, *Records,* p. 331.

received by the Church, to be purged from all blemishes and faults; to this end there was to be no departure from the ancient translation, unless the truth of the original text or emphasis demanded."[31] "Truly (good Christian Reader)," the translators declare in their Preface, "wee never thought from the beginning, that we should neede to make a new Translation, nor yet to make of a bad one a good one . . . but to make a good one better, or out of many good ones, one principall good one, not justly to be excepted against; that hath bene our indeavour, that our marke."[32] Their task was to make the gold of the English scriptures shine more brightly, "being rubbed and polished." The text of the Great Bible, accepted as standard, was continually before them, and departures from it, though numerous, were made only for good and definite reasons. On the whole one must admire the restraint of these four and fifty scholars, who zealously guarded the language of the scriptures to the end that they might "bee understood even of the very vulgar." It was one of the avowed principles of their translation not to use words in special and limited ecclesiastical senses. They would not say to certain words, "Stand up higher, have a place in the Bible alwayes, and to others of like qualitie, Get ye hence, be banished for ever." Niceness in words they counted to be the next step to trifling. How easy it would have been for them to indulge in literary preciosity, the fine writing of their own Preface clearly shows. "In a word," so runs their panegyric on the Bible, "it is a Panary of holesome foode, against fenowed traditions; a Physions-shop (Saint *Basill* calleth it) of preservatives against poisoned heresies; a Pandect of profitable lawes, against rebellious spirits; a

[31] *Report on the Making of the Version of 1611 Presented to the Synod of Dort,* in Pollard, *Records,* p. 339.
[32] *Preface,* in Pollard, *Records,* p. 369.

treasurie of most costly jewels, against beggarly rudiments; Finally a fountaine of most pure water springing up unto everlasting life." [33] Only in the last clause of this sentence were the authors of this Preface subdued to that in which they worked.

Reviewing these several stages through which the English Bible passed, one finds that after Tindale the most significant contributions to it were made by Coverdale. Especially in the Old Testament Coverdale treated the text very freely, at times, under the influence of the Zurich version producing paraphrase rather than translation. Most of Coverdale's expansions have been replaced in the Authorized Version by more exact translations, and the scholarly Genevan version occupies an important middle position between Coverdale's Old Testament and the Authorized Version of 1611. Coverdale did not think of himself as primarily a scholar, but in the modern term, as a popularizer. A variety of translations does not, he declares, make for "divisyon in the fayth and in the people of God." [34] On the contrary, the more translations the better. One man cannot always hit the mark, but now this shooter and now that comes nearest. In accordance with this spirit of eclecticism, Coverdale varied his translation, sometimes using Tindale's words, sometimes the traditional ecclesiastical words of the conservative translators. The particular mark which Coverdale himself attempted to hit was not so much that of literal exactness as ease and fluency in phrasing. Unlike Tindale, Coverdale was an experienced and successful popular preacher and exhorter, and some of the feeling for the round style of spoken discourse may be observed in his modification of Tindale's compact and sometimes angular English. Many of these stylistic expansions were removed by later, especially by the Genevan translators, but in the

[33] Pollard, *Records*, p. 348.

[34] Ibid., p. 203.

Psalter of the Prayer Book they have persisted to the present day. The psalms in the Prayer Book were originally taken directly from the Great Bible, and on the ground that Coverdale's psalms were "smoother and more easy to sing" than any of the later revisions, they have remained unaltered in the Prayer Book. One notes in these psalms not only a fuller phrasing than that of the version of 1611, but also a slightly stronger flavor of the broad popular style, as in Psalm x, 14, *Tush, thou God carest not for it,* which the Authorized Version renders more sedately, *thou wilt not require it* (Ps. x, 13).

In the New Testament Coverdale followed the model of Tindale very closely, but even here he made a great many minor additions which in a surprising number of instances were retained in the version of 1611. A few illustrations from the first Gospel will show how Tindale's texts were gradually made more easy and pliable.

Tindale, in Matt. i, 25, reads, *tyll she had brought forth hir fyrst sonne, and called hys name Jesus,* but Coverdale, translating the Greek πρωτότοκον more at length, has *fyrst borne sonne.* This is changed in the Great Bible to *hyr fyrst begotten sonne,* but the Authorized Version returns to Coverdale's first rendering. In Matt. iii, 4, Tindale translates, *This Jhon had hys garment of camels heer and a gerdell of a skynne aboute his loynes,* where Coverdale, again more literally and also more smoothly, reads, *a lethren gerdell.* The Great Bible, the Genevan and the Rhemish New Testament all return to Tindale's rendering, but the Authorized Version retains Coverdale's first translation. A striking illustration of the gradual formation of a smooth phrasing is afforded by Matt. vi, 34. Tindale reads here: *Care not then for the morow, but let the morow care for it selfe: for the daye present hath ever ynough of his awne trouble.* In Coverdale's Bible of 1535 this last clause reads,

Every daye hath ynough of his owne travayll, which is improved in the Great Bible: *Care not then for the morow, for to morowe day shall care for it selfe: sufficient unto the daye is the travayle therof.* The Genevan New Testament alters the first half of the verse for the better: *Care not then for the morow: for the morow shal care for it selfe: The day present hath ever inough to do with it owne grief.* The Rhemish version changes slightly: *Be not careful therfore for the morow. For the morow day shal be careful for it self: sufficient for the day is the evil thereof.* And the Authorized Version, accepting the best from the preceding versions and giving the whole a somewhat ampler rhythm, reads: *Take therefore no thought for the morrow: for the morrow shall take thought for the things of it selfe: sufficient unto the day is the evill thereof.* A further illustration may be cited from this Gospel. In Matt. xxv, 21, Tindale reads: *Then his master sayde unto him: well good servaunt and faithfull. Thou hast bene faithfull in lytell, I will make the ruler over moche: enter in into thy masters ioye.* Coverdale's rendering, as represented by the Great Bible, is as follows: *His lorde saide unto him: well thou good and faithfull servaunt. Thou hast bene faythfull over fewe thinges. I will make the ruler over many thinges. Entre thou into the ioye of thy lorde.* The Genevan Testament returns to Tindale, but the Rhemish version, with slight modification, follows Coverdale. And the Authorized Version, with one helpful change, also follows Coverdale: *His lord said unto him, Well done, good and faithfull servant, thou hast bene faithfull over a few things, I will make thee ruler over many things: enter thou into the joy of thy lord.* In Luke xviii, 13, Tindale reads: *And the publican stode afarre of and wolde not lyfte up his eyes to heven,* a close translation of the Greek. Coverdale, in the Great Bible, followed by the Rhemish and the Authorized Versions, changes the syntax for the sake of rhythm: *And the publycan stondyng a farre of, wolde not lyfte up hys eyes to heaven.* The play of the texts back and forth is interestingly illustrated by the translations of Luke xviii, 23. Tindale reads here: *When he heard that, he was hevy: for he was very ryche.* The Great Bible changes *hevy* to *sory,* which becomes in the Authorized Version, *very sorowfull.* The Genevan translation reads *very hevy* and *marvelous ryche,* and the Rhemish version is different from all others: *He hearing these things, was stroken sad: because he was very riche.* But in the succeeding verse the Authorized Version owes its reading, *How hardly shal they that have riches, enter into the kingdome of God?* mainly to the Rhemish translation, Tindale reading here, *with what difficulte shall they that have ryches enter into the kingdome of God?* It is interesting to note, however, that the Rhemish version reads *money* instead of *riches,* agreeing in this with the Great Bible. In Luke xviii, 26, Tindale translates, rather awkwardly, *Then sayde they that hearde that,* which reads more smoothly in the Great Bible and the Authorized Version, *And they that hearde it sayd.* One final illustration of the minute changes by means of which stylistic effect was gained may be cited from Luke xviii, 38. Tindale gives here a literal translation of the Greek, except that the pronoun subject of the verb is only implied in the form of the Greek verb, not specifically expressed: *And he cryed sayinge: Jesus the sonne of David, have thou mercy on me.* The Great Bible gains in dramatic force: *And he cryed, sayinge: Jesu thou sonne of David, have mercy on me.* The Genevan version as usual follows Tindale except that it changes the first word to *Then.* The Rhemish version also agrees with Tindale except that it omits the vocative pronoun altogether. And the Authorized Version follows the Great Bible exactly.

These illustrations have been cited to show the changes which Coverdale and the Authorized Version made in the text of Tindale's translation. Compared with the whole, they are relatively slight, and it is much easier to find passages in which the later versions agree with Tindale than passages in which they differ. Verse after verse of the Authorized Version follows Tindale almost without change, and such changes as are made, though as a whole they are improvements both in style and scholarly exactness, do not greatly alter the character of the book as it was first established by Tindale. Of a good book the later revisers made a better, as it was always their purpose to do, not a new translation.

II

The conception of a complete service-book in the native tongue for the use of the whole congregation of the church was of much later origin than the conception of a complete English Bible. Even Cranmer, to whom the final formulation of the Book of Common Prayer "after the use of the Church of England" is supposed to owe most, arrived at such a conception only slowly and gradually. His first plans contemplated only a remodeling of the traditional Latin service-books of the church. Later he approved the use of English for parts of the service, those parts which have to do with "mysteries" being still given in Latin. And finally, when the lay members of the church were granted that highest of all privileges, the privilege of partaking personally in the service of communion, even this last stronghold of Latin was given up by Cranmer. A complete English service-book, which differed in no respect from that in the hands of the officiating priest, was then for the first time put into the possession of the people.

Although the English people prior to the Reformation

had nothing equivalent to the Book of Common Prayer, they had certain books in English which were intended in some degree to take the place of an English service-book. Of this character was the Lay Folks Mass Book, as the work is called by its modern editor.[35] This was not a translation of the missal, though several parts of the service of the mass were retained, but rather an independent work with rubrics and devotions which run parallel to the mass and which were to be read silently by the lay people at the same time that the priest was celebrating the office aloud. The book is in English verse, and with the exception of the celebration of the sacrament of communion, in which the laity had no share, it provides a substitute for the various parts of the mass.

Another popular book of devotion was the Primer, or lay-folk's service book. Primers were written both in Latin and in English, and they were used not only as books for private devotions, but also as school-books for the instruction of children. Certain portions of the Primer were learned by heart, and, with the help of an alphabet often prefixed, at the same time the student learned how to read.[36] The contents of the Primers varied considerably, though they were originally derived mainly from the Hours of the Virgin. Other devotional matter was gradually added to the Hours, such as Psalms, a litany, certain occasional offices, and prayers, until the book became a kind of shortened breviary for the use of those who could read Latin or English, but who were not themselves clerics. One of the earliest English Primers extant was made about the year 1400. This Primer is extensive so far as its content goes, but in style it is crude and rudimentary. The same difficulties which confronted the translators of the Wiclifite

[35] Simmons, E.E.T.S., LXXI, 1879.

[36] See Watson, *The English Grammar School to 1660*, pp. 31-37.

Bible had also to be met by the compilers of a vernacular service-book. Such renderings as the following can hardly be counted satisfactory, or even intelligible English: "As it was in the bigynnynge and now and evere, in to the werldis of werldis," a literal translation of *Sicut erat in principio, et nunc, et semper, et in saecula saeculorum;* or the translation of the phrase from the Venite exultemus, *praeoccupemus faciem ejus in confessione* by "biforeocupie we his face in confessioun." [37]

But the Primer, unlike the Wiclifite Bible, continued in general use and underwent numerous revisions from time to time. It thus represents a gradual growth in the adaptation of the vernacular to the needs of the services of the church. In the second quarter of the sixteenth century, when the champions of the Reformation in England began to fight more in the open, it was natural that they should send forth certain Primers which were intended to serve as popular manuals of instruction in Protestant doctrine. Issued first without authority, these Primers were soon to receive episcopal and royal sanction. In the latter years of the reign of Henry VIII, three different versions of the Primer in English were printed, the first known as Marshall's Primer in 1534, the second in 1539 at Cromwell's direction. The third was known as the King's Primer, because it was published with Henry's sanction, in 1545, and with the command that no other was to be used throughout all his dominions. In these Primers we approach very near to the form of the Prayer Book by which they were soon to be supplanted. Marshall's Primer was the work of William Marshall, who translated and published various reform writings. In the first edition of his "Prymer in Englysshe" he had omitted the litany, but he adds it in the second edition "for the contentation of such weak minds"

[37] *The Prymer,* ed. Littlehales, Pt. I, p. 17.

as were disturbed by not finding it in the first edition. "Right doubtful it is, as I think," so he continues, "to pray unto all those that be mentioned, named and called saints in the common primers in Latin."[38] Besides the longer devotions for adults, Marshall's Primer contains a shorter primer for children, called *A fruitful and a very Christian instruction for children.* In this are given various prayers, the creed, graces before and after meals, at rising, at retiring, and for other occasions. The King's Primer was published first in English, being a "determinate form of praying in their own mother tongue, to the intent that such as are ignorant of any strange or foreign speech, may have what to pray in their own acquainted and familiar language with fruit and understanding."[39] To the English version was later added a Latin translation, and those who thought they could make their prayers with a more fervent spirit in that tongue, were given permission to use it. But King Henry's Primer was intended to supplement and not to replace the traditional service-books of the church.

With the accession of Edward VI a new impulse was given to that reformation of both doctrine and formula which had begun in the reign of his predecessor. Following the lead of the Continental ecclesiastic, Cardinal Francisco de Quiñones (Cardinal Quignon), Cranmer had already made experiments looking to the reformation and simplification of the Latin breviary. In the first years of Edward's reign a commission was appointed, with Archbishop Cranmer at its head, to examine the whole question of the formal services of the church. The conference met at Windsor, "a good number of the best learned men reputed within

[38] *Three Primers Put forth in the Reign of Henry VIII,* p. 124. Marshall's Primer was suppressed on the complaint of Convocation, cf. Watson, *The English Grammar Schools to 1660,* p. 33.

[39] *Three Primers,* p. 440.

this realm, some favoring the old, some the new learning," [40] and the results of their deliberations, laid before Parliament in 1549, were immediately accepted. These results were embodied in the First Prayer Book of Edward VI, and by the Act of Uniformity passed at the time, it was decreed that the "great diversitie in saying and synging in churches within this realme" which had prevailed hitherto, should now give place to this one use of the independent church of England. Three years later, in 1552, a revision, mainly doctrinal, of the First Prayer Book was made which brought it more into harmony with Protestant teachings at certain points. Queen Elizabeth's Prayer Book of 1559 represents a second revision, which differs but little from the First and Second Prayer Books of Edward VI. Later revisions were made by James I, in 1604, and a final one by Charles II, in 1662; but the changes in all these later revisions are relatively slight, and the book remains essentially as it was, so far at least as its literary character is concerned, when it left the hands of Cranmer and his associates in the days of Edward VI.

When one regards the Prayer Book from the point of view of the earlier traditional services of the church, the two most important steps taken by the authors of the book seem astonishingly radical. In the first place, a great mass of ritual observance which had gradually grown up in the course of centuries was ruthlessly set aside. The medieval church had developed an elaborate system of services, ordinary and occasional, for which appropriate forms had been devised. To control all the various service-books needed in the celebration of the different services taxed the capacity even of learned clerics, to say nothing of inexperienced laymen. Merely to turn the pages of the book was "so hard

[40] Gasquet and Bishop, *Edward the VI and the Book of Common Prayer*, p. 137.

and intricate a matter that many times there was more busines to fynd out what should be read, then to read it when it was founde out."[41] With the reformed service, "the curates shal nede none other bookes for their publique service, but this boke and the Bible." By an heroic act of compression, some of the traditional daily services of the church were omitted altogether, and the three services of matins, lauds, and prime were combined to form the service called matins in the First Prayer Book and morning prayer in the Second Book; and vespers and compline were united to form the only other daily service of the reformed church, called evensong in the First Prayer Book and evening prayer in the Second. But the services were not only few in number, they were also simple in outline. From a confused medley, rich in detail as a medieval cathedral, the reformers extracted a few leading principles, not much more than the skeleton of the mass-book, as Milton scornfully declared, the almsbasket of the prayers of the Roman church.[42] But the new service-book had this advantage, that it was comprehensible in its entirety, not only to the instructed clergy, but to every intelligent layman.

The second radical step of the authors of the Prayer Book was the choice of the vernacular for the language of the book. As was the case with the simplification of forms, the way for the use of English in all the services of the church had long been preparing. Through their layfolk's catechisms, mass-books, and primers, the popular mind had grown accustomed to the expression of devotional ideas in the mother tongue. And with the gradual acceptance of the notion of a democratic church, in which the priestly orders were the ministers and not the rulers of the congregation, it was logically necessary that the great

[41] *Preface,* in the First Prayer Book.
[42] *Prose Works,* ed. Symmons, I, 45, 262.

barrier of language should be removed so far as possible between priest and people. Nevertheless it was an act of great courage on the part of the learned men gathered at Windsor to set aside so completely the only language in which their ancestors had said the divine services for centuries and in which they themselves had been accustomed to hear them from the earliest days of their childhood. And it is all the more remarkable if, as Cranmer declares, it was agreed by all, "without controversy (not one saying contrary) that the service of the church ought to be in the mother tongue." [43] For the translation of the scriptures many precedents, from St. Jerome down, might be adduced, but in the defense of the native tongue as the appropriate language for a national church, the English church was making and not following precedent. The production of the English Prayer Book was but one more step in that slow progress towards complete national realization and expression which the English people for two centuries had now been entered upon.

Although the exact methods by which the English Prayer Book was produced seem not to have been recorded, it is certain that the moving personality, both in the construction and perhaps also in the actual composition of the book, was Archbishop Cranmer. Unlike Tindale's New Testament, the Prayer Book from the beginning enjoyed the good fortune of royal and episcopal favor. Something of the genial glow of the circumstances of its composition is reflected in the book itself. The task which lay before the commission assembled at Windsor was not one merely of devising a service-book intelligible to the plowman and the simple folk of England; in the mind of a scholar and writer of Cranmer's experience, the demands of simplicity and intelligibility were to be taken for granted. Equally im-

[43] Gasquet and Bishop, p. 137.

portant was the necessity of fashioning a book which should adequately express the dignity of a great national church, and which should have due regard to the feeling for form which had been fostered for generations by the stately services of the medieval church. It was not enough that the services of the reformed church should be simple and uniform, they must also be beautiful in themselves. In satisfying this demand, with rare discretion Cranmer and his associates avoided the extravagances of the fashionable and ephemeral literary styles of the time, and fixed their attention upon the purer and more permanent models of liturgical expression long traditional in the Latin services of the church.

The dignity of Cranmer's office and of the services which long familiarity must have made second nature to him raised him above petty mannerisms of style. In his homilies, published two years before the Prayer Book, for the use of licensed preachers in the church, Cranmer writes in a restrained, even manner, serene but not cold, and unfailingly appropriate to the somewhat formal purpose for which the homilies were intended. He eschews all obvious ornaments of style, such as alliteration, puns, doublets, fine words, and popular picturesque phrases. He never rises to heights of fervid eloquence, nor on the other hand, does he ever descend to a loose or careless or popular manner of writing. One admires throughout the homilies the evenness of tone and the fine feeling for words and for the cadences of phrasing in which the artist in language is revealed. This same disciplined and chastened literary feeling appears again in the composition of the Prayer Book.

It was no easy task to produce a book in the English language which should be popular, and at the same time compete in dignity and stateliness with the familiar Latin services. No literal translation would answer the purpose, for a literal translation of the Latin is cold and bare. The Latin services are both compact and at the same time large and dignified in the outline of their phrasing. The Latin words in themselves have a richness of flavor not often paralleled by an English equivalent, and a word for word substitution of English terms for the Latin makes the latter seem what they are not, hard and meager. On the other hand, mere ornament, compared with the severity of the Latin, must have seemed to Cranmer and his associates an unworthy and meretricious substitute for something better. The main problem before the authors of the book was therefore that of finding the proper cadences in English. By Cranmer's time the language was sufficiently rich in vocabulary to make the transference of ideas from one language to the other comparatively easy. But English words were prevailingly monosyllabic and were wanting in the sonority and fullness of the many-syllabled inflected words of the Latin. In the lack of exact equivalents in English, a substitute for the Latin words must be found.

This was done mainly by a process of expansion. The foundations of the Prayer Book, not only in content but in the spirit of the phrasing as well, were the older Latin service-books of the church, primarily the Salisbury Use, which was the one followed at Canterbury, and, after 1542, generally throughout the southern province of England. But the same principles of compression which were followed in the general structure of the services of the new Prayer Book could not be followed in the details of their expression. The brevity of the new services were compensated for in some measure by their warmth and breadth of feeling. So far as vocabulary is concerned, the authors of the first Prayer Book made use in the main of simple English words. Their diction is only slightly more Latinized than that of Tindale's New Testament. The English "almighty" is preferred to "omnipotent," "everlasting" to "sempiternal," and in general the effort of the authors of the Prayer Book seems to have been not to elevate the tone of the service-book by the employment of aureate terms, but to keep it as far as possible upon the plane of the current and generally intelligible speech. The stylistic devices which they did employ were various. What would have seemed abrupt in a literal translation of the Latin was often softened by the insertion of an exclamation at the opening of a sentence, e.g. *Domine, labia mea aperies,* which reads in the First Prayer Book, "O Lorde, open thou my lippes." And such additions are frequently made where the Latin has merely a vocative, or even where there is no vocative. Vivacity is also given to the English frequently by the expression of a pronoun which is merely implied in the Latin, as in the above and in *Benedicite omnia opera Domini Domino,* which becomes "O all ye workes of the Lorde, speake good of the Lorde." Or the bare name of the deity in the Latin is often amplified by the addition of some adjective like "almighty" or "everlasting." In general, however, the versicles are remarkable examples of compressed and faithful translation. Expansions like that of the opening sentence of the Litany, *Pater de coelis Deus, miserere nobis,* translated "O God the father of heaven, have mercy upon us miserable synners," are rare in the versicles and responses. In the prayers and collects, however, the changes are more numerous and striking. The English often becomes more concrete than the Latin, as when *qui contritorum non despicis gemitum* in the second prayer of the Litany becomes "that despisest not the syghyng of a contrite heart." A compact phrase of the Latin is often expanded; in this same prayer, the phrase *diabolicae fraudes* is rendered "the crafte and subteltie of the devyll." This habit of rounding out the phrasing of the English version by the pairing of almost synonymous words is well illustrated by the collect for the fourth Sunday in Advent. The Latin is extremely compact: *ut per auxilium gratiae tuae quod nostra peccata praepediunt, indulgentia tuae propitiationis acceleret.* This becomes in the English version: "that whereas, through our synnes and wickednes, we be soore lette and hindred, thy bountifull grace and mercye, through the satisfaccion of thy sonne our Lord, may spedily deliver us." Another illustration may be cited from the collect for the first Sunday after the Epiphany: *Vota, quaesumus, Domine, supplicantis populi coelesti pietate prosequere; ut et quae agenda sunt, videant; et ad implenda quae viderint, convalescant;* "Lorde we beseche the mercyfullye to receive the praiers of thy people which cal upon thee; and graunt that they maie both perceave and knowe what thinges they ought to do, and also have grace and power faithfully to fulfill the same." Sometimes phrases are introduced for which the original offers no equivalent, such as the words "in al our daungiers and necessities," in the collect for the third Sunday after the Epiphany; or when the last clause of the collect for Ascension Day, *ipsi quoque mente in coelestibus habitemus,* is rendered, "so we may also in heart and mind thither ascende, and with him continually dwell." The collect for the twelfth Sunday after Trinity is considerably expanded, but one phrase only need be cited: *effunde super nos misericordiam tuam,* which reads, "Powre downe upon us the aboundance of thy mercy." Similar illustrations of the way in which a compact and somewhat stern phrasing of the Latin service has been expanded in order to produce equivalent cadences in English might be cited indefinitely, but space permits only one more, the first of the group of collects which stand at the close of the communion service. This reads as follows in the original: *Adesto, Domine, supplicationibus nostris: et viam famulorum tuorum in salutis tuae prosperitate dispone: ut inter omnes viae et vitae hujus varietates, tuo semper protegantur auxilio.* Admirable in phrasing and diction as this prayer is, it cannot be said that the English version falls short of it: "Assist us mercifully, O Lord, in these our supplicacions and praiers, and dispose the way of thy servauntes toward the attainement of everlasting salvacion, that emong all the chaunges and chaunces of thys mortall lyfe, they maye ever bee defended by thy moste gracious and readye helpe."

Such was the spirit in which the authors of the Prayer Book set about the task of composing a common service for the use of the English people. The book which they constructed and the tone which they set in it have remained essentially unaltered since their day. Some additions were made in the first revision of 1552, notably the Exhortation and General Confession near the beginning of morning and evening prayer, with their familiar word-pairs, "acknowledge and confess," "synnes and wickedness," "dissemble nor cloke," "assemble and mete together," "erred and strayed," "devises and desyres," and others like these. But the tone of these original contributions to the Prayer Book, as they seem to be, does not differ from that established by the authors of the first version; nor do the changes and additions of Queen Elizabeth's Prayer Book of 1559, or the final revision of 1662, present anything new from the literary point of view. As a literary achievement the Prayer Book in its essentials is to be credited to Cranmer and his associates. And if we had no other testimony than that of time, we should have to grant that their work was well done. The latter clause of the statement attributed to James I, that the "Liturgie was taken out of the Masse Book, onely spoyled in the translation," has never found many supporters. It is true that Queen Elizabeth's dream of "an uniform uniformity" in the services of the English church has never been completely realized. From the days of its first composition, there were Puritan non-conformists who would have nothing to do with a prelatical Prayer Book, and there have always been numerous congregations of devout worshipers who have refused to accept the established forms. In spite of this, no single influence except that of the Bible has been so great as the influence of the Prayer Book upon all English devotional expression, whether public or private. Implicitly the Prayer Book has been accepted as a standard, and upon it have been modeled many varying, but not essentially different, forms of worship. The First Prayer Book of Edward VI expressed permanently one of the constant moods of the English people. It put an end to the period of experimentation by its invention of an adequate and satisfactory form of expression for the devotional feeling, and it became thereby one of the fixed stars in the literary firmament for the guidance of later generations of English people.

The English Bible and the English Prayer Book have a peculiar significance as the first classics of modern English literature. The *Morte Darthur* and the *Utopia* might suggest themselves as possible competitors for this distinction. But Malory is more medieval than modern, and is to be grouped rather with Chaucer than with Spenser. And the *Utopia,* originally written in Latin and never turned into English by its author, has persisted less as a classic of English literature than as one of universal literature. Neither the *Morte Darthur* nor the *Utopia* has enjoyed the permanent general interest of the relatively few great classics of the language, nor does either occupy one of those central pivotal positions in the development of English letters which lends to other works unusual historical significance. The Bible and the Prayer Book are to be regarded as the earliest English classics in the sense that they are the earliest books in the English tongue which have been uninterruptedly and generally read since the time of their composition, and which have been read substantially in the form which was given them in the middle of the sixteenth century. Whether we accept Tindale's New Testament or the Great Bible of 1539 as establishing the form of the English scriptures, we must recognize that this form was fixed and generally acknowledged two generations before it received final sanction in the Authorized Version. The Version of 1611 merely confirmed a tradition and did not establish it. In the same way the Prayer Book as an expression of the English genius must be dated from the year of the First Prayer Book of Edward VI. Official recognition helped to conserve what popular feeling would probably have maintained as tenaciously without public authority. The combination of the two, popular approval and public authority, resulted in the establishment of both Bible and Prayer Book in positions of extraordinary influence and power. The value of these two books in the maintenance of standards of propriety and sanity in English expression can hardly be overestimated. In the sixteenth century the English people were creating for themselves a new literary speech. They were driven to experimentation and to imitation which often led, in the absence of a standard literary idiom, to great extremes of literary styles. The scholars would have turned English into a kind of Anglicized Latin. The courtly experimenters, the Euphuists and Arcadians, would have exalted rhetorical artifice at the expense of naturalness and breadth of appeal. The advocates of a literary speech based entirely upon the native idiom would have sacrificed all dignity and variety of expression in the interests of a homely and often grotesque popular style. From all of these experiments much good resulted in the formation of the literary speech which the sixteenth century passed on to the seventeenth. But what was needed above all in the welter of experimentation was some sense of moderation, some feeling for a strong central idiom which should enable the writer of English to avoid both the extreme of artistic fantasy and of an ignoble Saxon bluntness. This need of a safe standard was supplied by the English Bible and the English Prayer Book. They were popular in the sense that they were intelligible to the great public and were cast in the forms of normal English speech. But they were literary, also, in that they were elevated above the ephemeral colloquial language, and in that they satisfied not only the intelligence of their readers, but also their feeling for propriety, and for dignity and beauty of expression. The direct influence of the Bible and the Prayer Book upon certain writers of the sixteenth and of later centuries has been very great. The ultimate significance of the books is to be found, however, in something deeper than the occasional and specific influence which they have exerted upon the style of individual writers. It is to be found in the fact that they were, for all Englishmen, unquestioned achievements of the English language. They became a great steadying, unifying tradition, and by their popular acceptance, one of the implicit conditions of all later use of English speech.

VI

THE COURTLY WRITERS

THE NEW LEARNING—INFLUENCE OF THE CLASSICS—AUREATE DICTION—CAXTON—SKELTON—THE 'TUMBLING' STYLE — WORD-BORROWING—CHEKE—ASCHAM—SIR THOMAS WILSON—THE RHETORICIANS—THE INGENIOUS STYLE—GUEVARA AND HIS INFLUENCE—LORD BERNERS—SIR THOMAS NORTH—THE INGENIOUS STYLE IN FICTION—THE SCHOOL OF LYLY—SIDNEY AND ARCADIANISM

I

THE ideal of the scholar and gentleman as mutually complementary sides of the perfect character greatly occupied the minds of Englishmen in the early sixteenth century. The new order of thought, as well as the old to which it stood in contrast, is illustrated in an anecdote of the time of Henry VIII. A certain great peer of the court expressed the opinion that "it was enough for noblemen's sons to wind their horn, and carry their hawk well, that study was for the children of a meaner rank." To this Pace, scholar and statesman, answered that "then noblemen must be content that their children may wind their horns and carry their hawks while meaner men's sons do wield the affairs of state."[1]

Similar warnings and counsels are expressed by another of Henry's servants. In one of his numerous treatises written for the profit of his "natural country," Sir Thomas

[1] Hall, "Quo Vadis," *Works,* ed. Wynter, IX, 538.

Elyot expounds his belief that the old chivalric rule of conduct must give place to a new one, not based on valor and courtesy, but on knowledge. That which soonest "helpeth a man to virtue," the one "sure and honest rule of livynge," Elyot declares, is learning. "All other thynges temporall be but tryfils and not of such value that there in we oughte to spende any studye." He then compares learning with "gentylnes of bloud," with fortune, with honor, with other virtues, but he returns to the opinion that learning is the most important of all.[2] That Elyot earnestly believed in these views, and all the more earnestly since they came to him with the sanction of Plutarch's approval, his own life bears ample witness. His "boke called the Governour," his "Castel of health," his "Dictionary," all his many publications were sent forth with the single intent of providing Englishmen of his day with the learning and with the principles of conduct befitting the cultivated scholar and gentleman.

But Elyot was not altogether the first by scholarly precept or example to set this new ideal of literary culture before Englishmen's eyes. Before his time Lydgate, Caxton, Berners, and Skelton had in some measure adumbrated the coming of a new scholarship and a new sense for literary form in England. Elyot was merely part of a general movement, he was one of many who added dignity to the practice of letters both by their scholarly standards in writing and by the distinguished social positions which they themselves held. In greater or less degree they realized the ideal set forth in Castiglione's description of the courtier as one who not only knew how "to ride and manage

[2] *The Education or bringinge up of children, translated oute of Plutarche by syr Thomas Eliot, knight.* Cap. V. The book is undated, but it was certainly written before 1540, since it is mentioned in *The Image of Goverance,* published in that year.

well his horse," but who was also "well spoken and fair languaged," who could write in prose or in verse, and who practiced the arts of the pen, like those of the sword, with grace and freedom.

The forces which brought about this changed attitude towards literature and learning, hitherto almost exclusively the pursuit of ecclesiastics, were of mixed native and foreign origin. In part they were closely bound up with the impulses which from the beginning of the fifteenth century had been changing the character of the popular English mind. When Occleve advised Sir John Oldcastle to rest content with the story of Launcelot de Lake or of the siege of Troy or Thebes,[3] he proved that he had understood neither the popular nor the learned tendencies of his time. The popular reformers could no longer be quieted with lifeless summaries of dogmatic doctrine. Nor could the lovers of imaginative writing and of good style content themselves with the faded plots and worn out literary devices of medieval romance. In Malory's *Morte Darthur* we have the last vanishing echoes from the din and uproar of primitive fighting, loving, feasting mankind, echoes that become, as is the nature of such sounds, purer and sweeter in quality as they become fainter and remoter from the actuality of their origin. New and fresh material was needed upon which the artistic imagination could vigorously exert itself. The cultivated writers of Renascence England wisely did not often try to breathe new life into the old stories of Arthur and Alexander, of Troy and of Thebes. Stronger attraction was exerted from a different direction.

In the earlier years of the English Renascence two constant elements in the development of the new literary art were admiration for the language and literature of classical antiquity and desire to transfer the qualities which dis-

[3] See above, p. 58.

tinguish the writings of the ancients to English, or at least to create their equivalents in the English vernacular. The position which French, the language of romance, had occupied in the fourteenth century, was now taken by Greek, and more especially by Latin. The constant effort of the early English humanists was to raise their English composition to the level of classical style. Even as early as Lydgate the tendency towards lofty style is elaborately exemplified, and the high esteem in which he was held by his contemporaries, and even by his successors of several generations later, as for example Caxton, Hawes, and Skelton, was due to the fact that he was regarded as herald of a new generation. In comparison Chaucer began to seem quaint and old and rude.

But though the writings of antiquity provided the general standards of excellence for English stylists, one does not find, either early or late, that they were very closely imitated as models. There were many admirers of Cicero among English courtly writers, but there was no English Cicero. In this respect English humanism differed from Italian, for in the writings of Bembo and the extremer Italian stylists, native spontaneity was completely stifled by iron-clad rules of servile imitation. Early English humanists were both less scholarly and in less degree animated by a passionate love of the fine art of writing than were the humanists of Italy during the corresponding period of the development of Italian literature. In Skelton, in Caxton, in Sir Thomas Elyot, one observes only a general and remote resemblance to Ciceronian eloquence. Even in writers like Bishop Fisher and Sir Thomas More, who were more immediately and consciously under the spell of Latin style, the form and rhetorical dress of classic expression are only in slight measure carried over into English. Ascham speaks of "that excellent perfitnesse" in speech and writing, "which was onely in Tullie or onelie in Tullies tyme."[4] But the most characteristic features of Cicero's style, his rhythms and cadences, are reproduced only in a very general way in Ascham's own writing. In their attitude towards Cicero, English humanists agreed in the main with Erasmus and with earlier Italian humanists like Petrarch, who, with all his admiration for Cicero, declared that his Latin was the Latin of Petrarch, not of Cicero.[5] So the writing of the early literary stylists in England always rested on a substantial foundation of native expression. What they got from the classics was rather the appreciation of form than specific models of form.

As English stylists continued to cultivate the graces of writing and as they developed a technic of their own, they departed farther and farther from classical standards. The shade of Cicero certainly would not recognize Lyly and Sidney as made in his image. Nor was any classical author other than Cicero made the determining model of the English stylists. They knew Seneca and studied him almost as zealously as they did Cicero. They cultivated Isocrates as well as Demosthenes and Plato. Their taste was eclectic, and indeed not very discriminating. They had a voracious appetite for everything that seemed to them to lend distinction to writing, but their feeling for classic art was enthusiastic and vague, rather than exact and scholarly.[6] Then again it must not be forgotten that the

[4] *Scholemaster,* ed. Arber, p. 144.

[5] Clark, *Ciceronianism,* in *English Literature and the Classics,* p. 135.

[6] English Latinists likewise exhibited moderation in their respect for classic models. Sir Thomas More was of course in agreement with the theory and practice of the more liberal humanists like Erasmus and Vives. But even professional Latinists, like Walter Haddon, whose Latin style seems to have been more highly esteemed than that of any other in the sixteenth century, were very moderate Ciceronians. It was Haddon who was called on to answer

break between medieval and Renascence culture in England was by no means complete. An art of fine writing had been elaborately practiced throughout the whole of the so-called Dark Ages, and it has already been pointed out how Wiclif was impelled to protest against it in the interests of simplicity. Many of the artifices of style employed by English writers in the sixteenth century seem to be merely transferred from medieval Latin style to the vernacular.[7] Not before the prose of Milton in the seventeenth century does one find what may be called a first-hand and adequate imitation of classical Latin prose in native English writing. Milton wrote a thoroughly scholarly style, and compared with him, the classicists of the sixteenth century seem amateurs and novices.

Among writers of English prose, the first significant cultivator of the learned tendencies of the new style was William Caxton, the father of English printing, though not of English prose. Born in the first quarter of the fifteenth century, Caxton is one of the connecting links between the medieval England of Chaucer, with its close French affiliations, and the Renascence England of the early sixteenth century. He was attracted to the trade of printing before he became interested in literary production, and afterwards he was driven to read, to write, and to translate in order to

Osorius, the Portuguese bishop, famous for his Ciceronian eloquence (see Preface, p. xi). Foxe (*Fox against Osorius, Tracts of the Anglican Reformers,* VIII, 327) declares that Walter Haddon daunted the haughty pride of Osorius "and utterly discomfited his vain-glorious peacock-like rhetoric with such gravity, wisdom, and so well disposed style" that the truth of the Gospel "might seem to have no need of any other patronage." Ascham (*Scholemaster,* ed. Arber, p. 112) advises Osorius to try to write "so straite, fast and temperate a style in latine" as Demosthenes wrote in Greek, and a preference for the plain style of Demosthenes is recorded by various other sixteenth century writers and scholars.

[7] This point is ably presented by Professor Morris Croll in an essay soon to appear, *Marte favente,* in *Englische Studien.*

supply his press with materials appropriate for publication. He thus became a literary experimenter. His work took the form mainly of prose translation or adaptation of French, Latin, Dutch, and of older English originals. He was always more of a literary craftsman than a literary artist. Not finding what he needed in contemporary or in past English literature, he set to work to supply the lack in a straightforward, workmanlike fashion, but always with shrewdness and literary discernment. The range of his interests was determined in large part by the demands of his public. The books which issued from his press were mainly romances and books of conduct for the courtly reader, editions or versions of what may be called the native classic literature of the times, Chaucer, Malory, Boethius, the stories of Troy, of Charlemagne, of the Æneid, many histories and lives of the saints, together with moral treatises and service-books of the church. He avoided doctrinal and controversial subjects, and the first English press gave little support to the popular movements that were transforming the character of English society. If not in his sympathies, at least in the choice of books for publication, Caxton was distinctly aristocratic and conservative. His originality, so far as it goes, was shown in the form of his writings and translations, not in their content. He conceived that what English needed was to broaden its horizon, to increase the volume and the power of its medium of expression. He has no hesitancy in parting from the old. The English, he declares, were born under the " dominacyon of the mone "; they are always seeking some new and strange thing, and their speech has changed so rapidly that the English of his boyhood differed greatly from that of his mature years. What Englishmen read a generation or two before his day, they could no longer read, or could read only with difficulty. The old style seemed to him obscure and rude, and no longer adequate for the uses to which English must be put.

The contrast between Caxton and Chaucer is instructive, and it shows why one is and the other is not of the new generation. Chaucer's art is highly traditional, and it differs from that of his contemporaries mainly in that it is more perfect than theirs. Early brought under the influence of French taste, Chaucer never greatly departed from his first models. It is difficult to point out any direct influence of Vergil or Ovid, of Dante, Petrarch, or Boccaccio upon Chaucer's growth as an artist. To all of these he was indebted for materials, but none of them can be called his liberator. His art grew deeper and richer in content and in form as he grew older, but there were no great revolutions in his taste. Lowell has said that Chaucer opened his windows to the south. Temperamentally he did so, and all the chambers of his house of poetry are flooded with the soft and genial radiance of his own personality. But Chaucer's was not a roving mind. He cultivated assiduously his own garden plot, decorated and beautified it with slips and seedlings from his neighboring France, some of which he improved in the transplanting, but he seldom allowed his gaze to wander far beyond his own garden walls.

Caxton himself misunderstood Chaucer in this respect. He regarded him as an innovator, as one who set about the task of enriching the English tongue and of providing it with a new courtly style as consciously as he himself was doing. "For tofore that he by labour embellished, ornated and made fair our English," says Caxton in a passage of the Proem to his edition of the Canterbury Tales which well illustrates his own conception of high style, "in this realm was had rude speech and incongruous, as yet it appeareth by old books, which at this day ought not to have place ne be compared among, ne to, his beauteous volumes and ornate writings, of whom he made many books and treatises of many a noble history, as well in metre as in rhyme and prose; and them so craftily made that he comprehended his matters in short, quick and high sentences, eschewing prolixity, casting away the chaff of superfluity, and shewing the picked grain of sentence, uttered by crafty and sugared eloquence." [8] But "sugared eloquence" and the reform of the English tongue were certainly not among Chaucer's ideals, and Caxton is led into his mistaken criticism merely by the fact that he finds many words of Romance origin in Chaucer such as he does not find in his "old books." Chaucer's foreign words, however, were not conscious innovations; they were the common property of good written and spoken English in his day. His English was that of the court, but it was not a newly invented and fashionable court language.

Though he expresses admiration for the virtue of compactness in Chaucer, Caxton himself cannot be said to have eschewed prolixity. He has only one device for elevating his style, and that is the multiplication of words. For form and structure his feeling is rudimentary. He escapes the monotony and simplicity of the medieval narrative style, but he does so at the expense often of being obscure, labored, and clumsy. He sought fullness, but the harmonious arrangement of parts in the structure of the sentence, which was to be the chief contribution of the classics to English style, was beyond his grasp. On the other hand the "fayr and straunge termes" of the originals from which he translated were within his comprehension, and these terms he brought over freely into English. When he was blamed for this, his answer on one occasion was that the "olde

[8] Pollard, *Fifteenth Century Prose and Verse*, p. 232. See also the epilog to the Boethius for another eulogy of Chaucer, Pollard, ibid., p. 222.

and homely termes" of the language were no longer intelligible, and furthermore that he translated not "for a rude uplondysh man to laboure therin," but for the clerk and gentleman. If these latter do not understand his new words, let them go read Vergil and other Latin writers, and then they will understand all.[9] A few sentences from the *Eneydos,* which was not translated from the original but from a degraded prose version in French, will illustrate Caxton's freedom in the use of new words, and his feeling for the heaping of words as an element of dignity in style:

"For to here opene and declare the matere of whiche hereafter shall be made mencyon: It behoveth to presuppose that Troye, the grete capytall cyte and thexcellentest of all the cytees of the countre & regyon of Asye, was constructe and edefyed by the ryght puyssaunt & renomed kyng Pryamus, sone of laomedon, descended of thauncyen stocke of Dardanus by many degrees, whiche was sone of Jubyter & of Electra his wyf, after the fyctions poetyque, And the fyrste orygynall begynnynge of the genealogye of kynges. And the sayd Troye was envyronned in fourme of siege and of excidyon by Agamenon, kynge in grece, brother of menelaus, whiche was husbonde to helayne. The whiche agamenon, assembled and accompanyed wyth many kynges, dukes, erles, and grete quantyte of other princes & grekes innumberable, hadde the magystracyon and unyversall governaunce of alle thexcersite and hoost to-fore Troye."[10]

This is Caxton at his best—or his worst, as one views it. Caxton could and often did write simply and naïvely, but when he wrote ambitiously, the above is a fair sample of his wares.

Another transitional writer who cultivated the courtly and learned style as zealously as Caxton was John Skelton. He was born in the third quarter of the fifteenth century and

[9] Preface to the *Eneydos* (1490).
[10] *Eneydos,* E.E.T.S., pp. 10-11.

he died in 1529. Skelton studied apparently at both universities, was ordained priest, and for some years was tutor to Prince Henry, afterwards Henry VIII. He exults in his title of *poeta laureatus,* assumed probably in virtue of a degree in grammar, including rhetoric and versification, which was conferred upon him by Oxford and again later by Cambridge. He also frequently calls himself *orator regius,*[11] but just how much this title means remains doubtful. Skelton's fame suffered a good deal from the tradition which made him merely a jester, the author of "merry tales" and abusive satirical poems. But in his day he was undoubtedly a person of distinction, a preacher, a scholar, a man of some consequence at the court, and a companion and associate of high ecclesiastical dignitaries. His scholarship is vouched for by Erasmus, but his eloquence made a deeper impression upon his generation than his scholarship. Caxton admired his translations of Cicero, of Diodorus Siculus, and of other Latin works into English, "not in rude and old language, but in polished and ornate terms craftily, as he that hath read Virgil, Ovid, Tully and all the other noble poets and orators to me unknown. And also he hath read the nine Muses, and understands their musical sciences, and to whom of them each science is appropred. I suppose he hath drunken of Helicon's well."[12] And Robert Whitinton, the grammarian, praises him with an enthusiasm and comprehensiveness that leaves nothing to be said for Demosthenes or any other of the orators of antiquity.[13] Thomas Churchyard, some years later, gives Skelton a lofty place among those who have "helpt our Englishe toung," praising especially his high judgment and the 'great practice' of his pen.

[11] Dyce, I, 132, 178, 179, 188, 191, 195, 197, 206, 408; II, 25.
[12] Pollard, *Fifteenth Century Prose and Verse,* p. 241.
[13] Dyce, I, xviii.

It is apparent from his own writings that Skelton was deeply interested in all questions of literary art. In spite of his amazing complacency, he usually speaks modestly of his own efforts in writing, especially in English. In the character of the heroine of the poem, he confesses in *Phyllyp Sparowe* that he cannot as yet find the " Englysh wordes elect " which his style requires. The native tongue is rude, and is so lacking in " pullysshed termes lusty," that he knows not where to find the words to serve his purpose if he should try to write ornately. Old poets, like Gower and Chaucer, he prizes for their matter, but men now bark at Chaucer's English. John Lydgate, however, writes after a higher rate, though some men say he " wryteth to haute," that is, in too high a style.[14] All this Skelton mentions in quite serious excuse of his own " Englysshe half abused," of his style " rude and playne," and " barreyne of eloquence."

As one might expect from Skelton's frequent apologies, his own writings show a zealous cultivation of the arts of style. Unfortunately most of Skelton's prose writings have been lost, and his literary aims can now be examined in large measure only in his metrical compositions. But even as poet, Skelton's practice is so illuminative of the developments of his time that it repays examination in a study of the style of English prose. Skelton very consciously cultivated two different styles of writing, the rude boisterous style of Pasquil the plain, and the ornate style of sugared eloquence. It is this latter, the learned style of Cicero, " with his tong of golde," that Skelton's admirers have in mind as his great achievement, but the other is no less characteristic. The difference can be best indicated by juxtaposing two stanzas from the *Garlande of Laurell,* one in

[14] Gower, Chaucer, and Lydgate are mentioned again in the same manner in the *Garlande of Laurell,* ll. 386 ff., Dyce, I, 377.

the popular, the other in the learned style. The first stanza is intentionally grotesque:

> "With a pellit of pevisshenes they had such a stroke,
> That all the dayes of ther lyfe shall stycke by ther rybbis;
> Foo, foisty bawdias! sum smellid of the smoke;
> I saw dyvers that were cariid away thens in cribbis,
> Dasyng after dotrellis, lyke drunkardis that dribbis;
> Theis titivyllis with taumpinnis were towchid and tappid;
> Moche mischefe, I hyght you, amonge theem ther happid." [15]

That the humorous character of the diction in this passage was not a necessary quality of the style is readily seen from many instances in sixteenth-century writing, which obviously were intended to be taken as serious eloquence. Thus Deus Pater in one of the Chester Plays [16] expresses himself in the same vein:

> "For all the mighte of the maiestye is magnified in me,
> Prince principall proved in my perpetuall prudens.
> I was never but one and ever one in three,
> set in substantiall sothenes within Caelestiall sapience.
> These three tryalls in a Trone and true Trynitie
> Be grounded in my godhead, exalted by my excellence;
> the mighte of my making is marked all in me,
> dissolved under a Dyademe by my divyne experyence."

The line in these passages of verse is the familiar alliterative long line of Langland and others, with the addition of rime. The alliteration is not consistently employed according to a strict system, but enough of the older method remains to preserve the swing of the lines. Moreover the alliteration is used to help produce that effect of volubility, of popular eloquence, which was noted as a chief characteristic of Langland's alliterative long line. The meter thus employed by Skelton and others is usually designated as tumbling verse in treatises on versification, and the general

[15] Ll. 637-643.
[16] *The Fall of Lucifer,* E.E.T.S., Extra Series, LXII, 10.

style, whether in prose or verse, may conveniently be known as the tumbling style. Frequent illustrations of it appear in the popular literature of the fifteenth and sixteenth centuries, sometimes as manifest corruptions of alliterative verse, but often also as the characteristic prose expression of the pulpit and other forms of popular eloquence.

In the stanza from the same poem of Skelton, chosen to illustrate the learned style, Skelton describes himself as commanded by certain great ladies to devise some "goodly conseyt"—

> "With proper captacyons of benevolence,
> Ornatly pullysshid after your faculte,
> Sith ye must nedis afforce it by pretence
> Of your professyoun unto umanyte,
> Commensyng your proces after there degre,
> To iche of them rendryng thankis commendable,
> With sentence fructuous and termes concovenable." [17]

In this style alliteration disappears, the lines scan as regular five-stress lines, and the popular vocabulary is replaced by a Latin aureate diction.[18]

This double tradition which Skelton followed reveals the twofold sources of his eloquence. On the one side he cultivated the new style with its ornate and aureate diction, tending in verse towards a regular numbered meter and in prose towards a clearly defined sentence structure; and on the other, he followed the old native tradition of a free alliterative long line, easily passing into a loose prose, and already in Piers Plowman used for bombastic and magnil-

[17] Ll. 815-821. The third line from the end means, "after the rank of the persons to be celebrated in the poem."

[18] Similar examples of this double style may be found in other of Skelton's poems, notably in *Magnyfycence,* which has been carefully studied in Ramsay's excellent edition for the E.E.T.S., London, 1908. Ramsay notes that the alliterative style is often used in this play "in passages designed to be especially impressive," and "in speeches of empty boasting."

oquent effects, which in Skelton, under the impulse of an unrestrained vatic enthusiasm, cross the bounds of eloquence into rant and even nonsense.[19] There can be no doubt that Skelton was seriously seeking in both of these directions for a method by which he could attain to a high style. He felt keenly the two tendencies of English expression in his day. As a scholar and a courtier, he was naturally attracted by the polished terms of the courtly aureate style. As *regius orator* and as plain speaker, he doubtless felt an equal admiration for the exuberant and ornamental popular style, which he must have known not only as a literary tradition, but also from the dithyrambic oratory of some of his eloquent contemporaries. For the popular style was never without its representatives. The pulpit kept it alive, and its influence always runs parallel to that of the classic ideals and models of eloquence.

It is unfortunate that none of Skelton's sermons or public discourses have survived, for they would probably illustrate clearly this popular native side of his theories and endeavors. The few passages of Skelton's prose still extant show, however, the way in which his tumbling verse passed into a tumbling prose. In his "Replycacion agaynst certayne yong scolers," prose and verse easily run into each other. The "Replycacion" is also interesting as showing Skelton's ingenuity in utilizing aureate and learned words for popular rhetorical effects:

"Over this, for a more ample processe to be farther delated and contynued, and of every true christenman laudably to be employed, iustifyed, and constantly mainteyned; as touchyng the tetrycall theologisacion of these demi divines, and stoicall studiantes, and friscaioly yonkerkyns, moche better bayned [limber-jointed] than brayned, basked and baththed in their wylde burblyng and boyling

[19] See the nonsense verses of Folly, Ramsay, pp. 56-57.

blode, fervently reboyled with the infatuate flames or their rechelesse youthe and wytlesse wantonnesse, embrased and enterlased with a moche fantasticall frenesy of their insensate sensualyte, surmysed unsurely in their perihermeniall principles, to prate and to preche proudly and leudly, and loudly to lye; and yet they were but febly enformed in maister Porphiris problemes, and have waded but weakly in his three maner of clerkly workes, analeticall, topicall and logycall: howbeit they were puffed so full of vaynglorious pompe and surcudant elacyon, that popholy and pevysshe presumpcion provoked them to publysshe and to preche to people imprudent perilously, howe it was idolatry to offre to ymages of our blessed lady, or to pray and go on pylgrimages, or to make oblacion to any ymages of sayntes in churches or els where."[20]

A passage of prose like this shows how far Skelton was from any just appreciation, or at least imitation, of the qualities of Ciceronian style. Like Caxton, Skelton would attain elevation of style by the heaping of big words and by robustious eloquence. For the rhythm of the Ciceronian period he probably had very little feeling. Indeed scarcely any trace of the direct influence of Cicero or other classical models can be found in the style of Skelton's writings. He appeals to "Retoricyons and oratours in freshe humanyte" for their "suffrage ornate," but his feeling for the humanities hardly went beyond a knowledge of "langagys divers"; and the manner of art in his conception is comprised under certain ornaments of style, especially rich vocabulary, metaphor, and allegory:

> "For trowthe in parabyll ye wantonlye pronounce,
> Langagys divers, yet undyr that dothe reste
> Maters more precious then the ryche jacounce."[21]

[20] Dyce, I, 208-209. Dyce, I, cxvii ff., cites a number of direct imitations of Skelton, but the "surcudant elacyon" of this style is found in many writers who do not get it from Skelton.

[21] "Speke Parrot," Dyce, II, 18, ll. 363-365. On the Renascence theory of the importance of metaphor and allegory, see below, pp. 306 ff.

II

The passion for fine diction, the beginning of which has been briefly indicated in the first section of this chapter, remained a constant feature of the higher English literary style of the latter fifteenth and sixteenth centuries. One of the most generally and the most savagely discussed questions in literary criticism of the time was that of the English vocabulary. The flood-gates of all European literature suddenly opened upon it, the English literary speech of the early Renascence was for a time in danger of being completely swamped. The extravagant admiration of foreign literatures and the desire to make English the equal of other languages led to an undue depreciation on the part of Englishmen of their native traditions. The work of enriching the vocabulary had been going on for centuries. Throughout the Middle English period new words and new forms of phrasing had been constantly added to the language. At the end of the fifteenth and in the sixteenth centuries, however, the manner of such additions changed. The earlier French borrowings were rarely conscious or literary. The Middle English poet used a French word because the custom of the language provided it for him as the natural word for the thought to be expressed. Chaucer, for example, rarely considered the origins of his words. He did not consciously pair a French word with an English, or an English with a French, as some historians have mistakenly asserted, but he used the traditional words of the courtly vocabulary of his day.

With Lydgate, with Caxton, Skelton, Sir Thomas Elyot, and other contemporary writers, however, begins the era of the conscious enriching and elevation of the language. As has already been pointed out, Caxton in his reading became enamored of the fair terms in French and Latin which he found there, and he set to work to transfer them bodily into English speech. Sir Thomas Elyot declares one of his purposes in the *Governour* to have been "to augment our Englyshe tongue" in order that men might more abundantly express the thought of their hearts, and also translate from Greek, Latin or any other tongue into English as adequately as from one foreign tongue into another.[22] His new terms he frequently explains by coupling with them their English equivalents, e.g. "animate or gyve courage," "inferiour or base," "adminiculation or aid," "obfuscate or hyd." [23] But often his new words are used without the appended glosses, and many an English reader must have been puzzled to know his meaning. The rhetorical writings of the times are full of criticisms of these inkhorn terms, as they were called, of English Italianate and English Latinate. Some of the most extravagant inkhornism made English into a kind of mongrel Latin-English which was frequently satirized by the writers of the time, but which, nevertheless, was a fashion cultivated in varying degrees by almost all admirers of good style. This fashion continued in full swing to the end of the sixteenth century, though it must be said that the courtly writers, as they acquired command over structure and form, more and more threw their influence in favor of the simple vocabulary, thus emphasizing a distinction between the easy courtly vocabulary and the pedantic learned vocabulary. Nevertheless a great many words which the learned Latinizers invented were generally accepted and have since passed current as good coin in the language. Thomas Nashe, for example, pours out all the vials of his wrath

[22] Proheme to his book *Of the knowledeg* [sic] *whiche maketh a wise man,* 1533.

[23] For other illustrations, see Moore, *Tudor-Stuart Views on the Growth, Status and Destiny of the English Language,* pp. 83 ff.

upon Gabriel Harvey's head because Harvey had used the phrase "villainy by connivance"—perfectly intelligible to-day, whatever else one may care to say about it. And in general the modern reader is surprised to find that so much of the verbal criticism of the times has now lost its point because the words which were the occasion of the criticism have become completely accepted and natural in the language.

The innovators of the sixteenth century could not have foreseen that this was to happen, nor would they have greatly cared if they had known it would not. They were carried away by the enthusiasm of invention and experiment. They enjoyed mixing new words as an artist does new colors. Sesquipedalianism was one of the exciting occupations of the times, and Harvey felt that he had delivered a telling blow upon his dearest enemy when he had invented for him the designation of a "polypragmaticall, parasitupocriticall and pantophainoudendeconticall Puppie." [24] Nashe, in turn, not without at least a grain of truth, declares of Harvey's phrase, "villainy by connivance," that "the Doctor lay a whole weeke and a day and a night entranced on his bed to bring [it] forth, and on the Munday evening late caused all the bels in the Parish where he then soiourned to be rong forth, for ioy that he was delivered of it." But Nashe is tarred with the same stick as his opponent, and almost any page of his writings would furnish examples more extreme than those he cites against Harvey. He himself boasts of his "huge woords," and declares that it is his "true vaine to be *tragicus orator,*" and that he does not care for "this demure soft *mediocre genius* that is like water and wine mixt togither." He would have "pure wine of itself and that begets good bloud, and heates the brain thorowly." As a sample of

[24] *Works,* ed. Grosart, III, 13.

this pure wine, we may decant a sentence from that amazing performance, *Nashes Lenten Stuffe,* itself a monstrous *tour de force* in praise of the red-herring:

" But how Yarmouth, of it selfe so innumerable populous and replenished, and in so barraine a plot seated, should not onely supply her inhabitants with plentifull purveyance of sustenance, but provant and victuall moreover this monstrous army of strangers, was a matter that egregiously bepuzled and entranced my apprehension."

Nashe's " plentifull purveyance of sustenance " has little advantage over Harvey's " villainy by connivance." But other examples of this brand of verbal magnificence may be found in places where one would scarcely expect it. Shakspere makes his Michael Williams, a type of the plain, blunt soldier, speak in the same vein:

" Now if these men do not die well, it will be a black matter for the King that led them to it; who to disobey were against all proportion of subjection." [25]

And Falstaff expresses the simple idea, Like master, like man, in the following high-sounding diction:

" Their spirits [i.e. of Justice Shallow and his servants] are so married in conjunction by the participation of society that they flock together in consent like so many wild geese." [26]

Similar examples might be added indefinitely, showing the conscious delight of the artist in the mere manipulation of big words. At its best, as usually with Shakspere, this cultivation of the aureate style resulted in that opulence of Elizabethan diction, that " pomp of speech," which later ages have admired, but seldom dared to imitate; at its worst it became nothing more than mere childish verbal pyro-

[25] *Henry V,* IV, 1, 150-153. [26] *2 Henry IV,* V, 1, 77.

technics, not unlike the unctuous rhetoric of popular oratory, or its more modern equivalent, the 'language' of an inspired 'ink-slinger' on a country newspaper.

The extreme measures of the Latinizers naturally stirred to activity an opposing conservative party which defended the use of a more chastened and a more largely native English vocabulary. It is not an accident that the earlier representatives of this conservative movement were generally friends of the Reformation, and men with more or less tendency towards the austere manner of life later to be known as Puritanism. In his own day Sir John Cheke was the acknowledged head of this party. His connections with the court began in the reign of Henry VIII, under whose patronage he was enabled to continue studies abroad already begun at that fruitful mother of Protestant doctrine and learning, St. John's College at Cambridge. In 1540, Cheke was made the first regius professor of Greek at Cambridge, and two years later he was made tutor to Prince Edward by Henry VIII. During the lifetime of Edward, Cheke remained one of his most intimate advisers, and after Edward's death, he was secretary of state during the brief supremacy of Lady Jane Grey. Under Mary, Cheke's career was clouded by persecution, and in the end by recantation of the opinions which he probably never ceased to believe, and by the acceptance of Catholicism. He died in 1557, without the opportunity of retrieving his self-respect under Mary's successor. Cheke was an accomplished scholar in Greek and Latin, and he possessed a fine feeling for Latin style. The greater number of his many works are either original compositions in Latin or translations from Greek into Latin. His most considerable work in English is his *Hurt of Sedition,* a controversial discussion of questions of government and religion, called forth by a popular insurrection of the times. Cheke writes here in a simple, unmannered style, with feeling for a short and rapid sentence structure and in a vocabulary carefully held in check, but not fantastically conservative. His translation from the New Testament, in which he applies in a more extreme way his views on the purity of the language, has already been mentioned.[27]

Cheke's influence as a teacher was much more important than his example as a writer. Indirectly his ideas can be traced in the opinions of two of his most interesting pupils, Sir Thomas Wilson and Roger Ascham, but the character of these ideas may be directly inferred from several of his own critical pronouncements. One of these is preserved by Ascham in *The Scholemaster,* under the discussion of Sallust. Cheke declared, says Ascham, that Sallust's writing was "neyther plaine for the matter, nor sensible for mens understanding."[28] And the reason why this was true, was that "in Salust writing is more Arte than nature, and more labor than Arte: and in his labor also, to moch toyle, as it were, with an uncontented care to write better than he could, a fault common to very many men." Cheke then, in Ascham's report of him, compares "naturall and plaine" writers with "artificiall and darke," finding the excellence of the former to arise from the fact that they were "daylie orators emonges the common people," and that they "gave themselves to use soch speach as the meanest should well understand and the wisest best allow." Similar in tone is a letter which Cheke wrote to Thomas Hoby, prefixed by Hoby to his published translation of Castiglione's *Courtier*. The burden of Cheke's criticism is that the English language should try to get along with its native resources, that it should be "unmixt and unmangeled with borowing of other tunges." He does not reprehend borrowing altogether, for the language, being imperfect, must improve itself in various

[27] See above, p. 248. [28] Arber's *Reprint,* p. 154.

ways. But preference is to be given to words formed in "the mould of our own tung," and to "the old denisoned wordes" of the language, before the writer of English ventures to use unknown words.

Among the disciples of Cheke, none was more enthusiastic than Roger Ascham. Although Ascham declares the Latin and Greek writers of antiquity to be the only possible models of eloquence for Englishmen, he insists upon the necessity of preserving the purity of the English tongue. Anyone who will write well, he says in his *Toxophilus*, must speak as the common people do, and think as wise men do.[29] "Many English writers," he adds, "have not done so, but usinge straunge wordes as latin, french and Italian, do make all thinges darke and harde."

In the *Scholemaster*, written some years later, Ascham presents his views with respect to the proper use of language much more fully. Style in writing is, to Ascham's mind, merely an aspect of moral conduct in general. He views with disfavor the tendency of many Englishmen to forget the simple native virtues of straightforwardness and honesty and to seek to replace them by foreign accomplishments of doubtful value. Yet Ascham also insists upon dignity and propriety in expression as in daily conduct. Affectation, whether of extreme refinement or of rudeness, is reprehensible in his sight. He regards a pure style as not only the best preservative of the content of writing, but also of the moral standards of the people to whom the writing is addressed. He enters a caution against making a divorce betwixt the tongue and the heart, and points out that when, in the Greek and Latin tongue, "apte and good wordes began to be neglected, and properties of those to tonges to be confounded, than also began ill deedes to spring, strange maners to oppresse good orders, newe

[29] *Toxophilus*, Arber's *Reprint*, p. 18.

and fond opinions to strive with olde and trewe doctrine, first in Philosophie and after in Religion, right judgement of all thinges to be perverted, and so vertue with learning is contemned, and studie left of." [30] Ascham's *Scholemaster* is, indeed, in many respects, a conduct book of the new kind, in which the ideals of the Reformation and the Renascence are united for the guidance of the youth of England. Truth of religion, honesty in living, and right order in learning are the three cardinal points of its doctrine, and Ascham's opinions on "the common goinge of Englishe men into Italie," on extravagance in dress, in behavior, and in diction, are all in harmony with his ideal of the dignified and well-ordered character.

But Ascham's own writings show that he was by no means disregardful of the more artful graces of style. He employed a simple vocabulary, but a barren or rude and popular manner of writing would have seemed, to himself as to others, out of harmony with his own important position. For he was not only a competent scholar, but also a man of some figure at court, enjoying almost uninterruptedly the good-will of four successive English sovereigns. Of his two important writings, the first, *Toxophilus,* was presented to Henry VIII, and the other, *The Scholemaster,* though not published until 1570, the year following his death, was probably finished in 1564, the sixth year of Elizabeth's reign. His ventures in authorship were incidental to what probably seemed to him his more important activities as lecturer on Greek in St. John's College, Cambridge, of which he was fellow, as tutor to the Princess Elizabeth, as public orator of his university, in succession to Sir John Cheke, as secretary to Sir Richard Morison on an important mission to the court of Charles V, and during the latter years of his life, as prebendary in York Cathedral. Ascham felt that

[30] Arber's *Reprint,* p. 118.

his own dignified position imposed certain obligations upon him. His *Toxophilus* was undertaken both for the purpose of showing his loyalty to his king and the love he bore his country, and likewise as a memorial of his learning. And though he declares it would have been "more easier and fit for mi trade in study"[31] to have written in Latin or Greek, he has preferred to write in English in order that he might provide some better example of English writing than those which passed currently in the hands of his countrymen. He defends also his choice of an apparently insignificant theme such as archery, instead of "Religion or Civill discipline," on the ground that a high title provokes great expectation, whereas a humbler subject permits that free and discursive treatment of the many topics in which Ascham was interested. In other words Ascham wished to write easily and humanely in the English tongue, treating profound moral questions with something of the literary grace which he found in his models, Cicero and the dialogues of Plato. The two persons in Ascham's dialogue are Philologus, lover of learning, and Toxophilus, lover of archery, "the Booke and the Bowe," representing the two important sides of the cultivated and well-balanced English character; for Toxophilus stands not merely for the lover of archery as a pastime, but also for sound, patriotic interest in all good national rites and customs.

Ascham obviously bestowed great care upon the elaboration of the form of English expression in which he sought to set forth his ideal of the just combination of learning and patriotism. In matters of vocabulary, as has been pointed out, he was moderate. He showed great restraint in avoiding learned coinages which, with his familiarity with Latin and Greek, he must continually have had thrust upon his attention. And on the other hand, he avoided

[31] *Toxophilus,* ed. Arber, p. 14.

any tendency towards the undue use of a quaint and archaistic vocabulary. He avoided also the obvious devices of the tumbling style, such for example as the heaping of synonymous terms, the excessive use of alliteration, of puns, verbal antitheses, and word-play in general. His feeling for dignified style was indeed based upon certain principles of sentence-structure, clearly perceived and firmly applied. In these respects Ascham shows a great advance over the earlier English stylists and connects directly with the ingenious writers of the third quarter of the century. The periodic sentence after the classic model he employed frequently and not without success, sometimes in sentences of considerable length, sometimes more compactly, as in the following:

> "What good thynges men speake of shoting and what good thinges shooting bringes to men, as my wit and knowlege will serve me, gladly shall I say my mind. But how the thing is to be learned I will surely leve to some other which bothe for greater experience in it, and also for their lerninge, can set it out better than I." [32]

Sentences of this formal character are varied, however, by the occasional use of crisp sentences of colloquial and conversational tone, appropriate to a dialogue. But more characteristic of Ascham's style than the periodic sentence, is the balanced and antithetic sentence. Of this an example, which Lyly himself might have written, may be cited from one of the prefatory addresses of the *Toxophilus:*

> "And so Cresus, hearyng not the true newes, but perceyving the wise mannes mynde and counsell, both gave then over makyng of his shyppes, and left also behynde him a wonderful example for all commune wealthes to folowe: that is evermore to regarde and set most by that

[32] *Toxophilus,* ed. Arber, p. 31.

thing whereunto nature hath made them moost apt and use hath made them moost fitte."[33]

Thomas Wilson had already called attention to and had illustrated this kind of balanced antithetic writing in his *Rhetorique,* under the heading "Egall numbers," noting that Isocrates "passeth in this behalfe."[34] And probably it was the "*suavitatem Isocratis*" which served Ascham directly as a model.[35] Wilson points out that in the balanced sentence the syllables need not be "of iust number, but that the eare might iudge them to be so egall, that there may appeare small difference." Ascham's writings show that he had fully grasped the possibilities of this form of sentence structure.

Another stylistic device in Ascham, that of repeating a word in the same or in slightly varying forms within the body of the same sentence or within a group of closely related sentences, is also noteworthy. Ascham may have learned this trick from the Spanish of Guevara, or from various other sources. It was so well known that Puttenham classified it among his ornaments of speech, giving it the name *traductio* in Latin or "the tranlacer" in English.[36] That this device was not due to poverty of

[33] *Toxophilus,* p. 16.

[34] *Rhetorique,* ed. Mair, p. 204.

[35] Even the severer stylists studied Isocrates, as is proved by Tindale's English translations from the Greek and Sir John Cheke's from Greek into Latin.

[36] "which is when ye turne and tranlace a word into many sundry shapes as the Tailor doth his garment, and after that sort do play with him in your dittie: as thus,

> Who lives in love his life is full of feares,
> To lose his love, livelode or libertie,
> But lively sprites, that young and recklesse be,
> Think that there is no living like to theirs . . .

Here ye see how in the former rime this word life is tranlaced into live, living, lively, livelode . . . which come all from one

vocabulary, but was intended as an ornament of style, its frequent employment sufficiently proves:

"To speake of shooting, Philologe, trulye I woulde I were so able, either as I my selfe am willing or yet as the matter deserveth, but seing with wisshing we can not have one nowe worthie, whiche so worthie a thinge can worthilie praise, and although I had rather have anie other to do it than my selfe, yet my selfe rather then no other. I wil not fail to saye in it what I can, wherein if I say litle, laye that of my litle habilitie, not of the matter it selfe which deserveth no lyttle thinge to be sayde of it."[37]

"Over ernest shooting surely I will not over ernestlye defende, for I ever thought shooting shoulde be a wayter upon lerning not a mastres over learning."[38]

"Englysh writers by diversitie of tyme, have taken diverse matters in hande."[39]

For the development of English style, Ascham was significant in several respects. As a theorizer and critic he saw clearly certain tendencies of English speech and writing in his day and formed his own opinions firmly and consistently. He exemplified in his writings a serious literary ideal which remained to the end of the century and which was frequently commended for imitation. He combined plainness of speech so far as words are concerned with the scholar's standard of solidly dignified and elevated writing. He produced little and probably wrote slowly and painfully, but his example served as a useful corrective of the loose, popular style of writing. His lack of lightness and vivacity are obvious defects, and his formality and emphasis on the

originall." Puttenham, *English Poesie* (1589), ed. Arber, pp. 213-214.

[37] *Toxophilus,* pp. 29-30.

[38] Ibid., p. 44.

[39] Ibid., p. 19.

art of writing were the first steps in the direction of the extravagance of certain later writers. Gabriel Harvey thought he heard the "siren of Isocrates" in the writings of Ascham, and certainly his ear did not deceive him. What Harvey found most admirable in Ascham was his "polished and refined eloquence," and he prefers the loosest period in Ascham or Sidney to the "tricksiest page of Euphues."[40] But the tricksiness of *Euphues* is already to a considerable extent implied in Ascham, and Lyly was quite as ardent an admirer of Ascham as Harvey. The difference between them was that Harvey would have held Ascham close to the classic models which he imitated, while Lyly followed the general tendency towards the further elaboration of the hints for the ingenious style which were already present in Ascham.

Sir Thomas Wilson, the pupil of Cheke and the friend of Ascham, was, like both of these, a supporter of Protestant doctrine and a man of importance in public affairs. He was sent on various embassies to the Continent, was elected to Parliament, and, as his highest public office, was appointed, in 1577, secretary of state to Queen Elizabeth. His most important publications were his *Rule of Reason, conteinyng the Arte of Logicke* (1551), his *Arte of Rhetorique* (1553), his translation into English of *Three Orations of Demosthenes* (1570), and his *Discourse uppon usurye* (1572).

Wilson declared the *Rule of Reason* to be the first logic in English and feared that the "fruict beyng of a straunge kinde," may at the first tasting seem somewhat rough and harsh. He defended the translation, however, on the ground that English is as capable for such uses as other languages. As was customary at the time, logic is but slightly distinguished from rhetoric, the only difference be-

[40] *Eliz. Crit. Essays,* ed. Gregory Smith, II, 274.

tween the two being, according to Wilson, "that Logike is occupied about all matters, and dooeth plainlie and nakedly set forth with apt wordes the sum of things, by the way of argumentacion," whereas, on the other hand, "Rhetorike useth gaie painted sentences, and setteth forthe those matters with freshe colours and goodly ornaments, and that at large."[41]

Wilson's opinions with respect to language are set forth more at length in his *Rhetorique,* not the first rhetoric in English, since it was preceded by Cox's *Arte or Crafte of Rhetorique* and Sherry's *Treatise of Schemes and Tropes,* but the first book to present rhetorical ideas with any fullness and personal coloring. For the present purpose, the most interesting parts of the *Rhetorique* are those in which Wilson discusses plainness of speech. Plainness, in Wilson's definition, consists in the avoidance of "straunge ynkehorne termes," and in speaking "as is commonly received."[42] He gives counsel against outlandish English and oversea language, against those who so "Latin their tongues that the simple can not but wonder at their talke." He speaks of the folly of "them that thinke Rhetorique to stande wholie upon darke wordes," and of those who think him to be a fine Englishman and a good rhetorician who can "catche an ynke horne terme by the taile." In his own writing, Wilson affects a somewhat colloquial style, not without some of the vigor and picturesqueness of Latimer, whom he several times mentions with admiration. Throughout the *Rhetorique,* as also in the *Rule of Reason,* Wilson's sympathy with the cause of the reformers appears frequently in his illustrations and examples.

Wilson's comparison of Demosthenes and Cicero is especially noteworthy. In the Preface to his *Three Orations* he condemns the man who wholly follows Cicero and

[41] *Rule of Reason,* fol. 3. [42] *Rhetorique,* ed. Mair, p. 162.

uses "his large veyne and vehement maner" of eloquence, and he exalts Demosthenes and his "playne familier maner of writing and speakyng." This work also contains an Epistle in which Wilson declares of Sir John Cheke that he had better skill "in our English speach to judge of the Phrases and properties of wordes and to divide sentences than any else had that I have knowne." With the name of Wilson, in this connection, may be joined that of Bishop Jewel, public orator of Oxford, and later bishop of Salisbury. Jewel delivered a lecture in Corpus Christi College, Oxford, before 1557, since he was ejected from Corpus Christi in that year, entitled *Oratio contra rhetoricam*. The oration is interesting as indicating an attitude of mind towards style and rhetoric which was certainly not the growing one in Jewel's day, except among those writers, the heralds of later Puritanism, whose interest in controversy and dialectic left little room for the more graceful side of the art of writing. Jewel declares the study of rhetoric to be useless, profitless, vain. Care in the seeking out and arrangement of words he considers a puerile waste of time. All men, he continues, are sufficiently instructed by nature for the needs of speaking. Men discussed important affairs among themselves long before Cicero and Demosthenes were born. What need is there of art, or of puerile ornaments? Truth is clear and simple, and it has little need of eloquence. Rhetoricians merely obscure truth, instead of revealing it more fully. Cicero has brought much evil upon the academic world in modern times; the study of him has, in fact, become a curse within the academic halls. Jewel closes his oration with an adjuration to the students of Oxford not to waste their time in vain rhetorical exercises, not to become mere beadles, heralds, and public bawlers, but to scorn all vain abundance of words and to turn their thoughts rather to the knowledge of learned matters. Though the work of a young man and itself a somewhat ambitious example of the art it contemns, Jewel's oration is instructive as an illustration of the earnest, though vain, opposition of some English scholars to the growing interest of Englishmen in the art of fine writing.[43]

Opinions like those of Ascham, Wilson, and Jewel were expressed by other purist writers and rhetoricians of the latter half of the sixteenth century. These later opinions are in the main patriotic protests against the tendency towards learned extravagance. Thus Gascoigne says that he prefers rather to have "faulted in keeping the olde English wordes (*quamvis iam obsoleta*) than in borrowing of other such Epithetes and Adjectives as smell of the Inkhorne."[44] In his notes on metrical composition, he thinks it not "amisse to forewarne you that you thrust as few wordes of many sillables into your verse as may be."[45] His endeavor is rather to make English commendable in itself than "gay with the feathers of straunge birdes." So far as vocabulary is concerned, Gascoigne's practice is in accord with his criticism, though in other features of style he does not fail to show his respect for the muse of gaudy English. In general Elizabethan critical opinion was at one in reprehending the pedantical and Latinized vocabulary. Henry Peacham, in his *Garden of Eloquence* (1577), gives the name Cacozelon to the practice of using big words for simple ideas, and among the illustrations cited is one which is quoted from Wilson's *Rhetorique*. Angel Day, in his *English Secretorie*,[46] gives an example of this "ridiculous

[43] Jewel's *Oratio* will be found in *Works*, Fourth Portion, ed. Ayre, for the Parker Society, pp. 1284-1291.

[44] *Posies* (1575), ed. Cunliffe, I, 5.

[45] Ibid., I, 468.

[46] First edition, 1586; I quote from the edition of 1595.

maner of writing" from the epistle to a book published by a doctor of physic who intended "to be very eloquent in words," the opening sentence of which ran:

"Egregious Doctors and masters of the eximious & Archane Science of Physicke, of your Urbanitie exasperate not your selves against mee, for making of this little volume of Physick, considering that my pretence is for an utilitie and a common wealth," etc.

The *Art of Poesie* (1589), ascribed to Puttenham, likewise reprehends the use of ill-affected terms brought in by men of learning, "darke wordes, and not usual nor well sounding, though they be daily spoken in court." And in the latter part of the century, the poets and satirical writers join the rhetoricians in ridicule of the high-sounding diction. Among the many instances of such satire may be mentioned the character of Rombus in Sir Philip Sidney's mask, *The Lady of May,* Don Armado in *Love's Labor's Lost,* Torquatus (Ben Jonson) in Marston's *Scourge of Villanie,* Amorphous in Jonson's *Cynthia's Revels,* and Crispinus in the *Poetaster,* Matzagente and Balardo in Marston's *Antonio and Mellida,* Emulo in Dekker's *Patient Grissil,* one of those men who "chew between their teeth terrible words," and finally, Severus, "extreame in eloquence," in one of Rowland's epigrams.[47] These characters were doubtless in part imitative of conventional types of fire-eating braggarts and pedantic scholars which had long been established in the traditions of the stage. But in part they also reflect the actual tendencies of English speech in Tudor times, and the fustian of the ex-

[47] *Works* (Hunterian Club), I, 41. Though Shakspere in general stood closer to the traditions of the elevated, learned style than to any other, he has a number of passages in which inflated and affected diction is satirized, cf. Lyly, *Works,* ed. Bond, I, 151-152.

travagant parodies was merely the extreme of a quality which many courtly writers admired and were eagerly cultivating.

Another influence making for the preservation and extension of the native resources of the language was the high esteem in which Chaucer was held among the courtly writers of the early sixteenth century. Thynne's first collected edition of Chaucer's works appeared in 1532, and though the text was not thoroughly understood, it was rightly felt that Chaucer represented a courtly tradition and that the mere existence of his writings lent dignity to the older forms of the language. It was partly this feeling which led Spenser to employ the archaistic style of his *Shepherd's Calendar,* not justified, as Sidney pointed out, by Sanazzaro. In doing so, according to Jonson, Spenser "writ no English," and indeed Spenser's archaic style is as little normal as that of the extremists among the Latinizers. Both sides were under the dominance of a theory of reform, and both made the true language suffer in the interests of their theories. Spenser's friend, E. K., was of the opinion that special praise was due the poet in that he "hath laboured to restore, as to theyre rightfull heritage, such good and naturall English words as have been long time out of use and almost cleane disherited." And E. K. is convinced that the right way to make English "ful enough for prose and stately enough for verse" is not to borrow words from abroad, but to bring back into the speech these old disherited words.

In practice, however, the theories of the conservatives and purists were not as powerful as the expanding and enriching tendencies of the time. It was in general a European and a Latin culture which the England of the sixteenth century was endeavoring to assimilate, and even the most ardent patriot neither was able nor desired to limit himself narrowly to the native resources of the language. No one-sided solution of the difficulty was possible. The English speech through its constant borrowings, beginning as far back as the twelfth century, had already become a bilingual language. It had a double personality, as it still has, and in harmony with the personality of the speaker or writer who uses it, now the one side and now the other side of its nature must come to the front. With the sensible man the main question has never been one of a pure Latin or a pure native vocabulary, for the Latinist must use native words and the purist must use words of foreign origin. The question has always been rather one of emphasis, of proportion and choice. So far as the problem can be disposed of theoretically, it was already successfully answered by more than one critic of the sixteenth century. Abraham Fraunce, for example, the author of the *Arcadian Rhetorike* (1588) and the *Lawiers Logike* (1588), takes the common-sense view of the question. In the *Lawiers Logike,* written for the learned lawyers of England and intended to be read after the "delicate and pleasant" studies of the university, Fraunce compares words for their inconstancy with the leaves of trees, and regarding logic as he does, in the manner of his time, not as a technical discipline but rather as the art of normal intelligible expression, he disapproves of all extravagance and obscurity of diction. He calls it therefore a fallacy "when unusuall and upstart woordes be foisted in," meaning thereby new and learned words, and on the other hand, as equally reprehensible "to affectate such woordes as were quite worne out at heeles and elbowes long before the nativitie of Geffrey Chawcer." [48] In his interesting eulogy on the excellency of the English tongue, R. Carew somewhat later compares English with Italian, French, Spanish, and Dutch,

[48] *Lawiers Logike,* Bk. I, Cap. IV.

and finds that English has gathered the honey of these languages and has left the dregs to themselves:

> "And thus, when substantiallnes combyneth with delightfulness, fullnes with fynes, seemlynes with portlynes, and courrantnes with staydnes, howe canne the languadge which consisteth of all these sounde other then most full of sweetnes? Againe, the longe wordes that wee borrowe, being intermingled with the shorte of our owne store, make up a perfitt harmonye, by culling from out which mixture (with Judgment) yow maye frame your speech according to the matter you must worke on, maiesticall, pleasaunte, delicate, or manly, more or lesse, in what sorte you please." [49]

III

Of all the devices employed for elevating the style of English writing, the extension of the vocabulary by means of the introduction of new and ornate words was one of the most obvious. Words lend not only color to writing, but they are as well the most immediate ways of approach to ideas. The aureate diction of the fifteenth and early sixteenth centuries was the result therefore of the combined influence of the naïve respect for high style and of admiration for the content of literatures other than English.

But diction, because it is so obvious, is not of itself sufficient to satisfy the requirements of a thoughtful and ingenious literary art. The high priests of literary culture in the sixteenth century sought after distinction and elegance of style, and these qualities were felt to be dependent not merely, or even mainly, upon fine words, but upon ornament less superficially applied, upon schemes and tropes, to use the terminology of the contemporary rhetorics. Schemes were figures of speech which arose from the manipulation of the sounds of speech, such as verbal

[49] Gregory Smith, *Eliz. Crit. Essays,* II, 293.

balance and antithesis, alliteration, rime, punning, all being "contrarie to the vulgare custome of our speech."[50] Tropes were figures, like metaphor and allegory, which arose from the manipulation of ideas or images, and which therefore rested upon a basis of signification. Schemes were obviously the more mechanical of the two kinds of ornament, and they were more fully developed in the artificial style of English courtly writers than were tropes. The rudiments of the cultivation of figures of speech dependent upon mechanical forms or structures have already been indicated in the discussion of Ascham's style. But the interest in this kind of ornament was by no means recent in Ascham's day. It goes back in fact both to certain classical writers and to the early church fathers, whose Latin style was often heavily incrusted with formal and mechanical ornament. From them it passed into the tradition of medieval rhetoric, and in the form of precepts and definitions, the features of the ingenious Latin style were elaborately set down in books which were intended to serve as guides in the art of composition. When rhetorics first began to be written in English, they carried over from the medieval books and from medieval practice many of the traditional rules and devices of writing. The rhetoricians of the sixteenth century undoubtedly exerted considerable direct influence in determining the practice of English prose writers when they came to write fine style in the vernacular. They are significant also, and call for a moment's notice, for their indications of the general drift of opinion with respect to high style.

The most generally held and perhaps the most influential of the theories of the rhetoricians was that literature is an esoteric art, with canons of composition as far removed as possible from every-day discourse. In poetry this was an

[50] Wilson, *Rhetorique,* ed. Mair, p. 176.

ancient tradition. Stephen Hawes, a diligent if not enlightened seeker after artistic effect in writing, bases the art of rhetoric mainly upon the use of remote figurative language,

> "Clokynge a trouthe wyth colour tenebrous."[51]

And he praises Lydgate as highly for keeping

> "ful close the moralyzacyon
> Of the trouth of his great intencyon"

as for his "depured rethoryke in Englysh language," which he drew, according to Hawes, from the well of fruitfulness in Vergil and Cicero.[52] Poetry, the most elevated and also the most ornate and figurative kind of writing, naturally affected the theory of artistic prose, for it was from poetry that rules and principles of writing could be most easily derived. Formal treatises which discussed the elements of style began to be written about the middle of the sixteenth

[51] *Pastime of Pleasure,* Percy Society, p. 29.

[52] This was essentially Sidney's theory of poetry, which has to do with things "not affirmatively but allegorically and figurativelie written" (*Apology,* in *Eliz. Crit. Essays,* I, 185). Petrarch's definition runs as follows: *officium (poetae) est fingere id est componere atque ornare et veritatem rerum vel mortalium vel naturalium vel quarumlibet aliarum artificiosis adumbrare coloribus, velo amoenae fictionis obnubere, quo remoto veritas elucescat, eo gratior inventu quo difficilior sit quaesitu, Ep. Sen.* XII, 2, quoted Koerting, *Petrarca's Leben und Werke,* p. 650. This definition, says Koerting, p. 651, is found almost literally in the early Latin Christian writers, especially in Lactantius (Inst. I, p. 36, ed. Bipont). It is objected to by Thomas Wilson, an advocate of plainness, who speaks scornfully of the "misticall wiseman and Poeticall Clerkes" who will "speake nothing but quaint Proverbes and blinde Allegories, delighting much in their owne darkenesse, especially when none can tell what they doe say," *Arte of Rhetorique,* ed. Mair, p. 162. This severe censure is considerably modified later (p. 195) when Wilson declares that "Poetes under colours shew much wisdome."

century.[53] The earliest was Richard Sherry's *Treatise of Schemes and Tropes* (1550). In his preface, Sherry defends the use of new words, such as the words *scheme* and *trope* in his title, and others like *paraphrasis, homelies, usurped,* and *abolyshed,* concluding that any idea whatsoever has "Englyshe oracion natural, and, holpen by art, wher by it may most eloquently be uttered." The way in which art is to help is manifestly by means of the schemes and tropes, which Sherry classifies and illustrates. He has various comments on style, one of the most illuminating being his definition of "vertue" or distinction in writing: "Vertue . . . is when the sentence is bewtyfied and lyfte up above the comen maner of speaking of the people." Thomas Wilson, in his *Arte of Rhetorique* (1553), takes on the whole the commonsense view of style, and insists upon plainness and intelligibility as the first requisite. In the *Rule of Reason* (1551), however, he had distinguished between plain logical and rhetorical writing, the latter alone making use of "gaie painted sentences" and "freshe colours and goodly ornaments." Richard Rainolde's *Booke called the Foundacion of Rhetorike* (1563) develops mainly the oration on the basis of the fable, which he defines as "a forged tale, containing in it by the colour of a lie a matter of truthe." Henry Peacham's *Garden of Eloquence* (1577) contains "all manner of Flowers, coulors [sic], ornaments, Exornations, Formes and Fashions of speech, very profitable for all those that be studious of Eloquence." A figure, according to Peacham's definition, is a "fashion of words, oration or sentence, made new by Arte, tourning from the common manner and custome of wryting or speaking." [54]

[53] *The Arte or Crafte of Rhetoryke,* by Leonard Cox, appeared about 1530, but it treats only the subject of invention.

[54] Fol. ^{b}i.

In the *Artes of Logike and Rethorike* (1584), Dudley Fenner also has much to say concerning figures. He defines rhetoric as "an Arte of speaking finelie," and he divides it into two parts, "Garnishing of speach, called Eloqution, and Garnishing of the manner of utterance, called Pronunciation." Abraham Fraunce, discussing the general precepts of rhetoric in his *Arcadian Rhetorike* (1588), divides the subject into two parts, congruity and bravery, comprising under the first head grammatical rules, omitted "for this time as being scarce resolved in this conceipt." "Braverie of speech consisteth in Tropes or turnings, and in Figures or fashionings," and it is with tropes and figures, their definition and illustration, that Fraunce's book is mainly concerned.

These ideals of fineness and bravery of speech are strikingly illustrated in a large group of prose writers of the latter half of the sixteenth century. The conception of a vernacular prose as an art of fine writing was new, and one is able to follow this prose through the stages of enthusiastic experiment to the point of its extremest elaboration in the writings of the most ingenious masters of the artificial style which the language has ever known. The development was indeed gradual, and no single model or set of models was followed. Picking up a trick here and a trick there, from medieval Latin style, from classical Greek and Latin, from the debased traditions of native English verse, and some from contemporary Continental stylists, the English courtly prose writers of the sixteenth century compounded a style which in the end was systematically and fully worked out. The prose of Lyly was the pre-eminent artistic prose of its period, the completest expression of a tendency that appeared in a school of writers. It was the first English prose to win acceptance in the literary world as exemplifying a satisfactory standard of expression. Lyly's contemporaries may have erred in their estimation of the value of his style, but they were in no doubt as to their admiration for it.

How far back one should go in tracing the origins of the Euphuistic style depends largely upon the definition which is given to the term Euphuism. In a broad etymological sense this word may designate, and it is often loosely used to designate, the excessive refinements of style in writing, no matter what their technical characteristics may be. Indeed in the use of the name Euphues by Ascham, which suggested to Lyly the name of the hero of his novel, the meaning is still broader. "Euphues," said Ascham,[55] "is he that is apte by goodnes of witte and appliable by readines of will to learning, having all other qualities of the minde and partes of the bodie that must an other day serve learning, not trobled, mangled and halfed, but sounde, whole, full and hable to do their office." It is Ascham's contention that learning and scholarship should not be the concern only of the "wretched, lame and deformed," but that they require the highest gifts of the mind and the body, that the true scholar is the complete gentleman. Accepting this definition of the terms Euphues and Euphuism, one might fairly include under them all the many endeavors towards the realization of an ideal courtly and scholarly character, in literature and in conduct, in the discussion of which the writings of the fifteenth and sixteenth centuries abound. But though these wider applications of the term need not be forgotten, it seems on the whole historically more justifiable, as it has been critically more customary, to limit the specific meaning of Euphuism to that manner of expression which finds its fullest illustration in the novels of Lyly.

It has often been pointed out that Euphuistic tendencies

[55] *Scholemaster*, ed. Arber, p. 38.

in writing are not peculiar to one age or people,[56] and that Lyly's progenitors extend all the way back to Ælfric, or even further, to Ælfric's models among the medieval Latin stylists. The peculiar thing about sixteenth-century English Euphuism is the systematic and elaborate way in which the tendencies of the style were carried out. Many writers were, to be sure, more or less Euphuistic without being thoroughgoing Euphuists. The *Life of Richard the Third,* attributed to More, shows definite anticipation of certain features of Lyly's style, and even the cruder stylists, like Caxton, Elyot, and Skelton, cannot be left altogether out of account. Ascham was decidedly more ingenious than any of his predecessors. Yet even Ascham's Euphuism was merely sporadic, and for the exuberant style as a persistent habit, he expresses strongest disapproval. In a young man "fulnes" does well enough, says Ascham, but "in farder aige," one's manner of writing is to be "temperated." He recommends those men who are "full of youthfull conditions," as was Sir Francis Bryan, one of the earliest ardent cultivators of a Euphuistic style, to "cut away the grosnesse that is in them." [57]

By the third quarter of the century, however, Ascham was beginning to seem a little heavy, to stand for the respectable but no longer fashionable virtues of an older generation. Under certain immediate influences, in part general and in at least one respect specific, Euphuistic writing grew rapidly in favor. The most important of the general influences, besides those already mentioned, was the breeding up of a generation of young university scholars who made a career not so much of scholarship as of 'wit.' Their extravagance in writing was only a part of a general

[56] See an interesting comparison between Lyly's *Euphues* and the Sanskrit romance *Vāsavadattā,* ed. Gray, pp. 33-35.

[57] *Scholemaster,* ed. Arber, p. 112.

expanding and loosening of the fancy and imagination. The sober learning of Ascham and his generation seemed dull and antiquated to these university fledglings who flocked to London in the third quarter of the century. Theology, hitherto the support and justification of scholarship, no longer interested them. They had discovered and were intent on cultivating more amusing interests and on turning them into sources of livelihood. The result of this was the sudden exploitation of fine writing for fine gentlemen.

The specific influence referred to was exerted from abroad by a writer who, more than any other individual, set the fashion towards Euphuism. This was Antonio de Guevara, who was introduced to those who read only English through the medium of the translations of Lord Berners, Sir Thomas North, and others. Guevara was a distinguished Spanish humanist, a man who had traveled widely, had held lofty positions in church and state, and through his writings had acquired an extraordinary literary popularity throughout Europe. He was born about 1480 and died in 1545. Of his various writings the one best known to Englishmen was his *Libro Aureo de Marco Aurelio.* Under this title the original Spanish had appeared in a first edition, which was pirated, according to Guevara, in 1528. This version was translated into French by René Bertaut de la Grise, whose book appeared in 1531, with the title *Liure dore de Marc Aurele.* It was from this French version that Bourchier's translation was made. In 1529 Guevara revised and amplified the unauthorized edition of 1528, and published the new version as *Libro llamado relox de principes enel qual va encorporado el muy famoso libro de Marco aurelio,* a title which was modified later to read, *Libro del emperador Marco aurelio con relox de principes.*[58] The French version of 1531 was then revised on the basis

[58] Feuillerat, *John Lyly,* p. 445.

of Guevara's enlarged edition, and this revision, appearing in 1540, served as the basis for a second English translation, Sir Thomas North's *Diall of Princes.*

In the language of Bourchier's translation, among other fictitious details Guevara asserts that he "founde this tretise in Florence, amonge the bokes left there by Cosme de Medicis," and that he has "reduced" it, not word for word, but thought for thought. He does not claim to be the principal author of the work, but takes particular credit to himself for having given high style to older and more rudely expressed high ideas: "for so hyghe sentences are not found at this presente tyme, nor to soo hyghe a style they of tyme past never atteyned."[59] As a matter of fact the book is in no sense historical, but connects rather with the history of the novel than that of historical or biographical writing. Its material was gathered from a variety of sources, from Plutarch, Xenophon, from Christian philosophical and meditative writers, in short from any source that might provide a thought, a sentiment, or an illustration. Of the writings of Marcus Aurelius himself, Guevara could have known nothing, since the first edition of them did not appear until 1559. He made some use of accessible biographical accounts of Marcus Aurelius, adding much from his own fancy and citing as his sources of information three imaginary biographers, who, he said, were his principal authorities.[60]

The book covers an extraordinary range of topics, and like other conduct books of the Renascence, it was designed to serve as a guide to the many possible duties, joys, and sorrows of the social life. In reading the *Libro Aureo,* it is not difficult to realize the source of its former popularity. The modern reader may sniff at the moral platitudes

[59] End of the Prologue.

[60] See Menendez y Pelayo, *Origenes de la Novela,* I, ccclxiv ff.

it contains, but a neatly dressed sentiment was as interesting in the sixteenth century as a cleverly turned situation in the plot of a novel to-day. And the moral doctrine of the *Libro Aureo* is not cast at the reader in an undigested mass. The whole is leavened by the aid of various animating devices. Speeches, letters, orations, dialogues between historical characters, often naturally presented, fables, anecdotes, proverbs, and allusions, all these, to say nothing of the sauce of the sweet style, lend life and interest to the narrative. At bottom the book is a kind of didactic romance with Marcus Aurelius always at the center of its many adventures into the realm of the spiritual life.

The style of the *Libro Aureo* contributed as much to the popularity of the book as its content. Fullness and ingenuity are the words which best describe this style. Guevara abounds in allusion, anecdote, and illustration. He polishes and amplifies his ideas to their extreme limits. Rhetorical questions, ejaculations, repetitions of syntax and phrasing at the beginnings of a set of clauses (anaphora), these and similar rhetorical devices are constantly employed. So far as the structure of the sentences is concerned, the most notable characteristic is the weighing and balancing of parallel or antithetic clauses. The periodic Ciceronian structure is not the prevailing type of sentence in the *Libro Aureo,* but the shorter two-part sentence or clause, with balanced halves. More purely verbal features of Guevara's style are the use of rime and assonance, employed often to emphasize balance and antithesis, of puns and word-echoes or 'tranlacing.' These characteristics of style will appear more specifically in the discussion of the use which Berners and North made of them. In passing it may be noted that Guevara did not employ alliteration or the so-called unnatural natural history of English Euphuism.

All of Lord Berners, Thomas Bourchier's, books are

courtly in character, are all translations, and were all written at Calais, where he was deputy governor from 1520 until his death in 1533. They consist of a translation of Froissart's *Chronicles,* finished in 1525; of the *Boke of Duke Huon of Burdeux* and the *History of the most noble and valyaunt Knight, Artheur of Lytell Brytaine,* both translated from the French; of the *Castell of Love,* from the Spanish of de San Pedro; and of the *Golden Boke of Marcus Aurelius,* translated from a French version of the first edition of Guevara's *Libro Aureo.*

Bourchier never acquired a consistent individual style and his various translations are interesting in different ways as illustrations of several tendencies in English courtly writing of the early sixteenth century. The translation of Froissart contains an original preface by Bourchier in praise of history, in which Bourchier exercises all his literary ingenuity to bring together, after the manner of Caxton, as many synonymous terms as possible. The writers of histories, says Bourchier, "shewe, open, manifest and declare to the reder, by example of olde antyquite, what we shulde enquere, desyre and folowe; and also, what we shulde eschewe, avoyde and utterly flye; for whan we (beynge unexpert of chaunces) se, beholde and rede the auncyent actes, gestes and dedes, howe and with what labours, daungers and paryls they were gested and done, they right greatly admonest, ensigne and teche us howe we maye lede forthe our lyves"—and so on to the reader's admiration and weariness. In this preface Bourchier was decidedly more artful than in the body of the book. When he came to translate the narrative itself, he followed the simple, unmannered style of his original. The translation is usually idiomatic, though now and then French locutions are followed slavishly. The vocabulary employed is on the whole simple, but it is enriched by an abundance of courtly and chivalric terms which the subject demanded. Stylistically there is little that is distinctive or significant in the book. It follows in the main the traditional methods of the later medieval prose romance, and though the writing is more virile than that of Malory, it is of the same kind, only cruder and less evenly maintained. The narrative produces a strong cumulative effect not by any structural unity or graces of expression, but by the unfailing vividness, reality, and variety of its separate episodes. In this book Bourchier wrote like the soldier and man of affairs he was, not gracefully or elegantly or learnedly, except in the preface, but concretely and solidly, sometimes crudely and bluntly.

The translation of Huon of Bordeaux was apparently undertaken from motives similar to those which led to the translation of Froissart, that is, the desire to provide a book of courtly entertainment, and at the same time, a picture of model knightly conduct. This romance is extremely long, and to a modern reader, tedious; but like all of Bourchier's writings, it maintains a dignified courtly tone. Like the Froissart, it is written in the naïve style of Malory, but again without Malory's grace and ease of phrasing. The style in general is unornamented, except for the use of synonymous doublets and triplets, and on the whole impresses one with a sense of impoverishment both in the cadences of phrasing and in vocabulary.

More interesting from the point of view of style than the Froissart or the Huon, is Bourchier's *Golden Boke of Marcus Aurelius,* which first appeared in print in 1535, the year after Bourchier's death. The great popularity of the work is indicated by the fact that fourteen editions of it were issued between 1535 and 1588. Bourchier was aware of the stylistic distinction of the book he undertook to translate, the quality of which was unescapable, even in a

French translation. The English version was published under the direction of Sir Francis Bryan, Bourchier's nephew, against whom Ascham had preferred the charge of eternal youth. It was at Bryan's instant desire, Bourchier declares, that he undertook the work. Bryan adds some comments at the end of the book in which he speaks of the undertaking as "a ryche and newe labour," and he thinks as much praise is to be accorded to the various translators of the book as to Marcus Aurelius, the reputed original author. "A ryghte precyous meate," says Bryan, "is the sentences of this boke: But finally the sauce of the sayd swete style moveth the appetite." There are many books full of "substancial meates," but they are "so rude and so unsavery and the style of so smal grace, that the fyrste morsell is lothesome and noyfull." It is the fate of such books to lie "hole and sounde" in libraries, but Bryan hopes a better fate may befall this *Golden Boke*.[61]

Of the characteristics of style of the original, the only one which is reproduced with any degree of success by Bourchier is balance and antithesis in phrasing. This appears constantly and with so little variety that a few simple examples will suffice as illustrations:

"Many tymes of wyse yonge men cometh olde fooles: And of yonge fooles customably cometh wise olde men." [62]

"Beleve me one thynge, that if a tree beareth not in Prymetyme his flowers, we hope not to have the fruyte in harveste rype: and a yonge man that hathe not passed his youthe with yonge people, we have noo hope that he shulde passe his age with olde men." [63]

"I am sure of one thynge, that if the yonge man be borne with foly, the olde man lyveth and dieth with covetyse." [64]

[61] F. 167, recto.
[62] F. 24, recto.
[63] F. 24, recto.
[64] F. 89, verso.

The system of alliteration, of which later English masters of the balanced and antithetic styles were to make such extensive use, is not in Guevara and was not elaborated by Bourchier. Neither does he employ rime. The device of 'tranlacing,' already mentioned in connection with Ascham, is reproduced to some extent in Bourchier's translation, but the results cannot be called successful. A few examples may be cited from the same passages as those from which the illustrations just quoted were taken:

"I am sore abasshed, that somme wyll be soo lordely and valiant in vertues, and so hygh mynded, and yet wyll make us beleve that they lyvynge in the flesshe and being of flesh, onely fele not the flesh. I can not tel if nature hath made other of an other nature than I am of, or me of an other nature thanne other be. For I being never so faste inclosed in the swete conversation of philosophy, yea in the best tyme, this false flesshe wolle calle atte the gate with his noughtye flesshe."

"This emperour was soo wyse in all thynges, that amonge theym that were mery, he was of great myrthe. And in verities he was very veritable."

"Therfore my sonne beware, be not extreme in extremities."

On the whole, Bourchier was quite as crude and awkward a stylist in his translation of Guevara as in his other writings. The hints supplied by his original he did not assimilate and apply to a stylistic method of his own. He reproduced what came easily in an English translation, but did not himself exert much ingenuity. The *Golden Boke*, in its English version, was not kept alive and made popular by its stylistic excellence or novelty. It was as a conduct book and as a collection of moral maxims, like Elyot's

Governor, Castiglione's *Courtier,* and similar books, that it was esteemed and read, and it was under cover of this interest that its literary influence was exerted.

Another writer of far greater literary importance than Bourchier who also came under the influence of Guevara, was Sir Thomas North. Born probably in the year which saw the publication of Bourchier's *Golden Boke,* North led an active life as soldier, scholar, and courtier. Though not without favor in court circles, he never held any very important offices, and his fame now rests mainly upon one of his literary works, his translation of Plutarch. His other writings, only two in number, were also translations. The earlier of these, *The Diall of Princes* (1557), was, as has been pointed out, a translation from the revised and amplified version of the French translation of Guevara's *Libro del emperador Marco aurelio con relox de principes.* A second edition of it appeared in 1568, to which was added a fourth book, "entituled the Favored Courtier, never heretofore imprinted in our vulgar tongue." A third edition appeared in 1582, and a fourth in 1619, after North's death. North's version was not made independently of Bourchier's, certain parts of the *Diall of Princes* being taken over almost literally from the earlier *Golden Boke.* Besides Berners and the revised French translation from the Spanish, North also had recourse to the original of Guevara, from which he translated parts not contained in the French version.

The main interest of the work to North as to Bourchier lay in its moral wisdom. In the dedicatory epistle prefixed to the translation, North praises Guevara's work because it is "so ful of highe doctrine, so adourned with auncient histories, so auctorised with grave sentences, and so beautified with apte simylitudes." He has nothing to say, however, with respect to the stylistic characteristics of Guevara's writings, now the main source of their historical interest both in the originals and in their translations. As with Berners the style of the *Libro Aureo* passes over into the *Diall of Princes* mainly in the use of the balanced and antithetic sentence and of tranlacing. An example which illustrates both devices is the following, extracted from North's translation of Guevara's prologue:

"The greatest vanitie that I finde in the worlde is, that vayne men are not onely contente to be vayne in their life, but also procure to leave a memorye of their vanitye after their death. For it is so thought good unto vayne and lyght men whiche serve the worlde in vayne workes: that at the houre of their deathe when they perceive they can doe no more, and that they can no lenger prevaile, they offer them selves unto deathe, which now they see approche uppon theim. Manye of the Worlde are so flesshed in the Worlde, that althoughe it forsaketh theim in deedes, yet they wyl not forsake it in their desires. And I durste sweare that if the world could graunt them perpetual life, they would promise it alwayes to remaine in their customable folye." [65]

It seems unnecessary to add further illustrations of North's transference of Guevara's mannerisms to his English translation. Much of the color and luxuriance of the original Spanish escapes in the passage through French

[65] Author's Prologue, fol. b II, recto. The Spanish of Guevara is as follows: "La mayor vanidad que hallo entre los hijos de vanidades: no contentos de ser vanos enla vida: procuran que aya memoria de sus vanidades despues dela muerte: porque paresce alos hombres vanos y limanos: que enla vida servieron al mundo con obras: desde la sepultura le offrezcan a mas no poder sus voluntades. Muchos delos del mundo estan tan encarniçados en el mundo: que si el los dexa a ellos de hecho: no dexan ellos a el con el desseo: porque yo jurare que juren los tales: que si el mundo pudiesse perpetuar les la vida: ellos le harian voto de permanescer para siempre en su locura." *Relox de principes* (ed. 1529), fol. vii, verso, quoted Feuillerat, *John Lyly,* p. 448.

into English, and the few rhetorical devices which North employs seem mechanical. It is interesting to note, however, that in North one begins to find distinct evidences of alliteration used to emphasize balance and antithesis in sentence structure. But the possibilities of this stylistic ornament seem not to have been realized or perhaps not to have interested North. He certainly did not regard his translation as mainly a stylistic experiment, but rather as an attempt to reproduce the content of the original with some regard for its form.

North's second venture in authorship, his *Morall Philosophie of Doni* (1570), took its title from the Italian original of which it is a translation. It is not, however, a philosophic work, but a western form of the well-known *Fables of Bidpai,* a collection of moral tales ultimately of Indian origin but extant in dozens of Asiatic and European versions. It is a slighter work than either *The Diall of Princes* or the Plutarch, and it seems to have been less popular in North's own day. As was the case with both *The Diall of Princes* and the translation of Plutarch, the moral sentiment of Doni's book was the immediate occasion of North's interest in it. The " marveylous benefite " which the translator promises to the reader is more likely to be found, however, in the easy familiarity of the tales themselves than in their moral lessons. The stories are mostly animal fables, but the various birds and beasts are quaintly and picturesquely drawn as types of human character. The vivacity of the narrative is specially heightened by the use of colloquial turns of phrasing, exclamations, and terms of address which often give the Oriental tales of the book an amusingly Elizabethan realistic color. Although the attentive reader might pick out passages from *The Morall Philosophie,* especially from the moralizing commentaries inserted between the tales, which exhibit some attention to literary artifice, mainly balance, alliteration and word-repetition, the book as a whole produces the effect of the free and easy style of colloquial speech. North does not employ the tricks of style which he might have learned from Guevara in any systematic way in his translation of Doni. He writes not an artificial style, but with the free idiomatic freshness and vigor of the independent and active-minded Elizabethan.

North's *Lives of the Noble Grecians and Romans* appeared first in 1579, and was printed only once again, in 1595, before North's death.[66] The translation was made from the French of Amyot, and here, as in his other books, North owes his form as well as his content to his source. The interest of the book for North lay in large measure in its didactic value. It also is a conduct book in the larger sense, teaching "honor, love, obedience, reverence, zeale, and devocion to Princes." It is better, North remarks, "to see learning in noble mens lives than to reade it in Philosophers writings." North himself, accordingly, has nothing to say independently. He followed Amyot closely in content, though somewhat freely in phrasing. Amyot wrote a slow-moving, dignified, and formal style, appropriate to his subject. His sentences were usually constructed after the model of the Ciceronian period. North, however, translated in an easier and more colloquial vein. His sentences are prevailingly long, though shorter than Amyot's, and variously membered, but they are not put together in regular periods. They are indeed very loosely constructed, sometimes without regard for strict grammatical coherence, though never without a feeling for cadence which saves them from the amorphous, sprawling structures of the

[66] Various modified and modernized versions of the book appeared later, and recently the text of the original edition has been republished, in Tudor Translations, ed. W. E. Henley.

medieval style. The rhythm of the prose of the translation is loose, but not naïve.

The vocabulary which North employed in the Plutarch was in the main lofty and dignified, but not the aureate vocabulary of the learned style. Neither was it a strikingly popular and colloquial vocabulary, though perhaps the most important difference between North and Amyot consists in the greater colloquial ease, even at times humorous familiarity, of the former as compared with his original. Thus Amyot's simple "il luy donna un souflet, et s'en alla," becomes the more vivacious picture in North, "Alcibiades up with his fiste, and gave him a good boxe on the eare, and went his way."[67] Where Amyot speaks of those "que estoyent demouriez à Rome," North amplifies into "the hometarriers and housedoves that kept Rome still."[68] Pericles, when he was about to place a garland of flowers upon the head of his dead son, in Amyot's words, "espandit sur l'heure grande quantité de larmes," but in North, "he burst out in tears, and cryed a mayne."[69] An infinite number of slight touches like these give to North's translation the familiar ease and picturesqueness so generally found in Elizabethan prose.

When North wrote independently he was inclined to be stylistically more formal and ambitious than when he translated. His use of balance and antithesis in the two-part sentence is the most noteworthy characteristic of his style when he writes in his own person. The following sentences from the short address to Queen Elizabeth prefixed to the Plutarch have an unmistakable similarity to Euphuistic rhythm:

"Therefore I humbly beseech your Majestie, to suffer the simpleness of my translation to be covered under the ampleness of your highnes protection."

[67] II, 96. [68] II, 158. [69] II, 46.

"Then well may the Readers thinke, if they have done this for heathen Kings, what should we doe for Christian Princes? If they have done this for glorye, what shoulde we doe for religion? If they have done this without hope of heaven, what shoulde we doe that looke for immortalitie? And so adding the encouragement of these exsamples to the forwardnes of their owne dispositions: what service is there in warre, what honor in peace, which they will not be ready to doe, for their worthy Queene?" [70]

From such passages one may perhaps infer that North might have developed an individual and personal style of his own if he had undertaken original composition on an extensive scale, and that this style would have had balance and antithesis as its fundamental features. But to speak of North as the founder of Euphuism is greatly to exaggerate his influence. Neither North nor Bourchier had that definite and certain feeling for expression which one looks for in the founder of an elaborate artificial style and which one finds in so marked a degree in Guevara. It was not Guevara the stylist who excited their deepest interest, but Guevara the preacher and moralist. At most Bourchier and North could but have pointed the way towards certain devices of style which later and more ingenious writers were to use with a fuller sense of their value. And of course it must not be forgotten that their translations were a symptom as well as a cause of interest in the originals of Guevara.

The channels through which the influence of Spanish style may have flowed into England need not be limited to the translations of Bourchier and North. With the arrival of Katharine of Aragon in England considerable direct interest in Spanish affairs and in Spanish literature was awakened. At the court a strong Spanish party was gradually formed, among its members being Bourchier and his nephew, Sir

[70] Henley's ed., I, 4-5.

Francis Bryan. Various Spaniards of distinction visited England from time to time, the notable scholar, Juan Luis Vives, for example, who was invited to Oxford in 1523 by Henry VIII and who remained until the fall of Wolsey in 1528, and Guevara himself, for a short time, in 1522.[71] Considering the esteem in which Guevara was held, it cannot be doubted that many Englishmen read his writings in their original Spanish, and that in this way the feeling for highly artificial literary style was fostered, even though Guevara's specific practices were not followed. Other translations of Guevara's works besides those already mentioned may be regarded as evidence of the attention which was paid to the author's Spanish writings. Sir Francis Bryan published in 1548 a translation made from a French version of Guevara's *Menosprecio de la Corte,* under the title, *A Dispraise of the life of a Courtier and a commendacion of the life of the labouring man.* In 1574 appeared Edward Hellowes' *Familiar Epistles of Sir Anthonie of Guevara,* a translation from the Spanish of the *Epistolas Familiares.* Though Hellowes declares that he lacks "both glosse and hewe of rare eloquence," his translation, as well as his own composition in his prefaces, shows some effort to reproduce the stylistic devices of his original. The following year, 1575, was published Geffrey Fenton's *Golden Epistles, contayning varietie of discourse, both Morall, Philosophicall and Divine, gathered as wel out of the remaynder of Guevaraes woorkes as other Authours, Latine, French and Italian.* This book was intended to serve as a supplement to Hellowes' *Familiar Epistles,* and though Fenton, like Hellowes, declares himself "not to be so curious to set out this work with elegancie of phrase and Rhetoricke, as to exhibite precepts to live wel," he also shows himself a not inexpert adapter of the Guevaristic tricks

[71] Gálvez, *Guevara in England,* p. 3.

of style. Other translations by Hellowes were *A Chronicle conteyning the liues of tenne Emperours of Rome* (1577), a version of Guevara's *Decada de las vidas de los x. Cesares,* and *A Booke of the Inuention of the Art of Nauigation* (1578), from Guevara's *Aguja de Marear y de sus inuentores.*[72]

The combining of moral purpose with imaginative narrative and with the quest after distinction of style, which Guevara's admirers noted approvingly in his biographical and didactic romance, remained one of the constant features of sixteenth-century courtly writing. As the art of imaginative narrative developed, drawing its materials more and more abundantly from classical, French and Italian sources, it continued to justify itself with professions of a moral seriousness which was a double inheritance from the English Reformation and from humanistic critical theory. The fancy was not allowed to play freely upon character and situation, and the doctrine of art for art's sake, or even of direct truth to nature, was probably never less esteemed than it was in the third quarter of the sixteenth century. The stylists were therefore not simply experimental; they sought a form pleasing to refined readers by means of which to convey moral lessons, but the moral intention was as prominent as the artistic. Striking illustrations of this combination of high style and morality are to be found in the various romances and collections of tales which began to appear abundantly after the middle of the century.[73]

[72] *The Mounte of Caluarie,* which appeared anonymously in 1595, is a translation of Guevara's *Misterios del Monte Caluario,* a book of pious meditations much more soberly written than the *Libro Aureo.* A later translation of the Epistolas Familiares was made by John Savage, in 1697, under the title *Spanish Letters.*

[73] The first Italian novel to be translated directly from the Italian (cf. Brie, *Englische Studien,* CXXIV, 46-57) was the 49th novel of Masuccio's *Novellino,* made by Henry Parker, ca. 1545. But this was not printed before Brie's text appeared, it was not a

One of the earliest collections of tales was William Painter's *Palace of Pleasure,* the first volume of which appeared in 1566 and the second the following year. The stories which Painter told were drawn mainly from Latin, Italian, and French sources, "recueled and bound together in this volume, under the title of the Palace of Pleasure," for the avowed purpose of providing profitable instruction in agreeable form. Even those stories which treat of unlawful love, against which Ascham inveighed so bitterly, are defended on the ground that by reading them "both old and yonge may learne how to avoyde the ruine, overthrow, inconvenience and displeasure, that lascivious desire and wanton wil doth bring to their suters and pursuers." [74] The tales are intermixed, however, with "pleasaunte discourses, merie talke, sportinge practises, deceitfull devises, and nipping tauntes" to exhilarate the reader's mind. In the telling of his tales, though he regrets that they are "not so set foorth or decked with eloquent stile, as this age more brave in tongue then manners dothe require," Painter shows plainly enough that he is interested in the artful devices of fine writing. In general his narrative method is simple and straightforward, though the sentences show some tendency to fall into the fixed cadences of the balanced and antithetic structure. He is fond of occasional learned words, which he sometimes uses in pairs, after the conventional fashion of the times, e.g. *decerped and chose, recueled and bound together, deserts and voide places,* etc. Alliteration is also

love intrigue story, and it was very crudely done. For the general bibliography of Italian translations, see Miss Scott's "Elizabethan Translations from the Italian," *Publications of the Modern Language Association,* X, 249-293; XI, 377-484; XIV, 42-153; 465-571. Tieje, "The Critical Heritage of Fiction in 1579" (*Englische Studien,* XLVII, 415-448) contains some discussion of the purposes avowed by sixteenth-century writers of fiction.

[74] *Palace of Pleasure,* ed. Jacobs, I, v.

consciously employed, as when he tells us that good example "prescribeth a directe pathe to treade the tracte of this present life"; [75] or when he declares that "No vertuous dede or zelous worke can want due prayse of the honest, though faulting fooles and youthly heades full ofte do chaunt the faultles checke that Momus mouth did once finde out in Venus slipper." [76] Such passages are sporadic, however, and Painter seems to have lacked the skill or the patience to employ his stylistic devices systematically.

In the year of Painter's second volume appeared *Certain Tragical Discourses of Bandello,* translated into English by Geffrey Fenton, who has already been mentioned as a translator of Guevara. The arguments which Painter had used in defense of his book appear again independently and more emphatically set forth in the dedicatory address of Fenton's work. The defense of history which is here made knows no distinction between authentic records of events and fictitious narrative, all being equally useful to the reader for reproof and counsel: "antiquitie gives choice of admonicions for obedience to his superiors, with charge to applie and employe all his care for the commoditye of his countrye." [77] Fenton is a much more thoroughgoing moralist than Painter, and he makes frequent additions and comments of a strongly Puritan color in the course of his narratives. Like Painter, he justifies his narratives of unlawful love on the ground that examples of evil to be avoided are as necessary as examples of good to be followed. In vocabulary Fenton does not follow the extreme of the enriching tendency, though he does not hesitate to coin new words at pleasure from Greek, Latin, French, and Italian. His style is more dependent for its main effect upon structural characteristics than upon the mere surface

[75] Jacobs, p. 10.
[76] Ibid., p. 10.
[77] *Bandello,* ed. Douglas, I, 4.

ornamentation of vocabulary. Such Euphuistic sentences as the following are of constant occurrence:

"Albeit as his presence often gave ympedimente to their metinge, so his absence restored their enterviewe." [78]

"Wherin, as the humor of his love seamed to excede the ordinarie impressions of men in that case, so he neyther was hable to resiste the hoate sommaunce of his newe appetit, nor kepe warre any tyme with the suggestion of his sodayne desire; but, as one that felt himselfe stricken with the thonderbolt of his destynie, gave place to his sentence, and entred into devise with himselfe what waye too use, to wynne the encounter of his fancie." [79]

Alliteration is sometimes used, either simply or according to the transverse pattern, for the sake of emphasis; but Fenton resembles Painter in that alliteration and the balanced and antithetic sentence are only occasional features of his style. He is, however, further significant in the development of Euphuistic writing for his frequent use of similes taken from natural history. His museum includes the chameleon, salamander, cockatrice, scorpion, elephant, tiger, leopard, ape, and other more familiar members of the animal kingdom. That this had long been a recognized kind of rhetorical amplification is evident from Wilson's inclusion of it in his *Arte of Rhetorique* (1553). After a brief discussion of the value of antithesis, Wilson proceeds:

"The like helpe we maie have by comparing like examples together, either of creatures living or of thinges not living: as in speaking of constancie, to shewe the Sunne, who ever keepeth one course: in speaking of inconstancie, to shewe the Moone which keepeth no certaine course. Againe, in young Storkes, we may take an example of love towards their damme, for when she is old, and not able for

[78] Douglas, I, 89.

[79] Ibid., pp. 24-25.

her crooked bill to picke meate, the yong ones feede her. In yong Vipers there is a contrary example (for as *Plinie* saieth) they eate out their dammes wombe, and so come forth. In Hennes there is a care to bring up their Chickens: in Egles the contrary, which cast out their Egges, if they have any moe then three: and all because they would not be troubled with bringing up of many." [80]

The year 1576 saw the publication of George Whetstone's *Rocke of Regard,* the first increase of his "barren braine" but to be followed by numerous others, among them *An Heptameron of Civill Discourses* (1582) which contains the Christmas exercise of "sundrie well Courted Gentlemen and Gentlewomen." *The Rocke of Regard* is divided into four parts which are given picturesque titles similar to the name of the book as a whole. The first part is called *The Castle of Delight,* and therein is reported "the wretched end of wanton and dissolute living." The second part is *The Garden of Unthriftinesse,* the third, the *Arbour of Vertue,* and the fourth, *The Orchard of Repentance,* titles which indicate sufficiently the moralizing tone of the whole. The book is made up of tales in verse and prose, and the same tricks of style, alliteration, puns, and other plays on words appear in both forms. Alliteration is usually simple, but sometimes it is employed in more complicated patterns, as when the author speaks of "the alluring beauties of brave ladies," or of one of his lovers who has "transformed his late liking unto such faythful love, as secretly he vowed that neyther change nor chaunce should (whiles life lasted) remove his affection." [81] Bal-

[80] Ed. Mair, p. 125. This whole passage on various methods of amplification reads like a description of Euphuism. The use of "brute beastes," of doves, cranes, dragon, dog, and lion, as "paterns and Images" is again recommended, pp. 191-194. See p. 77, where these precepts are exemplified in a specimen oration.

[81] *Rocke of Regard,* ed. Collier, p. 43.

ance in phrasing, sometimes helped out by alliteration, is not unfrequently employed by Whetstone, e.g. "the accidents of his evil fortunes might have forewarned other yonge gentlemen to have shunde the like follies." [82] But Whetstone's gifts were those of fluency and of the popular style rather than artistic ingenuity, and his stylistic mannerisms are crude and obvious. He speaks of the change he has made for the reader's delight, "of reading bad verse, with the proffer of worsser prose." [83] The prose is simpler than the verse, however, and for that reason better.[84]

Spiritually and artistically akin to Whetstone was George Gascoigne, whose writings for the most part appeared in print in the years 1575 and 1576. Gascoigne was poet and prose writer, and in the tale of intrigue and love adventure, *"The pleasant Fable of Ferdinando Jeronimi and Leonora de Valasco,"* he varies the prose, like Whetstone, by the introduction of occasional passages in verse.

[82] Collier, p. 276.

[83] Ibid., pp. 41-42.

[84] Certain other collections of tales dating from this period need only be mentioned by title. Thomas Fortescue's *Forest, or Collection of Historyes, no lesse profitable then pleasant and necessary* (1571), translated from a French version of an Italian translation of Pedro Mexia's *Silva de varia leccion,* has little narrative or stylistic interest. In 1577 appeared Robert Smyth's *Straunge, Lamentable and Tragicall Histories. Translated out of French into English;* and the year following, Henry Wotton's *Courtlie Controversie of Cupids Cautels: Conteyning five Tragicall Histories, very pithie, pleasant, pitiful and profitable. . . . Translated out of French as neare as our English phrase will permit. A Posie of Gilloflowers* (1580) by Humphrey Gifford contains "Divers briefe histories" in prose, though most of the book is in verse. According to Tanner, William Warner published in 1580 a translation of Bandello's *Novelle,* but no such book is now known; but Warner's *Pan his Syrinx or Pipe . . . seuen Tragical and Comicall Arguments* is extant in an edition of 1584 and another of 1597. These seven stories are rather short romances than novelle. Several interesting titles of books now lost are mentioned by Esdaile, *English Tales and Romances,* pp. xxxiii-xxxv.

Like Whetstone again, he is fond of picturesque alliterative titles, such as *The fruite of Fetters, The Droomme of Doomes day, A Delycate Diet for daintie mouthde Droonkardes,* etc. Gascoigne is a persistent moralist; even the light posies of his misguided youth he turns to account as beacons to assist the unwary "to avoyd the subtile sandes of wanton desires" and to direct them that they may not "runne upon the rockes of unlawfull lust." [85] But the motives which led Gascoigne to write were not simple. He delighted not only to exercise his pen in moral discourses but was deeply interested in literary experimentation of various kinds. His *Pleasant Fable of Ferdinando and Leonora* purports to be a translation from the Italian, but no Italian source has been found for it, and it seems to be an early attempt to tell in prose a complicated story of intrigue and adventure which may have had a basis in real life. In its narrative method, it is distinctly a forerunner of the novel of Lyly. His *Glasse of Government* is the first English prose comedy, his *Jocasta* the first tragedy translated from Italian into English, his *Steele Glas* the first regular English satire, and his *Certayne Notes of Instruction concerning the making of verse or ryme in English* the first treatise on poetry in English.

As a writer of prose, Gascoigne was an experimenter in the new field of the artificial style. He declares that he has "alwayes bene of opinion that it is not unpossible eyther in Poemes or in Prose too write both compendiously and perfectly in our Englishe tongue." [86] But the way to perfect writing in English is not to be sought by the borrowing of inkhorn terms from foreign languages; Gascoigne prefers, like the courtly writers in general, to err on the conservative side in retaining old English words of native origin. This ideal of verbal simplicity was con-

[85] *Posies,* ed. Cunliffe, p. 12.

[86] Ibid., p. 5.

sistently maintained by Gascoigne, and in general he shows literary discernment in the avoidance of the more obvious mannerisms of style of the time. Alliteration he uses freely, but not with crude insistence. Synonymous word-pairs and the tumbling or heaping passages of the popular oratorical style he rejects altogether. In his effort to attain distinction of style he exercises his ingenuity mainly upon the structure of his English sentences, and these he manages with considerable skill. Neatness and brevity are the distinguishing characteristics of his sentence structure, and these qualities are often re-enforced by the employment of the formal devices of balance of phrase in cadence and antithesis of thought. Gascoigne also indulges in the occasional use of similes from the natural world, e.g. the stork, "which feedeth the damme in age, of whom it selfe received nouriture beeing young in the neast"; [87] and the industrious bee which gathers honey out of the "most stinking weede," while the "malicious Spider may also gather poyson out of the fayrest floure that growes." [88]

The popular style seems, however, to have grown upon Gascoigne, more than the courtly. In the later treatises, *The Droomme of Doomes day* and *A Delycate Diet,* he assumes frankly the rôle of Puritan pamphleteer, and in *A Delycate Diet* utters a warning against "those Mermaydes of myschiefe, which pype so pleasantly in every Potte" with all the amplitude of picturesque phrase and alliteration of popular pulpit oratory.

This cleavage between fine style in fictitious narrative and fine style in undiluted didactic writing which has been observed in Whetstone and Gascoigne may be further examined in the practice of a writer of popular moral treatises who in his way was quite as ingenious as any of the practitioners

[87] *Glasse of Government,* ed. Cunliffe, p. 32.
[88] *Posies,* ed. Cunliffe, p. 12.

of the courtly style. This was Thomas Becon, born early in the second decade of the sixteenth century, later a student at St. John's College, Cambridge, and like many of his collegian contemporaries, an ardent advocate of reform in morals and religion. At various times he was under trial as a seditious preacher and fomenter of disturbance, and in 1543 he was compelled publicly to recant some of his opinions and to burn his published books. He held various livings, though he never attained to any high rank in the church, and seems to have died peacefully in 1567, probably at Canterbury. Under the pseudonym of Theodore Basil he published abundantly, and a few years before his death he gathered together his writings previously printed and issued them in a revised form in a folio edition of three parts or volumes.

Becon's writings are all theological or didactic in character. They were intended to be popular in tone, and their most distinctive literary quality arises from the attempt to make the subjects interesting by style and method of treatment. Very frequently the works are written in dialogue, and although the persons of the dialogue have little dramatic character, the interchange of speeches and the setting add some life to the treatises. In fact, they need only a slightly greater complication of plot to change them into moralities and didactic school-plays like Gascoigne's *Glasse of Government.* Becon was fond of ingenious figures as serving for the structure of his treatises and of giving them ingenious titles. *A Christmas Banquet* is a feast to which his friends are invited, the fare consisting altogether of scriptural texts, rolled on the tongue as voluptuously as though they were the most delicate morsels. *A Potation for Lent* is a companion piece to the *Banquet. The Pathway unto Prayer, The Flower of Godly Prayers,* and *The Pomander of Prayer* are self-explanatory titles.[89] *A Pleasant New Nosegay* is typical of a number of anthological treatises. Other picturesque titles are *The Jewel of Joy, The Castle of Comfort, The Solace of the Soul, The Fortress of the Faithful,* and *The Sick Man's Salve*. His longest work is *The Catechism,* in reality a general conduct book, touching various sides of life from many different points of view. It is interesting as giving the rules of living which were acceptable to a somewhat stern reformer, as distinguished from those so abundantly supplied for higher grades of society by the numerous courtly conduct books of the times.

Becon's sympathies with the severer aspects of the Reformation in England, with men like Sir John Cheke, Ascham, Wilson, and others, appears not only in his generally pious and didactic tone, but in many specific ways. His true gentleman is not precisely the popular Bible-man of Lollard days, but he is one whose life nevertheless is largely governed by his reading of the scriptures. Music is a "more vain and trifling science than it becometh a man, born and appointed to matters of gravity, to spend much time about it"; and Becon has only words of scorn for those who "have not spared to spend much riches in nourishing many idle singing-men to bleat in their chapels." A Christian man's melody is in his heart, when he recites psalms, hymns, and spiritual songs—"all outward melody is vain and transitory." Elsewhere Becon inveighs against

[89] This fashion in titles was followed by many. To those already mentioned may be added William Averell, "student in Diuinitie and Schoolemaister," who published, in 1584, *A Dyall for dainty Darlings, rockt in the Cradle of Securitie.* Among the treatises of John Norden, a devotional writer, are *A Sinful Man's Solace* (1585), *A Pensive Man's Practice* (1585), *A Mirror for the Multitude* (1586), *Progress of Piety, or Harberer of Heartsease* (1596). Becon's *Sick Man's Salve* is alluded to satirically in Jonson's *Silent Woman,* Act IV, Sc. II, and in *Eastward Hoe,* Act V, Sc. II.

the building of "gorgeous houses and sumptuous mansions." And the refined fashions in dress introduced into England from abroad are equally reprehensible in his sight: "O, what a monster and a beast of many heads is the Englishman now become! To whom may he be compared worthily but to Esop's crow? . . . He is an Englishman: he is also an Italian, a Spaniard, a Turk, a Frenchman, a Scot, a Venetian, and at the last, what not?" [90]

Curiously combined with this hard and repressive attitude towards the graces and luxuries of life is Becon's respect for eloquence and the exuberant and ornate style of literary expression. He longs for "the most pleasant speech and sugared eloquence" of Pericles, and declares that from his early youth he has been trained up "in the court of Lady Mnemosyne and her daughters and exercised in the wrestling-place of Apollo." [91] For this reason he thinks it not unfitting that he should bring forth some "literal lucubration" profitable to his countrymen. But one's surprise at Becon's assiduous cultivation of the literary graces is lessened when one realizes that he is not aping the accomplishments of the courtly writers, but is following certain traditions of fine writing current in didactic and moral discourse from the time of the church fathers. Becon cites Cicero as "most worthy to be embraced and both in tongue and pen to be followed," [92] but it is quite certain that he was more at home in the church fathers than he was in classical Latin or Greek literature. The robustious style of popular pulpit oratory also influenced Becon, mainly in the employment of the traditional features of the tumbling style, long catalogues of words, often carried to inordinate length, synonyms grouped in pairs and triplets

[90] *The Catechism,* ed. Ayre, p. 438. See also *Early Works,* p. 204.
[91] *Early Works,* p. 236.
[92] *Catechism,* p. 386.

and quadruplets, fantastic word-coinages, of both native and learned elements, and crudely insistent alliteration.

Some of Becon's rhetorical ornaments which depend on the manipulation of verbal harmony, the schemes of the medieval rhetoric, must be noted more in detail in order to bring out clearly their similarity in general spirit to the schemes of Euphuism, and at the same time their difference from the particular schemes which Euphuism made the distinctive features of its style. Alliteration, for example, is used very loosely by Becon. Alliterating words are often grouped together in long sequences, e.g. "but I know not whether your gay, gaudy, gallant, gorgeous, game-players garments . . ."; [93] or sometimes they are used only in pairs, e.g. "painful passion, dreadful death and royal resurrection." [94] But beyond this one finds little endeavor to employ alliteration in ingenious patterns. End-rime also occurs now and then in Becon, sometimes in combination with alliteration. Puns are made, even in the most serious passages, with amazing frequency. These verbal echoes are sometimes close, sometimes imperfect and far-fetched, for example, "pulpit" and "coal-pit"; or the statement that speech must not be "so polited that the heart be polluted." [95] Modern taste has made the pun so execrable that it is well to remember that the sixteenth-century writer, with the example of the reverend fathers of the church, from Tertullian down,[96] to support him, felt differently about it. Even so, however, it is doubtful if any courtly writer would have used puns as insistently and crudely as Becon has done. Slightly more complicated is Becon's use of verbal balance and antithesis. This is sometimes simple and rep-

[93] *Prayers and Other Pieces,* p. 215.
[94] *Early Works,* p. 1.
[95] *Catechism,* p. 350.
[96] See Norden, *Antike Kunstprosa,* p. 614.

resents a real antithesis of thought, as when he speaks of those who "had fallen from that joyful state into this sorrowful misery." More often, however, the antithesis is purely verbal and the words form a kind of linguistic compound proportion. Thus we have such phrasing as "bounteous liberality and liberal bounty"; [97] "the crown of glorious immortality and immortal glory"; [98] "O cruel fury and furious cruelness"; [99] "what studious diligence and diligent study, what painful labor and laborious pain." [100]

Such rhetorical flowers as have been illustrated occur abundantly in Becon's writings, and many of them are also found in the writings of the true Euphuists. What distinguishes Becon from Lyly and his immediate school is the fact that Becon never established the balanced and antithetic sentence as the fixed norm of his expression. His style never acquired the neatness and precision of the fully developed Euphuistic style, but at bottom it is the natural and loose style of popular oratory, decked out with some of the traditional schemes of medieval rhetoric. It was Becon's desire to edify his readers, not to drive them "into an admiration or stupor," but it would seem that his love of fine diction and ingenious figure frequently seduced him from his main intention. His endeavor apparently was to combine humanity and morality, fine writing and didacticism. All liberal sciences, in his opinion, were "to be studied and learned even that they might not depress but avance the true religion of God"; and eloquence without godliness is "as a ring in a swine's snout." [101] It was Becon's purpose to show that the vanities of the world were not the only material upon which the literary artist's ingenuity could be exercised. Moral truth to his mind

[97] *Early Works,* p. 1.
[98] Ibid., p. 30.
[99] Ibid., p. 53.
[100] *Catechism,* p. 6.
[101] Ibid., p. 382.

offered as distinguished and interesting a body of content as the tales of love and adventure of the worldly writers. All that the moral virtues needed was the charm of an attractive dress to enable them to satisfy the esthetic interests of the complete Christian gentleman. This may seem to have been a vain hope, but it was not an unreasonable ideal at a time when the children of the imagination had not yet justified themselves by their works.

The contrast between a popular stylist like Becon, with his obvious art and obvious morality, and a fine gentleman like George Pettie, in the main is surprisingly slight. In many respects they accepted similar standards, though they appealed to widely different audiences. Pettie was born about the middle of the century, was a student at Oxford, traveled abroad for some time, and died at Plymouth in 1589, being then, in the words of Wood, "a captain and a man of note." Wood also mentions the fact that Pettie first won recognition as a writer by his "passionate penning of amorous stories," and that he was "as much commended for his neat stile as any of his time."[102] Pettie wrote only two books, the first a collection of twelve prose tales after the model of Painter, entitled *A Petite Pallace of Pettie his Pleasure containing many pretie histories by him set forth in comely colours and most delightfully discoursed.* It appeared in two editions in 1576, the year of its publication, and other editions followed to the number of at least four before the end of the century. His second book appeared in print five years after the *Petite Pallace,* a translation through the French of the Italian *La Civil Conversatione* of Stefano Guazzo. The title of the English version is *The Civile Conversation of M. Stephen Guazzo* (1581), and in its first form, it contained only the first three books of Guazzo's work. The fourth book was added by Barthol-

[102] *Athen. Oxon.,* I, col. 553.

omew Young in a second edition which appeared in 1586. Guazzo's *Civile Conversation* belongs to the general type of conduct books of which Castiglione's *Courtier* is the best known example. It covers a wide field, discoursing in the second book on all those points which should be observed out of their own houses in company "betweene young men and olde, Gentlemen and yeomen, Princes and private persons, learned and unlearned, Citizens and strangers, Religious and Secular, men and women," and in the third book, the order to be observed in conversation within doors "betweene the husband and the wife, the father and the sonne, brother and brother, the maister and the servant." In short the book covers very much the same ground as Becon's *Catechism,* though the point of view is different.

The most interesting and the only original part of Pettie's version of Guazzo is contained in *The Preface to the Readers.* This preface opens with a defense of the art of writing, and of learning and scholarship as necessary accomplishments in the perfect gentleman. "Alasse, you wil be but ungentle Gentlemen, if you bee no schollers." Pettie himself seems to have been blamed for having devoted time to literary pursuits, and especially for having published the fruits of his labors. He considers learning, however, to be as necessary for a soldier as for any other man, and he reprehends the gentleman who strives to "cloake his art and skill in everie thing and to seeme to doe all things of his owne mother wit as it were." But study and industry are necessary before excellence can be attained in anything, and why is it a shame to show to be that, asks Pettie, which it is a shame not to be? "Therefore (Gentlemen) never denie your selves to bee schollers, never be ashamed to shew your learning, confesse it, professe it, imbrace it, honour it: for it is it which honoreth you, it is onelie it which maketh you men, it is onelie it which maketh you Gentlemen."

This eloquent and reasonable defense of learning leads Pettie over to the second point of his preface, the justification of his writing in English, and here again, he shows critical discernment. He is not of those who, returning from their travels abroad, find nothing at home good enough for them. On the contrary, he believes his own country to be "the civilest Countrie in the world," and as for the barbarousness of the English tongue, he declares it to be much the worse for those curious fellows who do not know in what the real excellence of a language consists. If he were furnished with learning otherwise, Pettie asserts that he would undertake to write in English "as copiouslie for varietie, as compendiously for brevitie, as choicely for words, as pithilie for sentences, as pleasantlie for figures, and everie waie as eloquentlie as anie writer should do in anie vulgar tongue whatsoever." Particularly interesting are the sensible views which Pettie expresses with respect to vocabulary. He is no enemy of inkhorn terms, nor, on the other hand, is he a narrow partisan of the native vocabulary. His position is that of the intelligent man of the world who is familiar with the usages of good society. "If a thing be of it selfe ill, I see not how the oldnesse of it can make it good, and if it be of it selfe good, I see not how the newnesse of it can make it naught." He finds a place for new words, therefore, provided they serve a useful purpose, and his only principle is to use all the resources of the language as effectively as possible. In these opinions Pettie has indicated the great advantages which have accrued to the English language through the practice in writing of the gentleman who was also a scholar. The merely learned, especially in Pettie's day, tended toward the pedantic in vocabulary, and the narrow patriot was inclined to restrict too much the resources of the language. The golden mean was to be found, where it always has been found, in the standards approved by the normal usage of good society. This intelligent respect for the accepted idiomatic vocabulary was a permanent gain for the language, and for their recognition of this, Pettie and his courtly contemporaries deserve great credit. They would have deserved still greater credit if they had also recognized that extravagant rhetorical artifice, whatever the weight of precedent, is no more necessary than extravagance in vocabulary for the formation of a literary style.

The *Civile Conversation* was a work of Pettie's maturer judgment and stands in sharp contrast to his *Petite Pallace*. In the *Petite Pallace,* Pettie tells his "tragical trifles" under the most transparent cloak of serious moral intention. All is airy, graceful, worldly, and instead of preaching, we have persiflage. Conventional morality gives place to a somewhat cynical didacticism. The dedicatory address of the book is To the Gentle Gentlewomen Readers, and the ladies are directly appealed to throughout. Their infirmities are held up to their eyes in a vein of witty cynicism which seems to have been intended, and accepted, as complimentary. I could preach better to you in a more pleasant matter, says Pettie, after a passage of mock moralizing; but the more pleasant, the less proper. In an age of literal repetition and of blunt didacticism, it is refreshing to find Pettie treating the traditional material of classic and of Italian story with something of Ovid's and Chaucer's humor and lightness of touch. But the temper of the times was not favorable to such moods, and after this first effort of his youth, Pettie's playful fancy gives way to serious didacticism. He feels it necessary in the *Civile Conversation* to apologize for his earlier "trifling worke" whereby he has won such fame as "hee which fired the Temple of Diana," and to purchase for himself some better fame by some better work and to countervail his former vanity by some formal gravity.[103]

Writing as an accomplished man of the world, Pettie makes use, in the *Petite Pallace,* of the many arts and graces of the courtly style more consistently, more ingeniously and effectively than any writer who had preceded him. Alliteration, transverse and simple, balance, and antithesis are the fundamentals of his style, and to these he adds rimes, puns, and all manner of half-suggested plays on words. His aim being neatness and precision of effect, he avoids the pompous learned vocabulary, the grouping of synonyms in couples and triplets, and the long cataloguing passages of the popular oratorical style. In one of his self-criticisms, Pettie seems to imply that his stories were first told orally and afterwards written down. But if so, they must have changed form greatly in the process of written composition, for only by the taking of much thought could so intricate a style have been evolved. To be sure, some of the tricks of style are easy and are applied crudely and obviously. Alliteration, so thickly laid on, hardly adds to the pathos of the following:

"And is my Curiatius slain? then care come, cut in sunder my corps, then dole deliver me to the dreadful darts of death."[104]

Or rime and alliteration combined in the following lament:

"Did true Thisbe gore her gorgeous body with the same sword wherewith princely Pyramus had pricked himself to the heart; and are not my hands strong enough to do the like? Did Julietta die upon the corpse of her Romeo, and

[103] *Civile Conversation,* Preface to the Readers.
[104] *Petite Pallace,* ed. Gollancz, II, 47.

shall my body remain on earth, Sinnatus being buried? No, gentle death! come with thy direful dart, and pierce my painful heart, and with one death rid me of a thousand deaths at once."[105]

Apparently Pettie wrote with a mind open to any kind of verbal association, and puns, alliteration, rime, and antithesis are often combined in one sentence:

"Nay, there was never bloody tiger that did so terribly tear the little lamb, as this tyrant did furiously fare with fair Philomela."[106]

Sometimes, as in the following sentence, the rhythmical combinations approach the music and cadence of verse:

"And surely in my judgment he reaped the right reward of his doating desire, for there only grafts of grief must needs grow, where such raw conceit doth set and such rank consent doth sow."[107]

The effects here lie on the surface. More subtle are those cadences which are not emphasized by alliteration or rime, but which result from the balancing of clauses of approximately equal length, like the lines of verse, and in the marking of the ends of the clauses by means of stressed and unstressed syllables, like masculine and feminine endings, forming thus a kind of prose stanza. To bring out the structural character of the passage, in the following illustration division has been made into lines of the length of the separate clauses and the lines are grouped according to the cadences of their endings:

"Sinorix, having heard this angel thus amiably pronouncing these
words,

[105] *Petite Pallace,* ed. Gollancz, I, 42. [106] Ibid., I, 60.
[107] Ibid., I, 122.

Was so wrapt in admiration of her wisdom,
And ravished in contemplation of her beauty,
that though she had not enjoined him to silence,
yet had he not had a word to say:

and lest his looks might bewray his love,
and his countenance discover his case,

he secretly and suddenly withdrew himself into his chamber,
to study what face to set on the matter." [108]

This manner of writing is not employed only in purple patches, but is inherent in Pettie's feeling for prose style. If it were worth while, the analyst might go through his writings and classify the various rhetorical devices in an elaborate system. Whether or not Pettie did this himself, it seems certain that his style was worked out consciously and intentionally. He must have determined his schemes of sentence structure and of his use of ornament very much as the poet establishes beforehand a form for his verses. These pattern units he then employed repeatedly and consistently. He was more, therefore, than a facile rhapsodizer in prose, he was a careful artist. On the basis of the principles he set for himself, he succeeded remarkably well. His error lay in the supposition that distinction and elegance in prose were to be attained by confining the subtle and infinitely varied cadences of prose within the bonds of normalized types of rhythm. Perhaps as satisfactory a statement as can be made of the difference between prose and verse is that prose is expression which is primarily organic, that is in which the expression responds immediately to the sinuosities of the thought, and secondarily manipulated, whereas verse is expression which is primarily manipulated and only secondarily organic. Now it is the characteristic of Pettie's style that the manipulation

[108] *Petite Pallace,* ed. Gollancz, I, 23.

is so apparent and persistent that what he writes ceases to be normal prose. The defense of Pettie's devices of style might be made that they emphasize points, logical similars, and antitheses. But intelligible and adequate prose expression does not often require such artificial aids as formal parallelism and antithesis, rime and alliteration, and when these devices are continually employed, they cease to represent immediate adjustments of form to thought. They add something extraneous and manipulated to the communication, and logic becomes thus, like the meter of verse, an applied ornament of style. The element of surprise plays a less important part in Pettie's style than that of wonder.

Though Pettie was the first fully to formulate an artificial prose style, it was John Lyly who made this style fashionable. All the elements of Lyly's style and literary method are to be found in earlier English writers, and Lyly, in the words of Gabriel Harvey, merely "hatched the egges that his elder freendes laide."[109] But Lyly's works bulked larger than those of his predecessors, both in amount and in the interest which they aroused in contemporary readers. The style which Lyly employed in them was peculiarly appropriate to his own character. As a student at Oxford he distinguished himself more by superficial brilliance and impudence than by any solid attainment or earnestness of purpose. Early in his career he laid his plans for climbing in the world through the favor and influence of those in high place. In pursuance of these plans, he left Oxford in 1575, having received the degree of Master of Arts in that year, and betook himself to London, the magnet which naturally drew all ambitious spirits to it. In London, Lyly made his residence at the Savoy, where he was sure of meeting good company. Here also

[109] *Works,* ed. Grosart, II, 124.

he was near to Cecil House, the palace of Lord Burleigh, the rung in the ladder of advancement to which he was clinging. From the Savoy was issued in 1578 Lyly's first work, *Euphues, The Anatomy of Wit.* This was followed in 1580 by a continuation entitled *Euphues and his England.* Besides this long romance in two parts, Lyly's other important writings were court comedies, eight in number and mainly in prose. The first of these comedies was published in 1584, though several may have been written earlier, and the last appeared in 1601. They were plays written for children's acting companies connected with the Chapel Royal and St. Paul's Cathedral, and they brought Lyly into the most important connections with the court to which he was able to attain. In the year 1589 Lyly entered parliament and for a number of years he held a seat in that body. His persistence, however, never won for him any court appointment of significance, and he died in 1606 with his main ambition in life unsatisfied.[110]

Whatever preliminary studies Lyly may have made in the formation of his style seem to have been suppressed. His first publication, *Euphues, The Anatomy of Wit,* is not experimental, but on the contrary the completest exemplification among all Lyly's works of the principles in writing for which his name has been remembered. The book sprang into immediate popularity, and deservedly so, since it made skillful use of the three most effective literary interests of the times. These three interests were didactic romance, gentlemanly scholarship, and distinction in style.

[110] The dates of the many editions of Lyly's novel are an indication of its continued popularity. The *Anatomy of Wit* appeared in 1578 in one edition, in two editions in 1579, and in one in 1580. *Euphues and his England* appeared in three editions in 1580. The two parts united appeared in 1581, 1582, 1584, 1585, 1587, 1595?, 1597, 1605, 1606, 1607, 1609, 1613, 1617, 1623, 1630, 1631, 1636, then a break to 1716, 1718. See Esdaile, pp. 93-96.

As a didactic romance, *Euphues* had predecessors in English, which had fixed the feeling for the type. North's *Diall of Princes,* which Lyly knew and to some extent followed, was essentially a work of this sort. There is, to be sure, no plot in *The Diall of Princes,* but such characters as appear are conceived imaginatively, not historically, and the sentiments and ideas expressed were such as could readily be applied to the situations and complications of contemporary life. The courtly books of conduct, such as Castiglione's *Il Cortegiano,* accessible in Hoby's translation, Elyot's *Governor,* and even Becon's *Catechism,* were all in some degree preparatory to *Euphues.* From Ascham Lyly derived much, both in thought and in feeling for style. For the main part of the plot of *Euphues* he was indebted to Boccaccio's tale of *Tito and Gisippo,* a well-known and very popular story in Lyly's day.[111] And through Gascoigne, Whetstone, Pettie, and other sources, he was brought directly into connection with the Italian novelle.[112] Lyly was original, however, in combining character and plot more intimately with didacticism, scholarship, and philosophic reflection than his predecessors had done.

Euphues is a young Englishman, presented by Lyly under the guise of a young Athenian, who goes to Italy in the manner of cultivated young Englishmen of the day, and there meets with experiences which offer Lyly opportunity

[111] See Wolff, *Source of Euphues, The Anatomy of Wit,* in *Modern Philology,* VII, 577-585. In an article in *The Library,* X, 337-361 (Oct., 1909), Mr. J. D. Wilson connects Lyly's *Euphues* with the school drama *Acolastus* and with the prodigal son theme in general, but the connection is not nearly so close as this essay would make it out to be.

[112] John Grange's *Golden Aphroditis,* London, 1577, has many points of similarity to Lyly's *Euphues,* according to Long, *Kittredge Memorial Papers,* pp. 371-376. Direct dependence of Lyly upon Grange is not certain, however, since Euphuism was in the air when both were writing.

for the display of much patriotic feeling and sententious wisdom. A young gallant "of more wit then wealth and yet of more wealth then wisdome," Euphues arrives at Naples, "a place of more pleasure then profit and yet of more profit then pietie," and here he determines to make his abode. At Naples he meets with a wise old gentleman who is moved to pity at the sight of such innocence and inexperience in the haunts of luxury and iniquity. The old gentleman's counsels have little effect upon Euphues, however, for he is determined to surrender himself to all the experiences, good and bad, of the fascinating city. In this manner, Lyly prepares the way for that familiar method of his day of teaching virtue by exploiting evil. In the character of Euphues he declares his intention to present as well "the vanities of his love as the vertues of his lyfe," and his defense is that the fairest leopard is set down with his spots. Euphues becomes bosom friends with a young Neapolitan, named Philautus, but his principles are so far undermined that he soon after abuses the confidence of his friend and steals from him the affection of his lady love, Lucilla. A true Neapolitan, however, Lucilla soon transfers her love from Euphues to another aspirant, named Curio. His own treachery brought home to him in this way, Euphues begins to take account of himself. He makes friends again with Philautus, and addresses to him a general disquisition against love, entitled "A Cooling Carde for Philautus and all fond lovers." He sees also that he has done wrong in leaving his native land, "the nourse of wisdome," in order to dwell at Naples, "the nourisher of wantonnesse." He determines to return home and to give himself up to study and the practice of virtuous living. As a kind of appendage to the story of Euphues in Italy, Lyly then adds a discourse entitled "Euphues and his Ephoebus," in which he sets down his opinions with respect to the education of youth, and which he concludes with an address " to the Gentlemen schollers in Athens," a disguise under which he attacks the University of Oxford. Then follows a second discourse, " Euphues and Atheos," " concerning God," and this first part of Lyly's work closes with " Certeine Letters writ by Euphues to his friendes," after the manner of the epistles of Guevara.

The didacticism of *Euphues* is not assumed or external, but inherent in Lyly's conception of his subject. He is endeavoring here to present an anatomy of wit, to analyze the character of the gentleman of knowledge and influence as that character should be. Like Ascham's *Toxophilus* and *Scholemaster,* with which it frequently agrees in thought, Lyly's *Euphues* is, from one point of view, a tractate on education. He conceives of the true English gentleman as a man of learning who prefers the simpler customs of his native land to the vicious refinements and luxuries of the Continent, who leads a life of virtue in all his social relations, and who, finally, is free from any suspicion of the atheism which the sterner English moralists of the sixteenth century beheld with horror in papistical Italy. These ideas were not original with Lyly—in fact they are all contained in Ascham—nor is it probable that Lyly felt the significance of them very sincerely or deeply. To him they were little more than conventional literary materials, and he borrowed them from his predecessors in the same way that he borrowed his scholarship and his style.

A clear indication that Lyly was not fundamentally a serious moralist is to be seen in the ease with which the didactic program of *Euphues, The Anatomy of Wit,* was given up in the second part of the romance, *Euphues and his England.* In this change of emphasis, Lyly doubtless responded in part to the pressure which his readers brought to bear upon him. *Euphues* was favorably received less for its obvious morality than for its delicate and witty handling of sentimental and courtly situations. The characters also stood out with greater fullness and reality in *Euphues* than in any English writings since Chaucer's *Troilus and Criseyde*. Frankly seizing his opportunity, in *Euphues and his England* Lyly threw off the restraints of didacticism, and appealed primarily to his readers' interest in real life and in the playful and witty analysis of emotion and sentiment. At the opening of the book, Euphues and Philautus are on the point of arriving in England. Having mastered all science, all knowledge, all the mystery of philosophy and religion, Euphues continues for some time to dispense good counsel abundantly to his friend. Soon, however, a rupture takes place in the friendship of the two. Euphues goes into retirement, there to spend his time in study; and in spite of its title, for the greater part of the volume, the real hero of *Euphues and his England* is not Euphues but Philautus. His adventures form the central theme of the action, and in the characters of Philautus and the friends he makes in England, Lyly gives himself up unreservedly to the discussion of delicate questions of sentiment and social conduct. The plot is simple. Philautus is in love with Camilla, and the progress of his passion is displayed in confidential confessions, in lengthy monologues, in letters and all the other familiar machinery of the conventional love story. Camilla does not return his affection, however, and Philautus is compelled, after much debating back and forth with himself on the fine points of constancy and honor in love, to turn his attention to the Lady Flavia, one of Camilla's friends. In the end Philautus is happily contracted to the Lady Flavia and settles down in England, while as the reward of his virtue, Euphues sits "musing in the bottome of the Mountaine Silixsedra" in contemplation of his old griefs. In *Euphues, The Anatomy of Wit,* the actual narrative of the fortunes of Euphues, Philautus, and Lucilla occupies but a minor part of the whole book, the greater part being made up of letters and moral discourses added to the story. But in *Euphues and his England,* though there is no lack of moralizing and sententious didacticism in the course of the narrative, the story is not made to carry as its sequel a burden of didactic treatises. The matters here raised and discussed are such courtly topics as the proposition that beautiful women are ever merciful; or the question whether it be "convenient for women to haunt such places where Gentlemen are, or for men to have accesse to gentlewomen"; or the difficult choice whether it be better to have as a lover "one that shoulde be secreate though fickle then a blabbe though constant." [113]

But nowhere does Lyly's change of front in *Euphues and his England* appear more clearly than in the address prefixed to the volume "To the Ladies and Gentlewoemen of England." The future of the nation no longer rests heavily upon Lyly's heart. He has no intention of troubling ladies with such serious matters. If they read his book at all, let them read it at such times as they spend playing with their little dogs; and so far as the author is concerned, he will be content that their dogs lie in their laps, if *Euphues* be in their hands. Indeed he declares that "*Euphues* had rather lye shut in a Ladyes casket, then open in a Schollers studie." He commends it to the ladies not for its seriousness, but for its lightness. "There is nothing lyghter then a feather, yet is it sette a loft in a woemans hatte, nothing slighter then haire, yet is it most frisled in a Ladies head, so that I am in good hope, though their be nothing of lesse accounte than *Euphues,* yet he shall be marked with Ladies eyes and lyked sometimes in

[113] Arber's ed., p. 416.

their eares." [114] In his later writings Lyly never returned to the heavy moral rôle which he assumed in his *Anatomy of Wit*. *Euphues and his England* was his only other venture in the field of romance, but in the comedies which soon followed, the prevailing note is still one of lightness, fancy, and gallantry.

Scholarship as an element of distinction in writing was as zealously cultivated as didacticism by Lyly, and with much the same degree of sincerity. Again he agrees in theory with Ascham that learning should not be a thing apart, not the technical profession of a specialist, but rather the perfectly assimilated accomplishment of the complete gentleman. Its function is to lend dignity to character and it is to be utilized in such a way that the wisdom of the ancient world shall shed light upon all the thoughts and sentiments of the immediate present. Lyly's scholarship is therefore an applied scholarship. He has no interest in antiquarian or philological learning for its own sake, nor does he ever interrupt the course of his narrative merely to display his own stores of information. The cultivated gentleman, in his conception, may not neglect scholarship, nor may he be dominated by it. He may use it to heighten the charm, the interest, and the wisdom of his utterances, but he must never forget that the mere facts of ancient learning are dead bones unless they are vivified by modern

[114] *Works*, ed. Bond, II, 10. The similar dedication of Pettie's *Petite Pallace* has been noted above; and Barnabe Rich, in *Riche his Farewell to Militarie profession* (London, 1581, but written before 1579 in Ireland), dedicates his book "to the courteous Gentlewomen bothe of England and Ireland," declaring that it is "lesse painfull to followe a fiddle in a gentlewoman's chamber, then to marche after a drumme in the feeld" (p. 3). *Riche his Farewell* is a collection of eight love tales, the second of which was used by Shakspere in *Twelfth Night;* stylistically the stories show artificial traits, but not so markedly as in Pettie and Lyly. Cf. also Sidney, below, p. 366.

wit. This indeed was the attitude of many of the most serious-minded Englishmen of the sixteenth century, the difference between men like Cheke, Ascham, and Wilson, who all held this view, and Lyly consisting in their different conceptions of the kind of learning and wit which were thus to be brought into new and living combinations.

With Lyly, the materials of scholarship served mainly for purposes of illustration. The Renascence veneration for the classics had carried with it a respect for all the thoughts expressed and all the models of conduct contained in classical literature. A doubtful proposition needed only the support of a classical quotation or a classical example to secure its unquestioned acceptance, and even simple and obvious truths which seemingly would require nothing more than their mere statement, took on an added significance when the authority of Aristotle or Cicero or Quintilian could be quoted in support of them. There thus developed a conventional feeling for classical example as not essential to the content of the expression but as a kind of figurative ornament of style. And it is in this way that Lyly makes use of his learning. Compared with the great scholars of the earlier sixteenth century, with Erasmus, Scaliger or Budaeus, or even with Englishmen like Colet, More, and Cheke, Lyly's scholarly equipment seems slight and trivial. Considered, however, from the point of view of the aptness and persistency with which he has used every scrap of information he could rake together, Lyly displays remarkable ingenuity. There is scarcely a sentiment expressed which does not enjoy the authority of some classical parallel. The heroes of Homer and Vergil, the gods and goddesses of mythology, the various kings and captains of ancient history, the poets, scholars, the characters of story and fiction, in short any name that has about it the glow of classical association, all these Lyly invoked as continually and quite as aptly as contemporary theological writers cited passages from the scriptures.

Another kind of learning which Lyly used with equal persistence and for the same purposes, consists of the facts of natural science or pseudo-science. These facts range from the obvious phenomena of nature, which pass before everyone's eyes, to such impossible marvels as the "fugitive stone in Cyzico, which runneth away if it be not fastened to some post,"[115] or the serpent Amphisbena, "which having at ech ende a sting, hurteth both wayes."[116] This kind of natural history is often combined with classical allusion in a way which shows that in Lyly's mind they were of equal value:

"Thinke this with thy selfe, that the sweete songes of Calipso, were subtill snares to entice Ulysses, that the Crabbe then catcheth the Oyster, when the Sunne shineth, that Hiena, when she speaketh lyke a man deviseth most mischiefe, that women when they be most pleasaunt, pretend most trecherie."[117]

These marvels and pretended observations of nature, to a large extent ultimately derived from Pliny, are used with an abandon and recklessness which imply a complete lack of scientific interest on Lyly's part. Their value in his eyes consists entirely in their picturesqueness and in their aptness as illustrations and parallels. As in his treatment of examples from history, he has accepted and utilized the mere form of statement of the genuine scholar, who having ascertained a fact, is eager to preserve it for posterity. But with Lyly the manner becomes a shallow rhetorical artifice, and the stores of scholarly or supposedly scholarly fact having become by this time abundant and easily accessible,

[115] *Works,* ed. Bond, II, 221. [116] Ibid., II, 64.
[117] Ibid., I, 250.

it was an artifice which could be put into practice without the expense of much exertion. It satisfied merely a conventional feeling for scholarship, just as the didacticism of *Euphues* satisfied a conventional feeling for morality. Learning divorced from seriousness of purpose became, in Lyly's hands, the slave of his own wanton wit.

In structural technic, as in other respects, Lyly's style is less remarkable for its originality than for the skillful and consistent use of certain rhetorical devices which his predecessors had already successfully employed. These devices were all intended to heighten the effects of antithesis, of parallelism, and balance of statement which were the constant moulds in which his thought was cast. Lyly's sentences are sometimes long, but rarely involved and periodic. The unit ideas of which they are composed are definite and compact, and amplitude of rhythm and phrasing are secured by combining similar or antithetic ideas in groups which are held together mainly by the structural symmetry of the separate parts of the combination. In the shorter sentences the effect produced is that of an aphoristic and epigrammatic kind of writing; in the longer sentences, as has been pointed out in connection with Pettie, the effect is that of an approximately equivalent set of sentence clauses or members not unlike the stanzaic structure of verse. And the total impression is always one of neatness and precision of statement, of pointedness often carried beyond the limits of logical necessity. Merely verbal devices of style, such as alliteration, assonance, rime, and punning are employed sometimes for their own sakes, more often for the purpose of emphasizing structural antithesis or parallelism. All these various features of Lyly's method in writing have been frequently studied and have been classified under the heads of an elaborate rhetorical terminology. The artificial character of the style lends itself readily to such analytic treatment, for the effects aimed at are so apparent and unmistakable that formal analysis is capable of laying bare their essential qualities, as it could not do with a more sutble style. The obviousness of Lyly's artifices and the persistency with which he employed them are, as one would expect, the sources of the main defects of his writing. No matter how skillfully it is managed, and in this respect one must acknowledge that Lyly surpasses any of his imitators or predecessors, one tires of continual alliterative balance and antithesis, of a manner of writing that easily detaches itself from the matter. Ingenuity and cleverness cannot lend dignity or abiding charm to shallow artifice. The mechanism of Lyly's style was clearly thought out, but his form tends to take on the rigidity of machinery. The characteristic Euphuistic sentence is sounded as a keynote at the opening of *Euphues,* and thereafter no surprises greet the ear except in the ingenuity with which this type sentence is amplified and embroidered:

"There dwelt in Athens a young gentleman of great patrimonie, and of so comely a personage, that it was doubted whether he were more bound to Nature for the liniaments of his person, or to fortune for the encrease of his possessions."

The machinery of this sentence permits of a number of obvious ornaments, of which the one most persistently applied is alliteration. This figure is frequently employed in patterns, ranging from simple pairs, as in

"O ye gods, have ye ordayned for everye maladye a medicine, for every sore a salve, for every payne a plaister, leving only love remedilesse?" [118]

to such ingenious transverse or crossed combination, as in the two following sentences:

[118] *Works,* ed. Bond, I, 208.

"Heere, yea, heere Euphues, maiste thou see not the *c*arved *v*isarde of a *l*ewde *w*oman, but the in*c*arnate *v*isage of a *l*ascivious *w*anton, not the *s*haddowe of *l*ove, but the *s*ubstance of *l*ust." [119]

"I leave to *n*ame thy *s*innes, which no *S*yphers can *n*umber." [120]

Assonance, rime, verbal repetition, and puns all combine in Lyly's skillful practice to the same general end, to produce an English style "like Arras, full of devise which was Broade-cloth, full of workmanshippe." [121]

It should be said, however, that Lyly himself outgrew to some extent the style by which his name is remembered. This style is most fully and most extravagantly exemplified in the narrative part of *Euphues, The Anatomy of Wit,* his first book. The story there recounted is a novella after the fashion of the tales contained in Pettie's *Petite Pallace,* by which a tradition of fine writing in narrative had become established. In the didactic and moral treatises which are appended to this story, Euphuistic traits of style are still present, but less abundantly and obtrusively. So also in *Euphues and his England* one finds the formulas of the ingenious style less constantly applied. By practice Lyly's manner of writing became less mechanical, and thus the virtues of his style became more manifest. For after all is said any disposition of the style of Lyly, and of this type of courtly writing in general, without a word of commendation would be unfair and historically one-sided. It is true that there is always too much "workmanshippe" in it, but it is also true that certain elements of Euphuistic writing were valuable contributions to the development of English style. The main defects of earlier prose and of popular

[119] *Works,* ed. Bond, I, 189.
[120] Ibid., II, 89.
[121] Prologue to *Midas, Works,* ed. Bond, III, 115.

prose writing were formlessness, or when form was consciously cultivated, heaviness. The courtly writers of the school of Lyly developed point and precision, lightness and melody. They broke up the long sentence into manageable fragments and made their writing easy without making it colloquial. When his artifices are not too apparent, as often in the second part of the story of Euphues and in the comedies which followed, Lyly's phrasing has a limpid charm altogether admirable. The following passage, on the theme that there is " no greater enchauntment in love then temperaunce, wisdome, beautie & chastitie," strikes a happy balance between art and simplicity:

" Fond therefore is the opinion of those that thinke the minde to be tyed to Magick, and the practise of those filthy, that seeke those meanes.

Love dwelleth in the minde, in the will, and in the hearts, which neyther Coniurer canne alter nor Phisicke. For as credible it is, that *Cupid* shooteth his Arowe and hytteth the heart, as that hearbes have the force to bewitch the heart, onelye this difference there is, that the one was a fiction of poetrie, the other of superstition. The will is placed in the soule, and who canne enter there, but hee that created the soule?

No no Gentle-men what-soever you have heard touching this, beleeve nothing: for they in myne opinion which imagine that the mynde is eyther by incantation or excantation to bee ruled, are as far from trueth, as the East from the West, and as neere impietie against God, as they are to shame among men, and so contrary is it to the profession of a Christian, as *Paganisme.*" [122]

This becomes the prevailing style in the comedies, and though the artifices of Lyly's ingenious manner are by no means forgotten, they take their proper place as occasional

[122] *Works,* ed. Bond, II, 118.

ornaments. "Didst thou never see Cupid?" asks Ceres in *Loves Metamorphoses,* to which Nisa answers:

"No: but I have heard him described at the full, and, as I imagined, foolishly. First, that he should bee a god blind and naked, with wings, with bowe, with arrowes, with firebrands; swimming sometimes in the Sea, & playing sometimes on the shore; with many other devices, which the Painters, being the Poets Apes, have taken as great paines to shaddow, as they to lie. Can I thinke that gods that commaund all things, would goe naked? What should he doe with wings that knowes not where to flie? Or what with arrowes, that sees not how to ayme? The heart is a narrow marke to hit, and rather requireth Argus eyes to take level, then a blind boy to shoote at random. If he were fire, the Sea would quench those coles, or the flame turne him into cinders." [123]

Lyly's stylistic mannerisms were of a kind both to encourage and to prevent imitation. As a readily comprehensible system they offered a complete model for the writer who conceived artistic expression to rest upon the application of formulated rules of composition. For here were rules both for structure and for ornament, here was a style which possessed all the qualities of "bravery" and distinction from the commonplace, and which at the same time followed a method easily observed and acquired. On the other hand, so perfectly had Lyly realized all the possibilities of his method, that he left little for his followers to do except merely to imitate. To Euphuize was easy, but when the model could not be surpassed, was not greatly creditable. The time was not yet come when English courtly writers could boldly reject the excesses of Lyly's style and make those merits of clearness, precision, and melody which it abundantly possessed, the foundation and

[123] *Works,* ed. Bond, III, 307-308.

principle of their writing. The vogue of Euphuism as a fashion among the wits was consequently short. Obvious traces of its influence are to be seen upon many writers of the last two decades of the century, upon Greene, Nashe, Lodge, and others,[124] but no writers were so persistently and consistently Euphuistic as Lyly. Its influence was wide rather than lasting. Pulpit discourse was not unaffected by it.[125] The style also made its way down to the 'fine writing' intended for the less cultivated classes, as in Deloney's novels of citizen life. It seems even to have affected speech, and to "Parley Euphuesime" [126] for a time was a necessary accomplishment in polite circles. The affectations of Euphuism soon suggested themselves as fit material for the satirist and parodist, and it is not surprising to see Shakspere treat with ridicule the mannerisms of a style from the better qualities of which he gained much.[127]

IV

To Sidney and to his following more than to any other of Lyly's contemporaries, is to be assigned the credit of checking fashionable imitations of Euphuism, or at least

[124] But Nashe, writing in 1592, already declares a long-standing emancipation from Euphuism: "*Euphues* I readd when I was a little ape in Cambridge, and then I thought it was *Ipse ille;* it may be excellent good still for ought I know, for I lookt not on it this ten yeare: but to imitate it I abhorre . . . ," *Eliz. Crit. Essays,* II, 243.

[125] See the sermons of Aylmer, Bishop of London, as quoted in Strype, *Life of Bishop Aylmer,* pp. 180-181, p. 182.

[126] *Six Court Comedies,* ed. Blount (1632), quoted by Feuillerat, *John Lyly,* p. 95.

[127] A parody of Euphuism occurs in 1 *Henry IV,* II, 4, 438 ff. For other contemporary criticisms of Euphuism, see Lyly, *Works,* ed. Bond, I, 133; and for a just estimate of the influence of Lyly upon Shakspere, see Bond, I, 150-154.

of dividing the current of it. A section of Sidney's *Apologie for Poetrie* (written about 1583, printed first in 1595) criticised severely those writers who disguise "honny-flowing Matron Eloquence" in a "painted affectation,"[128] sometimes with far-fetched words, sometimes "with coursing of a Letter, as if they were bound to followe the method of a Dictionary," and in general with the over-elaboration of ornament, "like those Indians, not content to weare eare-rings at the fit and naturall place of the eares, but they will thrust Jewels through their nose and lippes, because they will be sure to be fine." Lyly's similes from natural history are also ridiculed by Sidney, "all stories of Beasts, Foules, and Fishes"; and he adds the sound criticism that these similes are usually quite beside the point, "rather over-swaying the memory from the purpose whereto they were applyed then any whit informing the judgement, already eyther satisfied, or by similitudes not to be satisfied." Such writers, says Sidney, are dancing to their own music, and are "noted by the audience more careful to speake curiously then to speake truly." A counter-irritant to Euphuism more effective than these critical precepts, however, was Sidney's own example in providing in his *Arcadia* the model of a new kind of courtly style which soon found as enthusiastic imitators as Euphuism.

Sidney's two important works were his *Apologie for Poetrie,* also called *The Defence of Poesie,* and the book described on the title-page of the first edition as *The Countesse of Pembrokes Arcadia, written by Sir Philippe Sidnei.* Neither of these works was printed during Sidney's life, but both were circulated in manuscript among Sidney's friends, probably from the time of their composition. Though the

[128] Gregory Smith, *Eliz. Crit. Essays,* I, 202; for Harvey's opinions of Lyly, see ibid., II, 268 ff.

Apologie for Poetrie was in the first intention a defense of poetry called forth by Puritan attacks upon poetry and the drama, and perhaps specifically by Stephen Gosson's *Schoole of Abuse* (1579), its tone is not narrowly controversial, and Sidney took the occasion to present in a broadly critical and philosophic way his theories of the various kinds of literary composition. Particularly interesting with respect to English prose, is Sidney's theory that verse is merely an accidental accompaniment of poetry. Most poets, as he notes, "have apparelled their poeticall inventions in that numbrous kinde of writing which is called verse";[129] but the verse, according to Sidney, is to be regarded merely as apparel, "verse being but an ornament and no cause to Poetry." Certain writings of Xenophon and Heliodorus are then cited as examples of genuine poems, written nevertheless in prose. These are mentioned, says Sidney, "to shew that it is not riming and versing that maketh a Poet, no more than a long gowne maketh an Advocate, who though he pleaded in armor should be an Advocate and no Souldier." Positively Sidney's definition of poetry is given, briefly but broadly, as "that fayning notable images of vertues, vices, or what els, with that delightfull teaching, which must be the right describing note to know a Poet by."[130] It is the function of poetry "to lead and draw us to as high a perfection as our degenerate soules, made worse by theyr clayey lodgings, can be capable of." It should be noted that this definition of poetry provides no place for prose-poetry, as that term is often understood. Sidney does not advocate the mixing of the conventions of verse with those of prose; neither does he state that mere ornament and apparel can raise prose to the level of poetry. Whether the form be prose or verse, the essen-

[129] Gregory Smith, *Eliz. Crit. Essays,* I, 159.
[130] Ibid., p. 160.

tial quality of poetry is to be found in the dignity, the richness, and delightfulness of the ideas and images which are expressed. If, therefore, Sidney regarded his prose *Arcadia* as a poem, he did so not because of the rhetorical richness or ingenuity of the style, but because the subject seemed to him essentially poetical and therefore appropriate to be treated ornamentally.

The *Apologie for Poetry* not being a poetical theme, Sidney did not endeavor to treat it ornamentally or rhetorically. Occasional passages strike one as perhaps unconscious echoes of Euphuism, but on the whole in the *Apologie* Sidney wrote in a familiar and unmannered, yet dignified style. The easy tone of it suggests the dialogues of Plato, though the cadences are often Ciceronian. The essay opens with the conventional Renascence anecdote, and the discussion continues in the first person with a pleasant epistolary flavor that never descends to the level of the merely colloquial. Sidney's scholarship is evident in every paragraph, but he is as careful to avoid pedantic display of learning as he is to avoid affectation of style. According to modern taste the *Apologie* admirably realizes the ideal of gravity, charm, and distinction which the courtly authors of the time were so generally striving to attain. One is surprised that Sidney, having written so well here, should write so badly in the *Arcadia.* But the prose style that seemed adequate for a critical essay, perhaps seemed inadequate to Sidney for a work of a higher and imaginative kind. Though he regarded the essence of poetry as inherent in the subject, with other Elizabethan stylists he shared the opinion that an elevated theme, like that of the *Arcadia,* called for a rhetorical and artful style. Time has not altogether justified Sidney in this opinion, and his significance in the development of English prose would have been vastly increased if he had written his most important work with the sound feeling for prose style which he exhibited in the *Apologie*.

The exact date at which Sidney began the composition of his *Arcadia* cannot be determined, but it is certain that by the year 1580 he had completed a romance of this title, divided into five books and with eclogues between the various books. This work was not published, though it was widely circulated in manuscript. Later Sidney began a revision and enlargement of this "Old Arcadia," as it has been called,[131] which was not completed at the time of his death in 1586. In its incomplete form, this second revision of the *Arcadia* was published in 1590; though unfinished, even in its fragmentary state it is a long book and, stylistically at least, it adequately represents everything Sidney was endeavoring to do in the *Arcadia*. Three years later, with the approval of the Countess of Pembroke, a second edition of the unfinished *Arcadia* appeared containing large additions from the "Old Arcadia," and this form of the work has been frequently reprinted.[132]

According to Sidney's own statement, he did not write the *Arcadia* for publication, and one of his last requests was that the manuscript should be destroyed. In a brief letter to his sister, the Countess of Pembroke, which appears in the first printed version of the work, he reminds her that

[131] See Mr. Bertram Dobell's *New Light upon Sir Philip Sidney's "Arcadia,"* in the *Quarterly Review*, July, 1909, pp. 74-100. Mr. Dobell gives a full analysis of the Old Arcadia, which is simpler both in action and in style than the later published versions. But of course it was not through the Old Arcadia, but through the later versions that the influence of the romance was exerted. See also Wolff, *Greek Romances in Elizabethan Fiction*, pp. 345 ff., pp. 370 ff.

[132] The edition of 1590 has been reproduced in photographic facsimile by Sommer (London, 1891). Three manuscript copies of the "Old Arcadia" have been discovered, but none has been published. *The Countesse of Pembrokes Arcadia*, ed. Feuillerat, Cambridge, 1912, is an excellent edition of the text of 1590

it was intended only for her eyes, not for those of severer judges. He reminds her also, in the conventional vein, of the manner in which it was written, "being done in loose sheetes of paper, most of it in your presence, the rest, by sheetes, sent unto you as fast as they were done." Being but a trifle, "and that triflinglie handled," Sidney hopes that his sister will keep it to herself, or give it only to friends "who will weigh errors in the ballaunce of good will." Its chief safety "shalbe the not walking abroad." "Read it then," the letter concludes, "at your idle tymes, and the follyes your good judgement wil finde in it, blame not, but laugh at. And so, looking for no better stuffe then, as in an Haberdashers shoppe, glasses, or feathers, you will continue to love the writer, who doth exceedinglie love you; and most hartelie praies you may long live, to be a principall ornament to the familie of the Sidneis." This hardly reads like a serious apology.

Though Sidney did not specifically avow any moral purpose in the composition of the *Arcadia,* one can scarcely doubt that it was intended to be more than light pastime for idle moments, and more than a mere echo of traditional chivalric romance. Of the two adjectives, vain and amatorious, which Milton applied to the work,[133] the second is descriptive, for the story is mainly one of love adventure. As to its vanity, there is room for difference of opinion. According to Sidney's friend, Fulke Greville, Sidney's purpose in the *Arcadia* was to provide "not vanishing pleasure alone, but morall images and examples—as directing threds—to guide every man through the confused labyrinth of his own desires and life." [134] At another place he declares that "in all these creatures of his making," Sidney strove to turn "the barren philosophy precepts into pregnant

[133] *Prose Works,* ed. Symmons, II, 408.
[134] Greville, *Works,* ed. Grosart, IV, 222.

images of life" so that men might see, as in a glass, "how to set a good countenance upon all the discountenance of adversitie and a stay upon the exorbitant smilings of Chance."[135] Another of Sidney's friends, Gabriel Harvey, not inadequately describes the *Arcadia* as "a gallant Legendary, full of pleasurable accidents, and proffitable discourses; for three thinges especially very notable; for amorous Courting (he [i.e. Sidney] was young in yeeres;) for sage counselling, (he was ripe in judgement;) and for valorous fighting, (his sovraine profession was Armes:) and delightfull pastime by way of Pastorall exercises may passe for the fourth."[136] Throughout the *Apologie* Sidney had made much of the poet as teacher, and it is certain that theoretically at least he would not have regarded narrative and characterization as sufficiently important in themselves to constitute a great poetic theme. It seems not untrue therefore to Sidney's probable intention if the *Arcadia* is regarded as a courtly didactic romance, intended to interest the same general public as the one to which Lyly made his appeal.

In his choice of a chivalric and romantic theme for his *Arcadia,* Sidney may have been influenced by several considerations. He may have held opinions like those of Ascham and other moralists, that it was time for the English to set their faces against the tragical trifles and tales of wanton love which his immediate predecessors had borrowed so abundantly from Continental sources. These stories, both because of their brevity and their subject-matter, must have seemed to Sidney not to measure up to the dignity of poetic themes. On the other hand one may feel some surprise that he did not seek for his materials in classical sources, in the stories of Troy or Thebes. The

[135] Greville, *Works,* ed. Grosart, IV, 19.
[136] Harvey, *Works,* ed. Grosart, II, 100.

setting of the *Arcadia,* so far as names and machinery are concerned, is Greek, but the spirit of it is entirely chivalric and medieval. The story has, to be sure, little connection with the real world at any time, though it has as much reality as the *Fairy Queen,* in which Spenser, a few years later, was to combine didactic romance with the chivalric traditions of King Arthur. In his treatment of his chivalric material, Sidney may also have had in mind the criticism of Du Bellay,[137] who reprehended the retelling of romances merely for the entertainment of ladies. Du Bellay would have these romances treated seriously and learnedly, and he advises the writers of romances to employ their eloquence upon the ancient fragmentary histories and traditions of the French people, in order that out of them they might construct the complete body of a fair history, mingling therewith fair orations and addresses after the fashion of Thucydides, Sallust, and other good authors. With the exception that his story was not drawn from national chronicles, Sidney followed the method recommended by Du Bellay. He did attempt to construct the complete body of a fair history, to write, according to his own conception, a sustained and complex 'poem,' and he inserted in the course of his narrative, many orations, speeches, and ornaments of style to enliven it.

The plot of the *Arcadia* is extremely complicated, not in its main structure, but through the interpolation of numerous long episodes, narrations, and digressions. The earliest form of the story in the Old Arcadia is relatively simple and direct, but in the revision Sidney exerted himself to secure epic fullness and variety. The story opens *in medias res.* Two young princes, Pyrocles and Musidorus, have been separated by shipwreck on a voyage the purpose of

[137] *Defence et Illustration de la langue francoyse,* ed. Chamard, pp. 236-239.

which is explained later. Their various wanderings and wonderful feats of valor are followed separately until both arrive at the court of Basilius, king of Arcadia. For reasons which are withheld from the reader's curiosity, Basilius is living in rustic but luxurious seclusion in a region where " falls not hail or rain or any snow "—the days there are like one long summer's afternoon. To this happy retreat Pyrocles gains admission in the disguise of a woman and under the name of Zelmane, Musidorus as a shepherd's servant, under the name of Dorus. Basilius has two daughters, Philoclea and Pamela, the objects of the courtly, and in the end, successful wooing of Pyrocles and Musidorus. Complications are introduced by the passion of Basilius for Zelmane, whom he takes to be a woman, and for the equally mad infatuation of his queen, Gynecia, with the same person, whom she recognizes, in spite of his disguise, to be a man. In the end, the reader learns that Basilius has retired to the pastoral seclusion of his retreat in Arcadia in order to avoid the fulfillment of an oracle, which nevertheless, in the completed forms of the story, is fulfilled in a sufficiently unexpected manner. The two daughters are happily married to their faithful lovers, Basilius and Gynecia come to their senses, and the story ends happily.

This bare sketch can give no indication of the wealth of detail and characterization with which the main story is enriched and often encumbered. In this " gallant legendary " there are over one hundred characters who are not merely figures in the action, but are clearly individualized. This art of character portrayal Sidney seems to have learned from the Greek romance of Achilles Tatius, his large and intricate plot on the other hand being more in the manner of Heliodorus. Even insignificant characters are often analyzed in much greater detail than is required by their place in the action. This psychological element in the treatment of character helps, however, to give to the *Arcadia* that quality of seriousness and importance with which it impressed contemporary readers. The direct didacticism of the conventional Elizabethan romantic narrative is not found in the *Arcadia.* Sidney was apparently not concerned to present a precise code of conduct for daily living, but rather types of human character and action on an epic scale for the philosophic contemplation of those whose spirits moved in ample sweeps. His characters range from rude clowns and gentle shepherds to rebellious princes and models of all the knightly virtues. The subject of love is presented from an astonishing variety of points of view, including morbid, exaggerated, and evil passion as well as the simpler and more natural aspects of romantic love. Propriety or decorum in conduct is always part of the indirect teaching of the story, and the few passages of the narrative intended to be humorous usually turn upon situations in which a humble character ventures to aspire to the courtly privileges of love-making and fighting. The knightly virtues of valor, loyalty, and devotion are fully illustrated, and courtly accomplishments are exemplified in combats, debates, letters, poems, and conversations. The sentiments are often spun very fine, but not infrequently the reader is rewarded by coming upon admirably-phrased precepts of wisdom and elevated conduct.

The *Arcadia* had its English as well as its foreign antecedents. Interest in romantic narrative had never died out since the time of its introduction into England in the form of Middle English translations from the French. The early printers, Caxton, Wynkyn de Worde, and Copland, found much of the material with which to feed their presses in late prose versions of the earlier metrical romances. All three, for example, published editions of *The Four Sons of*

Aymon and of Malory's *Morte Darthur.* Later translations helped to keep alive the interest in chivalric material. Lord Berners' *Boke of Duke Huon of Burdeux* and *The History of the most noble and valyaunt Knight, Artheur of Lytell Brytaine* were both translated from French, his *Castell of Love* from Spanish. *The XI Bookes of the Golden Asse* of Apuleius, translated by William Adlington, appeared in 1566, and three later editions in the same century testify to the favor with which Sidney's generation regarded this enchanting medley of romance and satire. Parts of the *Amadis of Gaul* appeared in an English dress in 1567-1568, though Anthony Munday's fuller translations were not published until after Sidney had written his *Arcadia.* James Sanford published in 1567 *The Amorous and Tragicall Tales of Plutarch. Wherevnto is annexed the Hystorie of Cariclea and Theogenes and the sayings of the Greeke Philosophers,* being passages from Plutarch's *Moralia* and Heliodorus' *Ethiopica.* In 1569 appeared Thomas Underdowne's version of Heliodorus under the title *An Æthiopian Historie.*[138] Another favorite story which may, however, as easily be grouped with the Italian novels as with the romances of the period, was the *Eurialus and Lucresia* of Aeneas Sylvius, which had been printed in an early English version by van Doesborgh at Antwerp, and again in 1560, under the title *The goodly History of the moste noble and beautyful Ladye Lucres of Scene in Tuskan & of her louer Eurialus very pleasaunt and delectable vnto the reder.*[139] Some of these translations combined pleasure with the

[138] Other editions followed in 1577, 1587, 1605, 1606, 1622, and 1627.

[139] Four editions of this tale appeared between 1560 and 1570, another in 1596, and later ones. The story was sufficiently spicy to interest Pepys, who owned a copy of an edition of 1567, reprinted in *The Hystorie of the Moste Noble Knight Plasidas and other rare pieces,* Roxburghe Club, 1873.

profit of acquiring foreign tongues, as in the *Histoire de Aurelio et Isabelle* of Juan de Flores, "nyeuly translatede In foure langagies, Frenche, Italien, Spanishe and Inglishe," in 1566. James Sanford's *Garden of Pleasure* (1573), consisting of "most pleasante Tales, worthy deedes and witty sayings of noble Princes & learned Philosophers" translated from Guicciardini, also contained "divers Verses and Sentences in Italian, with the Englishe to the same, for the benefit of students in both tongs." *The Pretie and wittie Historie of Arnalt and Lucenda* (1575) likewise contains Italian and English "set foorth for the learner of th' Italian tong" by Claudius Hollyband.[140]

Of the works of Boccaccio, the *Filocolo* alone appeared in English before Sidney's *Arcadia*.[141] The *Amorous Fiametta,* translated by Bartholomew Young, was not published until 1587, and the *Decameron* not until the first quarter of the next century. After the *Arcadia* had strengthened the taste for romance appeared the various translations of Anthony Munday, Emanuel Forde, and many others. Bartholomew Young added to his *Amorous Fiametta* a translation of Montemayor's *Diana* in 1598. A translation of the *Daphnis and Chloe* of Longus, made from the French of Amyot by Angel Day, was published in 1587. The *Clitophon and Leucippe* of Achilles Tatius appeared first in English in William Burton's translation (1597), but earlier French, Italian, and Latin versions of the tale were accessible to Sidney, who was certainly familiar with it.

Among the immediate sources from which Sidney drew most freely, for general tone, for incident, and even for the

[140] Originally written in Spanish by Diego de San Pedro; see Menendez y Pelayo, *Origenes de la Novela,* I, cccxvii. On Juan de Flores, see ibid., pp. cccxxxvii ff.

[141] Editions of the *Filocolo* in English appeared in 1566, 1567, 1571, and 1587.

details of expression, the most important were chivalric romances like *Amadis of Gaul,* the pastoral novel, *Arcadia,* of Sanazzaro, the *Diana Enamorada* of Sanazzaro's imitator, Jorge de Montemayor, and above all the *Aethiopica* of Heliodorus and the *Clitophon and Leucippe* of Achilles Tatius.[142] The most important single source for the *Arcadia* seems to have been the *Aethiopica* of Heliodorus, and though one may hesitate to go so far as to say that Sidney "has deliberately written Greek Romance in English,"[143] it is certain that upon the basis of the Greek romances he developed his theme in order to give it the complexity and magnitude of epic action.

The style of the *Arcadia* was carefully chosen to fit the subject. Sidney's purpose being to write a sustained and elevated narrative, one also in which the events moved with the freedom and often the apparent confusion of the complications of life, he appropriately took as the basis of his style a long and complicated sentence structure. The neat epigrammatic and antithetic style of Lyly he knew and occasionally employed, but it was not made the fundamental style of the *Arcadia.* Nor is Sidney's characteristic sentence the formally constructed period of the Ciceronian tradition. Perhaps it can best be described as an episodic sentence structure, loose but not chaotic. The elements of which his thought was composed were not broken up into separate logical points, but groups of detail are presented in the interwoven, often parenthetic, and yet progressive pattern of natural thinking in which a whole action is held in solution. The following is typical:

[142] For a detailed study of Sidney's borrowings from Greek romance, see Wolff, *Greek Romances in Elizabethan Fiction,* pp. 308-366.

[143] Wolff, ibid., p. 365.

"But then, Demagoras assuring himselfe, that now Parthenia was her owne, she would never be his, and receiving as much by her owne determinate answere, not more desiring his owne happines, then envying Argalus, whom he saw with narrow eyes, even ready to enjoy the perfection of his desires; strengthning his conceite with all the mischievous counsels which disdayned love, and envious pride could geve unto him; the wicked wretch (taking a time that Argalus was gone to his countrie, to fetch some of his principall frendes to honour the marriage, which Parthenia had most joyfully consented unto,) the wicked Demagoras (I say) desiring to speake with her, with unmercifull force, (her weake armes in vaine resisting) rubd all over her face a most horrible poyson: the effect whereof was such, that never leaper lookt more ugly then she did: which done, having his men and horses ready, departed away in spite of her servants, as redy to revenge as they could be, in such an unexpected mischiefe." [144]

This synthetic sentence structure lends to Sidney's narrative a largeness of movement which he doubtless deliberately cultivated as appropriate to the scale on which the whole work was planned. As a compromise between a severely architectural and learned sentence and the dapper, often mechanical and narrowly formal Euphuistic style, Sidney's sentence has much to recommend it. Natural without being naïve, it reads easily and is capable of a great variety of cadences. The parentheses and participles which Sidney employs so freely, and the linking of clause to clause in loose sequence, may seem to the modern reader to imply a disregard of clear and orderly thinking on Sidney's part, as though he omitted to take the trouble to digest his ideas before he set them down. But this criticism would be unfair to Sidney. The modern feeling for sentence structure is highly analytic; and though Sidney would have placed himself more immediately in the line of de-

[144] *Arcadia* (1590), p. 21^b.

velopment of English prose if he had completed the tendencies in this direction already begun by Pettie and Lyly, his own ideal of a style which was ample and dignified, yet not pedantically formal, was one which he could have evolved only after conscientious and careful reflection. In the *Apologie* Sidney employed a simpler sentence structure, but for the high style of a great work which was to combine scholarly dignity with the power of pleasing the courtly, cultivated reader, he was in accord with the common opinion of his age in thinking that something more was required. His faults are faults of intention, not of neglect.

The long episodic sentence, varying in the degree of its complexity, is the ground tone of Sidney's style, and upon this somewhat elaborate structural framework he has applied many minor ornaments of expression. Among the most notable are his fine and ingenious forms of phrasing. The heroines, for example, when they wish to retire for the night do not simply undress, but impoverish their clothes to enrich their bed. And the youth Kalander recovers from a sickness so rapidly, "that in six weekes the excellencie of his returned beautie was a credible embassadour of his health."[145] A lady enters an arbor "whose branches so lovingly interlaced one the other, that it could resist the strongest violence of eye-sight."[146] This lady, who turns out to be one of the heroes of the story disguised as an Amazon, sings a song and is discovered by his friend, Musidorus, who calls for explanations:

"So that Pyrocles (who had as much shame as Musidorus had sorrow) rising to him, would have formed substantiall excuse; but his insinuation being of blushinge, and his division of sighes, his whole oration stood upon a short narration, what was the causer of this Metamorphosis."[147]

[145] *Arcadia*, p. 9. [146] P. 50^{b}. [147] P. 51^{b}.

Conceits of this sort sometimes run through whole passages, as in the following:

"O my Philoclea, is hee a person to write these words? and are these words lightly to be regarded? But if you had seene, when with trembling hand he had delivered it [a letter], how hee went away, as if he had beene but the coffin that carried himselfe to his sepulcher. Two times I must confesse I was about to take curtesie into mine eyes; but both times the former resolution stopt the entrie of it: so that he departed without obtaining any further kindnesse. But he was no sooner out of the doore, but that I looked to the doore kindly; and truely the feare of him ever since hath put me into such perplexitie, as now you found me. Ah my Pamela (said Philoclea) leave sorrow. The river of your teares will soone loose his fountaine; it is in your hand as well to stitch up his life againe, as it was before to rent it. And so (though with self-grieved mind) she comforted her sister, till sleepe came to bath himself in Pamelaes faire weeping eyes." [148]

Somewhat similar is that form of poetic paraphrase recommended by Du Bellay under the name of Antonomasia,[149] which consists in naming objects or stating actions not directly but by circumlocutions, as when dusk is described as "about the time that the candle begins to inherit the Suns office," [150] or dawn as the time when "the morning did strow roses and violets in the heavenly floore against the comming of the Sun." [151] The trees are said to form a pleasant refuge from "the cholericke looke of Phoebus," [152] and when the Arcadians are about to go to sleep, they "recommend themselves to the elder brother of death." [153] Though set descriptive passages of great

[148] Pp. 124ᵃ-124ᵇ.
[149] *Defence,* ed. Chamard, p. 285.
[150] P. 40ᵇ.
[151] P. 7ᵃ.
[152] P. 81ᵃ.
[153] P. 97ᵇ.

beauty occur throughout the *Arcadia,* they are seldom entirely free from such conscious artifices of a high poetic style. Often poetic elaboration takes the form of that sentimental treatment of inanimate objects which Ruskin called the pathetic fallacy. A well-known instance is that where the Lady Pamela is "woorking uppon a purse certaine Roses and Lillies" with her needle, "which with so prety a maner made his careers to and fro through the cloth, as if the needle it selfe would have bene loth to have gone fromward such a mistres, but that it hoped to return thenceward very quickly againe: the cloth loking with many eies upon her, and lovingly embracing the wounds she gave it: the sheares also were at hand to behead the silke that was growne to short."[154] The description does not stop here, but continues with an elaboration of the conceit through all its possibilities.

Merely verbal devices are also extensively employed in the interest of the poetic style. Poetic compounds of a kind prescribed by Renascence theorists and employed by many Elizabethan poets, frequently occur, such as "day-shining stars"; "hony-flowing speach";[155] "sun-stayning excellencie";[156] "wrong-caused sorrow";[157] "an unthought-on songe"; "blame-worthinesse";[158] "eye-ravished lover."[159] The vocabulary otherwise is in general not oppressively learned, though it is always elevated, and, as will be evident from the illustrations already quoted, sometimes hyper-distinguished. But occasionally Sidney also employs plain native words, for example, *hurtlessly, foregoers,* meaning "ancestors," and similar terms in a way which shows that he shared, to some extent at least, Spenser's respect for the native resources of the language.

[154] P. 278ª.
[155] P. 2ᵇ.
[156] P. 3.
[157] P. 7.
[158] P. 17ᵇ.
[159] P. 22.

But such words are not numerous and Sidney never cultivates a rustic or archaic simplicity.[160]

Sidney's other tricks of style, though not so persistently employed as Lyly's, are in general of the same kind. Occasionally sentences occur which might have been taken bodily from *Euphues,* as for example:

"and so growes that to be the last excuse of his fault which seemed to have been the first foundation of his faith"; [161]

"he had yielded to seeke the recovery of health, onely for that he might the sooner go seeke the deliverie of Pyrocles"; [162]

"we thought it lesse evil to spare a foe then spoyle a friend"; [163]

"And so, I that waited here to do you service, have now my self most need of succor." [164]

Riming and punning, on the other hand, and on the whole alliteration, are held well in check by Sidney. Nor does he employ classical allusion and illustrations from natural history in Lyly's extravagant manner. More characteristic of Arcadian style are certain tricks of merely verbal ingenuity. One of these is that known to the early rhetoricians as climbing, or climax, whereby a word of one phrase is repeated as the leading idea of the next, through a sequence of phrases:

"Now then, our Basilius being so publickly happie as to be a Prince, and so happie in that happinesse as to be a

[160] In the *Apologie, Eliz. Crit. Essays,* I, 196, he blames Spenser for "framing of his stile to an old rustick language" in the *Shepherd's Calendar,* citing the contrary practice of Theocritus, Vergil, and Sanazzaro in support of his own view that an archaic vocabulary was not to be employed.

[161] P. 15b.

[162] P. 33b.

[163] P. 210b.

[164] P. 78b.

beloved Prince, and so in his private blessed as to have so excellent a wife, and so over-excellent children, hath of late taken a course which yet makes him more spoken of then all these blessings." [165]

Another ' ladder ' of this kind is the following:

" No, no, let us thinke with consideration, and consider with acknowledging, and acknowledge with admiration, and admire with love, and love with joy in the midst of all woes: let us in such sorte thinke, I say, that our poore eyes were so inriched as to behold, and our low hearts so exalted as to love, a maide, who is such, that as the greatest thing the world can shewe, is her beautie, so the least thing that may be praysed in her, is her beautie." [166]

What was intended for ornament in this ' tranlacing,' often suggests poverty of vocabulary to the modern reader, as in the following repetitions:

" For finding himselfe not onely unhappy, but unhappie after being falne from all happinesse: and to be falne from all happines, not by any misconceiving, but by his own fault, and his fault to be done to no other but to *Pamela:* he did not tender his owne estate, but despised it; greedily drawing into his minde, all conceipts which might more and more torment him." [167]

Transverse verbal balance, as in Becon, is another figure frequently employed by Sidney, e.g. " the sweetest fairenesse and fairest sweetnesse "; [168] " the one wanting no store, th' other having no store but of want "; [169] " foolish fortune or unfortunate follie "; [170] " rather angry with fighting then fighting for anger ; [171] " had shewed such furie in his force and yet such stay in his furie "; [172] " but the universall lamenting his absented presence, assured him of

[165] P. 12ª.
[166] P. 2ᵇ.
[167] P. 245ª.
[168] P. 2ª.
[169] P. 7ª.
[170] P. 64ª.
[171] P. 288ᵇ.
[172] P. 289ª.

his present absence." [173] Often these verbal figures rest upon an ingenious antithesis of images or ideas, as in the description of the fire on the ship which drove Pyrocles and Musidorus "rather to committe themselves to the cold mercie of the sea, then to abide the hote crueltie of the fire"; [174] or of the delightful country of Laconia, where the houses are so distributed as to make "a shew, as it were, of an accompanable solitariness and of a civil wildnes"; [175] or in the following variation on the main theme of the book:

"But while we were thus full of wearinesse of what was past, and doubt of what was to follow, Love (that I thinke in the course of my life hath a sporte sometimes to poison me with roses, sometimes to heale me with worme-wood) brought forth a remedy unto us." [176]

An analysis of style such as the *Arcadia* has been subjected to inevitably brings the extravagances of the writing into stronger relief than its merits. Enough has been said to show that when Sidney broke down the barrier between poetry and prose, he had no intention of bringing either poetry or literary prose down to the level of everyday discourse. The high style in prose offered to him as broad a field for the exercise of rhetorical ingenuity as verse, and he agreed with his courtly contemporaries in the opinion that a prose style worthy of the scholar and of a lofty theme demanded such bravery of speech as would set it apart from the common speech of men. At the same time it is not difficult to separate the more extreme mannerisms and rhetorical ornaments of Sidney's style as mere surface display from a background of sound and genuine prose expression. His sentences are not always long paragraphs,

[173] P. 49^b.
[174] P. 4^a.
[175] P. 7^a.
[176] P. 193^a.

his conceits and verbal tricks do not adorn every line with their false glitter. In the main he wrote easily and unaffectedly, lightly and gracefully. He fashioned a speech appropriate to the conversation of gentlemen, neither too weighty with learning nor too bluntly familiar and colloquial. This he did whenever he relaxed in his misguided effort to do something better.

The writings of Lyly and Sidney represent the farthest swing of the pendulum in the development of an artistic English prose in the sixteenth century. Both had their imitators, but no other models of fine style appeared to take their place. In *Euphues* and in the *Arcadia* experimentation had been carried to the farthest limits, and the natural tendency towards the end of the sixteenth and in the seventeenth century was to react in favor of a simpler style. Plainness of speech now began to be cultivated and to be commended even for writing of literary pretensions. But the plainness of speech of the seventeenth century was a very different matter from the plainness which had been advocated by many theorists in the second quarter of the sixteenth century. The whole language had been elevated by the learned and courtly stylists. The vocabulary had been enormously increased, methods of figurative adornment had been elaborated, sentence structure had been made pointed and easy. The conservative reaction towards plainness was in no danger of exalting a rustic or medieval simplicity; its task was merely to restrain some of the rhetorical extravagances of the period of artful experiment. Of the various types of prose style cultivated in the sixteenth century, the most influential for the future literary uses of the language was the courtly style. It provided models for the middle kind of the three classical *genera dicendi,* the plain, the mean, and the grand. The plain style of Tindale, Latimer, and many others, with its picturesque colloquial flavor in diction and in form, was an almost universal gift of Elizabethan writers and one that even the most ingenious stylists did not permit to fall into complete disuse. But this plain style lacked distinction and literary tone. Employed unambitiously, it became merely matter-of-fact, familiar, and lowly; elaborated by means of the various devices of the tumbling style, it developed into a robustious, turgid kind of writing which seemed rude and popular when it was measured by the standards of classical literature. At the other extreme stood the formal periodic style in which many writers made experiments and which found its first adequate master in Hooker. This was an appropriate kind of writing for scholarly and serious subjects, but its dignity and stateliness lifted it above the lighter and more graceful moods of the polite world. The courtly writers occupied a middle ground. In vocabulary they shunned the extremes of pedantry and of innovation, and in phrasing they struck a compromise between the shapelessness of the naïve style and the architectural formality of the period. They applied ornament extravagantly, but the ornament was not really the essential quality of their style. It belonged to an age when even men adorned their persons with feathers and with chains of gold and dressed themselves in silks and velvet. Beneath all the frippery of this rhetorical dress there lay a permanent contribution to the development of English prose in the greater ease, the greater variety of modulation which the courtly writers introduced into it. Apart from its short-lived fashionable absurdities their style was admirably adapted to the expression of the opinions, the changing sentiments and actions of cultivated social life. Dryden declared that Beaumont and Fletcher understood and imitated the conversation of gentlemen better than Shakspere. And it is true that the prevailing level of expression in Shakspere is poetical and "aureate," not merely ornamental as in Lyly and Sidney, but elevated both in feeling and phrase to the plane of the grand style. Lyly and Sidney, however, were directly in the line of development which led to Beaumont and Fletcher, to Dryden, to Addison, to all cultivators of a graceful English literary style raised above the colloquial speech, yet not so exalted or so artfully labored as to destroy the sense of ease and reality.

VII

HISTORY AND ANTIQUITY

MEDIEVAL HISTORIANS—THE CITY CHRONICLES—THE BRUT—FABYAN—FROISSART—POLYDORE VERGIL—HALL—GRAFTON—HOLINSHED—SPEED—THEORY OF HISTORICAL WRITING—EARLY BIOGRAPHICAL HISTORIES—CAVENDISH'S "WOLSEY"—HAYWARD—BACON'S "HENRY VII"—RALEIGH—TRANSLATIONS—JOHN LELAND—LAMBARDE—STOWE'S "SURVEY"—CAMDEN—CONCLUSIONS

I

THE tradition of historical writing which the early modern English historians inherited from medieval times was a venerable, if not highly differentiated one. At no time after its composition was the existence of the Old English *Chronicle* forgotten, and the name and writings of Bede were revered by many a later historian of far less ability than Bede. But Bede never had any genuine successors, and with the close of the Old English period, the patriotic impulse which had led to the composition of the vernacular *Chronicle* suffered a decline, and the *Chronicle* itself, in its latest continuations, tails off ignominiously in a bad Latin.

For a time little history of any kind, whether in Latin or in English, was written. With the beginning of the twelfth century, however, an abundant historical literature sprang up in England, mainly written in Latin prose and under monastic auspices. Soon also romantic metrical histories in the vernacular began to appear. At the end of the twelfth or early in the thirteenth century was written the English metrical history of Layamon, known as the *Brut,* and about a century later, the English metrical chronicle of Robert of Gloucester. Another English metrical history was that of Robert Mannyng, written soon after Robert of Gloucester's chronicle, and in the third quarter of the fourteenth century, in the north of England appeared the *Bruce* of John Barbour. At the same time Latin continued to flourish as the language of prose historical composition, notably in the histories of Roger of Hoveden, of Matthew Paris, in the work traditionally ascribed to Matthew of Westminster, in the writings of Roger of Wendover, and of Ralph Higden, whose *Polychronicon* was "the standard work on general history in the fourteenth and fifteenth centuries."[1]

The writing of prose histories in English begins with Trevisa's translation of Higden's *Polychronicon,* made in 1387, and with Capgrave's more original work, written about the middle of the following century. But this new English history was not a return to or a continuation of the national *Chronicle* of the Old English period, nor had it learned much from the many Latin histories of the intervening period. Capgrave, following the usual encyclopedic method of the times, begins his history with the Creation, and he has quite as much to record concerning Hebrew history between the Creation and the Flood as he has concerning English history between the coming of Hengest and Horsa and the Norman Conquest. The whole history of Alfred is summed up in the following brief paragraph:

"In this tyme regned Alured in Yngland, the fourt son of Adelwold. He began to regn in the yere of our Lord

[1] Babington, Rolls Series, p. xlii.

DCCCLXXII. This man, be the councelle of Saint Ned, mad an open Scole of divers sciens at Oxenford. He had many batailes with Danes; and aftir many conflictes in which he had the wers, at the last he ovircam hem, and be his trety Godrus,[2] here Kyng, was baptized and went hom with his puple. XXVIII yere he regned, and died the servaunt of God." [3]

Brief as they are, we see in these records a complete mingling of fact and fable. Alfred is not realized as an actual historical personage, and the figures in the record move like the dim and half-forgotten actors in some old romance. Such was the naïve feeling for English history which Capgrave, "one of the most learned men of his time," [4] had in the fifteenth century.[5]

One chief cause of the inadequacy of the work of these medieval and belated medieval historians was that they attempted too much. An encyclopedic history from the Creation down could scarcely be expected to rest throughout on a sound foundation of documentary or traditional evidence. The mere remoteness of the periods covered was in itself sufficient to account for the loose methods employed. What English history needed was to narrow its circle of inclusion, to discover some foundation of solid reality upon which to rest its feet. This foundation Englishmen discovered in their own cities, especially the city of London, an apparent and inspiring fact, and one about which were centering more and more the nation's traditions

[2] A nominative after the Latin form, made on the supposition that Godrum, from Guthrum, was an accusative.

[3] *The Chronicle of England by John Capgrave,* ed. Hingeston, p. 113.

[4] Ibid., p. xii.

[5] For a valuable summary of the historical writings of this period, see Kingsford, *English Historical Literature in the Fifteenth Century,* Oxford, 1913. Contemporary with Capgrave was the belated medieval rimed *Chronicle* of John Hardyng.

of greatness. It was London which restored to English historians the sense for fact, and it is in the chroniclers of the city of London, and in less degree of other cities, that one must seek for the beginnings of modern English historical writing.

The city chronicles, which were very numerous, are not themselves very exciting forms of composition. They were written sometimes in French and Latin, but the later ones usually in English. The *Chronicles of the Mayors and Sheriffs of London AD. 1188 to AD. 1274,* and the *French Chronicle of London AD. 1259 to AD. 1343,*[6] are typical examples of early city chronicles. The materials are ordered under the heads of the successive officials of the city, and no attempt at connected narrative is made. Some attention is given to national affairs, but the main concern of the chroniclers is with the city and its citizens. Many details of a legal character are mentioned, both of a private nature and such as are connected with the liberties of the city. Taxes and coinage, as one might expect, are frequently matters of comment. And trivial incidents of local importance, for example the severe winter and great frost in 1268, and the "great fire at St. Botolph's" in 1278, occasionally give that gossipy flavor to the records which is a constant feature of English fifteenth- and sixteenth-century chronicles. These chronicles also contain interesting references to the Jews and their place in London life.

From the historical memoranda of John Stowe have been published certain collections evidently taken from some city chronicle.[7] They consist mainly of brief records of

[6] Published in English translation by Riley, London, 1863.

[7] Edited by Gairdner, *Three Fifteenth-Century Chronicles,* Camden Society, 1880. See also *Two London Chronicles from the Collections of John Stow,* ed. Kingsford, Camden Miscellany, XII (1910). These are brief but characteristic historical memoranda of the first half of the sixteenth century.

official business of the city and the kingdom, mingled with some amusing city gossip. Sir John White, for example, is reprehended because, being mayor, he wore both a long beard, whereas it had been the custom for the mayor to be shaven, and also a round cap that weighed not four ounces, "whiche seemyd to all men, in consyderation of ye auncient bonyt, to be very uncomly."[8] The *Historical Collections of a Citizen of London*[9] contain a good example of fifteenth-century city chronicling. The probable author of this chronicle was William Gregory, mayor of London in 1451. It begins with 1189 and extends to 1469, the entries for the last few years being probably by a continuator. Events are narrated by years in simple chronicle fashion, headed by the names of mayors, bailiffs, sheriffs, and other city officers. Insignificant matters and marvels are not omitted, and a good deal of attention is given to national as well as local affairs. One can see how such a city chronicle, by some extension of interest, could easily develop into a national chronicle. The marvels of royal feastings and celebrations seem to have aroused great enthusiasm on the part of the chronicler, and he describes them with all of the citizen's pride in the magnificence of the court maintained by the taxes which he paid. For the dinner at the coronation of Henry VI the whole bill of fare is given, among other delightful dishes in the second course being "Gely wrytyn and notyd, Te Deum Laudamus." There was also "Pygge in doory," and "A lybarde ys hedde whythe ij esterygys fetherys." Abundant details are given as to precedence, points of procedure on ceremonial occasions, conduct of trials and combats, and other weighty matters such as must have troubled the peace of mind of a fifteenth-century London mayor. Disturbances

[8] Gairdner, pp. 127-128.
[9] Also edited by Gairdner, Camden Society, 1876.

in the city are noted, such as the hanging of a thief, the burning of a heretic, and such notable happenings as that in 1466 "the mayre beryd [his] lady, and his scheryffe and his swyrdeberer."[10] One may smile at the simplicity of these early city chroniclers, but after much reading of medieval histories, amusement will be tempered by a sense of relief that historical writing is beginning to escape from the encyclopedic inclusiveness and the monastic and legendary traditions of the medieval period, and is beginning to acquire some feeling for color and locality and for the immediate setting of character and life in which events take place. If these early chronicles read rather like diaries than histories, it should be remembered that the intimate sense of reality of the diary or the book of memoirs was the very thing which historical writing at this time most needed. Another important achievement of the city chronicles was that they finally detached historical writing from Latin and made the familiar language of the vernacular the customary medium for historical composition.

The materials contained in the London chronicles were utilized towards the middle and the latter part of the fifteenth century in the composition of a number of popular English histories which followed a more consecutive and more comprehensive narrative method than the earlier city chronicles had done. Of these one of the most popular was *The Brut, or the Chronicles of England,*[11] written in a simple, naïve prose and extant in a great variety of forms and manuscripts. A version of *The Brut* was printed by Caxton in his *Chronicles of England* in 1480, and thus became "the first of our printed histories."[12] Another development from the London chronicles was the

[10] P. 233.
[11] Ed. Brie, E.E.T.S., 1906-1908.
[12] Kingsford, l. c., *The Brut,* pp. 113-139.

work of Robert Fabyan, who endeavored to enlarge his plan so as to make, in some measure, a general English history of his book. A clothier and member of the Drapers Company, alderman of the ward of Farringdon Without, and in 1493 sheriff, Fabyan no doubt was a typical, comfortable London citizen. His will, which is still extant, is a long detailed document, an interesting illustration of middle-class pomposity in the testator's day, with elaborate provisions for all kinds of prayers and feastings, month's minds and alms-givings, to be performed on the occasion of his death. Fabyan's book was first printed in 1516, three years after his death. A second edition, revised in many details, appeared in 1533.[13] It was called *The Concordance of Histories,* and though mainly devoted to British history, it contained also large sections on France. The work was elaborately conceived, and the sources which Fabyan used, both French and English, were numerous. It is divided into seven parts, chronologically, the early sections being developed at greatest length. In structure, however, and to a large extent in spirit also, it remains a city history, with scope broadened. The annals are headed by the names of city officials, and the narrative itself is simple and naïve. There is little feeling for connected story, and no seeking after the eloquent and grandiose style of some later English chroniclers. On the whole, Fabyan seems to have been an industrious, conservative citizen, with little animation or literary skill. Occasional passages of crude verse are inserted in the midst of the prose, sometimes translation, sometimes original, and often of a pious character. The author speaks of his work as rude and preliminary:

> "So have I nowe sette out this rude werke,
> As rough as the stone nat commen to the square,

[13] Edited by Ellis, 1811, from both forms.

> That the lerned and the studyed clerke
> May it over polysshe and clene do it pare." [14]

His purpose in writing he declares to be not "for any pompe or yet for great mede," but only to spread the "famous honour of this Fertyle Ile." Fabyan's patriotic fervor was not sufficiently great, however, to impart any considerable degree of warmth to his narrative of national events. The most interesting parts of the history are those in which he treats of matters which touched him more nearly than affairs of state. There are various passages in praise of London, and frequent references, in the first edition always unsympathetic, to Lollards and heretics. When John Badby was burned at Smithfield for heresy, Fabyan dismisses the affair with the laconic remark, "wherfore he had as he deserved." [15] In later editions of the book, following the general tendency of the times, these anti-reforming passages were either omitted or modified. Among the city details mentioned, many are of antiquarian interest, as for example the beginning of the market called the Stocks, but many also are of merely casual or local interest, as when we are told of the remarkable fact that the river Thames was in flood twice in one year. In a day when newspapers were not, the chronicle served various uses which seem now scarcely compatible with the dignity of the muse of history.

A few years after the publication of Fabyan's *Chronicles,* two works appeared in print, neither originally written in English, but both of which were soon to exert a strong influence in elevating the literary tone of English historical writing. The first of these was Froissart's *Chronicles* in Berners' translation, the first volume of which appeared in 1523, the second in 1525, and the other was Polydore Vergil's *Anglicae Historiae Libri XXVI,* first published at

[14] P. 3.

[15] P. 574.

Basel in 1534. Although Englishmen were not unacquainted with Froissart before Berners' translation appeared, the translation undoubtedly brought home to them the significance of the book and compelled a comparison with their own historical writings. It was undertaken at the request of Henry VIII, and when it was finished, it was dedicated to him. In a preface placed before the translation Berners expressed eloquently his sense of the dignity of the historian's calling. He is in harmony with the best thought of his time when he makes the chief function of history to be a moral one, that is, the providing of examples of character and action from past times for the guidance of those living in the present. History he says may well be called a divine providence, since in it are embraced all human actions. "The most profytable thyng in this worlde," he adds, "for the instytution of the humayne lyfe is hystorie." All other monuments in process of time by "varyable chaunces" are confused and lost; history alone abides, for time, which consumes everything else, is the keeper and guardian of history.

After this preface, however, Berners wisely permits the teaching of the book to be conveyed not by direct precept, but implicitly. If the book provides models of knightly conduct, it does so because the materials of it were originally chosen with a consistent feeling for the lofty and the dignified. It is throughout a history of the actions of men who were governed by the chivalric code of conduct. The humble and the familiar find little place in it, and though the book is unfailingly picturesque and vivid, the scene is always set for the higher actions of state or for tales of knightly adventure. Without being a romance and without sacrificing the feeling for security in the fact, Froissart's *Chronicles* produces on the whole the effect of romantic history. From Berners' translation of Froissart, the observant Englishman of the time could have learned both how to carry his story more freely and currently than the English chroniclers had been accustomed to do, and also how to lift his narrative to a level of interest to which historical writing in English had not hitherto aspired.

The work of Polydore Vergil commands respect both for the excellent Latin literary style which it exhibits and for the critical spirit with which the sources of English history are treated. An Italian acquainted with the best results of Renascence scholarship, Polydore Vergil came to England in 1501 or 1502 as sub-collector of Peter's Pence—a connection with the papal court that did not enhance his credit in the eyes of the increasingly numerous group of reformers in England. He received various ecclesiastical preferments and soon became friends with the most distinguished English scholars. He died in Italy, probably in 1555, whither he had returned a short time before to spend the remaining period of his life.

Polydore Vergil's history of England was written at the suggestion of Henry VII, who, in 1505, requested him to undertake such a work. Vergil seems to have set about the task methodically and seriously, collecting and sifting all available sources of information. In 1525 he edited Gildas, the first edition of that author ever made. In 1534 his *Anglicae Historiae Libri XXVI* was published at Basel. If we count from the avowed date of its inception in 1505, Vergil was at work twenty-nine years upon this volume. A second edition appeared in 1546, a third in 1555, and numerous later ones. The first two editions come down to the year 1509, but the third, in twenty-eight books, comes down to 1538. A fragmentary English translation of the work appeared in the latter part of the reign of Henry VIII by an unknown translator.[16]

[16] Published by Ellis, Camden Society, 1844 and 1846.

The history opens with a general description of Britain and the surrounding islands. This large theme is broadly and ably handled. Vergil's own investigations are included and often show indications of keen and independent observation. He notes, for example, that the English avoid the hills and open spaces for their dwellings, and, in the words of the English translation, choose the "delectable valleys," where the inhabitants, especially the nobles, have their houses: "whoe accordinge to their aunciente usage, do not so greatlie affecte citties as the commodious nearenes of dales and brookes." From this Vergil notes the result that "theruralls and common people, bie the entercourse and daylye conference which they have with the nobilitie, confuselie dwellinge emonge them, are made verie civill, and so consequentlie their citties nothinge famous."[17] He has observed also the clannish pride of the Scots of the Highlands, who "avoydinge travayle even in their extreme penurie, boste of their nobilite, as whoe shoulde saye, better it weare that a man in gentil bloode shoulde wante than bie crafte or science to gather for his livinge."[18] Among the products of the land, Vergil gives the chief place to the oxen and wethers—"but beafe is peereles, especiallie being a fewe dayse poudered with salte." He notes the similarity in the speech of Wales, Scotland, Ireland, and Cornwall, and he prefers English to Welsh because the Welsh "speake not soe smothelie nor pleasantlie as the Englishe people. For Welchemen, as I suppose, speake more in the throate; but contrarie wise, Englishmen, resemblinge more the Latinistes, drawe theire voice onelie a litle within their lippes, which sounde is pleasaunte and likinge to the hearer."[19]

In the narrative parts of the history one finds the facts

[17] Ellis, p. 4. [18] Ibid., p. 11. [19] Ibid., p. 13.

well ordered and the events presented with considerable skill. Throughout the book, the tone of the writing is distinguished and it shows that Vergil had formed his style upon the best classical models. He is fond of introducing formal set portraits of characters, in the classic manner, a device often imitated by his English followers. His treatment of English affairs is impartial, and even in the discussion of religious matters, though he is no friend of Wiclif or the Lollards, he does not show himself an intolerant enemy. Personally he probably had no very deep religious convictions, and seems to have viewed the religious and theological disturbances of the times with a disinterestedness and a worldly detachment which was not uncommon among cultivated Italians of the sixteenth century, and which was, in the eyes of severe English judges, like Ascham, for example, almost as bad as out and out atheism. Impartiality was scarcely an intelligible virtue to Englishmen of Ascham's day. No abuse was too great, if one may judge from the utterances of English writers of this time, to be heaped upon the name of Polydore Vergil. Bale, for example, in his *Chronicle of Lord Cobham* (1544), has a good deal to say about Polydore Vergil and his history. He earnestly desires that someone should set forth the English Chronicles "in their right shape," and he wants this to be done mainly as a corrective of "Romish blasphemy." He accuses Vergil of "polluting our English Chronicles most shamefully with his Romish lies and other Italish beggarys."[20] But Polydore Vergil offended not only the religious prejudices of Englishmen—he also touched them very nearly in a tender patriotic spot. He called in question the authenticity of Geoffrey of Monmouth's history, with its romantic stories of the Brut, of Arthur and his achievements, stories which, long since

[20] *Select Works*, ed. Christmas, p. 8.

mellowed by native tradition, had come to seem an inalienable right of the British people. The battle over Geoffrey was a long and bitter one, and though Polydore Vergil's critical position was to be established in the end, it was only after much rancorous shedding of ink and after the death of the prime mover in the conflict. Englishmen, however, were not slow to derive some profit by the example of the foreigner whom they did not hesitate to malign. Vergil suffered the fate which almost inevitably falls to the lot of the author who meddles with the intimate affairs of a country not his own. But perhaps because he irritated Englishmen of the time, he was the more influential. Certainly his historical method, his general skill as a writer, and his broad and disinterested view of affairs were far in advance of anything that had appeared in English historical writing before his day, and just as certainly they exerted a great influence on later writers of English history.

The first English historian to profit by Polydore Vergil's performance was Edward Hall. He published the first edition of his *Union of the two noble and illustre Famelies of Lancastre and Yorke* in 1542, and a second edition, edited by Richard Grafton, appeared in 1548, the year after Hall's death. No complete copy of the first edition is now extant. A third edition appeared in 1550, also under the editorial supervision of Richard Grafton, who says that Hall finished his chronicle to the year 1532 and that he left among his papers a number of notes which Grafton declares he put together without any additions of his own. It is doubtful, however, as will appear later, if all of the book traditionally ascribed to Hall was written by him.

Having completed his earlier education at Eton and at King's College, Cambridge, Hall settled down to the profession of the law in London. He was an ardent supporter of the cause of the reformers and of the policies of Henry VIII. The theme of his chronicle, as it is stated in the title to the second edition, is the union of the houses of York and Lancaster, "beginnyng at the tyme of Kyng Henry the Fowerth, the first aucthor of this devision, and so successively proceadyng to the reigne of the high and prudent prince Kyng Henry the Eight, the undubitate flower and very heire of both the sayd linages." Impelled by these motives of loyalty and also by the purer desire of the historian to save past events from oblivion, Hall writes with a sense of the dignity of his great subject, and exerts, even strains himself to make the style worthy of the theme. His scholarly bent is made apparent in many ways. He shows a fondness for long speeches and formal orations, of the kind recommended by Thucydides,[21] which the characters deliver in their proper persons. He frequently employs the rhetorical device of doublets, such as "dolour and lamentacion"; "culpe and cause"; "breake and violate all lawes"; "an hundred mo injuries . . . he remitted and sepulted in oblivion." These, however, are but mild examples of Hall's tendency to use fine and wordy phrases. The following sentence describing the character of Henry VII is fairly typical:

"He havyng both the ingenious forcast of the subtyl serpent and also fearyng the burning fire like an infant that is a little synged with a small flame: and farther vigilantly forseyng & prudently providyng for doubtes that might accidentally ensue: devysed, studyed and compassed to extirpate and eradicate all interior sedicions and apparant presumpcions whiche might move any tumulteous route or sedicious conjuracion against him within his realme in tyme to come." [22]

[21] Dale's translation, I, 13.
[22] Edition of Ellis, London, 1809, p. 422.

It was this kind of writing which brought upon Hall the condemnation of Ascham, who declared that in the chronicle "moch good matter is quite marde with Indenture English," and that anyone who would improve the style of the book must first "change strange and inkhorne tearmes into proper and commonlie used wordes: next specially to wede out that that is superfluous and idle, not onelie where wordes be vainlie heaped one upon an other, but also where many sentences of one meaning be so clowted up together as though M. Hall had bene, not writing the storie of England, but varying a sentence in Hitching schole." [23]

As further aids in elevating his style, Hall frequently employs rhetorical questions, ejaculations, and addresses to the reader; alliteration is not uncommon, as when he describes Joan of Arc as the "pevishe painted Puzel"; and often the phrasing has a true Euphuistic turn, as when he speaks of a "lamentable chance & lachrimable loss," [24] or of the French king's death as ending "the poynt of his fatall fine." [25] He is fond of introducing set portraits of characters, a trick probably learned from Polydore Vergil, of whose work frequent passages of Hall are scarcely more than translations.[26] On the other hand, although there are numerous brief passages of general moralizing and of sententious wisdom which interrupt the narrative, Hall indulges in practically no personal references to himself or in details of merely gossipy interest. He omits all descriptions of feasts and ceremonies, usually remarking that it would take too long to describe them in detail, and he omits much of the picturesque side of the popular religious innovations of the times, probably from a feeling that the ac-

[23] *The Scholemaster,* Arber's reprint, pp. 111-112.
[24] Ellis, p. 497.
[25] Ibid., p. 249.
[26] Gairdner, *Early Chronicles,* p. 304.

tivities of the humbler disturbers of the peace were not fitly to be included in so dignified a narrative.

The above description, however, applies to the book only to the beginning of the history of Henry VIII. All the first part extending to the death of Henry VII is formal, dignified, somewhat pedantic, but well told in its way, with a sense of the largeness of movement of the subject. And it is this part, especially the account of the reign of Henry VII, which shows most the influence of Polydore Vergil. With the beginning of the reign of Henry VIII the tone of the writing completely changes. It becomes much simpler and less rhetorical, and though it does not become gossipy or trivial, it does become much more humanly interesting. Much more attention is paid to the popular side of theological opinion, and it is here that we find recorded the amusing story of Tunstall's treatment of Tindale's Bibles.[27] The narrative frequently exhibits a feeling for the humorous and the picturesque which is quite lacking in the earlier parts. The account of the early years of Henry's reign is particularly animated. The chronicler tells with evident enjoyment how in the eleventh year of Henry's reign, at the request of the King's counsellors, certain "young menne whiche were called the kynges minions" were dismissed, and in their stead "foure sad and auncient knightes" were assigned to the King's privy chamber. He continues with a description of a mask wherein the dancers "daunsed with Ladies sadly, and communed not with the ladies after the fashion of Maskers, but behaved theimselfes sadly. Wherefore the quene plucked of their visours," when it appeared that "the youngest man was fiftie at the least. The Ladies had good sporte to se these

[27] Turning on the point that the more Bibles Tunstall bought and destroyed, the more money Tindale acquired from the profits of the sale with which to print new and larger editions.

auncient persones Maskers."[28] Feasts and pageants and ceremonies are all elaborately described, and the chronicler enters joyfully into all the gayety of the court. A riot of color runs over the pages of the narrative, "blewe satten pauned with Sipres, powdered with spangles of Bullion," cloth of silver and cloth of gold, "hed of damaske gold set with diamondes," "broched satten," pearls and precious stones, "flowers of silk," "crimosin velvet," and a dazzling wealth of similar opulent detail. The writer of this part of the chronicle has also a feeling for poetry, as when he tells of the twelve noblemen dressed "in shorte cotes of Kentishe Kendal" who appear, as it were out of the blue sky, before the queen and her ladies, and after dancing, take their departure; or of the king when in the second year of his reign, with all his knights, squires, and gentlemen in white satin and all his guard and yeomen of the crown in white sarcenet, he "rose in the mornynge very early to fetche May or grene bows." It is difficult to believe that the person who wrote the "indenture English" of the earlier part of Hall's *Chronicle* could also have written the graceful and animated account of the reign of Henry VIII. Who the author of this section of the book was seems not to be definitely ascertainable, though not improbably the account of the reign of Henry VIII is to be credited to Richard Grafton, editor and continuator of Hall.[29]

After Hall and next in the succession of English chronicle writers came Richard Grafton, whose *Abridgement of the Chronicles of England* first appeared in print in 1562 and several times later. In 1569, however, Grafton published an amplified history which he called *A Chronicle*

[28] Ellis, p. 599.

[29] The grounds for this statement are presented in an article which will appear in a forthcoming number of *Modern Language Notes*.

at Large and meere History of the Affayres of Englande. Grafton apologizes for adding one more to the "many books alreadie set forth, bearing the names and tytles of Chronicles of Englande," but justifies his own work on the ground that others have either been too brief or too detailed, some have "intermyngled the affaires of other forreyne Nations with the matters of Englande," and still others, "namely strangers" (the allusion is probably to Polydore Vergil), have "slaunderously written and erred from the manifest truth." It is Grafton's intention to do what he declares has never before been done, to write a "playne and meere Englishe historie," and not to "intermix" his story with foreign affairs. Nevertheless Grafton's history begins with the Creation, the explanation being given that England had the same time of creation that the rest of the world had, and that consequently its history begins with the beginning of the world. The specific story of England opens with the arrival of Brute in Britain, whose legend Grafton accepts without question. The earlier parts of the history, however, are passed over rapidly, and it is only with the reign of William the Conqueror that the narrative is fully elaborated. In those parts for which Hall was available Grafton follows Hall very closely. But he used various sources, and gives a list of seventy-four authors who are "alleged in this history." In the earlier parts especially he assigns many passages to their specific sources. In its own day Grafton's work was highly esteemed, and apart from any question of its historical value, the reason for its popularity is not difficult to find. It tells its story currently and animatedly, and as writing, it is much more mature than Fabyan and far less affected and pedantic than Hall. It was the best example of chronicle writing which had so far appeared in English.

Before the publication of Grafton's *Chronicle at Large,*

his *Abridgement* had to compete with the similar work of a contemporary rival historian, John Stowe's *Summarie of Englyshe Chronicles,* the first edition of which appeared in 1565. This was followed by numerous later editions, and by editions of a version of the *Summarie* abridged. But Stowe, following Grafton's example, also published an amplified form of the *Summarie* in his *Chronicle of England* in 1580, which in its final and fullest published form in 1592 was entitled the *Annales of England.* The *Annales* was several times reprinted, and after Stowe's death the book was continued by Edmond Howes. As Howes remarks in his preface, the reader need expect in this work "no fyled phrases, Ink-horne termes, uncouth wordes, nor fantastique speeches, but good playne English without affectation, rightly befitting Chronologie." Stowe wrote with industry and with the propriety which became a sober London citizen, but his *Annales* is not an inspired work. By temper Stowe was an antiquary rather than an historian, and his *Survey of London* is to-day much more important than any of his historical writings.

With Grafton's *Abridgement* and Stowe's *Summarie* may be grouped Thomas Cooper's *Epitome of Chronicles,* first published in 1549 and a number of times later. This work is a continuation of a chronicle of the world, begun by Thomas Lanquet, but carried by Lanquet only from the Creation to the year 17 at the time of his death. The major part of the work is therefore Cooper's, since he brought down the epitome to his own times. It is of slight importance now, either as history or literature, but it contains some interesting prefatory remarks on the significance of historical writing, borrowed mainly from Cicero, and perhaps it deserves at least to be mentioned both as an example of a kind of compilation popular in its time and later condemned by Bacon, and as one of the works of the author of 'Cooper's Dictionary' and of several polemical tracts that figured in the Marprelate controversy.

The apex of English chronicle writing was reached with the publication of Holinshed's *Chronicles* in 1577. The published parts of this work, however, were but the merest fragment of the plan of the whole as it was originally conceived. Under the influence probably of the *Cosmographia Universalis* of the famous Hebraist and geographer, Sebastian Münster, which was published at Basel in 1544, Reginald Wolfe, a fellow countryman of Münster and a native of Strassburg, but as early as 1537 established in London as printer and publisher, projected "an universall Cosmographie of the whole world," and "therewith also certaine particular histories of every knowne nation." As Holinshed states in a letter prefixed to the third volume of the *Chronicles,* he together with others was engaged to assist Wolfe in the composition of this great work. Unfortunately Wolfe died in 1573 before any part of the plan had been brought to completion, and in default of a publisher brave enough to assume the burden of so great an undertaking as Wolfe had planned, the whole project lapsed. Encouraged by friends, Holinshed later continued his historical labors, and in 1577 was enabled to publish in two folio volumes a modification of the original scheme containing histories of England, Ireland, and Scotland, with descriptions prefixed. Ten years later, after the death of Holinshed, this first edition, "collected and published by Raphaell Holinshed, William Harrison and others," "newlie augmented . . . to the yeare 1586," was printed again by John Hooker of Exeter, the uncle of Richard Hooker, who had had a share in the original edition. The book, as the title indicates, was the result of the collaboration of various authors. John Hooker contributed a translation of Giraldus Cambrensis on the conquest of Ireland, and some further articles concerning Ireland. Holinshed himself wrote the continuation of the history of Ireland from the point where Giraldus left off to 1509. This was continued in the first edition by Richard Stanihurst to the year 1547, and in the second edition by the same contributor to the year 1586. Stanihurst's verbal eccentricities in writing contrast markedly with the simple style of the other contributors. In the second edition the history of Scotland, which Holinshed had carried down to 1571, was continued by Francis Botevile. But aside from Holinshed's share in the book, the most important contribution was the description of England by William Harrison, a native of London who had studied at Westminster School and later at Oxford and Cambridge, but the greater part of whose life was spent in the seclusion of country livings in Essex. Unlike most of the antiquaries of his time, for Harrison was antiquary rather than historian, Harrison himself was not a traveler. A journey of forty miles seemed to him a momentous occasion. Nevertheless, with the aid of Leland's manuscripts and the assistance of friends by correspondence and conversation, he gathered together the materials of his *Description* and made of them a well-ordered and entertaining book. He speaks very modestly of his achievement. He protests earnestly that he "never made any choise of stile or words, neither regarded to handle this Treatise in such precise order and method as manie other would have done, thinking it sufficient truelie and plainelie to set foorth such things as I minded to intreat of, rather than with vaine affectation of eloquence to paint out a rotten sepulchre"; and a little later he hopes "that this foule frizeled Treatise of mine will prove a spur to others better learned." But Harrison writes picturesquely without effort, and perhaps was at an advantage over more learned antiquaries in that he was not hampered by theories of a fine style or by an unmanageable mass of detail. His *Description* is not merely a list of facts, but he stops occasionally to deliver his own comments and opinions in an engagingly free and intimate way.

As to Holinshed's share in the book, little need be said. The traditions of English chronicle writing, by this time become conventional, are followed, and the narratives attempt to present little more than an epitome of historical events with some attention to setting. Holinshed maintains his style on the middle level, neither high nor low. He writes simply and clearly, but never eloquently. Indeed he expressly disclaims any attempt at "rhetoricall shew of eloquence, having rather a regard to simple truth than to decking words." His work shines more from the reflected glory of its use by Shakspere than from any splendor of its own.

Though Holinshed's was the most elaborate attempt at chronicle writing in England, perhaps the distinction of being the most perfect English chronicle from the point of view of execution belongs to John Speed's *History of Great Britaine*. Speed made good use of the fully developed technic of chronicle writing with which the traditions of the form provided him, but he added nothing essentially new. His flamboyant style, however, is sometimes not without a certain finish and charm of phrasing not found in the earlier chroniclers. Like his predecessor Stowe, Speed was a London craftsman, "brought up to his father's trade of tailoring." Through the assistance of Sir Fulke Greville, however, in 1614, when he was a little over sixty years old, Speed's hand was set free "from the daily imployments of a manuall trade" by the acquisition of a landed estate. As early as 1598 Speed had busied himself in making maps of the various counties of England, and these were collected and published with an accompanying descriptive text in the year 1611 under the title *Theatre of the Empire of Greate Britaine.* Later editions bear the title *A Prospect of the most Famous Parts of the World,* and open with a *Generall Description of the World,* wherein the author shows " how the whole earth which at first knew but one Land-lord, hath beene since rent into severall parcels, which Kings and Nations call their owne." [30] In the year 1611 also appeared the first edition of Speed's *History,* which covers the history of England from the conquests of the Romans to the reign of King James. The *Prospect* was often printed with editions of the *History,* providing thus a complete chorographical as well as historical account of Britain. At the end of the *History,* Speed gives a *Summary Conclusion of the Whole,* in which he acknowledges his debt to various books and persons. But he himself, he declares, has journeyed throughout England, " whose beautie and benefits, not a farre off, as Moses saw Canaan from Pisgah, but by my owne travels through every province of England and Wales mine eyes have beheld." The materials of the history proper are well ordered and compactly narrated, though sometimes with a straining after rhetorical effect which seems more like " fusty foolery " than the high style which Speed thought he was writing. The garment of fine writing always sits awkwardly on these citizen chroniclers.

The development of historical writing in the sixteenth century was on the whole slow and meager. The chronicles differ from one another to some extent in the degree of literary skill which their authors exhibit, but the general purposes and standards which governed their composition remained much the same. The chief defect of the chroni-

[30] Edition of 1631, p. 2.

clers lay in their lack of insight into the significance of events. Fraudulent invention of detail with intent to deceive was not frequent, but the sense of distinction between romance and history or philosophy and history was not keen. The opinion expressed by Isaac Casaubon that history "is nothing else but a kind of Philosophy using Examples,"[31] "a Metropolis of Philosophy," was very generally held. And the defense of history so frequently made that it provided the models of good and bad behavior to be chosen or shunned by posterity was one which the writers of pure fiction could as appropriately offer in defense of their work, for contemporary romance likewise rested upon an ethical basis. Between didactic fiction and history Geffrey Fenton makes practically no distinction in the prefatory letter to his *Certain Tragical Discourses of Bandello* (1567). These tragical discourses or 'histories' are modern tales told as though they were based on fact and justified because they yield us "frelye presidentes for all cases that maye happen." Apparently any narrative of events with moral applications satisfied Fenton's conception of history. A famous instance of the confusion of romance and history may be noted in the discussion which centered about Guevara's *Dial of Princes.* In this work, Guevara asserted that he was translating from a Florentine manuscript, which it appeared on investigation neither he nor anyone else had ever seen. In answer to the charges of fraud that were brought against him, Guevara maintained "that all ancient profane history was no more true than his romance of Marcus Aurelius, and that he had as good a right to invent for his own high purposes as Herodotus or Livy."[32] And a similar point of view is exemplified, if

[31] See Bolton's *Hypercritica,* ed. Spingarn, *Critical Essays of the Seventeenth Century,* I, 98.

[32] See Ticknor, *History of Spanish Literature,* II, 17.

not expressed, in the romances of Lyly, where historical anecdote and episode are utilized merely for the sake of their moral or illustrative significance and with no regard at all for their historical verity. History of this kind differs very little from that of the *Gesta Romanorum.* The writings of the chroniclers were to be sure not so uncritical as those of the professed romancers, because the chronicles usually rest directly upon manuscript sources. But the sources themselves were rarely regarded with a questioning eye and were used as storehouses of edifying narrative, not in order to verify events.

The broad scope of the chroniclers likewise tended to prevent them from gaining an intimate realization of character or of the causes of events and the human motives which are the occasions of events. Their story was of wars and battles, of the births, marriages, and deaths of kings, or if they descended to matters more familiar, it was only too likely to be in the manner of "your lay Chronigraphers," who write of nothing but of "Mayors and Sheriefs and the deare yeere and the great Frost." [33] They lacked not only "the wings of choise words to fly to heaven," but also ideas to be put into words. Edmund Bolton speaks of their "vast vulgar tomes," of their "tumultuary and centonical writings" as resembling "some huge disproportionable Temple, whose Architect was not his Arts Master." [34]

From the middle of the sixteenth century, the theory of historical writing had occupied the minds of many Italian writers, and in 1574 Thomas Blundeville had published a book of precepts derived from Patrizzi's *Della Istoria* (1560) and from an unpublished work of Jacopo Acontio.[35]

[33] Nash, *Pierce Penilesse,* in McKerrow, *Works,* I, 194.
[34] *Hypercritica,* l. c., p. 98.
[35] *The True Order and Method of writing and reading Histories*

The notion of a constructive and rigorous historical method, however, seems not to have become very definitely established in England until towards the end of the sixteenth and in the first quarter of the seventeenth century. One begins then to meet with frequent expressions of discontent with what had previously been accomplished in the field of English history. Sir Henry Savile, for example, who five years before had published a translation of four books of the *Histories* of Tacitus, remarks in the dedicatory epistle of his *Rerum Anglicarum Scriptores* (1596) that the writers of English history, "being of the Dregs of the Common People," have merely "stain'd and defiled" while they have endeavored "to adorn the Majesty of so great a Work." [36] And Thomas Lodge, in a prefatory address To the Courteous Reader in his translation of *The Famous and Memorable Workes of Josephus* (1602), though he sets forth the usual theory that history should serve as a storehouse of examples, places special stress on the thought that the judgment must be called into play to determine the significance of the examples, history in the narrow sense merely supplying the material upon which the judgment is to operate.[37]

In the *Advancement of Learning,* published in 1605, appeared Bacon's well-known analytical discussion of the kinds of history and of the methods appropriate to them. To the three parts of human understanding, according to Bacon's classification, memory, imagination, and reason,

according to the Precepts of Francisco Patricio and Acontio Tridentino, London, 1574. See Einstein, *Italian Renaissance in England,* pp. 309-313, for an account of the content of Blundeville's book. Sidney has some interesting observations on the qualifications of the historian in a letter written to his brother in 1580, reprinted in Collins, *Critical Essays and Literary Fragments* (Arber's *English Garner*), pp. 6-8.

[36] Bolton's translation of Savile, in *Hypercritica,* l. c., I, 96.

[37] Lodge, *Complete Works,* Hunterian Club, IV, 23-27.

the three appropriate kinds of expression are history, poetry, and philosophy. History may be natural, civil, ecclesiastical, or literary. Of these four, the first kind, the history of the physical world, Bacon finds to have been only inadequately attempted, and the last not at all. His comments on ecclesiastical history are relatively brief, but what he has to say about civil history is full and carefully thought out. Of the epitomes or chronological summaries which were popular at the time, he speaks harshly, calling them the corruptions and moths of history. Just or perfect history may consist of chronicles, of lives, or of narrations or relations. Chronicles he also calls the history of times, and while granting that they are the most complete and absolute kind of history, he maintains that they are inferior to lives or biographies in usefulness and to narrations of particular actions in truthfulness. For the histories of England that were already in existence, he has little respect. Conceding that the history of England, which should include that of Scotland, from the beginning to modern times, might be an undertaking difficult to manage, because of the length of time to be covered, he recommends "an excellent period of a much smaller compass of time as to the story of England; that is to say from the uniting of the roses to the uniting of the kingdoms." In conclusion of this section of his discussion, Bacon calls attention to various kinds of mixed history, reprehending the practice, so dear to the chroniclers, of intermingling "matters of triumph, or matters of ceremony, or matters of novelty with matters of state." He speaks approvingly of cosmography as a kind of history compounded of natural and civil history. Some of the ideas contained in these passages of the *Advancement of Learning* appear also in a set of paragraphs written earlier as introductory to a history of England from the beginning of the reign of Henry VIII, "near unto the present time wherein Queen Elizabeth reigneth in good felicity,"[38] which Bacon purposed to write. He declares here that he may undertake this task of trying to write an English history without apology, since he will not be writing again that which others have already done well. "For those which I am to follow are such as I may rather fear the reproach of coming into their number, than the opinion of presumption if I hope to do better than they." Although the full plan as it is here outlined by Bacon was never carried to completion, only a few years later he gave a practical demonstration of these theories in a work which established a new standard for English historical writing, his history of the reign of Henry VII.

Shortly after the publication of Bacon's *Advancement of Learning* appeared Samuel Daniel's *Collection of the History of England* (1612). Daniel declares that he undertook to write a history because England was held "to come behind other Nations in this kind," and that he has "made choyce to deliver onely those affaires of action that most concerne the government."[39] He puts in an appendix all "treaties, letters, articles, charters, ordinances," and similar documentary evidence. The arrangement of Daniel's *Collection* is narrowly chronological, and though the events are rapidly and compactly told, the narrative exhibits little life, or color, or considering his theories, little insight into the subject. The book is rather an expanded epitome than a history. Daniel's *Civil Wars,* like the historical poems of Drayton, is more significant in the history of epic poetry than in that of historical writing, though in general these historical poets kept close to the facts of history as they were recorded in the chroniclers and other historians.

One more critical discussion of history may be noticed,

[38] *Works,* ed. Spedding, XI, 34. [39] *Works,* ed. Grosart, IV, 76.

a dissertation written after Bacon's *Henry VII* was completed but before it had appeared in print. Though not published until later, Edmund Bolton's *Hypercritica, or A Rule of Judgment for writing or reading our History's* was composed about 1618. Bolton declares that though England has enjoyed all other honors, it still is without a history, and he agrees in the main with Sir Henry Savile that not any of the English histories " discharge that Office which the Titles promise." To Speed he gives rather qualified praise when he says with respect to his style and industry that " for one who (as Martial speaks) hath neither a *Graecum χαῖρε* nor an *Ave Latinum,* [he] is perhaps without many Fellows in Europe." [40] The gravest defects of English historical writing he declares to be the want of art and style, and in the course of his essay he proceeds to lay down the principles which he thinks should govern the composition of history. The most difficult duty of historians he considers to be that of showing how the will of God has operated in the affairs of men. Of English historians he is of the opinion that Sir Thomas More has come nearest to realizing this duty. A valiant defense of the necessity of truth and of " indifferency and even dealing " is presented; if one will set his hand to paper, " then the Nobility of the office commands him rather to die then with the Injury of Truth to humour Times and Readers, and content himself." [41] A principal duty of the historian is " to handle the counsels and causes of Affairs," and Bolton then proceeds to point out the places " where the most universal Shipwracks are made," as the English historian endeavors " to make his course through the great Sea and Archipelago of so noble and magnificent a work." After some discussion of the proper style and language to be employed, Bolton closes with a summary of the qualities

[40] L. c., I, 98.

[41] L. c., p. 95.

requisite in the good historian. He must write as a "Christian Cosmopolite, to discover God's Assistances, Disappointments, and Overruling in human affairs"; as a "Christian Patriot to disclose the Causes and Authours" of his country's good or evil, to establish thereby the lawful liberty of nations; as a Christian subject, to show "the benefit of Obedience and Damage of Rebellions"; and finally as a "Christian *Paterfamilias*," not neglecting his private affairs, since "Labours of this noble Nature are fitter to get Renown then Riches, which they will need, not amplyfy." [42]

Though the high demands of theory were not practically realized in any pre-eminent English history during the period under consideration, there were nevertheless a number of attempts which reveal a profounder sense for historical narrative than the conventional epitome or chronicle. Several of these fall within the earlier years of the sixteenth century, for example, *The First English Life of King Henry the Fifth, written in 1513 by an anonymous Author known commonly as The Translator of Livius*,[43] Sir Thomas More's *History of King Richard III*, and Cavendish's *Life of Wolsey;* later come Bacon's *Henry VII* and his fragmentary historical writings, and noteworthy for their intention at least, if not for their performance, the various historical works of Sir John Hayward. Most of these writings, it will be observed, are in the field of historical biography, a limitation of plan which made possible a more thorough and unified treatment than the chronicle histories had usually attempted. *The First English Life of King Henry the Fifth* is mainly a translation of Tito Livio's *Vita Henrici Quinti* (1438) "out of facound Latine" by a writer who speaks

[42] Ibid., p. 114. [43] Ed. Kingsford, Oxford, 1911.

of himself as one "from whome all pratique and famous inditinge is farr exiled." Other sources are also employed by the author and are indicated in his marginal comments. His own additions are mostly moral and general ejaculations on the subject-matter. The book is a conscientious but pedantic piece of work, its chief merit consisting in the fact that the materials taken from various sources are really fused into an attempt at a united and connected narrative.

The History of King Richard III, usually ascribed to Sir Thomas More,[44] in its first published form is a fragment, breaking off abruptly in the tale of the conspiracy between the Duke of Buckingham and Cardinal Morton. In the modern edition of the work,[45] the conclusion, to the death of Richard, is taken from the version inserted by Grafton in his continuation of Hardynge's *Chronicle.* The tone of the writing in this latter part changes and shows clearly that it is by a different and less artful writer. The earlier part, which may be assumed to be from More's pen, is hostile to Richard throughout, following the source of which it is a loose translation, but it maintains a dignified literary tone. The central thread of the narrative is never lost, the unity of detail adding greatly to the dramatic effect. The only excursus of any significance is that in which the writer dwells for a moment on the fate of Jane Shore, and even here he apologizes for mentioning such a subject in a serious history. Stylistically the narrative is well managed. Orations and set speeches are introduced, and often the action is made vivacious by means of dialogue. The sentences frequently betray classic influence in the use of periodic structure and of formal balance and antithesis.

[44] See p. 83 for the question of authorship.

[45] *More's History of King Richard III,* ed. Lumby, Cambridge, 1883.

But they are also often admirably compact and epigrammatic in form. On the whole the biography afforded an excellent model of historical narrative from the point of view of its style and structure. The same praise cannot be given to it for its temper. It presents a set portrait of Richard clearly and sharply defined, but certainly overdrawn and partisan. It seems to have been written less in the spirit of the disinterested seeker after truth than in that of the political pamphleteer, intent on strengthening the cause of Richard's vanquishers. The "bad eminence" which the name of Richard held through the chroniclers, in Shakspere, and which it has held down to the present day, is a direct inheritance from this history. One may doubt if Richard was as black as he is painted; but there can be no difference of opinion as to the dramatic power of the picture which is here presented, and the fascination which it has exerted upon the minds of all later generations.

In striking contrast to the tone of the *History of Richard III* stands George Cavendish's *Life and Death of Cardinal Wolsey*. Cavendish also is a special pleader, but he presents his case for Wolsey with such restraint and modesty that his story seems almost a perfect example of historical narrative. Cavendish would have been the first perhaps to disclaim artistry, and the reader is often in doubt whether the best effects in the book are gained by the conscious mastery of technic or are the result of that rarer kind of excellence in writing, the natural expression of a clear and transparent nature. Certain it is that Cavendish was not a skilled professional writer. His *Life* was the work of a man of one book, a book into which he put the fruits of all his own reflection and experience. The one event of his life was his connection with the great cardinal. Born of a good Suffolk family in 1500, at the age of twenty-four he was married to Margery Kemp, niece of Sir Thomas More. Two years later, in Wolsey's words, "abandoning his own country, wife and children, his own home and family, his rest and quietness, only to serve me," Cavendish entered the cardinal's service as gentleman usher. He remained with Wolsey throughout the remainder of Wolsey's career, and was with him at his death in November, 1530, at Leicester. His faithfulness to his master was highly commended by Henry VIII, who promised to take him into his service and who rewarded him with a gift of twenty pounds, besides paying to him ten pounds of unpaid wages and granting him permission to choose six of the best "amongst all my lord's cart horses, with a cart to carry my stuff, and five marks for my costs homewards."[46] The Duke of Norfolk also would gladly have taken Cavendish into his service. But apparently Cavendish had seen enough of the life of the court, for he never again attempted to make a career for himself. With his six cart horses and his stuff, and with a heart full of food for many years' meditation, he retired to the seclusion of his home at Glemsford in Suffolk, from which he never reappeared.

It was almost thirty years later when Cavendish began to set down in writing the story which doubtless long before had taken form in his mind. Internal evidence in the *Life and Death* indicates that it was written in 1557, and doubtless the counter-reforms of Mary made the time seem propitious for the preparation of a defense of the great opponent of protestant reform. The accession of Elizabeth, however, rendered the publication of the work impracticable, and though it was widely circulated in manuscript and in this form may have been known to the authors of the Shaksperean *Henry VIII,* it was not until the middle

[46] *Life and Death,* ed. Ellis (1899), p. 256.

of the eighteenth century that a representative manuscript appeared in print.[47]

The purpose which moved Cavendish to write his story of Wolsey's life and death is briefly stated at the opening of the work. He declares his intention to be to tell of Wolsey's "ascending and descending from honorous estate," partly from his own knowledge and partly from other persons' information. He refuses controversy and will not answer the "divers and sundry surmises and imagined tales" which have circulated since Wolsey's death, but prefers to let them "remain still as lies." This dignified position the book consistently maintains. It tells its story simply, without violent accusation or partisan bias. Its undertone is not one of personal feeling, but of sober philosophy. The moral lesson of the vanity of ambition and worldly greatness, which Wolsey's life has so often been used to enforce, has nowhere been presented with greater sincerity and earnestness than in the *Life and Death*. The early life of Wolsey is very briefly described, but the picture of the magnificence of his prosperous period is elaborated in great detail, providing thus an artistic contrast with the longer half of the story of Wolsey after his fall. Cavendish was an undisguised admirer of Wolsey and, by reason of the simplicity and warmth of his feeling, he succeeds in presenting an engaging portrait of him. He nevertheless sets down frankly the faults of his master, faults of pride, of ostentation, of worldliness, and neglect

[47] Stowe in his *Annals* printed extracts from Cavendish, and a garbled version was printed in 1641. In 1761 appeared Grove's edition from a manuscript. The first standard edition was by Singer, 1815; a second edition appeared in 1827. Singer's text is reproduced in Morley's Universal Library. In 1893 Mr. F. S. Ellis published an edition for the Kelmscott Press, and in 1899 reproduced this text, with modernized spelling, for the Temple Classics edition. The edition of Boston, 1905, contains a composite text made up from Singer and Ellis.

of spiritual opportunities. But there is no lachrymose sentimentality, no post-mortem familiarity on the part of the author. He writes as a simple retainer should write of one whom rank and fortune have placed above him, and he makes no attempt to set himself up as judge or to acquire a vicarious importance by reason of the greatness of his master. He is not for a moment garrulous, and though there are occasional brief passages of a general moralizing character on the vanity of ambition, the burden, as it were, of the song, there is much less of this than one might expect in a writer of the time. The story closes appropriately with the report of Wolsey's death which Cavendish made to Henry VIII and to the council in London. No general judgment of praise or blame is passed, though at the time Cavendish was writing, the temptation to speak harshly of Henry VIII must have been great. Even in matters of religion Cavendish never speaks bitterly or meddles with questions of state that did not concern him. He does not conceal his opposition to the protestant reform, but on the other hand, he is not a violent partisan. His book is the work of a simple, honest man, writing with a sure sense of the proprieties of the situation and with the serenity and gravity of one looking back over a long period of meditation. It has consequently somewhat the tone of a book of memoirs, and as is often the case with such books, it perhaps becomes a work of art less by intention than by what one might call the happy accident of its truth and directness. Cavendish wrote with the vividness and concreteness of one whose prime concern was to put down in writing what he had seen and known, and his work thus became quite as much a life of himself as of his subject.

Though tortuous and uncontrolled sentences sometimes occur and clauses are not always grammatically relateable, Cavendish's style on the whole is simple and compact. He has a naïve way of opening a subject, like a medieval romancer, with "Now will I declare unto you," or some similar phrase. He often reproduces the exact tone of conversation, and probably the exact words. Yet his skill, when he sets himself the task of elaborate description or portraiture, is by no means slight. For the conventional chronicler he seems not to have had much respect. He scorns to describe the details of the funeral of Henry VII and the coronation of Henry VIII, leaving "the circumstances thereof to historiographers of chronicles of princes, the which is no part mine entendment."[48] And as to the complications of Henry's troubles with France, Cavendish refuses to say anything, speaking perhaps with the impatience of one who has been behind the scenes, of the "imaginations and inventions, even as men's fantasies served them, too long here to be rehearsed: the which I leave to the writers of chronicles."[49] One habit, however, Cavendish shares with the chroniclers, that of frequently commenting on the fickleness and lack of judgment of the people. In the minor details of style, Cavendish shows great restraint. Alliteration is sparingly used, and the artificial tricks of balance and antithesis, of the use of doublets and learned words appear not at all. The modesty which characterizes the spirit of the book governs the management of the technical details of expression. One may wonder if this twofold restraint and propriety was not the result of Cavendish's Catholic training and traditions, and if so, be led to reflect on what was lost to writing in sixteenth-century England through its rejection of Catholic discipline. The only piece of sixteenth-century historical writing which in its simple truth and restraint of feeling merits a place by the side of Cavendish's *Life* is the brief account of Sir Thomas More, by his son-in-law, Roper, and

[48] Ellis's edition, p. 10.

[49] Ibid., p. 43.

in both cases it was the piety of the writer that gave its peculiar charm to the writing. English style of this period was usually very highly colored and self-assertive. It tended to become either extravagantly popular or extravagantly literary and refined. Both in feeling and in the technic of expression, writers of the time often passed beyond the legitimate bounds of their subject. The excellence of Cavendish's *Life and Death* arises from the fact that the author clearly perceived the limits of his subject and held himself within them.

The first of the historical writings of John Hayward, who in 1619 became Sir John Hayward, appeared in the last year of the sixteenth century. This was entitled *The First Part of the Raigne of Henrie the IIII,* and to Hayward's misfortune, it was dedicated in highly laudatory terms to the Earl of Essex. The book aroused Queen Elizabeth's anger, who thought she saw in it, after the return of Essex from Ireland, allusions favorable to his cause. According to the story preserved by Bacon,[50] Elizabeth regarded it as a " seditious prelude to put into the people's heads boldness and faction," adding that " she had good opinion that there was treason in it." Elizabeth asked Bacon if he could not find sufficient cause in the book for preferring a charge of treason against the author; " whereto I answered," continues Bacon, " ' For treason surely I find none, but for felony very many.' And when her Majesty hastily asked me wherein, I told her, the author had committed very apparent theft; for he had taken most of the sentences of Cornelius Tacitus, and translated them into English, and put them into his text." But Elizabeth was not to be put off with a jest, and suspecting that Hayward was not the author of the book but merely a borrowed name to conceal the real author, she

[50] *Letters and Life,* III, 150.

wanted to rack him "to produce his author." "I replied," says Bacon, "'Nay, madam, he is a Doctor, never rack his person, but rack his style; let him have pen, ink and paper, and help of books, and be enjoined to continue the story where it breaketh off, and I will undertake by collecting the styles to judge whether he were the author or no.'" Though Hayward escaped the threatened racking, both of body and of style, he was kept in prison for several years, and it was not until the accession of James that he regained his liberty and was taken into favor. He was an ardent supporter of James, of the doctrine of the divine right of kings and of the hereditary succession. A university graduate of Cambridge and a student and practitioner of the law in London, Hayward was not without learning sufficient to enable him to set forth his arguments authoritatively in the several treatises which he published on these subjects. His distinction as a lawyer was greater than as an historian, and his elevation to the knighthood doubtless came in recognition of his legal attainments. In the later years of his life he also published several religious treatises, the most popular being his *Sanctuarie of a troubled Soule,* a book of prayers, of pious ejaculations, self-recriminations and meditations which produces a curious impression of fervor without genuine fire.

Besides the *First Part of the Raigne of Henrie IIII,* Hayward's historical writings consist of *The Lives of the III Normans, Kings of England, William the first, William the second, and Henrie the first* (1613), and two posthumous works published a few years after his death in 1627, *The Life and Raigne of King Edward the Sixth,* and *The Beginning of the Reigne of Queene Elizabeth.* In general Hayward strove to be an impartial historian. He is not a violent religious partisan, blaming Cranmer, for example, for insisting on the burning of two heretics, on the ground that "a good thing is not good, if it be immoderately desired or done."[51] On the whole he gives a very fair statement of the reasons for religious reformation in Edward the Sixth's reign, with much respect for all sides of the question. His first experience in connection with his *Raigne of Henrie IIII* doubtless impressed upon him the conviction which he expresses, that history should be a record of events and not a partisan account of affairs. He likewise has definite theories as to what should constitute "a true carried History." He takes issue in part with "a noble Writer in our time,"[52] who esteemed it to be "a maim in History, that the Acts of Parliament should not be recited." To this Hayward agrees in so far as parliamentary acts occasion "tumults or division, or some remarkable alteration in the state; otherwise, as I find them not regarded by most imitable Writers, so I account the relation of them both fruitlesse and improper for a true carried History."[53] A preface to *Henrie the IIII* again touches briefly on the art of writing histories—what things are to be suppressed, what lightly touched, and what to be treated at large, "what liberty a writer may use in framing speeches, and in declaring the causes, counsailes and events of things done," and other similar subjects. These are merely mentioned, however, as topics which Hayward says he might profitably have discussed if he had not been unwilling to make his gates wider than his town, and he closes "onely wishing that all our English Histories were drawne out of the drosse of rude and barbarous English: that by pleasure in reading them, the profit in knowing them, might more easily bee attained."[54]

[51] *Edward the Sixth,* 2nd ed. 1636, p. 16.

[52] Bacon is meant, who in his *Henry VII* (ed. Spedding, *Works,* XI, 147) defends this doctrine at some length.

[53] *Edward the Sixth,* p. 113.

[54] From the edition of 1642, where the preface is headed "A. P.

It was not for lack of effort on Hayward's part if his histories were not "drawne out of the drosse of rude and barbarous English." Many of the artful tricks of Euphuism and Arcadianism, by Hayward's time already become somewhat old-fashioned, he cultivates with more zeal than discretion. He is fond of 'tranlacing,' as when he speaks of the "common sorte," "which joyeth to see any hard happ happen to them whoe are extreme happy." [55] Alliteration is sometimes hard-worked, as when he declares that "many principall poyntes have not punctually beene performed." [56] He is particularly fond of the balanced antithetic sentence. The following, describing the grief of the two children of Henry VIII on hearing of the death of their father, might have come bodily out of *Euphues* or *Arcadia:*

"Never was sorrow more sweetly set forth, their faces seeming rather to beautifie their sorrow than their sorrow to clowd the beautie of their faces. Their young yeares, their excellent beauties, their lovely and lively enterchange of complaints, in such sort graced their griefe, as the most yron eies at that time present were drawne thereby into societie of their teares." [57]

He is not averse to puns, and cheap alliterative phrases are not uncommon, e.g. "stiffe stubbornness and filthy flattery," "vile vulgars," and "vague villaines," meaning the people; and speaking of one Bell, put to death at Tyburn, he describes him as "a man nittily needy." He follows the usual fashion of the chroniclers in his frequent scornful references to the "vulgar multitude," in the in-

To the Reader." There is no indication who A. P. was, but the passage reads like Hayward.

[55] *Annals of Elizabeth,* ed. Bruce, p. 24.

[56] Ibid., p. 35.

[57] *Edward the Sixth,* p. 9.

sertion of set speeches of his own invention, and even occasionally in allusions to such prodigies as the mare that brought forth a foal with one body and two heads. He pauses in the narrative not infrequently for brief passages of moral or political wisdom, and he often cites precedents very learnedly and elaborately from Greek, Roman, Hebrew, and general Asiatic history. Unquestionably Hayward had a feeling for historical narrative as distinguished from mere chronicle writing, but his literary taste was not sufficiently formed to enable him to write histories which might serve as models of permanent value.

Bacon's *History of the Reign of Henry VII* was composed in the summer of 1621 and appeared in print the following year. It was the first work completed by Bacon after his fall, and as soon as it was finished, a fair copy, still preserved in the British Museum, was made and sent to James. But though Bacon evidently had some intention of pleasing the king by the composition of this history, the reading of it is sufficient to show that he did not strive to accomplish this end by flattery. The *History* is not a eulogy of Henry VII, nor a veiled eulogy of King James. It is a serious endeavor to realize in practice certain principles of historical writing which Bacon had long held theoretically. In the *Advancement of Learning* he had proposed as a worthy subject for an English historian the history of England from the Union of the Roses to the Union of the Crowns. The *History of the Reign of Henry VII* was the first section of this broader plan, and though the whole was never carried to completion, a fragment of a history of the reign of Henry VIII and another of the reign of James I show that the project was never long out of Bacon's mind. His reasons for choosing this period of English history are specifically given. He refrained from going "higher to more ancient times" because the farther back one goes, the fewer documents and original sources of information there are available. Moreover the later times are more profitable for the historian to study, since in them the matter of history is not great wars and conquests, but rather the events of times "refined in policies and industries." This period also offers something "altogether unknown to antiquity," that is, the changes "in matters of religion and the state ecclesiastical." Bacon adds various other happenings of interest within the realm and without as justifying his intention to write a history of approximately his own times, concluding with "the new discoveries and navigations abroad, the new provisions of laws and precedents of state at home, and the accidents memorable both of state and of court." The only doubt that occurs to him is that the times of which he proposes to write may be "of too fresh memory." But he sets this doubt aside by assuring himself that the truthful historian of contemporary events, if he does not win the praise of his own day, is at least secure of that of posterity.[58]

The method of Bacon's *Reign of Henry VII* does not differ greatly from that of earlier biographical English histories. The center of the action is always the king and his counsellors or followers. The character of the king is analyzed to the minutest detail, and all the doings of state at home and abroad are duly recorded. The people rarely appear in Bacon's narrative except as rebels, as attendants on the king's celebrations, or as taxpayers from whom the royal revenues are derived. In other words, Bacon attempts no more than his predecessors the composition of a social or economic history of the times of Henry VII. The nearest he comes to this is in the recital of the laws passed in the various parliaments of the reign, a procedure he recommends to all writers of histories, since

[58] *Works,* ed. Spedding, XI, 34-37.

laws are "the principal acts of peace." Even here, however, though the laws discussed are in their effects often of a popular character, Bacon seems to be interested in them mainly from the point of view of the development of legal history or theory. In certain formal respects, also, the *Reign of Henry VII* is like earlier histories. One finds in it the usual invented speeches, put into the mouths of the characters,[59] the formal character portrait, and though this is in the main done implicitly and without specific comment, the same feeling for the moral and didactic value of biography. The one, but all-sufficient, characteristic which lifts the *Reign of Henry VII* out of its class is the greatness of mind of the author of the work. Here, for the first time in the development of English historical writing, one feels that the historian is not only completely master of the details of his history with respect to narrative arrangement and order, but also with respect to the full biographical and political significance of the details. Bacon's history becomes therefore not primarily a narrative of events, but a revelation of character, an analysis of principles and theories of government. It tells the story of Henry's life in accordance with Bacon's personal interpretation of the evidence afforded by the records. Henry is neither a picturesque villain nor an exalted saint in Bacon's eyes, but a human being of mixed character whose actions are in themselves interesting, and for those who care to ponder over them, may be edifying. The spirit of Bacon's history is as far removed as possible from the romantic. It is the work of one who knows himself firmly fixed in a world of realities, of one who sees deeply into the motives which actuate men, and who by reason of the clearness of his

[59] See Morley, *Critical Miscellanies,* IV, 101, for a discussion of the set speech in Renascence historians, carried back to Thucydides.

vision has lost some of the glamour of life. Human nature does not need to be highly colored to interest Bacon, and the familiar, even the ignoble, does not move him to scornful invective. Like the Italians Machiavelli and Guicciardini, with whose methods he was certainly acquainted, Bacon writes with something of the dispassionateness of the judge whose concern is primarily to make a full and complete statement of the case. Yet at the end of the history, it cannot be denied that Bacon has passed sentence on Henry VII. The drawing of the indictment is a sentence, not of absolute condemnation or acquittal, but the many-sided sentence which is the only one of any significance to the historian. When one compares Bacon as historian with preceding chroniclers and historical writers, one can give the earlier writers credit for industry in the collection of detail, for occasional picturesqueness in narrative and richness in description, in which respects they often surpass Bacon, but nowhere can one find such grasp of general situation and of individual character, such richness of thought in so brief compass, as in Bacon's *Henry VII*. It was Bacon's achievement to show that stories of great wars and conquests of kings and princes, or descriptions of royal progresses and feastings, no matter how richly embroidered, were not adequate to impart dignity to historical writing. The true dignity of history, as men might learn from Bacon's example, depends less upon the greatness of the action of which it treats than it does upon the degree of wisdom displayed by the historian in his grasp of character and in his comprehension of the significance of events.

A curious contrast is presented when one turns from Bacon's closely reasoned *Henry VII* to Raleigh's grandiose *History of the World*. This work realizes in some respects the philosophical idea of history which the scholarship of the seventeenth century was beginning to inculcate; it at least attempts to take account, as Bolton recommended, of the ways of God to man. But on the other hand it may also be grouped with the encyclopedic and cosmographical treatises of the kind fragmentarily represented by Holinshed's *Chronicle*. It may even have been influenced in its origins by still earlier and medieval forms of universal history, the *Historia Scholastica* of Peter Comestor and the *Compendious History of the World* by Orosius. There is more than a trace of medievalism both in the conception and in the treatment of the materials of Raleigh's *History*. His authorities, of which he cites over six hundred, are often of a kind that even the critical knowledge of his day should have taught him to reject. And though the Bible is unquestionably an historical document of very great importance, Raleigh represents an extreme point of view when he declares that the Biblical narratives, by virtue of their sacred character, are the tests and touchstones of truthful record with which all other historical evidence must be made to concur. On the other hand, the *History* is a peculiarly contemporary expression of Raleigh's own spirit and the spirit of his day. The wonder never grows less that the great minds of the sixteenth century should have been at once so rich in detail and so broadly inclusive. Raleigh was a poet, a courtier, a soldier, a sailor, a daring explorer, even a philosopher (if we may use the term to describe one who has thought widely on the moral aspects of human life), and in all these varied activities, a man of rare energy and distinction. His mind moved freely and in large circles, and it is not surprising that one who had committed himself, as Raleigh had done, to the bold adventure of determining the outline and structure of the physical world should also undertake the still bolder adventure of tracing the growth and form of human civilization. Whatever may be its imperfections of execution, Raleigh's *History* in its conception exhibits the quality of greatness which later generations have not always been able to share with the Elizabethans.

The immediate popularity of the book is a proof that it met a contemporary need. It was written between 1607 and 1614, while Raleigh was in prison, and it appeared first in print in two editions in 1614. New editions appeared at intervals of a few years throughout the seventeenth century, attesting a continued interest in the book which has now been lost, but which is by no means unintelligible to anyone who may be led to read it. The *History* begins with the Creation, and extends only to the year 130 B.C. This, however, was but one section of the whole as originally planned, which was to consist of three parts or volumes, carrying the history of the great nations of the world down to Raleigh's own times. Of the whole plan the first part alone was finished, and this treats only of Jewish, Greek, and Roman history. This first part is itself a long work, testifying to Raleigh's industry during the seven years in which it was written. It has a unity of its own, and though at the end of it, Raleigh declares that he has already "hewn out" a second and third volume, the lack of the later parts in no way impairs the interest of the earlier. The modern reader may regret that Raleigh did not begin by writing a history of those events in which he himself took so prominent a part, and in his *Preface* he acknowledges that it might have been better if he, as one who had been "permitted to draw water as near the well-head as another," had attempted rather to put together "the unjointed frame of our English affairs than of the universal." "To this I answer," says Raleigh, "that whosoever in writing modern history shall follow truth too near the heels, it may haply strike out his teeth."[60] With his final conclusion the average reader of the seventeenth century, eager for some connected story of the history of the great nations, the great captains and heroes of antiquity, would doubtless have agreed; and though a contemporary history would certainly have gained in dramatic interest, it could hardly have retained the broad philosophic movement, the moral and political wisdom, which are the distinguishing characteristics of the *History* as it stands.

His own conception of history Raleigh presents in some detail in the *Preface* to his book. The obvious ideas of the immortality of history, "that it hath given us life in our understanding since the world itself had life and beginning," and that it provides for mankind edifying examples of virtue and of vice, Raleigh passes over lightly. His main point is that the writing of history consists in tracing the judgments of God, and the chief lesson of history is that all human greatness is mutable and transitory. Though kings and princes of the world have labored to make themselves and their issue masters of the world, "yet hath Babylon, Persia, Syria, Macedon, Carthage, Rome and the rest, no fruit, flower, grass, nor leaf, springing upon the face of the earth of those seeds:—No; their very roots and ruins do hardly remain."[61] Of the ultimate purpose of God in thus exalting and degrading the nations and princes of the earth, Raleigh does not venture to speak. He simply notes that the history of the world is the story of a sequence of tragedies, the word tragedy being understood in its medieval sense, of the ascent and the fall of princes. Of one thing, however, he is quite certain, and that is that wickedness shall not go unpunished. He finds that God is "the same God in Spain, as in England and

[60] *History* (Edinburgh, 1820), I, lviii.
[61] Ibid., p. vi.

France," a just God, but an avenging God, visiting his wrath upon the third and fourth generations. The figure of the stage constantly recurs. Man plays out his little part before the public gaze, but the end of it always is tragedy. Death stands ever at the end of the path, and all winds drive us to the port of death, "when by letting fall that fatal anchor, which can never be weighed again, the navigation of this life takes end."[62] And since God is the author of all our tragedies, since it is He who has "written out for us and appointed us all the parts we are to play,"[63] and since He has shown his impartiality by visiting the greatest misfortunes upon the greatest princes, no man, not even the most humble, can complain of wrong. "Certainly there is no other account to be made of this ridiculous world than to resolve that the change of fortune on the great theatre is but as the change of garments on the less."[64] A manly philosophy, certainly, if somewhat melancholy in its combination of stoicism and helplessness.

In pursuance of his general plan of displaying the tragedy of human life, Raleigh begins with the first great tragic story of the creation and fall of man. The whole Biblical story from Adam to Noah and the sons of Noah is narrated with a great wealth of learned illustration. But Raleigh does not feel himself bound to follow, undeviatingly, the thread of his narrative. He acknowledges that he makes many digressions, "which if they shall be laid to my charge, I must cast the fault into the great heap of human error."[65] For this human error of wandering from the subject, the reader of the *History* to-day will be grateful, since the digressions are frequently the most interesting parts of the narrative. Although acknowledging that "the matter is of no great weight as touching his kind," Raleigh

[62] *History,* p. xxxv.
[63] Ibid., p. xxxix.
[64] Ibid., p. xl.
[65] Ibid., p. lvii.

devotes a whole section to the discussion of the question whether or not the tree of life in the garden of Paradise was the same as the Ficus Indicus, or banian-tree, reputedly a rare tree, though he declares that he himself had seen "twenty thousand of them in one valley not far from Paria in America." He has seen them also "in those seas of the Indies where oysters breed," and by pulling up one of the cords of the tree entangled in the beds of oysters, he has seen "five hundred oysters hanging in a heap thereon; whereof the report came, that oysters grew on trees in India." [66] At another place, having narrated some of the evil works of the devil in the world, Raleigh pauses to describe in a passage of stately oratorical beauty the last refuges of the devil, since in these latter days "he cannot play upon the open stage of the world" as in former times. Now he "finds it more for his advantage to creep into the minds of men; and inhabiting in the temples of their hearts, works them to a more effectual adoration of himself than ever." Instead of the images and idols of old, dead stones cut into the faces of beasts and birds, "he now sets before them the high and shining idol of glory, the all-commanding image of bright *gold*." [67] These digressions are sometimes of considerable length, as when the story of the giving of the law to Moses leads over into a general treatise on the origin and nature of law. Raleigh discusses the name and meaning of the words law and right, defines the eternal law of God as Hooker, whom he quotes, had done before him, with the aid of Thomas Aquinas and St. Augustine, distinguishes between the law of nature, the written and the unwritten law of God, and various other theoretical and administrative aspects of the law. Sometimes also the digressions are interesting as containing the results of Raleigh's own practical experience and observa-

[66] *History,* I, 145. [67] Ibid., I, 203.

tion. Thus in discussing the relative advantages of the Carthaginians and Romans for warfare in Sicily, he shows by modern instances how commanders who could avail themselves of the means of maritime transportation were enabled to overcome and outwit their enemies. "And to say the truth," he continues, "it is impossible for any maritime country, not having the coasts admirably fortified, to defend itself against a powerful enemy that is master of the sea. Hereof I had rather that Spain, than England, should be an example."[68] Another interesting digression occurs in the account of the funeral games held by Scipio in honor of the memory of his father and his uncle. A part of these games consisting of a duel between two Spaniards, Raleigh is easily led into a long discussion of the history of dueling and of the points of honor involved in the dueling code. For the "mystical curiosities" of the latter he has great scorn, as for the rule that it is a far greater dishonor "to receive from an enemy a slight touch with a cane than a sound blow with a sword; the one having relation to a slave, the other to a soldier." "I confess," adds Raleigh,[69] "that the difference is pretty; though, for mine own part, if I had had any such *Italianated* enemy in former times, I should willingly have made with him such an exchange, and have given him the point of honour to boot."

Numerous though the digressions are, so large is the general movement of the book that they do not appreciably retard the narrative. In a somewhat complicated pattern the action moves steadily forward, the main thesis by gradual accretion becoming more and more powerful. The reader is always a spectator before the stage of the world and the author is the showman. His method is not so crude as that of the earlier narrators of the falls of princes, but the spirit informing it is not dissimilar. Raleigh en-

[68] *History,* V, 56.

[69] Ibid., V, 467.

deavors to infuse feeling and thought into the bare records of antiquity, and in doing so, he often looks at his subject from the point of view of the poet. Like the "tragical poets" of whom he himself speaks, Raleigh's tale is "against infidelity, time, destiny; and, most of all, against the variable success of worldly things, and instability of fortune."[70] His theme is moral and didactic only in the largest sense, and his story, like those of the tragedians, is intended to purge and purify the emotions, not to lay down precepts of action. The most eloquent passages of the book are those in which Raleigh displays the vanity of ambition, "which plougheth up the air and soweth in the wind," and the blind ignorance of man who will not know himself until death compels him to turn his eyes inward:

> "O eloquent, just, and mighty Death! whom none could advise, thou hast persuaded; what none hath dared, thou hast done; and whom all the world hath flattered, thou only hast cast out of the world and despised;—thou hast drawn together all the far-stretched greatness, all the pride, cruelty, and ambition of man, and covered it all over with these two narrow words, Hic jacet."[71]

Bacon raised history to a dignified level by intellect, Raleigh elevated it by his poetic feeling. His *History of the World* was without question the most moving account of human events that had so far appeared in England.

Original historical composition during the English Renascence was almost exclusively devoted to English subjects. The history of foreign nations, however, especially the nations of antiquity, was not inadequately represented in translations. A translation of Xenophon by William Barker, containing six books, appeared in 1560 (?), and enlarged to eight books in a second edition in 1567. This

[70] *History,* VI, 368. [71] Ibid., VI, 370.

translation was made, according to Barker, "out of Greeke into Englishe." Later translations were those of John Bingham (1623) and of Philemon Holland (1632). Herodotus appeared in a partial translation in *The Famous Hystory of Herodotus . . . Deuided into nine Bookes, entituled with the names of the nine Muses* (1584), translated by one who signs himself B. R. Thucydides came earlier in a version made from a French translation by Thomas Nicolls (1550), the only one to appear apparently before the translation made by Hobbes, "Immediately out of the Greeke," in 1629. The *Moralia* of Plutarch interested Elizabethan translators more than the *Lives,* the only translation of which was Sir Thomas North's (1579), made not from the Greek but from the French of Amyot. Polybius is represented by a translation made by C. Watson (1568), to which the translator added an abstract of the life of Henry V, and by a later version by Edward Grimeston (1633). Herodian's history of the Roman Emperors was translated by Nicholas Smith and published by Copland (1550?), the translation being made not from the original Greek but from the Latin version of Politian. A later version (1629), "Interpreted out of the Greeke Originall," was one of the numerous works of James Maxwell, author of many historical and religious writings in the first half of the seventeenth century. Aelian is represented by *A registre of Hystories* translated "as well according to the truth of the Greeke text as of the Latine" by Abraham Fleming (1576). The Roman history of Appian is represented by *An auncient Historie and exquisite Chronicle of the Romane warres* (1578), with continuations from a source not specified.

The Latin historians were usually translated directly from the Latin originals. Of Caesar "as much as concernyth thys realm of England" was translated and published by an unknown author in 1530. Arthur Golding issued *The eyght bookes of Caius Julius Cæsar* in 1565, but no other translations of Caesar appeared, probably because no need was felt for English translations of so well-known a book, until the English versions of Sir Clement Edmondes in the first decade of the next century. Extracts from Livy by Antony Cope were published in 1544, but no completer version appeared until that made by the professional translator, Philemon Holland, in 1600. The first translations from Tacitus appear to have been the *Fower bookes of the Histories of Cornelius Tacitus* (1591) by Sir Henry Savile. *The Annales of Cornelius Tacitus,* with the *Germania,* by R. Grenewey, appeared in 1598, and this and the preceding book passed through a number of editions. Sallust was translated by Alexander Barclay and published by Pynson (1520?). Later translations were made by Thomas Heywood (1608) and William Cross (1629). Suetonius first received the favor of an English dress from Philemon Holland (1606). Eutropius, "Englished by Nicolas Haward," stands alone in an edition of 1564, as does Diodorus Siculus, "Translated out of French into Englysh by Thomas Stocker" (1569). A version of Diodorus Siculus by Skelton, still extant in manuscript, has never been printed. The abridgment of Trogus Pompeius by Justin was translated and published (1564) by Arthur Golding, the translator of Cæsar. Extracts by Thomas Norton had appeared earlier (1560?), and a later translation was made by G. W. (1606). Arthur Golding also published a translation of Pomponius Mela (1585). Ammianus Marcellinus was not translated until he fell into the hands of Philemon Holland (1609).[72] To this list of

[72] For some minor translations and for additional bibliographical detail, cf. Palmer, *List of English Editions and Translations of Greek and Latin Classics printed before 1641,* London, 1911.

translations from the classics may be added a version of Dares Phrygius by Thomas Paynell (1553), which had previously been versified by Lydgate on the basis of Guido della Colonne's Latin prose. Josephus was first made available in English in the translation of Thomas Lodge (1602).

Translations from Italian historians were not numerous. John Shute published *Two very notable Commentaries, the one of the originall of the Turcks and Empire of the house of Ottomanno . . . and thother of the warres of the Turcke against George Scanderbeg* (1562), the first part of which is a translation from the Italian of the Turkish history of Andrea Cambini. To the list of Arthur Golding's translations already mentioned is to be added *The Historie of Leonard Aretine, concerning the Warres betwene the Imperialls and the Gothes for the possession of Italy* (1563). *A notable Historye of the Saracens* (1575) was "Drawen out of Augustine Curie and sundry other good Authours" by Thomas Newton, translator and editor of Seneca and a distinguished Latinist of the times. Curio's original was written in Latin from which Newton made his translation. Turkish history was again represented by *The History of the Warres betweene the Turks and the Persians* (1595), translated from the Italian of Tommaso Minadoi by Abraham Hartwell, and by Ralph Carr's *Mahumetane or Turkish Hystorye* (1600), "translated from the French and Italian tongues." Of the greater Italian historians, Guicciardini was the earliest to be translated, his history of Italy having been "Reduced into English" by Geffrey Fenton as *The Historie of Guicciardin* (1579). Machiavelli first appeared in English in Peter Whitehorne's *Arte of Warre* (1560), a translation of Machiavelli's book of the same title and one of a number of similar treatises on military practice and drill which were translated from various Italian authors. Of the historical writings of Machiavelli the earliest representative was Thomas Bedingfield's *Florentine Historie* (1595). The *Discorsi* were translated by Edmund Dacres, under the title *Machiavel's Discourses upon the first decade of T. Livius* (1636), and the same translator published in 1640 the first English version of Machiavelli's *Il Principe*.[73] Of translations from the French, the most important, after Berners' Froissart, was *The Historie of Philip de Commines* (1596), admirably translated by Thomas Danett.[74] With the books derived from French sources, however, may perhaps be grouped Richard Knolles' *Generall Historie of the Turkes* (1603 and a number of later editions), a dignified and slow-moving narrative, largely based upon Boissard's *Vitae et Icones Sultanorum Turcicorum* (1596).

II

Antiquarianism and history were two closely related subjects in the mind of the sixteenth-century scholar, and the same writers often cultivated both fields. The impulse to the study of English antiquities came partly through the desire to follow back to their origins English laws and legal traditions; partly from students of theological questions, who often endeavored to give authority to the new teachings of the Reformation by showing that they were not really new but merely an inheritance from ancient practice; partly also from the purely patriotic motive of seeing that the records of the nation were preserved and restored; and

[73] For other translations from the Italian, see the bibliography by Miss Scott, *Pub. of the Modern Language Association*, XIV, 485-524.

[74] Edited by Charles Whibley for the Tudor Translation Series. For minor translations from French, see Upham, *French Influence in English Literature*, pp. 471-505.

finally in a considerable degree from the humanistic desire to imitate in English everything that had been done in classical literature. As England had her disciples of Cicero, Ovid, and Vergil, so she must also have her followers of Strabo, Pausanias, and Varro. With such models to lend distinction to the endeavor, the writing of works on English antiquities came to be regarded as worthy the attention of the most learned and important scholars. And undoubtedly there must have been a fascination in entering so virgin a territory. To put down on record for the first time the name of a writer or the name of a river or town had some of the interest of original discovery. In the composition of books of antiquity and of topographical detail, England was really discovering herself, not merely scattered notices of past times, but the country and the people with a unified and unbroken history.

It was about the middle of the sixteenth century when such books first began to appear. In 1548 John Bale published his catalogue of English writers under the title *Illustrium Majoris Britanniae Scriptorum Summarium.* Bale felt keenly the neglect of English antiquities, and especially the heedlessness which permitted the destruction of ancient books and manuscripts by the very Englishmen who should have been the first to care for their preservation. At the dissolution of the monasteries, he saw vast numbers of books either utterly destroyed or carried out of the country into lands where their value was better understood. Hindered by "ungentyll poverte" from rescuing these books by purchase, he could only stand helplessly by and raise his voice in protest. And though he is violent enough against the "laysy lubbers and popyshe belly-goddes" of the monasteries for their neglect of their manuscripts, he confesses that the English are now doing worse, since they not merely neglect but sell and destroy the manuscripts of the old libraries.[75]

The first professional English antiquary was John Leland. He was born in the first decade of the sixteenth century, studied at St. Paul's School under William Lyly, later at Cambridge, at Oxford, and at Paris, where he knew well Budaeus and other famous French scholars. In 1533 he was made "king's antiquary," an office created for him in which he had neither predecessor nor successor. In the same year, by royal commission, he began the task of collecting materials for what was to be a great work on the history and antiquities of the English nation. His journeyings in quest of antiquarian lore were extensive. He had authority to enter the libraries of all cathedrals, abbeys, priories, colleges, and other places where records, writings, and secrets of antiquity were deposited; and he declares "that there is almost neyther cape nor baye, haven, creke or pere, ryver or confluence of ryvers, breches, washes, lakes, meres, fenny waters, mountaynes, valleys, mores, hethes, forestes, woodes, cyties, burges, castels, pryncypall manor places, monasteryes, and colleges, but I have seane them, and noted in so doynge a whole worlde of thynges verye memorable."[76] This journey, according to Leland's statement, occupied six years, but a longer time elapsed before he made any report on his activities. In 1545 he addressed a little pamphlet to Henry VIII, described as *A New Years Gift,*[77] in which he gave an account of his plans and intentions. He intends, he declares, to call his history "*de*

[75] *The Laboryouse Journey,* 1549. The pages are unnumbered.

[76] *A New Years Gift.*

[77] Published again by Bale in 1549, with comment by Bale, under the title, *The Laboryouse Journey and serche of John Leylande, for Englandes Antiquitees, geven of hym as a newe years gyfte to Kynge Henry the VIII. in the XXXVII. yeare of his Reygne, with declaracyons enlarged by Johan Bale.*

Antiquitate Britannica, or els *Civilis historia.*" There are to be as many books as there are shires in England and Wales, "so that I esteme that thys volume wyl enclude a fyfty bokes." There are then to be six books on the islands adjacent to Britain, and finally he expects "to superadde a worke as an ornament and a ryght comely garlande," in three books, to be entitled *De nobilitate Britannica.* He comments on the general neglect of English antiquities, and accounts for the fact on the ground that old works have not been printed, "and also because men of eloquence hath not enterprised to set them fourth in a flouryshynge style, in some tymes past not commenly used in Englande of writers otherwise wele learned, and now in such estymacyon, that except truth be delycately clothed in purpure her written verytees can scant fynde a reader." Bale's comment on this is that the endeavor to satisfy "delycate eares and wyttes" with a more eloquent style "myghte wele be spared." And on Leland's general plans for the writing of books, he remarks that "it wolde have byn a wondre (yea, a myracle to the worlde) to have redde them."

Leland did not succeed in carrying any part of his great plan to a conclusion, and the little *New Years Gift* is the only English writing that he completed. When Bale published his edition of the *New Years Gift* in 1549, Leland had already become insane, in which condition he died three years later. Bale charges Leland with being "vayneglоryouse," probably meaning thereby that he set his mark higher than was needful; and he declares that Leland had "a poetycall wytt, whyche I lament, for I judge it one of the chefest thynges that caused hym to fall besydes his ryghte dyscernynges." In this there may be an element of truth. Leland had written a considerable body of Latin occasional verse and was interested in the graces of expression. The task, therefore, of assembling and of setting forth in "a flouryshynge style" the mountain of facts which he had collected may well have been beyond his ability. He left them merely as detached notes, which were to be useful to many later chroniclers, antiquaries, and historians, but which are entirely without literary quality.[78]

A more successful, though less ambitious attempt than that of Leland, was William Lambarde's *Perambulation of Kent.* Lambarde was a Londoner who, at the death of his father, inherited the manor of Westcombe in Greenwich, Kent. He had been a student of law at Lincoln's Inn, and had there devoted some time to the study of Anglo-Saxon and of history with Laurence Nowell, one of the early restorers of Anglo-Saxon studies in England. His first publication, *Αρχαιονομία, sive de priscis Anglorum legibus* (1568), was the result of his interest in these subjects. Two years later he completed his *Perambulation,* though it was not printed until 1576. He later published several more books on legal subjects, held various public offices, among which was that of keeper of the records in the Tower, and died in the first year of the new century.

Lambarde had begun the collection of materials, arranged in alphabetical order, for a Topographical Dictionary, covering not one, but many shires,[79] but he tells us that "after that it had pleased God to provide for me in Kent," he determined to begin his publication with that shire. He writes with becoming modesty, fearing lest he may have "shaped such a peece as is more meete to be condemned to the kitchen than worthy to be admitted or have place in the parlor."[80] The content of his book is

[78] See Hearne's edition of the *Itinerary,* 1710 (re-edited by Miss Lucy Toulmin Smith, 1906-8), and of the *Collectanea,* 1715.

[79] Not printed in Lambarde's lifetime, but issued in 1730, as *Dictionarium Angliae Topographicum et Historicum.*

[80] *Perambulation,* p. vi.

naturally miscellaneous. He describes the geographical characteristics of Kent, the products, the people of the county and their activities, but mainly places, towns, castles, and similar memorials. He offers etymologies for most of the place-names he mentions, carrying the names back to Anglo-Saxon or Celtic originals in a way which is often picturesque but quite as often incorrect. He makes use of the privilege of the local chronicler in recording trivial events, as that Lenham long since "had market upon the Tuesday, which even to this day it enjoieth," [81] or the story of the orphan boy, William Sennock, who lived to become mayor of the city of London.[82] The gentle bucolic spirit of the book breaks, however, when Lambarde speaks of matters of religion. For he is a violent partisan, and often stops to revile the monks or to expose their frauds. Although Lambarde by no means writes in dictionary style and has a constant care for picturesque phrasing, he does not descend to petty artifices and mannerisms of style. There is a pleasant charm in all his descriptions, whether he talks of "Seacoastes, Rivers, Creekes, Waterings and Rills," or of the more important places of human habitation. And with it all, Lambarde never loses the sense of the importance of his subject. He was doing something which had never been done before, and thereby was uniting himself in fellowship to Tacitus and Cæsar. He writes with the threefold interest of the scholar, the writer, and the gentleman, and though such a task undertaken with the same seriousness to-day might seem prosy, at the end neither Lambarde nor his modern reader is dissatisfied with this "Xenogogie and Perambulation of Kent, the first and onely Shyre" that its author has described.

Lambarde's book, the first local history written in English, had many successors, but none more interesting than the

[81] *Perambulation,* p. 292. [82] Ibid., p. 469.

work suggested by it, that perambulation of London and its suburbs by John Stowe, known as the *Survey of London.* Stowe's life was spent in London. He was born in 1525, the son of a tallow-chandler, and he himself was a tailor. Such time and money as he could abstract from the necessities of his calling he devoted to the pursuit of studies in divinity, astrology, and poetry. His interest in the first two of these subjects, dangerous matters for a man of his fortune to meddle with, seems to have got him into trouble and thereafter to have declined. His interest in poetry bore fruit, however, in the publication of his first work, an edition of *The Workes of Geffrey Chaucer* (1561). This was followed by the publication of his various historical works, and a few years before his death, by his *Survey of London,* in 1598.

In his perambulation of London, Stowe describes all the city's gates, towers, castles, bridges, churches, springs, streams, wells, together with any other notable thing that had come to his attention. It is a highly detailed picture of London, more however of the physical London than the city of men and women. Nevertheless the book gives one a sense of the reality of city life in England in the latter part of the sixteenth century such as can be paralleled elsewhere only in the realistic writings of Nashe, Greene, Deloney, and Dekker. Stowe, however, was not consciously part of any literary movement of the time, and if he shows some of the tendencies which appear in naturalist and realistic professional writers, the explanation is to be found in the common origin of these tendencies, that is, in the emergence into literature of the middle classes and their social interests. Stowe shares with many other contemporary antiquaries and historians the gift of lending life and human interest to what might easily have been a dry catalogue of detail. The convention of impersonality which the modern printed book seems to impose upon most authors was not then so powerful as it soon became. Stowe takes the reader into his confidence, chats discursively about this or that, quotes as it were from his personal diary, and if the spirit moves him, even enters into the details of his private life. The writing as a result may seem garrulous, but it is not likely to seem stupid. Moreover, as one who had spent the better part of a century in London, Stowe could write with something of the privilege of an oldest inhabitant. He had seen many and notable changes take place, and knowing by experience how difficult it was to recover the truth with respect to past happenings, he realized to the full the importance of his own contemporary observations.

"This Hogge lane," he notes reminiscently, "stretcheth North toward Saint Marie Spitle without Bishopsgate, and within these fortie yeares, had on both sides fayre hedgerowes of Elme trees, with Bridges and easie stiles to passe over into the pleasant fieldes, very commodious for Citizens therein to walke, shoote, and otherwise recreate and refresh their dulled spirites in the sweete and wholesome ayre, which is now within few yeares made a continuall building throughout, of Garden houses, and small Cottages: and the fields on either side be turned into Garden plottes, teynter yardes, Bowling Allyes, and such like, from Houndes ditch in the West, so farre as white Chappell, and further towards the East." [83]

Sometimes the recollections have little more than their antiquity to commend them, as when, speaking of the church of St. Lawrence in the Jewry, he records:

"I my selfe more than 70. yeares since have seene in this church the shanke bone of a man (as it is taken) and also a tooth of a very greate bignes hanged up for shew in chaines of iron." This shank bone was twenty-five inches long, "of a man as is said, but might be of an Oliphant." [84]

[83] *Survey,* ed. Kingsford, I, 127. [84] Ibid., I, 275.

These passages are typical of Stowe. He always writes as the credulous citizen, meetly, soberly, gossipingly, with occasional quiet charm, and even with some conscious quaintness and humor. But he is never ambitious or straining, and to his credit be it said, never affectedly literary.

The position which Holinshed's *Chronicle* occupies among English chronicles, William Camden's *Britannia* holds in the line of development of antiquarian and chorographical writing. In the ambitiousness of its scheme and in the inclusiveness of its detail, it is the result and the summary of much preceding effort. The burden consequently under which Leland staggered and succumbed, Camden was enabled to carry lightly. He is said to have begun making collections for his great work as early as his twentieth year, when, in 1571, he returned from Oxford to his home in London. In 1575 he became second master in Westminster School, utilizing the free periods of vacations for journeying about England and adding to his collections. On his thirty-fifth birthday, May 2, 1586, appeared the first edition of his *Britannia,* a lasting testimony of his admirable industry and skill. Various editions of the work appeared later, the last for which Camden was responsible being that of 1607. In the mean time Camden had become head-master of Westminster School, had published a Greek grammar for use in the school, in 1597 had been made Clarenceux king-of-arms, and had otherwise been active as scholar, antiquary, and herald. In 1615 appeared his *Annales rerum Anglicarum et Hibernicarum, regnante Elizabetha,* which was later several times translated into English. The first English translation of *Britannia* was made by Philemon Holland, in 1610, and according to the statement of the title page, with additions and revision by Camden. Camden lived to be seventy-two years old, and among his friends he numbered not only the pioneers in historical and antiquarian English scholarship, but also such representatives of the more exact, but dryer, learning of the first half of the seventeenth century as Sir Henry Savile, Sir Henry Spelman, and John Selden.

Camden chose not to write in English and now pays the penalty for this choice in that the modern reader is more likely to turn to Philemon Holland's translation of the *Britannia* than to the excellent Latin of the original. As a Latin stylist, Camden speaks apologetically of his writing. He declares that he has not weighed every word in goldsmith's scales, and that it is not his intention to pick flowers in the gardens of eloquence. But this disclaimer need not be taken too seriously, for it is quite evident that Camden was not a negligent student of the technic of expression. The freshness, the picturesqueness, and the charm of Holland's translation are in the main all found in the original. What Holland has added is a certain quaint and idiomatic English flavor, unmistakably Elizabethan, which doubtless Camden himself would have given to his narrative if he had written in the vernacular.

The *Britannia* begins with an account of the races that have dwelt in Britain, of the political divisions of the country, of the different ranks of English society, of the law courts of the land, and then proceeds to a minuter description of England by shires. All topographical features are indicated, as well as climate, occupations, and any marvels that came to Camden's notice. Much attention is given to etymologies, but even these details are not dryly presented. The descriptions often show not merely knowledge about a place but feeling for it. Speaking of Taunton in Somerset, in Holland's words he says:

"From thence with a soft streame and gentle fall, Thone runneth by *Thonton,* commonly *Taunton,* and giveth it his name. A verie fine and proper towne this is indeed, and most pleasantly seated: in a word, one of the eies of this shire. . . . The Countrey here, most delectable on every side with greene medowes; flourishing with pleasant Gardens and Orchards, and replenished with faire Mannour houses; wonderfully contenteth the eyes of the beholders." [85]

Some of the etymologies are more ingenious than convincing. The town Goodmanchester, a name which Camden takes to be a popular error for Gormonchester, is carried back in its origins to

"the verie same City which Antonine the Emperour termed Duroliponte, amisse, instead of *Durosiponte*. For *Durosi-ponte* (pardon mee I pray you for changing one letter) soundeth in the British tongue, *A Bridge over the water Ose*. And that this river is named indifferently and without distinction Use, Ise, Ose, and Ouse, all men confesse. But when this name was under the Danes quite abolished, it beganne to be called *Gormancester*, of *Gormon* the Dane, unto whom after agreement of peace, king *Aelfred* graunted these provinces." [86]

Popular traditions and tales are accepted and repeated by Camden with an amazing simplicity. In his account of Whitby he includes all the local superstitions about jet which had there flowered in the people's imaginations. He speaks also of "certaine stones faschioned like serpents folded and wrapped round as in a wreathe, even the very pastimes of Nature disporting her selfe." Some of the stones are "shaped round in maner of a Globe," in which, if you break them, "are found stony serpents enwrapped round like a wreath. but most of them are headless." [87] This region was particularly rich in wonders. For not far away the Irt, a little river, "maketh way toward the sea, wherein the muscles and cochles, after they have with a

[85] P. 223. [86] P. 510. [87] P. 721.

kinde of yawning or gaping sucked in dew, which they lust after to conceive by, bring forth pearles, or to speake as the Poet doth, *Shell-berries,* which the inhabitants thereby search after at a low water, and our Lapidaries and Jewellers buy of the poore needy people for a little, but sell againe at an high rate."[88] Thus is the hard path of science and etymology made pleasant and easy. The book as a whole is a monument to Camden's industry and to a wide and humane, if extremely uncritical, scholarship. But learning had not yet grown into the hard mistress she was soon to become. Whether the details of Camden's scholarship are exact or inexact, they are always kept alive by a pleasant personal note. He makes scholarship, if not a precise, at least an amiable pursuit.

Descriptions of English antiquities and of English regions, like those of Leland, Lambarde, Harrison, Stowe, and Camden, were of course only reflections of a general interest in the bounds of the physical world. This interest extended from the period of antiquity to the latest contemporary voyage of adventure and discovery. Arthur Golding's translation of Pomponius Mela (1585), "concerninge the Situation of the world," was not merely a work of scholarship, but was designed to be of practical benefit to "Gentlemen, Marchants, Mariners and Travellers." A few years earlier Thomas Twine had published a translation of Dionysius Periegetes under the title of *The Surueye of the World* (1572), containing not only descriptions of the principal countries, kingdoms, peoples, cities, towns, ports, promontories, hills, woods, mountains,

[88] P. 765. The Latin of this (from the edition of 1590, p. 629), runs as follows: Superius Irton amniculus mare petit in quo conchae cum rorem, quem veluti maritum appetunt, oscitatione quadam hauserint, fiunt gravidae, margaritasque sive, ut cum Poeta loquar, baccas concheas pariunt, quae accolae cum resederit aqua venantur, gemmariique nostri minimo ab egenis emunt & maximo revendunt.

valleys, rivers, and fountains of the inhabited world, but also of the seas, "with their Clyffes, Reaches, Turnings, Elbows, Quicksands, Rocks, Flattes, Shelves and Shoares," a work which was said to be "very necessary and delectable for students of Geographie, Saylers, and others." With the progress of discovery in the sixteenth century, contemporary descriptions of the outlying regions of the world were written by most of the notable captains and explorers who sailed forth into the unknown from all the ports of Europe. Many of these were gathered together by Richard Eden, who published part of his materials in *A Treatyse of the newe India with other new founde landes and Islands* (1553), from Sebastian Münster's *Cosmographia Universalis,* and *The Decades of the Newe Worlde or West India* (1555), from Peter Martyr. The voyages of the great English discoverers, of Drake, Hawkins, Gilbert, Frobisher, Raleigh, and others, resulted in the publication of descriptions and records of mixed scientific, commercial, and romantic interest. As the bulk of this literature increased, it inspired Richard Hakluyt to attempt a collection of it. The fruit of his labors appeared in his *Principall Navigations, Voiages and Discoveries of the English Nation,* a first edition in 1589 and a second, largely increased, in 1600. The book is a compilation from various sources, partly translated and partly adapted from the original narratives of English explorers and adventurers. It is not, however, a digested history of exploration, but rather a library of documents and descriptions from which a history could be written. The project of telling the story of the extension of man's knowledge of the world upon which he lives was one to stir the imagination, but the purpose and plan of Hakluyt's work are more romantic than the execution. The collection contains much information, much sturdy, straightforward narrative, and by reading between the lines, one can catch some of the glow of great achievement in the age of Elizabethan exploration. The materials of an epic of exploration are contained in Hakluyt, but they were not sufficiently fused and refined by passage through a literary imagination to form either a history or a poem.

If one endeavors now in retrospect to measure the achievements of the writers of history and of the antiquaries of the sixteenth century in relation to the traditions of these subjects as they were inherited from their medieval predecessors, one finds that the great advances were made in two opposite directions. In the first place, the writers of English history in the Renascence acquired a deeper understanding of the comprehensiveness and of the dignity of historical narrative than had hitherto prevailed. Medieval history was comprehensive so far as chronological inclusiveness was concerned, but there is apparent in the cyclical chronicles of the earlier period little imaginative feeling for the structure of the whole. A good deal of the spirit of medieval chronicle writing survives, even to the end of the sixteenth century, but in Hall, Holinshed, Stowe, and others, there is also evident striving to write history with attention to the unity and consecutiveness of events, and in consequence with a larger sense of its dignity. The task of the historian, as it gradually came to be regarded, was not to fill a treasure-house of fact with a mere catalogue of events, but to tell a connected story. And towards the end of the century the province of the historian was still further enlarged by the annexation of some parts of the field of the philosopher and theologian in providing explanations of the causes and of the course of events. Parallel to this widening of the bounds of the intellectual world in history ran the expansion of the historian's grasp of the limits of the physical world, as evidenced in the cosmographical descriptions and local perambulations of the antiquaries. The two combined gave to the historical writer of the time an inspiring and confident assurance of the dignity and importance of his subject.

On the other hand English history made great advances in the sixteenth century in its command over a variety of minute historical fact and in its sense of the reality of the materials out of which history is made. Much of the Elizabethan historian's detail is indeed trivial, and only slowly was the lesson learned of the difference between detail which was genuinely significant, which really gave the personal coloring to character and action, and that which was of ephemeral or of merely ornamental interest. Nevertheless historical writing did gradually become more immediate and personal in its interests, more and more a record of credible human beings in a world of credible circumstances. One finds in sixteenth-century historians a much clearer realization of the life of the state than had hitherto existed, both with respect to the development of internal policies and privileges, and with respect to the relations of England to foreign nations. The histories of the time clearly reflect the growth of the English national consciousness. Even in ecclesiastical matters, which were the prime and often the exclusive concern of medieval historians, the sixteenth-century historian, as Bacon pointed out, had an entirely new story to tell, a story, too, which came much nearer to common humanity in its daily acts and experiences than the chroniclings of the monastic historians had ever done. And finally, with historians like More, Cavendish, and Bacon, one finds human character analyzed with a realization of its subtleties and shades of meaning such as the historians of the medieval school never remotely approached. In some respects it was an advantage to the English historians of the sixteenth century that they concerned themselves relatively so little with the philosophic interpretation of events. By keeping their attention directed to concrete detail and to specific character and motive they gave to their writing a much to be desired solidity and reality which otherwise it might have lacked.

These two characteristics combined, the new sense of the largeness of the meaning of history and the new feeling for the reality of the characters, the setting and the events of historical narrative, appear as the distinctive merits of the histories of the sixteenth century when they are compared with the cruder historical writings of the earlier centuries. They are also the condition of the special applications of the art of English prose writing to historical composition in this period. The lofty seriousness with which history was regarded encouraged the historian in the cultivation of a dignified and substantial technic in writing, at the same time restraining in him, to a very considerable degree, the strong tendency of the age towards extravagance and artificiality of style. The feeling for varied life and color in detail also gave to the historical literature of the period a much greater vivacity of effect, a much greater illusion of truth and reality than the earlier historians were capable of producing. The objective existence of the world of history exercised, on the whole, a beneficial effect upon the historians' command of the technical art of composition. It kept them in the middle way, providing them with abundant materials for the exercise of their art, and steadying them also with the sense of a duty towards these materials to be soberly and worthily performed. It would be too much to expect, even of historians, that they should forego all extravagance and fantasy in style, but compared with the writers of fictitious narrative, they remained engagingly natural and simple.

VIII

THE MODERNISTS

Modernism and Realism—Realism in the Drama—Ben Jonson—Economic and Social Discussion—Medicine and Quackery—Merry Jests and Tales—Rogue Tracts—Modernism and Villainy—Nashe—Greene—Peele—Lodge—Dekker—Deloney

Readers of Shakspere will not need to be reminded that the Elizabethan sense of the word 'modern' was not the same as it is in present-day English. To the Elizabethan, the adjective meant approximately 'commonplace,' 'familiar,' and Elizabethan modernism, as a literary style, may fairly be equated with nineteenth-century realism. But realism, like M. Jourdain's prose, is ever with us, waiting only for the philosopher to give it a name. The mere process of naming it, however, often makes realistic writing seem to mean more than was intended. Realists who would have recognized themselves as such and who were professed practitioners of a cult are not to be found until much later than the period covered by this book. Before critical opinion had formulated a theory with respect to it, realistic writing was in the main merely an occasional outcropping of the rock bottom of daily life. It would be a vain refinement, therefore, to attempt to state clearly what had not yet taken clear form, and in the present chapter many writers will be mentioned whose work was not consistently or prevailingly, sometimes not even intentionally realistic.

Though realism, or modernism, in the sixteenth century is not susceptible of a sharp and clear definition, there is little difficulty in recognizing the numerous manifestations of the realistic spirit when they appear; and perhaps it will be sufficient to say that in the following discussion the term realism will be used, somewhat loosely from the philosophic point of view, to designate the reflection of the world of sensible fact and of everyday human experience in literature, whether presented in a simply descriptive spirit, or as reflections of the anti-heroic endeavor to escape from the idealistic refinements of poetry and romance.

Towards the end of the sixteenth century there were some indications that the experiences and circumstances of familiar life were coming to be recognized more clearly than ever before as valuable material for literary purposes, and indications also that at this time something like a realistic school was beginning to be formed. In his hostile discussion of what he called modernism and villainy, Gabriel Harvey even gave a name to these tendencies. But the time was not ripe for the full apprehension of the possibilities of a realistic method, and the literary pictures of London life in Dekker, Greene, Nashe, and others, were continued only in slight sketches which served as settings for popular anecdotes. When the young Milton sought for a great subject, it was not London that occurred to him, not the moral struggles of men facing the troubles and complications of contemporary life, but instead the misty King Arthur and the battles of the angels in heaven.

Certain kinds of writing not originally devised to hold a realistic content, by their nature are more open to the reception of such materials than others. The drama especially has proved to be a peculiarly favorable medium for the reproduction of the setting and characters of real life. In the sixteenth century meter was the form imperatively prescribed by tradition for all serious dramatic efforts, and from this prescription Elizabethan drama successfully freed itself in but relatively few instances. Interesting parallelisms can be observed, however, in the use of prose in the drama and in the development of the feeling for realistic effect. The mysteries, moralities, and interludes of the earliest English drama were written mainly in a four-stress line ultimately derived from the Old English alliterative line. In its Middle English and early Modern English developments, this four-stress line followed two tendencies, the one a regularizing and restraining tendency, leading towards a fixed seven- or eight-syllable line with weak cæsura and little alliteration but with clearly marked rime, and the other a free and expanding tendency, resulting in a line with an irregular number of unstressed syllables, a clearly marked break or cæsura in the line, and a considerable retention of the native ornament of alliteration with a correspondingly weak sense for rime. It was this latter kind of verse, known as tumbling verse, which connects directly, as has already been pointed out,[1] with the development of a certain type of English prose. In the mysteries and moralities, in the interludes and early comedies, this tumbling verse, often passing over into a tumbling prose, was frequently employed in passages of boasting, of exhortation, of popular and sometimes realistically humorous volubility. It is often difficult to tell where the metrical intention leaves off and the prose begins in this kind of writing. The persistence of this style in the popular drama is remarkable, so late a comedy as *The Taming of a Shrew* (1594) exhibiting a thorough confusion between prose and tumbling verse. The differentiation and separation of a popular tumbling prose from tumbling verse never became complete, however, and the significance of the tumbling

[1] See above, p. 15.

style in the present discussion lies mainly in the fact that it was one of the ways in which the tradition of familiar expression established by *Piers Plowman* was kept alive.

For the earliest consistent and artistic use of prose in dramatic writing one must turn not to the popular drama but to the court comedies of Lyly. In his two romances Lyly had previously worked out a form of expression suitable for the conversation of the polite world, and this style, freed from some of its more extravagant mannerisms, he transferred to his comedies. The influence of Lyly's example upon later dramatic writing was very great, both upon comedy and the more serious drama. It did not establish prose as the standard form in any kind of dramatic writing, but it certainly led to the freer use of prose in all kinds. The comedies of Shakspere show manifest traces of this influence, and as for the tragedies it is doubtful if Shakspere would ever have written certain of the more familiar passages in *Hamlet* in prose, or the charming vignette of social life in which the visit of the Lady Valeria to Volumnia and Virgilia in *Coriolanus* is described, if Lyly had not prepared the way for him. In the Elizabethan masques and entertainments, also, the traces of the influence of Lyly's prose are very marked. By reason of their lightness and informality, dramatic compositions of this type found in prose a peculiarly congenial form of expression, and in them are contained some of the most faithful transcripts of Elizabethan manners and sentiments.

In the period of the great names in the Elizabethan drama, one finds prose used with an increasingly certain sense of its values and proprieties. Marlowe used little prose—least of all in his heroic plays. Ignoble characters occasionally use prose in *The Massacre of Paris,* only however in planning or discussing murders. In *Tamburlaine* prose is used in several passages of comic character or of commonplace narration. After Bajazet has committed suicide, Zabina's grief passes beyond the restraints of verse into prose. In *Faustus* prose is more extensively used, mainly in scenes of humorous, satirical, and realistic coloring. The Seven Deadly Sins use it exclusively. The character Ithamore uses prose almost altogether in *The Jew of Malta,* though he breaks into verse when occasion offers, as in his description of the beauties of Greece; but in general when sordid subjects are discussed, such as the lending of money, or when the less dignified characters take part in the action, the narrative passes from verse to prose.

Marlowe's contemporaries, Greene, Peele, and Kyd, all used prose to a certain extent and according to a scheme more or less well defined. Greene's *Comical History of Alphonsus* is entirely in verse, and his *Orlando Furioso* has very little prose in it. But in his *Looking Glass for London, Frier Bacon and Frier Bongay, James the Fourth,* and *The Pinner of Wakefield,* prose is very freely employed. Peele's prose is found mainly in his *Edward the First, The Old Wives Tale,* and *Sir Clyomen and Sir Clamydes.* Kyd's *Spanish Tragedy* contains a few prose passages, brief moments of relief from the crude horrors of the play.

Greene seems to have had a carefully thought out plan for the use of prose. His noble characters express themselves in verse, the ignoble characters speak prose, and the middle-class characters sometimes employ verse and sometimes prose, according to the circumstances. In only one instance does he cause a woman to speak prose, this being the character of the Smith's Wife in *The Looking Glass for London.* Elsewhere his women speak verse, even when men of corresponding rank speak prose. Thus Alcon speaks prose, though Sannia, his wife, employs verse; Margaret, the keeper's daughter, and Joan, a country wench, and The Hostess of the Bell at Henley, all speak verse, in *Frier*

Bacon, though Miles, the two Friars, and other humble male characters use prose. While other dramatists did not follow this convention as strictly as Greene, the general tendency was to give female characters a dignified treatment for which verse was the fitting medium of expression. The free use of prose by Portia and Nerissa in the *Merchant of Venice,* of Rosalind and Celia in *As You Like It,* of Helena in *All's Well,* and of other female characters in Shakspere's early and middle comedy, was perhaps due to the influence of the comedy of Lyly, and is not found in the more serious plays and in the later comedy.

Greene's *Looking Glasse for London and Englande,* written in collaboration with Thomas Lodge, is a satirical and didactic survey of London life, having for its main structural framework the deeds of the Machiavellian Rasni, king of Nineveh, a prince who follows his star through bloodshed and destruction. The main action of the play is in verse, but inserted at various stages of the main story are realistic descriptive scenes of familiar life in prose. The first gives a picture of drunkenness and the violence resulting therefrom, the second illustrates the evils of usury, and the others are similar transcripts of London characters and situations. Occasional echoes of the cony-catching pamphlets occur and throughout these amusing interludes one realizes that Greene knew at least his London thoroughly. *Frier Bacon and Frier Bongay* is a play of varied interest, but the story of Lacy, the Earl of Lincoln's wooing of Margaret, the lovely maid of Fresingfield, a humble dairymaid raised to elevated position, is noteworthy for its charming pictures of simple English life. Broad comedy situations are provided by Miles, Friar Bacon's poor scholar, by Rafe Simnell, a court fool, and by various "clowns," or rustics, as this term is understood by Greene. *The Scottish Historie of James the Fourth* is primarily a love romance, but here again realistic comedy relief is provided by Bohan, a cynical Scotchman, by Nano, a dwarf, and Slipper, a rogue, and by various other humble characters. One would like to be sure that Greene also wrote *George a Greene, The Pinner of Wakefield,* doubtfully assigned to him. The play centers about a redoubtable hero of Bradford, George a Greene, the town pounder, and it presents an attractive picture of village life in "Merry England" against a background of kings and nobles. The change from verse to prose in the play corresponds in general to the social plane upon which the action for the time being moves. Though it is a patriotic and loyal play, its main purpose is to exalt the people and to illustrate their valor. Much of the color of town and country life is given in the course of the action, by George himself and his sweetheart Bettris, by her father Grime, by Jenkin, George's man, and Willy, his boy, by various townsmen, shoemakers, and others. The play is one of hearty, though somewhat heavy humor, and was certainly written by one who understood and enjoyed the simple life of old England.

The most engaging qualities of Thomas Dekker appear more fully in his plays than in his other writings, especially in *The Shoemakers Holiday* (1600) and *Patient Grissill* (registered in 1600 but not published until 1603), both of which are written in prose. The plot of *The Shoemakers Holiday,* derived mainly from Thomas Deloney's novel, *The Gentle Craft,* tells the story of Simon Eyre, who rises from humble position to be Lord Mayor of London. It presents a pleasant picture of citizen life in London, a hearty, stirring life, neither too boisterous nor too subtly refined. *Patient Grissill,* written in collaboration with Chettle and Haughton, is based on the old story of Griselda as Chaucer had told it in the Clerk's Tale, but various sub-plots and characters are added. Dekker is generally supposed to have been responsible for the character of Babulo, the old servant of Grissill's father, and for Laureo, her poor-scholar brother. Both are admirable character studies, and Babulo fills an especially important part in the play by emphasizing the human side of the occasionally somewhat far-fetched pastoral situations. The play as a whole presents a charming picture of family life among humble, hard-working villagers, not poetized beyond recognition like a fanciful shepherd idyl, but still lifted above the sordid by much tender feeling and good humor.

Thomas Heywood, in many respects spiritually akin to Dekker, followed the more usual custom in his plays of mixing prose and verse. His *Woman Killed with Kindness* (about 1603) is a domestic tragedy in which the story is simply and naturally told without effort at high style. The prose and verse are about equally divided, the superior characters speaking blank verse, though the style in general is so direct that the transition from their verse to prose is never violent. In considering tragedies of this type, which deal with middle-class characters and familiar contemporary situations, one is surprised to find that prose is not more extensively used. Even servants and ruffians sometimes employ verse in *Arden of Feversham*. But perhaps the explanation is that the established literary convention of metrical form for tragedy was less likely to be set aside in a somewhat crudely popular kind of writing like the domestic tragedy than elsewhere, the popular taste clinging to a mechanical, even stilted, distinction of form in spite of its inappropriateness.

Heywood's other plays resemble *A Woman Killed with Kindness* in containing a mixture of prose and verse. *The Fair Maid of the West* is a romantic comedy, the leading characters being Bess Bridges, a tanner's daughter and barmaid, and her true lover, Spencer, an English gentleman.

The play is full of interesting pictures of sea-captains, pirates, merchants, and swaggering gentlemen, an exciting medley of adventures in England, on the high seas, and in Morocco. *The English Traveller* is another domestic tragedy, in blank verse with the humbler parts in prose. *The Wise Woman of Hogsden* is a comedy of intrigue dealing with London characters and written largely in prose, though with some verse. Heywood always wrote a remarkably free and unaffected style, whether in prose or verse, and is always fresh and direct in feeling. His characters are the familiar ones of English life, drawn with great verisimilitude and treated realistically, not heroically. The power of the metrical convention in Elizabethan drama may be estimated from the fact that even Heywood was not able to rise superior to it.

With the so-called later Elizabethans, for example with Massinger, Beaumont, and Fletcher, the general tendency prevailed of adhering to the convention of meter in dramatic composition. Even Shakspere uses prose less freely in his later plays than he had done in the comedies and tragedies of his early and middle periods. The verse of the later Elizabethan drama is, to be sure, a much looser and freer metrical form than the earlier blank verse of the Marlowe tradition. If the drama did not accept prose as the accredited form in which dramatic writings were to be composed, at any rate it modified its verse form in order to give it some of the qualities of ease and variety characteristic of prose. Massinger employed prose in only one play, *The Virgin Martyr,* mostly in verse but with prose passages in which the low-life characters, Hircius and Spungius, take part. Beaumont and Fletcher have many plays entirely in verse, some in mixed prose and verse, but none altogether in prose. Their command over both forms is remarkable, and a play like *Philaster,* or *The Knight of the Burning Pestle,* passes from one form to the other easily and effectively.

In general prose was used in the Elizabethan drama for purposes of artistic contrast with verse. This was, in the main, Shakspere's use of prose. The only one of his plays which is predominantly prose is the *Merry Wives of Windsor,* and the content and expression of this play belong distinctly to the middle-class and familiar style to which Harvey applied the terms modernism and villainy. Otherwise in Shakspere, as in other Elizabethan dramatists, prose occurs only sporadically, and generally as a relief from more severe or poetic expression. At times, in passages of frenzied and incoherent emotion, prose was employed even in moments of highest dramatic tension, the vehicle of verse breaking down under the strain of the passion. Usually, however, the prose parts of a play present the comedy relief to more serious or more elevated action, the comedy of clowns, servants, artisans, and country boobies. Often these comedy characters are raised to the level of expression in verse when they come into contact with characters of higher rank, and the reverse is also true. Queen Elinor, for example, in *Edward the First,* changes from verse to prose when she addresses the Potter's Wife. The higher themes, such as hate and revenge, romantic love, the beauties of nature, as well as all set passages of oratorical quality, almost universally took metrical form, but humble and homely or sordid and grotesque situations were often presented in prose. On the whole the use of prose was remarkably flexible, and within certain limits effective. One might expect these limits to have been more widely extended than they were, but the critical canon which connected serious drama with epic poetry, and in general the feeling for literary distinction in style were powerful checks on the free development of a dramatic English prose in this period.

In the discussion of the prose of the Elizabethan drama, Ben Jonson occupies a place apart. No dramatist used prose more artfully or consciously than Jonson, and few used it less successfully. The main defect of Jonson's dramatic prose is that it is so slightly dramatic, or in equivalent terms, so little in the spirit of easy, natural conversation. This criticism is as old as Dryden, who objected to Jonson's language, especially in his comedies, that "he weaved it too laboriously." Jonson, he adds, was "the Virgil, the pattern of elaborate writing."[2] And Jonson was quite as elaborately simple in his prose as in his verse.

As a prose stylist Jonson formed himself neither upon the popular tradition of the loose, familiar, and picturesque manner, nor upon the more ornamental courtly style of Lyly and his followers. He stands with Bacon, whom he highly commends, in his admiration of "a strict and succinct style." He quotes approvingly the statement of Aulus Gellius that he "would rather have a plaine downright wisdome, then a foolish and affected eloquence."[3] "Nothing is fashionable till it bee deform'd," he says elsewhere, in a passage which seems to be original; "and this is to write like a *Gentleman.*"[4] He was annoyed at the distinction often made between the scholar and the gentleman, "as if a *Scholler* were no *Gentleman,*" and delivered himself to the effect that to write like a gentleman will in time "become all one as to write like an Asse."[5] He agrees that the language of the "true Artificer" must differ from the vulgar somewhat, but it "shall not fly from all humanity, with the *Tamerlanes* and *Tamer-chams* of the late Age, which had nothing in them but the *scenicall* strutting and furious vociferation to

[2] *Essay of Dramatic Poesy,* ed. Arnold, pp. 70-71.
[3] *Discoveries,* ed. Castelain, p. 19.
[4] Ibid., p. 33.
[5] *Staple of Newes,* Act IV, Sc. II. These are the words of Shunfield, but seem to be the opinions of Jonson.

warrant them to the ignorant gapers." [6] And he even took the pains to go through his own plays after they were written and prune away the more luxuriant passages. According to the report of a conversation with Drummond, Jonson wrote all his verses first in prose, and was also of the opinion that verses "stood by sense without either colours or accent—*which yett other tymes he denied.*" [7] But though Jonson set his face against the richly ornamented literary style, in prose or verse, it was by no means a naïve simplicity which he cultivated. He aimed at a chiseled distinctness of form which can be attained only by the highest art.

Aside from the plays, the only extended pieces by Jonson entirely in prose are a few critical prefaces and introductions to the plays, his *English Grammar,* and his *Timber or Discoveries.* The *English Grammar* is a brief sketch which offered little opportunity for literary amplification. *Discoveries* was made up largely of translations from Latin writers, though with additions by Jonson. It was a kind of commonplace book, a collection of "dispersed meditations," like Bacon's *Essays.* The thoughts contained in it were not mere jottings, however, but were carefully elaborated as to form. They continually remind one of Bacon in the early editions of his *Essays,* and many passages might be transferred to the *Essays* bodily without seeming out of place. Except for occasional learned words, the meditations are expressed in that "pure and neat language" which Jonson professes he loved. Ornament was so carefully excluded that the very lack of it becomes a stylistic distinction. The "laborious terseness of expression" which Swinburne found so characteristic of Jonson, is nowhere more marked than in these brief comments and criticisms.

Only two of Jonson's plays, *Epicoene* and *Bartholomew*

[6] *Discoveries,* p. 41. [7] *Works,* ed. Cunningham, III, 486.

Fair, were written altogether in prose. Some were written entirely in verse—*Catiline* and *Sejanus,* as a matter of course, but also comedies, like *The Alchemist, The Devil is an Ass, The New Inn,* and others. A number of the plays contain a mixture of verse and prose, the prose in some of them, for example *Every Man in his Humour* and *Every Man out of his Humour,* being so much greater in extent than the verse that they are practically prose plays. In many of the masques and entertainments prose is also extensively employed, and in these informal dramatic compositions occur many pleasant sketches of humble English life, of city artisans and their wives, of humorous Irish, Welsh, and Dutch comedy characters. The prose of the masques is on the whole unusually free and easy for Jonsonian prose. In these lighter productions he seems to have abated a little of the severity of his literary ideals. In the more ambitious plays, however, one is constantly aware of Jonson's intention to write like a scholar. It is not so much that he obtrudes his professional learning upon the reader's attention or that he is lacking in truthful observation. His plays, on the contrary, are an inexhaustible mine of comment on the details of contemporary middle-class life. But Jonson's own attitude towards the life he describes is one of aloofness, the voices of his characters fall thinly and remotely upon the ear. His purpose was to present not individuals and concrete realities but rather generalizations of realities. He employed abundantly therefore the materials of realism, and he even strove zealously to make his dialogue a faithful record of colloquial conversation. He was careful to indicate the clipped and abbreviated forms of spoken expression, to employ abundantly the expletives and current smart metaphors of familiar speech, and in many detailed ways to reproduce photographically popular syntax and phonetics. But the result seems overdone. The very abundance of concrete detail, as often in modern dialect stories, leads the reader to look upon it as linguistically curious, true to literal fact, but cold and lifeless. Much of Jonson's detail is not individually appropriate to the character employing it, but only generally to his type or class of person. One constantly feels with respect to Jonson's characters that the showman is exhibiting them, that they are not acting or speaking as their own spirit gives them utterance. Though theoretically it might seem that this ought to make them more real, Jonson's abstraction of sentiment and romance from his characters has probably also added to the effect of their unreality. In spite of his thoroughgoing realistic method, none of Jonson's characters seem as convincing as many of Shakspere's or Dekker's or Heywood's, perhaps because none of them arouse the immediate sympathy of the imagination which is the dramatist's most effective aid in producing the illusion of reality. Jonson's own age was not greatly interested in his plays, and later generations have rather inclined to regard them with respectful admiration than with affection. Perhaps the explanation lies, in part at least, in the feeling that a theoretical realism like Jonson's is more in the spirit of science than of literature, and that therefore the plays call for little emotional or personal response.

A second group of sixteenth-century writings which frequently took a realistic coloring is that which had to do with general moral, social, and economic conditions. Technical treatises on government, such as Sir John Fortescue's *Governance of England,*[8] or Cheke's *Hurt of Sedition,* afforded few opportunities for the introduction of picturesque detail, though Fortescue's description of poverty in France [9]

[8] Edited by Plummer, Oxford, 1885; written between 1471 and 1476, but first printed in 1714.

[9] Plummer, p. 114.

is a vigorous and concrete piece of writing. *A Discourse of the Common Weal of this Realm of England,* written by John Hales, a man of some importance in civil affairs, has more literary quality.[10] It is written in the form of a dialogue in which a knight, a merchant, a doctor of theology, and a craftsman take part. These four, whose characters are well maintained, discuss mainly the economic state of England, enclosures and grazing, money and coinage, and similar topics. The dialogue is pleasantly written, with some humor, a gentlemanly give and take of opinion, and a considerable sense for the contemporary conditions of English life.

It was the Reformation, however, which was most effective in opening men's eyes not only to new truths within but also to the existence of realities without. Simon Fish's *Supplication for the Beggars* and similar supplications have already been mentioned. Henry Brinklow's *Complaynt of Roderyck Mors* is an impassioned plea for the poor people of England. It calls attention to the exorbitant rents demanded by landlords, a subject discussed at length also in Hales, to the lack of alms-giving, to the fact that the people are worse off economically under Henry than they had been under the papacy. Much is said against proud bishops: "What lordes have more gorgyos houses than thei have?",[11] and the complaint is in general in behalf of the "comynaltye," "the body of this reame." Another work of Brinklow's is his *Lamentacyon of a Christen agaynst the Cytye of London.* The irreligion and immorality of the city are here portrayed, the wretchedness of the poor who "lye in their howses in most grevous paynes and dye for lacke of ayde

[10] Written in 1549, but first published in 1581; also known as *A brief conceipt of English policy.* It has been edited by Miss Elizabeth Lamond, Cambridge, 1893, and also by A-C. Tersen, Avallon, 1907, with a French translation.

[11] Cowper, E.E.T.S., Extra Series 22, p. 69.

of the riche," the wickedness of aldermen whom, if they repent not, "I will, yf God lende me lyfe, in an other worke name you,"[12] and other conditions that called loudly for reform. Not infrequently, also, the controversial dialogues of the time, as in Sir Thomas More, are enlivened by touches of genuine description and humor. And of course for vivid realistic detail it would be difficult to surpass Foxe's *Acts and Monuments*. William Turner, botanist, physician, preacher, and religious controversialist, transferred a good deal of the racy humor of his preaching to his controversial dialogues. He enjoyed a full share of that power of vivid, concrete expression which characterizes the preachers of the early Reformation, men like Latimer, Lever, and Bradford. As time passed, however, the drift both in preaching and in controversy was towards a more dignified and learned method than that which had been employed by the earlier leaders. Popular preachers were never lacking, but Hooker, Andrewes, and Donne established standards which put most popular preaching quite beyond the literary pale, and after the first flush of the Reformation, controversy occupied itself with the least real of all things, with the subtleties of theological doctrine.

Among other professions, the incentives to literary expression seem to have been less powerful. Treatises on botany, mathematics, astrology, alchemy, agriculture, on military subjects, on sword play, on riding the great horse, and similar subjects abound, but they seldom rise above the level of the literal and matter-of-fact. Among the more learned professions, doctors and lawyers perhaps have the fullest opportunity of viewing human nature unveiled, but the Elizabethan lawyer, with exceptions like Sir Thomas More and his controversial opponent, Christopher St. German, seldom

[12] Cowper, ibid., p. 91.

utilized his experiences for active literary purposes, though his profession supplied the passive material for much realistic satire and description. The profession of medicine on the other hand had strong humanistic associations which encouraged the popularization of medical lore, and as diversion from severer professional pursuits, the exercise of the pen in many an engaging sketch of men and manners. Among early humanist doctors the name of Linacre occupies an honorable place, though he wrote little or nothing in English. William Turner has already been noticed in connection with his controversial pamphlets; he deserves mention also as "the first Englishman who studied plants scientifically."[13] As a part of his general program of education, Sir Thomas Elyot wrote his *Castel of Helth,* which appeared first in 1534, and again in 1541, "in some places augmented by the first author therof." In the Proheme, Elyot defends himself against the charge of meddling in undertaking to write about medicine. He declares that his only purpose is to serve the public and benefit it, as did Henry VIII himself, who did not disdain "to be the chiefe author and setter foorth of an Introduction into grammer for the children of his lovyng subjectes." And if physicians are angry because he has treated of their science in English, let them remember, says Elyot, "that the grekes wrate in greke, the Romains in latin, Avicenna and the other in Arabike, which were their owne proper and maternall tongues." Very naïvely Elyot tells how he has collected his medical lore from various bookish sources. His knowledge is not often of the kind which maketh a wise man in medicine, nor is it presented with much attention to literary form. On the whole the book is a mechanical compilation, significant merely as an early attempt to popularize technical knowledge.

[13] On Turner as herbalist, see Arber, *Herbals,* pp. 100-108.

A more entertaining observer of men and manners was a contemporary of Elyot's, Andrew Borde, "of Physicke Doctor." He studied abroad, at "all the unyversyties and scoles approbated, and beynge within the precinct of chrystendome."[14] Being at Montpellier, "the well-hed of Physycke," he consulted "with many egregyous Doctours of Physycke" what matter he should write, and as a result produced his *Compendious Regyment or A Dyetary of Helth* (1542). Except in the aureate Preface, from which the quotations given above are taken, the *Compendious Regyment* is as crudely written as Elyot's *Castel of Helth.* It was intended to serve as a book of information and its occasional quaintnesses due to the credulity of the author are not often intended. A further fruit of Borde's travels abroad was his *Fyrst Boke of the Introduction of Knowledge,* a book of traveler's reminiscences, criticisms, and directions. Its purpose is to "teache a man to speake parte of all maner of languages, and to know the usage and fashion of all maner of countreys." His method in attempting to carry out this ambitious program was to give first a woodcut presentation of an Englishman, or Frenchman, or German, to follow this with a metrical account of the land of the English or the French or the Germans, and then to conclude with a prose account of the same, with a few directions how to speak the various languages, lists of common phrases, the values of coins, and other such simple wisdom. Though a book covering so wide a field must necessarily be thin and scattering, Borde often writes picturesquely, as one with his eye upon the fact.

"The people of Hygh Almayne," he observes, "they be rude and rustycall, and very boystous in theyr speche, and humbly in their apparell; yet yf some of them can get a fox

[14] *A Compendious Regyment,* ed. Furnivall, pp. 225-226.

tale or two, or thre fox tayles, standyng up ryght upon theyr cappe, set up with styckes, or that he maye have a capons feder, or a goose feder, or any long feder on his cap, than he is called a 'yonker.'" [15]

The best of all things he finds in England, except its speech, which he confesses is "a base speche to other noble speches, as Italion, Castylion and Frenche; howbeit the speche of Englande is of late dayes amended." [16] He observes that in Cornwall there are two speeches: "the one is naughty Englyshe, and the other is Cornyshe speche." With true English pride he believes that "the noble citie of London precelleth al other, not onely of that region, but of all other regyons . . . And as for the ordre of the citie in maners and good fashyons & curtasy, it excelleth al other cities and townes. And there is such a brydge of pulchritudnes, that in all the worlde there is none lyke." [17]

William Bullein, born early in the reign of Henry VIII, also traveled on the Continent to study medicine. He published, in 1558-59, *A newe booke entituled the Governement of Healthe,* and several years later his *Bulwarke of defence againste all sicknes, Sornes, and woundes that dooe daily assaulte mankinde.* Other professional writings of Bullein's were *A comfortable Regiment . . . against the moste perilous Pleurisie,* and *A briefe and short discourse of the Vertue and Operation of Balsame.* But his most interesting, and from the literary point of view his most important effort, was his *Dialogue bothe pleasaunte and pietifull, wherein is a goodly regimente against the fever Pestilence, with a consolacion and comfort against death* (1564). The book, as

[15] *Fyrst Boke,* ed. Furnivall, p. 160.

[16] Ibid., p. 122.

[17] Ibid., p. 119. Borde wrote several other books, among them a treatise on beards of which so little is known that it is impossible to tell whether it was a waggish or a supposedly scientific performance.

Bullein says, doth "intreate of sonderie thynges,"[18] and is indeed a curious jumble of various matters, though the author seems to have had specially in mind a practical purpose of helping his "poore nedie brothers povertie." Twelve persons take part in the conversation, and the dialogues are presented in succession almost like the scenes of a drama. Yet it is characteristic of the unformed literary standards of the author that the work also suggests Smollett and the rambling type of novel. A citizen and his wife are the central figures and about them are grouped a number of other characters, a beggar, a doctor, a miser, several roguish servants and others. There is a good deal of satire in the course of the narrative, upon quackery in medicine, upon lawyers and usurers, upon worldly prelates. Some serious information as to drugs and the treatment of diseases is given. Mingled with the lighter matter occur serious philosophic reflections and a discussion of the psychology of the will and the soul. A critical estimate is given of "Old Morall Goore" of "Wittie Chaucer," of "Lamenting Lidgate," of "Bartlet [i.e. Barclay] with an hoopyng Russet, long coate," and of "Sir Davie Linse."[19] But the main framework of the dialogue is a charmingly simple and natural picture of life in contemporary England. We see the merchant and his quick-tempered wife leaving London in a time of pestilence in search of a place of safety in the country. We breathe in with them the odors of the "sweete feeldes, garnished with faire plantes and flowers," so refreshing after the deadly air of the city. Her good husband kindly explains to his wife the sights as they pass through villages upon which she comments with urban superiority. She is greatly troubled at a "greate smoke" in a wood, but the merchant relieves her fears by explaining that "it is

[18] *A Dialogue,* etc., ed. Bullen, E.E.T.S., Extra Series, 52, p. 1.
[19] Ibid., pp. 16-18.

nothyng but makyng of charcole in that place." "Why, is Charcole made?" says the wife. "I had thought all thynges had been made at London, yet I did never see no Charcoles made there: by my troth, I had thought that thei did growen upon trees, and had not been made."[20] This amusing motive of urban simplicity in the country is well maintained. As they travel leisurely along, the refugees pass the time by listening to anecdotes and stories told by Roger, their man. At an inn they meet with Mendax, who entertains the merchant, experienced in traveler's tales, but angers the simple-minded wife, with accounts of the wonders he has seen in the new world, how they "gather up Carbuncles and Diamondes with rakes under the spice trees," and how in the Torrida Zona a great rain falling upon "many hundred carte loades of good Hoppes," blown down by the wind, formed "through the help of muche spice" a drink equaled neither by "Hipocras wine nor Beere."[21] A Utopia is alluringly described by Mendax called Nodol in the land Taerg Natrib, but like these names, the characteristics of this delectable region are the reverse of those actually found in London and Britain. So the travelers proceed pleasantly until a great cloud comes out of the sky. A passage of remarkable dramatic power and eloquence then describes the approach of Mors and the death of the citizen, and the dialogue closes with a comforting disquisition from Theologus. The whole is a curious mixture of scientific treatise, satire, morality play, merry tales, and truthful delineation of characters and actions. Bullein was a writer of varied powers and in a clearly defined literary form might have produced a work of lasting importance.[22]

[20] *A Dialogue*, etc., p. 59.

[21] Ibid., p. 101.

[22] A somewhat similar medley is Thomas Lupton's *Sivqila* (i.e. Aliquis), 1580-81. It is described in detail by F. Brie, in the

A more narrowly satirical purpose appears in John Halle's *Historiall Expostulation against the beastlye Abusers, bothe of Chyrurgerie and Physyke in oure tyme* (1565), the aim of which is to reveal the frauds and tricks of quack practitioners. Halle refers to other works of like kind, "a little booke called a Galley late come into Englande from Terra Nova, laden with Phisitiens, Apothecaries, and Chirurgiens, &c.," "a little worke entitled A Poesie made in forme of a vision, &c.," and "maister Bulleyne, in his Bulwarke."[23] But he not only shows up frauds, he also tells good practitioners how to conduct themselves, and versifies some of his precepts "for the better instruction of all yonge chirurgiens." At the end of his book he adds some prayers "mete for chirurgiens." The didactic purpose usually lies very near to the surface in these professional and pseudo-scientific writings and frequently gets the better of the other interests.[24]

A kind of realism appears in literature as an occasional manifestation of elements which are persistent on non-literary levels. The popular tale, for example, has always existed, and when it appears in literary forms, it frequently carries with it some of the color and business of actual life. By emphasis upon some of his broader narratives, Chaucer acquired a traditional reputation as leader and master in this style. Naturally enough it came to pass that the accepted antithesis to this kind of writing in the sixteenth century was not romance, but decency and

Festschrift in honor of Wilhelm Viëtor, Marburg, 1910. Lupton wrote other works of a somewhat archaic literary character.

[23] Percy Society, p. 26.

[24] Hall's *Historiall Expostulation* was part of a larger book entitled *A most excellent and Learned Woorke of Chirurgerie Called Chirurgia parua Lanfranci,* which, according to Hall, was "reduced from dyvers translations to our vulgar or usuall frase."

morality. In a prose work written at the end of his brief career, Greene represents Chaucer and Gower as appearing to him in a vision, Chaucer defending merry tales and Gower seriousness and morality. To enforce their opinions, each tells a story. Chaucer's tale is a picturesque sketch of country manners and life with several Cambridge students figuring in the action. The plot is of the familiar kind in which a clever wife outwits a fond and jealous husband. In the setting of the story, much attention is given to descriptive detail. Tomkins the wheelwright at Grantchester and his wife Kate who sold cream in Cambridge are portraits at full length of the same school as those of the carpenter and his young wife, with her body "gent and smal," in Chaucer's *Millers Tale*. It is apparent from Greene's comment, as well as from the story which he puts into the mouth of Chaucer, that he thinks of Chaucer as above all the poet of popular life, the teller of merry jests in which the mirth was not held in check by considerations of decency. As a contrast to Chaucer's story of Tomkins and Kate, Greene has Gower tell the moral tale of Theodora and Alexander, typically illustrative, in its turn, of the traditional conception of Gower.

Early in the sixteenth century collections of broad tales, usually in prose, began to appear in print. One of the earliest was the group of crude stories known as the *C. Mery Talys* (c. 1526). A few years later appeared *Mery Tales, Wittie questions and quicke answers* (c. 1535). The translation of the German jest-book, *Till Eulenspiegel*, which appeared under the English title of *Tyll Howleglas*, was an important contribution to this form of literature.[25] At the same time the German *Pfarrer von Kalenberg* appeared in an English version entitled the *Parson of Kalen-*

[25] It was printed at Antwerp, 1519?, and in three editions by Copland; Esdaile, p. 79.

borowe. English collections after a time came to be attached to the names of native eponymous heroes of jest cycles. *Merrie Tales Newly Imprinted,* attributed to Skelton, was licensed for printing in 1566-67, but the date of the earlier edition indicated by the title, if there was one, is not known. The preceding year the *Geystes of Skoggon* had been licensed, though the earliest edition extant is one of 1613. Popular books of this character must often have been simply worn out of existence by much use. A variant on the usual form of these collections appeared in the *XII. Mery Jests of the Wyddow Edyth* (1573), the central figure of the tales being a woman of Exeter to pleasure inclined. In 1582, and in a number of later editions, appeared the *Life and Pranks of Long Meg of Westminster,* which provided Deloney with some of the materials for one of his novels of London life. A collection of short comic stories in prose, containing the story of the Induction in the *Taming of the Shrew* and ascribed to Richard Edwardes, was printed in 1570, but is now extant only in a fragment of an edition of the early seventeenth century.[26] Among later collections may be mentioned *Tarltons newes out of Purgatorie* (1590 and later editions), *The Cobler of Caunterburie, or an Inuective against Tarltons Newes out of Purgatorie* (1590 and later), *The Merrie Conceited Jests of George Peele* (1607), *Dobsons Drie Bobbes* (1607), Richard Johnson's *Pleasant Conceits of Old Hobson the merry Londoner* (1607), less popular than the same author's *Seauen Champions of Christendome* (1596 and frequently later), and *Tarltons Jests* (1611). *The Cobler of Caunterburie,* the authorship of which Greene indignantly repudiated, invokes the name of "old Father Chaucer," the stories being supposed, in imitation of the Canterbury Tales, to have been told by passengers on a barge plying between Billingsgate

[26] Esdaile, p. 44.

and Gravesend. The *Merrie Conceited Jests of George Peele* of course were not written by Peele, but they have a homogeneity which results from a clearly defined conception of Peele's character.

These collections of merry tales and anecdotes, the list of which might be increased,[27] contain stories which shade from bare outlines of anecdotes, like the medieval exempla, to carefully elaborated and realistic pictures of life. That they should deal largely with roguery and indecency one might expect from their popular origins. Their realistic detail arises from no theoretical interest in realism as material for the literary artist, but merely from the desire of the raconteur to make his story as convincing as possible. A good story is always the better for being provided with a recognizable local seat and habitation. At the same time the popular anecdote provided a method from which the literary artist could and did learn much, and we shall find the literary prose novelle of the later sixteenth century as deeply indebted to it as was Chaucer in his metrical tales of common life. Indirectly, also, the popular anecdote exerted an influence on other forms of expression. The clown of the earlier Elizabethan drama, like the end-man of the modern minstrel show and the monologue artist of vaudeville, transferred much of the spirit of the realistic tale and the merry jest to the stage. It was not by accident that collections of jests and tales came to be attached to the names of comic actors like Kemp and Tarlton. Launce with his dog, in *The Two Gentlemen of Verona,* is an illustration of the kind of comedy in which the actor occupied the stage alone and kept the audience amused as long as his acquired stock or

[27] See Chandler, *The Literature of Roguery,* I, 59-70; Schulz, *Die Englischen Schwankbücher bis herab zu "Dobson's Drie Bobs"* (1607), Palaestra 117, Berlin, 1912; Aydelotte, *Elizabethan Rogues and Vagabonds, and their representation in contemporary literature,* Oxford, 1913.

his inventive ingenuity lasted. Ready wit, unimpeded flow of language, and an easy familiarity with the audience were the qualities required above all in such acting. According to a well-known story, Sir Thomas More, whom popular tradition remembered, as it did Chaucer, chiefly as a jester, sometimes took his place among the actors on the stage and improvised a part for himself as he went along. And it has already been pointed out how the methods of the early comedians exerted a leavening influence on prose controversial writing in certain of the Marprelate tracts.[28]

The world of the semi-respectable or of the entirely submerged provided the material for still another kind of realistic writing popular in the latter half of the sixteenth century. These were books describing the practices of scamps and vagabonds, professedly for the behoof of innocent citizens and youth, but really no doubt in large measure in satisfaction of the perennial curiosity of the respectable and prosperous as to the doings of the underworld. One of the earliest of these tracts was *A Manifest detection of the moste vyle and detestable use of Diceplay* (1552).[29] A long line of rogue pamphlets was inaugurated when John Awdeley published in 1561 his *Fraternitye of Vacabondes, as wel of ruflying Vacabondes, as of beggerly, of women as of men, of Gyrles as of Boyes, with their proper names and qualities.* A continuation of Awdeley's book appeared in Thomas Harman's *Caveat or Warening for Common Cursetors vulgarely called Vagabones,* the first edition of which, no longer extant, was published in 1566 or 1567. Harman devotes considerable space to "the leud, lousey language of these lewtering Luskes and lasy Lorrels," which he thinks was invented not more than

[28] See above, pp. 128-130.

[29] Reprinted by Halliwell, Percy Society, XXIX (1850).

thirty years before.[30] He gives a dictionary of this "Peddlers Frenche" which was amplified by later writers of rogue tracts. Though he professes to use no art, and that he "never tasted Helycon," Harman's own English is learned and careful, as for example in the use of cursetors "in the intytelynge" of his book as a learned equivalent for vagabonds. He mentions older names for his cursetors, such as "leud leuterars, Faytores, Robardesmen, Drawlatches and valyant beggares," but these words he considers old-fashioned, and such as, if he had used them, might have caused his readers to say, "Oh, what a grose, barberous fellow have we here!"

Harman's *Caveat* passed through a number of editions which kept alive popular interest in his rogues. The theme became a standard one in later Elizabethan literature, and writers who were living on their wits and their pens, Greene, Dekker, Rowlands, and others, often turned to it with the certainty of being gladly read. These later rogue pamphlets are of greater literary significance than Awdeley's or Harman's crude efforts, and more will be said of them in connection with the general literary career of their authors.

At the entry of the last quarter of the sixteenth century, however, it was not the underworld which supplied the most popular and the most widely used material for the storyteller's art, but rather the world of fashion and refined sentiment. The Italian novella translated into English brought with it interest in the analysis and description of shades of feeling and subtleties of action hitherto unknown in English literature. It is a little difficult to say just how much of this writing should properly be characterized as realistic. Lyly's *Euphues,* for example, which is merely an expanded novella, is primarily a sentimental romance, yet it

[30] *A Caveat,* etc., ed. Viles and Furnivall, p. 23.

must often have suggested to contemporary Englishmen their own gilded youth. With all its extravagances and artificialities, *Euphues* shows feeling for the reality of life as its comedy was acted out on the stage of the polite world. The book has social sense in greater degree than any English book before it ever had, and it is, of course, much less " romantic " than Sidney's *Arcadia.* It would be pushing the definition of realism too far, perhaps, to make *Euphues* a realistic work, but there is some significance, at least, in the temptation to do so. The *Arcadia,* on the other hand, could not by any possibility be regarded as a realistic story. Realism of a kind there is in the *Arcadia,* but it is the artful realism of humble characters employed merely as foils for the gentlemen and ladies whose fine sentiments are the main interest of the book. These humble characters are often treated with an astonishing brutality and coarseness of feeling on Sidney's part, perhaps because Sidney was aware that they were not genuinely human and real.

Romance, whether of the school of Lyly or of Sidney, did not long remain in the ascendency. Unmistakable echoes of these two models continue to be heard until much later, but before the end of the century both the genteel sentiment of the romancers and the staid scholarly ideals of the old school of Ascham had to compete with a rising generation of city wits whose effort was to popularize, or as some of their critics thought, to vulgarize literature. The court and the university no longer provided the only reading publics, but now London, grown prosperous and self-confident, gave support and encouragement to a whole disorderly army of dramatists, ballad-writers, pamphleteers, and story-tellers. Perhaps nowhere better than in the literary quarrel between Gabriel Harvey and Thomas Nashe do we get a view of the changing ideals of the last decade of the century. Harvey was a man of very substantial scholarly attainments. In his earlier years he lectured on rhetoric at Cambridge, and he showed good sense in at least one respect by changing from a strict Ciceronian to the school of Erasmus and Vives. He lived to a good old age but never wrote any books of importance. The chief event in his life, so far as literary history is concerned, was his quarrel with Nashe. The specific details, even the immediate occasion of this quarrel are of no permanent interest, but the general clash of personality and ideal are significant. Nashe was a wit; he depended on inspiration, fire, enthusiasm. He cultivated volubility and unrestraint, and was determined to be entertaining at any cost. Harvey defended a more dignified, more scholarly, orderly, and serious attitude towards literature. The virtues he inculcated were those which, when carried to excess, became the vices of the pedant. His witty opponents made of him, indeed, the typical pedant of his day, but to an impartial contemporary observer there could have been no question that the cause he supported stood in need of defense, and it must not be forgotten that Harvey was the friend of Sidney and Spenser. The clash of opinion between Harvey and Nashe was of course not peculiar to them or their day. It was akin to the old debate of the relative merits of nature and nurture, of natural gifts and discipline. The hero in Lyly's *Euphues* puts the case for nature, but Lyly himself, in his rôle of moralist, speaks for nurture.[31] The same side of the debate is assumed by Harvey. "Right artificiality," so he writes in one of his *Foure Letters,* "(whereat I once aimed to the uttermost power of my slender capacity) is not mad-brained, or ridiculous or absurd, or blasphemous, or monstrous; but deep-conceited, but pleasurable, but delicate, but exquisite, but gracious, but admirable: not according to the fantastical mould of

[31] *Euphues,* ed. Arber, pp. 43-47.

Aretine or *Rabelays,* but according to the fine modell of *Orpheus, Homer, Pindarus,* & the excellentest wittes of Greece, and of the lande that flowed with milke and hony." [32] He speaks scornfully of "cutting Huffe-snuffes," and declares that he borrows not his "phrase of knave or queane," but is debtor to the "Civill quill." With regret he looks back to the time when Cheke, Smith, Haddon, and Ascham flourished, a vanished golden age of scholarship. In Ascham's day, men cultivated "a kind of smooth and clenly and neate and fine elegancy," "but alacke, nothing livelie and mightie, like the brave *vino de monte,* till his [Nashe's] penne began to play the sprite of the buttry, and to teach his mother-tongue such lusty gambolds, as may make the gallantest French, Italian or Spanish gagliards to blushe, for extreame shame of their ideot simplicitie." [33]

Elsewhere Harvey states what he supposes would be a contemporary defense of Nashe, the main point of it being that men do not now want study or learning or sobriety, but cleverness, wit, and "villainy." Writing is not now a gentleman's profession, but a villain's. "Life is a gaming," so runs this supposed defense, "a jugling, a scoulding, a lawing, a skirmishing, a warre; a Comedie, a Tragedy: the sturring witt, a quintessence of quicksilver: and there is noe dead fleshe in affection or courage. You may discourse of Hermes ascending spirit; of Orpheus enchanting harpe; of Homers divine furie; of Tyrtaeus enraging trumpet; of Pericles bounsinge thunderclaps; of Platos enthusiasticall ravishment; and I wott not of what marvelous egges in mooneshine: but a flye for all your flying speculations, when one good fellow with his odd jestes or one madd knave with his awke hibber-gibber, is able to putt down

[32] *Foure Letters, Works,* ed. Grosart, I, 218.
[33] *Works,* II, 50.

twentye of your smuggest artificiall men, that simper it so nicely and coylie in their curious pointes. Try, when you meane to be disgraced: & never give me credit, if Sanguine witt putt not Melancholy Arte to bedd." [34] With this defense Harvey is of course not in agreement. He declares that they who will "seeke out the Archmistery of the busiest Modernistes shall find it nether more nor lesse then a certayne pragmaticall secret, called Villany." It is the villainist who knocks the nail on the head, and "spurreth cutt farther in a day then the quickest Artist in a week." [35]

The arch-villainist among these modernists, Thomas Nashe, after a troubled career of only thirty-four years, left a strange variety of writings behind him as claims to future fame. He took his first degree at St. John's College, Cambridge, and could have been a fellow, he says, if he would. Instead he seems to have preferred the more stirring life of literary adventurer in London, where he had settled as early as his twenty-first year, in 1588. He was the friend of some of the most active wits of his day, of Greene, Lodge, Daniel, Marlowe, and others, but extreme poverty always attended his footsteps.

His first independent publication, his *Anatomie of Absurdities* (1589), is mainly a satire on women, but it contains much about the weakness and vices of other kinds of persons, and comments bitterly on the lack of reward which the scholar received at the hands of the rich and great. This theme is continued in *Pierce Penilesse* (1592), with many others confusedly thrown together. The more important of the remaining works of Nashe are his *Terrors of the Night* (1594), a discussion of dreams, visions, and supernatural appearances; his novel, *The Unfortunate Traveller* (1594); *Christ's Tears over Jerusalem* (1594), which contains some highly rhetorical description of the

[34] *Works,* II, 62.

[35] Ibid., II, 63.

fall of Jerusalem and satire on London; various pamphlets in the quarrel between Nashe and the Harveys; a lost comedy, *The Isle of Dogs;* and his last work, Nashe's *Lenten Stuffe* (1599), a sort of prose epic of the red-herring, descriptive, humorous, and satirical, with many excursions, but on the whole sticking remarkably close to the subject.

Nashe's vein was mainly that of railing satire, "the railipotent Nashe" is Harvey's name for him, and his chief characteristic as a writer was his verbosity. He admired above all lightness and agility in a writer. He scorns "grosse-braind formalitie"[36] and adjures Englishmen not to have "Leade and Tynne Muses" because they have lead and tin mines. "For shame, bury not your spyrits in Biefe-pots."[37] In his address "To the Gentlemen Students of Both Universities," prefixed to Greene's *Menaphon,* one of his earliest writings, he derides those labored writers who afford "the presse a pamphlet or two in an age," and praises "the man whose extemporall veine in any humour will excell our greatest Art-maisters deliberate thoughts."[38] There is no credit, he declares, in threshing corn out of full sheaves, but out of "drie stubble to make an after harvest, and a plentifull croppe without sowing, and wring juice out of a flint"—that is the "right trick of a workman."[39] Even "Zeale and Religion" cannot compensate for lack of wit, and the preachers, too, must "arte-enamel" their speech if religion is not to reap infamy.[40]

In Nashe's earlier writings, in the *Anatomie of Absurdities* for example, one observes obvious traces of the influence of the style of Lyly. As he became surer of himself, however, Nashe developed a style more his own. The

[36] *Works,* ed. McKerrow, II, 10.
[37] Ibid., II, 122.
[38] Ibid., III, 312.
[39] Ibid., III, 152.
[40] Ibid., II, 124.

most striking feature of this style is the abundant use of long and outlandish words. To the "ploddinger sort of unlearned Zoilists about London" this seemed a "puft-up stile and full of prophane eloquence." Others made objections to Nashe's multitude of "boystrous compound words" and to his "often coyning of Italionate verbes which end all in Ize, as mummianize, tympanize, tirannize." [41] But Nashe maintains that his style is no more puffed-up than any man's would be "which writes with any Spirite"; and as to his boisterousness, "no speech or wordes of any power or force to confute or perswade but mustbee swelling and boystrous." The English tongue, of all languages, "most swarmeth with the single money of monasillables," and these, in Nashe's opinion, are the "onely scandall of it." [42] Nashe's standards, in a word, were those of the bravo. He was a literary ruffler, a "roaring boy" with the pen. He aroused attention by giving and taking offense and delighted in shocking the sensibilities of his readers.

Nashe's literary dependencies were various, though in the main he was the natural product of the life of his day. He was one of a group of university wits who had accumulated the materials of scholarship but who had very few serious scholarly interests and who were yet confronted with the serious problem of getting a living out of their university training. Such scholars were readily drawn into the whirlpool of London life, where they only too often sacrificed not only their scholarship, but all sense of decency and morality to a false notion of genius. Yet Nashe, child of his age though he was, manifestly falls in line with a long established English tradition. He takes his place with the

[41] *Works,* ed. McKerrow, II, 183. The word "mummianize" he had used in the phrase, "Ierusalems mummianized earth," and explains this to mean, "Ierusalems earth manured with mans flesh," II, 185.

[42] Ibid., II, 184.

ancient ranting and railing masters of eloquence, of whom examples are to be found as far back as Piers Plowman. His method is akin to that of Skelton, of the popular orators like Latimer and Bradford, of all practitioners of robustious eloquence. At bottom the foundation of all such writing is the plain and popular style, the English of colloquial discourse, broad and free. In spite of his huge words, Nashe's style is less learned and Latinized than the style of many a courtly contemporary who seems verbally less striking. In harmony with his general anti-heroic attitude, Nashe's writings are all conversational and familiar in tone. They are all dramatic monologues, in which the author stands before his audience and speaks in the first person. He declared that he borrowed nothing from Tarleton, the comic actor. But he often used devices of dramatic personal address, noisy exclamation, popular and coarse epithet which, if not derived from Tarleton, were sufficiently like Tarleton's methods to be noticeable to contemporaries. He speaks warmly of Pietro Aretino, whom he admires chiefly for his wit, his virtuosity, but it is doubtful if he was a close student of Aretino's writings.[43] There is also some resemblance between Nashe and Rabelais, likewise noted by Nashe's contemporaries. But here again the resemblance is general. Nashe indeed is representative of a widely distributed Renascence type. He is a kind of English Horribilicribrifax, intent on verbal ingenuity, and above all an admirer of verbal abundance. With this he joins the unheroic and realistic view of life, exploiting not the graceful and sentimental possibilities of his themes, but the sordid and ridiculous.

In considering Nashe as realist, one must dwell for a moment on what time has shown to be his one work of last-

[43] Professor McKerrow finds no direct influence of Aretino upon Nashe's style.

ing interest, his *Unfortunate Traveller*. This short novel, a little over one hundred pages, appeared in its first edition in 1594. Nashe calls it "a cleare different vaine from other my former courses in writing."[44] And in this work he seems to have thought out for himself a more definitely realistic method than in any other of his writings. The book, however, is by no means a pure example of realistic fiction, but rather a medley of familiar and traditional literary motives. It tells the story of Jack Wilton, "a certain kind of an appendix or page, belonging or appertaining in or unto the confines of the English court." The time of the action is supposed to be about fifty years before the time of writing, that is, in Nashe's intention, practically contemporary. Jack is a gentleman (he claims this title) who follows his various masters in camp and court through France, Germany, and Italy. He knows all the shifty tricks and vices of pages, and practices them, too, with frank admiration of his own cunning. The world is his orange, and he busies himself to get as much juice out of it as possible. He is not held by any bonds of loyalty to his masters, or indeed of honest dealing. He is a page of fortune, as his masters were soldiers of fortune. He is a fresh, good-looking, spirited youth, not altogether a scamp, but with no higher principles than his kind were supposed to have. When he is guilty of irregular conduct, it is more because of the wickedness of this world than from any natural depravity.

The setting of the story is concrete and detailed, with many pictures of the life of the camp, and later, of Venice. Yet the descriptions are not minute, and it is uncertain whether or not Nashe had seen the places he describes. A long episode descriptive of Rome in plague time is powerful, but highly colored and fanciful—a description of the

[44] McKerrow, *Works*, II, 201.

imagination, not of the observing eye. This passage contains a story of murder and revenge like the familiar "tragical tale" of the Italian novelle. A considerable section of the *Unfortunate Traveller* is also taken up with conventional moralizing, in the manner of Lyly, on the evils of travel, the wickedness of the Italians, and the absurdity of foreign customs in general. And Jack Wilton, after his foreign experiences, like Euphues, returns to England and swears "upon an English Chronicle never to bee out-landish Chronicler more" while he lives.[45] Before this he has married his mistress and made resolutions looking toward a more virtuous life. Many long speeches and orations occur in the progress of the story quite in the manner of Lyly, and there is Euphuistic satire of the universities, of scholars, "the leaden headed Germans first" and of Englishmen who have "surfetted of their absurd imitation."[46] On the whole one finds a surprising parallelism between the story of Jack Wilton and the miscellaneous kind of romance popularized by *Euphues*. But here, as ever, Nashe takes the unheroic view of his material, and this gives to his story some resemblance to a picaresque narrative. Yet Jack, though he is always poor, is not a rogue nor does he forget that he is a gentleman. He sees mostly the seamy side of life, and one of the "good fellowes" who live "as merry as cup and can," he passes from adventure to adventure with devil-may-care easiness. The shady character of Jack gives to the story a general flavor of realism and makes the romantic parts seem like episodes, though in fact they constitute a considerable part of the whole. The most important romantic episode is the fanciful and ethereal story of the Earl of Surrey's love for Geraldine. Jack happens at one time to be in the service of Henry Howard, Earl of Surrey, and

[45] McKerrow, *Works,* II, 328.

[46] Ibid., p. 251.

thus has opportunity to descant upon the Earl of Surrey's passion. In strong contrast with this courtly romance is the love affair of Jack himself with his mistress, later his wife. This story is not idealized, not poetized, and indeed one may feel that in his own story Jack has substituted mere coarseness for reality, that the realism of his story is as extreme as the romance of the Earl of Surrey's. But this is the kind of violent contrast in which Nashe delighted.

When Nashe wrote of the "different vaine" of his story, he perhaps had also in mind the style of it, which is not so robustious as in his other writings. There are fewer big words, fewer compounds, and fewer passages of rhetorical display. Nashe plainly endeavored to fit an appropriate style to Jack Wilton, light, picturesque, and not infrequently coarse. Occasional puns and Euphuistic conceits survive, but in the main the harmony between the character of the hero and the style of the story is fairly complete.

The *Unfortunate Traveller* is, therefore, a composite, made up of various familiar motives. The most original element is the character of Jack, who is really not a picaresque hero, but merely a young English gentleman viewed from the reverse side. It was Nashe's constant habit to take the burlesque point of view. He rarely sought effects of charm and grace, rarely idealized characters or descriptions, but as plain speaker, he brought everything down to his own irreverent level. This accounts for the fact that, with all his admiration for lofty diction, he never attained to anything better than occasional patches of huf-snuf rhetorical brilliance. He never freed himself from the spirit of mockery, from the habit of taking a derisive view of situations which others had made familiar in a more conventionally pleasing way. Realism which rests upon a dispassionate observation of nature, or upon a genuine sympathy with the simple, homely experiences of life, never appealed to him. The fool's fire which he followed, which seemed to him worthy the pursuit of genius, was a much more coruscating and iridescent affair.

One of the "good fellowes" with whom Nashe wasted his time in London was Robert Greene, probably the son of a saddler in Norwich, and a fellow collegian of Nashe's at St. John's, though not an exact contemporary. Greene came to London as a free lance, deserting his wife and child in the country, and after a few years of a life which even his friends did not attempt to defend, he died in 1592, at about the age of thirty-two, "by a surfeit taken of pickled herrings and Rhenish wine; as witnesseth Thomas Nash, who was at the fatal banquet."[47] Perhaps no writer of this group of aspiring wits paid more dearly in shame and suffering for his belief in the sufficiency of genius than did Greene. The strong wine of freedom and inspiration went to his head, and only in the last few years of his short life did he come to himself in what seems to have been a fit of repentance as violent as his former wild life had been.

Almost two score titles are to be found in the list of Greene's works, a surprising fertility considering the brevity of his literary career. Most of these titles, however, designate short works, written under the spur of immediate need. Nashe says that Greene would "yark up" a pamphlet "in a night and a day" when the fit was on him. He began his literary career with shameless imitation of *Euphues*. His *Mamillia, A Mirrour or lookingglasse for the Ladies of Englande,* licensed for printing in 1580, a year after the appearance of *Euphues,* in its

[47] Meres, *Palladis Tamia,* in Collins, *Critical Essays and Literary Fragments* (Arber, *English Garner*), p. 19.

"sugred happie style" which in "English prose doth climbe the skie," almost out-Euphuizes Euphues. It is significant, however, of Greene's chief gift, that of the story-teller, that the plot of *Mamillia* is more clearly defined and less interrupted by subsidiary actions than that of *Euphues*. Other love tales, in the conventional fashion, followed *Mamillia*. It was Greene's custom to make copy by inserting short stories in any work upon which he happened to be engaged. In his *Planetomachia* (1585), which treats of "the essence, nature and influence" of the seven planets, he has enlivened his astronomical discourse "with pleasaunt Tragedies." And in *Penelopes Web* (1584) the account of this "Christall Myrror of faeminine perfection" is "interlaced with three severall and Comicall Histories." The most enduring of Greene's novels was his *Pandosto* (1588), known to-day chiefly because Shakspere used it in the *Winter's Tale,* but formerly so popular that at least twenty-four editions appeared between the date of publication and 1735.[48] When Sidney's *Arcadia,* first passed around in manuscript and after 1590 accessible in a printed form, had somewhat impaired the fame of *Euphues* and had established a new fashion, Greene was ready at hand to satisfy the new demand with his *Menaphon* (1589) and various other Arcadian pastorals and romances. Nashe praised Greene's "Arcadian Menaphon" as an example of "that *temperatum dicendi genus,* which *Tullie* in his *Orator* tearmeth true eloquence."[49] And Thomas Brabine, in verses addressed to the author, bids all "witts that vaunt the pompe of speach" to view in *Menaphon* a note beyond their reach. All this high praise is for a shepherd romance in obvious imitation of Sidney's style, with songs interspersed and eclogues and poems of various kinds.

About the year 1590 Greene seems to have experienced a

[48] Esdaile, pp. 69-71. [49] Greene, *Works,* ed. Grosart, VI, 11.

change of heart which led to a choice of entirely new materials for literary exploitation. In that year he published his *Mourning Garment,* at the end of which there is an apology wherein Greene says that this is the last of his "trifling Pamphlets." In the same year also appeared *Greenes Never too late,* which purports to reveal "the fraudulent effects of Venus trumperies." With this and with *Francescoes Fortunes, or The Second part of Greenes Never too late* (1590), Greene was definitely launched upon his career of reform and repentance. The story of Francesco is a strange combination of romance and reality, in some respects not unlike Gascoigne's *Pleasant Fable of Ferdinando and Leonora.* It has an Italian setting, though it tells of "an English Historie acted and evented" in England. Francesco lives at Caerbranck (Brancaster in Norfolk?), a poor young man of wit and learning who had been at the university. He falls in love with Isabel, the daughter of a gentleman named Fregoso, who lives not far from Caerbranck. Fregoso opposes the match, but Francesco arranges with Isabel to meet him "upon Thursday next at night hard by the Orchard under the greatest Oake." Isabel keeps the tryst, clad "onely in her smocke and her peticoate with her fathers hat and an old cloake," and together they flee to Dunecastrum (Doncaster?) and are happily married. They live peacefully and humbly together, and their virtuous life causes even Fregoso to be reconciled to them. Francesco applied himself "to teaching of a Schoole, where by his industry he had not onelie great favour, but gote wealth to withstand fortune." And in due time there was born to this happy pair a son, "answerable to their own perfection." At length Francesco is compelled by "necessarie businesse" to go to the chief city of that island, called Troynovant. Knowing that he should have to spend the space of some nine weeks in Troynovant, on his arrival "he solde his horse and hired him a chamber." This is the beginning of his sorrows, for opposite him lives Infida, a courtezan, who gains such complete control over him that for him "there is no heaven but Infidaes house." Isabel has heard of Francesco's unfaithfulness and sends him a tender letter in which she says nothing of the life he has been leading, but dwells only on her loneliness. "The onely comfort that I have in thine absence," so she writes, "is thy child, who lies on his mothers knee, and smiles as wantonly as his father when he was a wooer." But Francesco scoffs at his wife's letter and shows it to Infida. For three years he remains under Infida's spell, and then, his money being all gone, she turns him adrift. Francesco is hard put to it to make a living. He cannot work with his hands, for the "care of his parents and of his owne honor perswaded him from making gaine by labour; he had never been brought up to any mechanicall course of life." He chances to fall in with some players who persuade him to try play-writing. In a short time he "grewe so exquisite in that facultie," that happy were the actors who could get any of his works. Now that he is prosperous, Infida tries to get him again into her toils, but vainly, Francesco's eyes having been too completely opened by her earlier faithlessness. In the meantime Isabel is in straits at home. She has been approached by a rich "Bourgomaster" of Caerbranck named Bernardo. Repulsed by Isabel, Bernardo hires a youth of the city to prefer false charges against her. When the moment comes, however, this youth is smitten in his conscience and reveals Bernardo's evil plan. Isabel's fame is thus increased, and reports of these happenings even reach Francesco in the city. He returns home after an absence of six years and is received without recrimination by Isabel. They live happily together ever afterward, and the story closes with a long pastoral tale told at the feast given to celebrate the home-coming of Francesco.

This story, which it was worth while to analyze in detail because it shows how the Italian novella could be made the vehicle for the portrayal of genuine English life, is undoubtedly in some measure autobiographical. Its parallelism to certain episodes in the life of Shakspere will not pass unnoticed, and indeed the main events of it are of a kind that must have been not infrequently exemplified in later Elizabethan London. The story, as Greene tells it, is overlaid with all the devices of the conventional romance, with high-sounding eloquence, figures of speech, classical allusions, quotations, and similar ingenious ornament. At bottom, however, it is felt to be real. The gentle and womanly Isabel, Francesco, the simple victim of city wickedness, the professional harlot Infida, all these are genuine transcripts of English life. The actions in which they figure are simple and natural, and the only reason why Greene did not write in *Francescoes Fortunes* a thoroughly realistic novel of London life was that he had at his command only a romantic mould in which to shape his material.

In pursuance of his program of reform, Greene struck a vein which brought him more popularity than any of his tales of idle love had ever done. In 1591 appeared his *Notable Discovery of Coosenage,* which constitutes the first part of the *Art of Connycatching* and the first of a long series of cony-catching pamphlets by Greene and his imitators. It begins with an account of various kinds of cheats and tricksters, and concludes with two stories, "How a Cookes wife in London did lately serve a Collier for his coosnage," and "How a Flaxe wife and her neighbours used a coosening Collier." The *Second Part of the Art of Connycatching* is really nothing more than a collection of such short stories, a group of tales in a cony-catching setting. These stories are narratives of episodes in London life, with actual places mentioned and often the names of persons. It is usually "a good fellow" who in the Christmas holidays came to see a play at the Bull within Bishopsgate, or "poor A. B. in Turnmill street" at Spilby fair, or some innocent apprentice at Newgate Market who falls victim to the practices of sharpers and thus provides the material of the story. Greene addresses himself in the *Notable Discovery* to the "yong gentlemen, Marchants, Apprentices, Farmers, and plain Countrymen" of England, and as the pamphlets were cheap, they were widely distributed among the class for whom they were intended. A tanner of Exeter, in one of the stories, announces that he has bought Greene's cony-catching pamphlet for threepence and has thus learned all the mysteries of that trade. Greene declares that his pamphlets had become so generally known that sharpers now had difficulty in finding victims and that they had even threatened him with violence. But Greene consoles himself with the reflection that "no pains nor danger [is] too great that groweth to the benefit" of his country.[50] His desire now is only to do good to his countrymen. "I am English borne," he writes, "and I have English thoughts, not a devill incarnate because I am Italianate, but hating the pride of Italie, because I know their peevishnes."[51] In harmony with his change of purpose he explains that he has adopted a new style, and to those who object that his new writings show "no eloquent phrases nor fine figurative conveiance" as his other works have done, he replies that a "certaine decorum is to bee kept in everie thing" and that it is not proper to "applie a

[50] "Epistle Dedicatorie" to the *Second Part of the Art of Connycatching*, *Works*, X, 69.
[51] Ibid., p. 5.

high stile in a base subject . . . Therefore humbly I crave pardon and desire I may write basely of such base wretches who live onely to live dishonestly."[52] The style is base, however, only in the sense that it is simple and unaffected and eschews Euphuistic and Arcadian ornament.

The theme thus successfully inaugurated by Greene in his *Art of Connycatching* was continued in several modified forms. In *A Disputation Betweene a Hee and a Shee Connycatcher* two practitioners of the art conversing together reveal themselves in a remarkably vivid and entertaining manner. As part of the *Disputation* Greene utilizes a short conventional love-romance, *A Watchword to Wanton Maidens,* written in the old style of such stories and evidently left over from his earlier period. In *The Defence of Connycatching,* Greene[53] writes under the guise of one who opposes him. He attacks here other kinds of knavery than cony-catching, the oppressions of usurers, the cheating of millers, alewives, chandlers, butchers, lawyers, false travelers, blackmailers, brokers, tailors, and other seemingly respectable members of society. There is much popular gossip about tradesmen and their ways, the effect of the pamphlet being to convince the people of the truth of what they will always believe, that there exists a general conspiracy of fraud against them among all tradesmen and purveyors.

In continuation of his new-found devotion to popular interests, Greene wrote *A Quip for an Upstart Courtier, or A Quaint dispute between Velvet breeches and Cloth-breeches* (1592). This engaging sketch was dedicated to Thomas Barnabie, Esq., as a "maintayner of Cloth breeches (I meane of the olde and worthie customes of the Gentilitie

[52] "Epistle Dedicatorie," p. 71.

[53] Or some imitator of Greene. The authorship of the pamphlet is not certain.

and yeomanrie of England)." The dispute turns on the relative merits of Velvet-breeches, adorned with rich ornaments, and Cloth-breeches, plain and simple, but serviceable. Cloth-breeches maintains not only that the gentleman may lose caste if he degenerates from his "auntient vertues," but also that the "churlish and servile" person may become a gentleman if "indued with learning or valour." Hence he concludes that gentility grows "not onely by propagation of nature, but by perfection of quality."[54] He discourses eloquently against the vices of Italy cultivated by Velvet-breeches, and lauds plain, honest English virtues. This is Ascham's old plaint, but the difference between Ascham and Greene is that Ascham was thinking only of gentlemen, whereas Greene's sympathies are really with the plain people. In the end a jury is made up, mainly of simple craftsmen, who decide in favor of Cloth-breeches, as "by many hundred yeares more antient, ever since *Brute* an inhabitant in this Island." Velvet-breeches, on the other hand, is an "upstart come out of Italy, begot of Pride, nursed up by selfe love & brought into this country by his companion Nufanglenesse."[55] The pamphlet undoubtedly made a strong popular appeal, and perhaps it expresses a genuine sympathy with the people on Greene's part. The only thing which begets doubt of Greene's entire sincerity is that he was now in the desperate position of a writer who must continually find a new public in order to live. No doubt Greene's romances were bought in greater numbers by middle-class readers than they were by courtiers, and one cannot help wondering whether or not his change of heart had anything to do with a realization of the practical wisdom of appealing directly to this popular public.

This doubt becomes acute when one turns to Greene's

[54] *Works,* XI, 225.

[55] Ibid., p. 294.

penitent pamphlets, written during his last days and published only after his death. The most important of these is *Greene's Groats-worth of Wit,* a last confession the bitterness of which is somewhat sweetened by several entertaining tales. In the address "To the Gentlemen Readers," Greene declares that henceforth he will write more useful pamphlets, "directing you how to live, yet not diswading you from love." Another last confession was *Greenes Vision: Written at the instant of his death. Conteyning a penitent passion for the folly of his Pen.* How popular these death-bed confessions were is shown by the publisher's note prefixed to the posthumous edition of the *Vision,* to the effect that "Manie have published repentaunces under his name," but that none was "more unfeigned than this, being everie word of his owne: his owne phrase, his own method." [56] It is in this vision that Chaucer and Gower appear before Greene and argue the merits of the two kinds of narrative with which their names had become traditionally identified. Chaucer defends merry tales, and tells Greene that poets' wits are free, and their words ought to be without check, that he has therefore "doone Schollerlike" in setting forth his pamphlets. Gower, on the other hand, defends serious and moral narrative. In the end Greene rejects Chaucer, Solomon then appears in the vision and counsels Greene to seek wisdom, to leave "effeminate fancies" and to give himself up entirely to theology. "Be a Divine, my Sonne," concludes Solomon, "for her documents are severitie, and her foode is the bread of life." When Greene awakes from his vision, he determines to "seeke after wisdome so highly commended

[56] One of those who made capital out of Greene's death was John Dickenson, who in 1598 published *Green in Conceipt. New raised from his graue to write the Tragique Historie of fair Valeria of London.* Dickenson had sponged on Lyly in an earlier work, *Arisbas, Euphues amidst his slumbers* (1594).

by Solomon," and he promises his readers that however the direction of his studies shall be limited, they shall have the fruits of his better labors. It seems, therefore, from these statements, that Greene was upon the point of giving up not only the courtly romance but also the tale of common life which he had cultivated in place of the romance. All that he had hitherto done seemed now to Greene but " wanton fancies," and had not death intervened, the next stage of his career might have seen him devoting his talents to religious meditations and pious pamphlets.

It was Greene's tendency to play insistently on only one string at a time. He first wrote Euphuistic romances, then Arcadian romances, and when these veins seemed exhausted, it came the turn of his rogue pamphlets, followed by his death-bed confessions. These last unhappily turned out to be almost literally death-bed confessions, though if further time had been granted him, no doubt this theme also would soon have given place to a new one. The truth appears to be that Greene was more intent on working the market than in realizing any firmly held literary or personal convictions of his own. And yet he seems at bottom to have had some genuine feeling for the life of the plain citizen, even the disreputable citizen. His many reflections of the life of merchants, apprentices, servants, farmers, and such simple folk are presented in their settings with all the fidelity of a Dutch genre picture; and when he treats of low-life characters and activities, of thieves, sharpers, courtezans, of the life of the ale-house and the suburbs, moral indignation does not obscure his vision of the picturesque fact. Much of this method he of course learned from the merry tale of the Chaucerian tradition, but on the other hand he not infrequently goes out of his way to express opinions, not conventional or literary, which lead one to suppose that Harvey's criticisms of " villainy " in literature formed no part of his artistic creed. And yet Greene wrote no comprehensive realistic work. His writings are all sketches, and his narrative gift, though excellent within the limits of the novella or anecdote, seems not to have been capable of sustained effort. He was apparently not completely aware of the vast narrative possibilities of the life of his humble public, and though his feeling for this public seems genuine so far as it goes, it does not go very far.

Two other London wits whose names are traditionally connected with those of Nashe and Greene are George Peele and Thomas Lodge. Of Peele little need be said in a discussion of realism. His *Old Wives Tale* is a romantic play, pieced together out of fragments of popular legendary material which it treats in the spirit of *Comus* and the *Midsummer Night's Dream. The Merry Conceited Jests of George Peele* were not written by Peele but about him. If the tales had any basis in fact, Peele must have been as knavish a rogue as ever cut purse. Lodge, on the other hand, seems at least to have made some effort to join the forces of the modernists. He was the son of a lord mayor of London, and was educated at the Merchant Taylors School and at Oxford. He began his literary career with *A Reply to Stephen Gosson's Schoole of Abuse* (1580), a short and itself somewhat abusive defense of poetry, music, and stage plays. Several years later he published *An Alarum against Usurers* (1584), to which was annexed the "delectable historie of Forbonius and Prisceria." This book, which is praised in some prefatory verses for its "pretie stile," presents, in the first part, the story of a young gallant who falls a prey to usurers, with the result that his own moral character deteriorates and he becomes himself a "gentleman broker." The story is told in an extremely Euphuistic manner, though it probably reflects some personal experiences of Lodge and betrays some interest in the law, of which he had become a student. The story of Forbonius and Prisceria is a conventional love romance, with Euphuistic and Arcadian features, monologues, letters, debates, shepherd motives, poems interspersed, and all the other furniture. In this kind, however, Lodge did better with his next romance, his *Rosalynde; Euphues golden legacie found after his death in his cell at Silexedra* (1590). The book, according to Lodge, was " feathered in the surges of many perillous seas," having been written " on a voyage to the Islands of Terceras & the Canaries.[57] Though he speaks modestly of it as a work " heawen down by a soldier with his curtleax, not bought with the allurement of a filed tongue," it is in fact an ornate romance adorned with all the refinements of the artificial style.

By the time *Rosalynde* had received its welcome, there were signs that the popularity of romance in general had begun to wane. Lodge made two attempts to join the new movement, neither of them successful. His *Famous, true and historicall life of Robert second Duke of Normandy, surnamed . . . Robin the Divell* (1591) is a crudely conceived story of the bloody acts of an impossible villain. The theme was too violent for a rogue pamphlet, in which there was always a certain element of humor, and the style in which it was written was merely that of the refined romance transferred to an inappropriate subject. Lodge's second venture in the popular manner was his *Life and Death of william Long beard, the most famous and witty English Traitor, borne in the Citty of London* (1593). This book, dedicated to the Lord Mayor of London, tells the story of a man of low birth who in the reign of Henry II attained to wealth and high position, but not to good

[57] *Works,* Hunterian Club, I, 4.

habits. To the main story are added "manye other most pleasant and prettie histories." But Lodge had really never gone to school to the popular tale, and these stories are all written in the slow and long movement of the style of romance. Lodge complains, in some introductory remarks, that fault is found "if the stile be not of the new stamp," and that men are "in thraldome to their fashionate manners." With respect to his own writing, he promises "to washe out the spots assoone as they are spied." But the spots of the romantic style in Lodge were like those of the leopard, which grow brighter by washing.

In his succeeding works, having become a Roman Catholic and having taken up the study of medicine, Lodge gave up the struggle and frankly descended to the level of the merely learned and pious. In *The Divel Conjured* (1596) he declares that now he cares not for style, and prefers that men should condemn him "for default in Rethoricke, then as in times past, commend my stile and lament my judgment." The book is a supposedly philosophical discussion of angels, devils, magic, and similar topics, and not a social pamphlet at all. *Prosopopoeia containing the teares of the holy, blessed and sanctified Marie* (1596), a book of meditations and ejaculations, is another work of repentance in which Lodge speaks sorrowfully of the "foule forepassed progenie" of his thoughts composed in the night of his error. *Wits Miserie and the Worlds Madness* (1596) contains highly elaborated but lifeless and medieval discussions of the seven deadly sins, illustrated by descriptions of typical characters. After this, besides some translations, Lodge produced only several medical tracts, *A Treatise of the Plague* (1603), sensible and learned, but not intended to be entertaining, and *The Poore Mans Talent* (1623?), a practical collection of prescriptions and of discussions of diseases.

It is with some relief that one turns from these "wanton wits," who all seem to have "look'd on truth askance and strangely," to Thomas Dekker, the most genuine of the end of the century depicters of London life. Curiously little is known about Dekker, except that he was a fertile producer of plays and prose pamphlets and that, though industrious, he was often in poverty and was probably improvident. He was born in London and, as his writings show, quite at home in the life of the city. He was not unlearned, since he quotes Latin freely and makes learned allusions; but he does not boast of having been at the university and probably did not belong to the group of university wits. He was a professional man of letters who lived close to the public for which he wrote. His pamphlets are full of vivid detail, and his sympathy with the simple aspects of London life, with citizens, tradesmen, apprentices, serving-maids, and other humble characters is frequently apparent. In his *Foure Birdes of Noahs Arke* (1609) he put together a book of prayers, for a school-boy, for an apprentice, for a maid-servant, for a mariner, a soldier, for the higher ranks as well, all of which are admirably simple, direct, and fresh in expression, but never so engagingly so as in the prayers for children, artisans, servants, prisoners, and other humble folk. He was a man also of unusual humanitarian sensibility, and his descriptions of the plague-stricken city are powerful in feeling. His pictures of low life are often sweetened by touches of poetry, not the poetry of unreal romance, but the poetry which inheres in the simplest of things for him who is able to extract it. Dekker's vein is not prevailingly satiric, but often sympathetic and humorous. His work in prose, like that of most prose writers of his time, suffers for lack of appropriate forms, and materials are often jumbled together in a way which seems to indicate hurried composition.

Necessity doubtless fostered in him a journalistic habit of filling space and of writing for the immediate occasion. With all its defects, however, his work presents a richer picture of London life than that of any other contemporary chronicler. A true child of the London of his day, he has given us the most attractive, perhaps also the most faithful picture of the life of the city.

That most terribly real of all happenings, the plague, provided Dekker with the material for his first prose pamphlet. This was called *The Wonderfull Yeare 1603. Wherein is shewed the picture of London, lying sicke of the Plague.* At the end of it, "like a mery Epilogue to a dull Play," certain tales are narrated, "of purpose to shorten the lives of long winter nights that lye watching in the darke for us." With such stories Dekker says he could fill a large volume and call it the second part of the hundred merry tales. But the mirth of these tales lies close to tragedy. Many touching incidents of the plague are vividly narrated, and the pathos of the accounts is increased by the mingling of "ridiculous stuffe" in the catalogue of horrors. The plague figures again, but less prominently, in Dekker's second original pamphlet, *The Seven deadly Sinnes of London* (1606), not the conventional medieval sins, but the sins of the author's day, such as intentional bankruptcy, whereby creditors are cheated, lying, "Candlelight," i.e. the sins that walk abroad under cover of night, sloth, apishness, shaving, i.e. trickery and oppression, and cruelty. These sins are not abstractly analyzed, but are typified by persons, "drawne in seven severall Coaches, Through the seven Severall Gates of the Citie Bringing the Plague with them." The treatment of the theme contrasts interestingly with Lodge's *Wits Miserie.* In *Newes from Hell* (1606), Dekker attempted a rather heavy-handed satirical description of hell, its horrors, punishments, and inhabitants, after the manner of Nashe's *Pierce Penilesse*. Nashe himself is addressed in terms of extravagant admiration and Dekker's "plump braynes" swell and burst in passages of expansive eloquence imitative of Nashe. This was not Dekker's true vein, however, and fortunately he soon abandoned it. A renewed outbreak of the plague in 1625 brought forth *A Rod for Run-awayes* (1625), the last of Dekker's prose pamphlets. This is a kind of newspaper report and description of the city and its misfortunes. Many incidents of the plague are related, some only briefly sketched, but even in outline powerfully suggestive of the pathos, the grim humor, and the tragedy of the situations.

Like Greene, Dekker found the most fruitful source of material for pamphleteering in the underworld of thieves and rogues. His *Belman of London: Bringing to Light the most notorious villanies that are now practised in the Kingdome* (1608) was an immediate popular success. It details the wickedness of night-prowlers, of various kinds of rogues, rufflers, anglers, and other picturesque rascals. Dekker declares his intention of devoting his life to the safety of his country until all such evil-doers are "hunted into the toyles of the Lawe." In *Lanthorne and Candle-Light. Or The Bell-Mans second Nights-walke* (1609) a "Brood of more strange Villanies" was revealed. Besides exposing various criminal practices, Dekker also discusses the canting language in some detail. In this pamphlet he took occasion to make some criticisms of Samuel Rowlands, an imitator of Greene and author of a number of realistic satirical poems and rogue pamphlets, who sought profit in the success of the Bell-man by publishing his *Martin Mark-All, Beadle of Bridewell; his defence and answere to the Belman of London* (1609). Rowlands comments on the popularity of the *Bel-man of London,* which, he says, is so well known that every "Jacke-boy now can say as well as the proudest of that fraternitie (will you wapp for a wyn, or tranie for a make)." He apparently tries to show that Dekker was heavily indebted to Harman's *Caveat* for his materials and that he had not given the fraternity of vagabonds a fair treatment. Dekker in turn charges Rowlands with being a usurper who has taken upon him the name of the Bell-man without being able to maintain that title, and who is "rather a Newter than a friend to the cause." In this latter charge there may have been some truth, for one feels constantly that the authors of these rogue pamphlets do protest their moral intentions too much, and that perhaps they were more at home with rogues and vagabonds than plain citizens had a right to be.

With Dekker's rogue pamphlets may be grouped a work devoted to rogues whose roguishness was not compensated for by their wit. The *Guls Horne-booke* (1609) contains a description of different kinds of fools, cast into the ironical form of a book of instructions for all such as would be complete gulls. It is a conduct book applied to the fool and man about town to teach the elements of the fool's conduct. Structurally it is divided into chapters, how a gallant should behave himself at the play, in the tavern, at an ordinary, in Paul's Walk, and various other situations which give Dekker an opportunity of describing different types of city rufflers and loungers. The book, says Dekker, "hath a relish of Grobianisme, and tastes very strongly of it in the beginning." [58] The reason was, as Dekker explains, that he had translated "many Bookes" of Dedekind's *Grobianus* into English verse, but not liking the subject, he altered the shape and "of a Dutchman fashioned a meere Englishman." Here as ever Dekker writes with his eye upon the object, and his "meere Englishman" is an invaluable social document, illustrating the life of Shakspere's London.

[58] *Non-Dramatic Works,* ed. Grosart, II, 199.

Most of the remaining pamphlets of Dekker are manifest catch-alls, written for the market. His *Jests to Make you Merie* (1607) is a collection of short tales with very little wit to grace them, to which are added "the discoveries made by Cock Wat, the walking Spirit of Newgate," a continuation of the cony-catching theme of Greene. *The Dead Terme* (1608), a dialogue between Westminster and London, is a jumble of antiquarian information, of satirical and moral reflections on the sins of the city, of descriptions of various notable objects, Paul's Steeple making a long complaint and statement of its history, the stews of the city, the Thames and its wonders, and similar matters of popular interest. It closes with a description of Stourbridge Fair and a merry tale dealing with an episode in plague-time. *Worke for Armourers: or The Peace is Broken* (1609) was written when the play-houses were empty because of the plague. In default of this customary resource, Dekker visits the Bear Garden and describes the baiting of the bear with more realization of the barbarous character of the sport than was common among his contemporaries. The greater part of the pamphlet, however, is a conflict, like a morality, between Money and Poverty, with occasional glimpses of actual life and manners. The *Ravens Almanacke* (1609) is another medley of various things, cast in the form of a mock almanac in which the writer prognosticates misfortunes such as plague, famine, and civil war for "this present yeare 1609." The pamphlet also contains merry tales, of a cobbler and his shrewish wife, of a usurer, of a rope-maker in Devonshire who was cured of cruelty by his wife, and others. Many interesting casual descriptions and echoes of real life keep the interest alive in the varied matter of the pamphlet. Like other pamphlets of similar character, it should not be judged too severely from the point of view of unity and coherence, since doubtless one of the main purposes of writings of this kind was to supply readers with the miscellaneous entertainment provided in modern times by magazines and newspapers. Or if Dekker had lived in the days of Addison and Steele he would undoubtedly have cast much of his materials into the form of periodical essays instead of huddling them together within the covers of a single book. So far as structure is concerned, however, Dekker's inventive skill was slight, and he apparently made little effort to elaborate a form which might appropriately have contained his realistic material.

Still further removed from the group of university wits and closer to the public for which he wrote was Thomas Deloney, sometimes extravagantly praised as the inventor of the realistic novel. Deloney seems to have been a silk-weaver by occupation, probably a native of Norwich, who took to literature as an additional means of support. Among his literary contemporaries he is usually referred to with more or less good-humored contempt. His contemporary popularity was established first by his ballads, in which he was first the rival and, after his death in 1592, the successor of Elderton. The themes of these ballads are usually sentimental incidents taken from English history, e.g. *A Mournfull Dittie on the death of Rosamond, King Henry the Seconds Concubine, The Lamentation of Shores Wife,* the story of Godiva of Coventry, of King Locrine, and others. Miscellaneous ballads tell of the destruction caused by a great wind in the market town of Beckles in Suffolk, of the death and execution of fourteen most wicked traitors in Lincoln's Inn Field, of the lamentation of "Mr. Pages Wife of Plimouth, who being forc'd to wed him, consented to his Murder," and much other "doleful matter merrily set down."

Deloney's novels are three in number, *The Most Pleasant*

and delectable Historie of John Winchcombe, otherwise called Jacke of Newberie, The Gentle Craft, in two parts, and *Thomas of Reading, or The Six Worthie Yeomen of the West,*[59] all written between 1596 and 1600. *Jacke of Newberie* deals with episodes in the life of a broadcloth weaver and others of his calling. The story is not closely compacted as to plot, but like all of Deloney's novels, is merely a string of episodes. It exemplifies in Jack of Newbery the author's conception of the good and honest tradesman who by his industry passes from poverty to comfort and from comfort to affluence. A good many stories of the type of the merry jest find a place in the course of the narrative. Tales of a high-strung romantic character are also inserted for relief, told in Deloney's version of the refined Euphuistic style with an amusing mixture of magniloquent English and flat statement. One observes a good many echoes from the chroniclers, who were probably Deloney's most sedulously read authors, in descriptions of feasts, entertainments, royal visitations, and similar incidents. The style also reminds one of Stowe's painful efforts to attain dignity and elegance. In spite of its composite character, however, there is at bottom a solid foundation of feeling for the realities of life and character in the book.

What has been said of *Jacke of Newberie* applies equally to Deloney's other novels, to *The Gentle Craft,* dealing with shoemakers, and to his third novel, the story of Thomas of Reading, who followed "the trade of clothing." The tales are all written from the popular point of view, but are not written down by a person who felt himself superior to his

[59] Plagiarized by Henry Roberts in his *Haigh for Deuonshire. A pleasant Discourse of sixe gallant Marchants of Deuonshire* (1600), according to Mr. Seccombe (DNB., s. v. Roberts), who refers to an article by W. B. Pye, *Western Antiquary,* Feb., 1885.

characters. The virtues commended are the simple virtues of the tradesman, industry, thrift, economy, shrewdness rather than generosity, and cleverness in driving a bargain, even to the loss of the man you are dealing with. Perhaps the women characters are more interestingly developed than the men. They consist of widows, serving-maids, roystering girls of the taverns, old gossips, and others of full habit. The typical situation is that in which a woman, a serving-maid, or a rich widow, woos a fresh and promising young apprentice or tradesman. In Deloney's view of life it is the male who is pursued, not the female. There is much of the free-spoken language of a coarse age, coarse rather than indecent, in the conversation of the characters, though when the proprieties are in evidence, nothing could be more proper than their bourgeois primness. The reader is given to understand, however, that this is merely surface decoration. The humor of the stories is mainly of the heavy style of practical joking, though some crude efforts are made at comic dialect characterization in very imperfectly indicated French and German. Some of the English characters are also marked by local characteristics of speech. The novels are placed in past time, *Jacke of Newberie* in "the daies of King Henrie the eight," *Thomas of Reading* in "the dayes of King Henry the first," while *The Gentle Craft,* in its beginnings, goes back to the time of "the renowned king of Powis, a noble Brittaine borne," who was the father of St. Hugh. But the life described is really that of Deloney's England. One sees the bustling, familiar, good-natured intercourse of prosperous citizens and their workmen in the daily round of tasks. There is much eating, drinking, singing, joking, to relieve the tedium of toil. It is the carefree, happy life of those who earn their daily bread, not in the sweat of their brows, but by the skill of their hands, of artisans who know trouble only when they feel it in their purses or their paunches. Compared with Dekker, Deloney's pictures of London life seem heavy and coarse. Deloney apparently saw only the boisterous side of middle-class life, only the hilarity of comfortable, well-fed citizens who give their animal spirits free rein in their hours of leisure. Dekker also knows the merry side of London life, but the lightness and grace with which he describes it are lacking in Deloney.

In no comprehensive sense can Deloney be characterized as the father of the realistic novel. What he did was to combine older methods and materials, the chronicle narrative with the merry jest and the debased courtly romance, into a succession of episodes held together loosely by a character or group of characters. His three novels are relatively very slight and are quite inadequate to give a full and real picture of the life he depicts. Nor was this probably Deloney's intention. He certainly had no theories of realistic narrative, but wrote to amuse his public, which was a public of apprentices, merchants, tradesmen, and craftsmen. He wrote, consequently, in a simple and naïve style, even when he tried to be fine. He was a man of the people writing for the people, and as an artistic achievement his work is of slight significance. Nevertheless, so far as it goes, Deloney's method was to a considerable extent that of realistic fiction, and one may perhaps reasonably inquire whether Deloney did not build better than he knew, whether without intending it, he did not in fact inaugurate a new literary method which later generations utilized and developed. The dates of the printed editions of Deloney's three novels lend some color to this opinion. Editions of *The Gentle Craft* are still extant which appeared at intervals of a few years to the middle of the eighteenth century, and of the other two novels editions appeared continuously to the end of the seventeenth century.[60] But the continued interest of the popular reading public in Deloney's novels is not in itself sufficient justification for applying the title of father of English realism to him. He must first be measured by the degree of his influence upon his literary successors, and it is apparent that such influence was slight. His novels were not the models for Defoe, Richardson, or any of the later masters of realism. His historical significance, like that of the other realistic writers of the end of the sixteenth century, lies in his reflection of a growing popular interest in reading in his day, and in the life of simple folk. Scholars and courtiers were then not the only supporters of literature, but the increasing class of prosperous townsmen were eager for literary entertainment and willing to pay for it. The people had always had a traditional oral literature of their own and reflections of this appear even in the romances of the age of chivalry. But in answer to this new demand, certain "villainists," many of whom had enjoyed the advantages of the academic and literary culture of England, condescended to bring printed literature down to the popular level. They told witty and indecent stories, they described the life of the streets, of respectable citizens and their despoilers of the underworld, they gave to literature the boisterous, huf-snuf, and anti-heroic eloquence which was the last cry in Elizabethan modernity. Yet with all this their constructive achievements were slight. Even the drama, the most appropriate container for their material, and one which, in its independent development, had evolved a clearly defined form, was only imperfectly and partially utilized. The merry tale did indeed contain the germ of the

[60] For bibliography, see Esdaile, pp. 38-43. Doubtless numerous editions of the novels appeared of which no copies have survived. Like the popular chap-books which they resemble, the novels were printed in cheap form and probably in small editions of which no copies escaped the wear and tear of time.

novel, and the elements of a realistic fiction are present in the elaborations of this type of narrative in the writings of Greene, Dekker, and Deloney. But not even Greene, whose short stories went farthest in this direction, seems to have had the courage of any profound realistic convictions, or perhaps to have realized the possibilities of the long and detailed narrative of real life. The conditions of London society called forth writings which revealed the possibilities of a realistic fiction, but it was left for later generations effectually to occupy this newly discovered literary world of the familiar and commonplace.

IX

BACON

Public Activities—Literary Interests—Early Writings—Methods of Self-Discipline—Philosophical Treatises — Composition and Growth of the "Essays"—Use of Latin—Literary Technic—Conclusions

The influences which molded the life of Francis Bacon developed not a talent, but a character. He finds his place in the history of literature largely by virtue of a single book, and that book one which he esteemed less highly than most of his other works. Nature did not deny to Bacon the gifts which might have made an author, but he preferred to be, as he would have regarded it, something more than merely a writer. For all sophistical practices of the craft of writing he had as great scorn as the profound thinker with whom this historical survey of English prose began. Not until all other passages for his activity were closed did Bacon become reconciled to the thought of devoting himself entirely to the profession of letters. Within a year or two of his death he resolved to spend his time wholly in writing, and "to put forth that poor talent, or half talent, or what it is that God hath given me, not as heretofore to particular exchanges, but to banks or mounts of perpetuity, that will not break."[1] But the choice was late and never whole-hearted. The literary talent he possessed Bacon cul-

[1] *Works,* XIII, 186.

tivated only as an aid to and as a relief from his more serious callings as lawyer, statesman, and philosopher.

Circumstances and family tradition inclined Bacon, even as a youth, to look upon himself as destined for a public career. The university had little part in his education. He entered Trinity College, Cambridge, in 1573, at the age of twelve years and three months, but his connection with Cambridge lasted only two years. His youth must have made impossible any deep influence of the university upon him at the time, and later he seems never to have felt an inclination to ally himself with any group of university wits, as ambitious young collegians of his day were wont to do. The most that Cambridge did was to beget in him a sentimental feeling for that university, and when disappointment and lack of advancement weighed heavy upon him, he often thought of retiring "with a couple of men to Cambridge," there to spend his life in "studies and contemplations, without looking back."[2] But these were only dreams, and it is doubtful if Bacon would have been as happy as he imagined in the cloistral quiet of the university. He was never content merely to speculate, and his philosophy always implied practical activity on a grand scale.

At the age of fifteen Bacon was admitted to Gray's Inn and began the study of the law. These studies were interrupted, however, by a residence of several years in the household of Sir Amias Paulet, Elizabeth's ambassador in Paris from 1576 to 1579. The reports which Sir Amias Paulet sent to Bacon's father in England show that Bacon was already comporting himself with characteristic discretion. On the death of his father in 1579, however, Bacon returned to England and faced the troublesome problem of choosing a permanent career for himself, a problem all the more difficult and pressing because he was under the neces-

[2] *Letters and Life,* I, 291.

sity of increasing his small income. The practice of his own profession of the law would naturally be the first thing to suggest itself, but for Bacon this would have been an unhappy solution of his difficulties. He had no desire to become merely a lawyer, not from any dislike of the law in itself, but one may suppose for the same reason that he did not want to become merely a writer; the acceptance and practice of any profession was a virtual confession of limitation. Instead of the sober law, he turned his mind to another field of endeavor, one in which success was perhaps less certain, but which offered hopes of larger returns and greater liberty. In 1584 he had entered his first Parliament, beginning thus a public activity which was to continue until his disgrace. In the same year he wrote a Letter of Advice to Queen Elizabeth, which may be taken as the outward evidence of his inward desire to serve the Queen in confidential capacities. Bacon sought for himself a place in the great world, a place from which he might exert a directing power upon the affairs of the nation, and as he dreamed, upon all the future of mankind. To attain this place, the first necessity was royal favor, and Bacon set himself the task of winning Elizabeth's ear and of seeming to be a man of importance among men before he really was, with an assiduity and self-assurance not always entirely pleasing. But even so, advancement came slowly, and though she did not altogether discourage him, Elizabeth kept him dangling always at a distance from the object of his desires.

These weary years of waiting were not, however, a time of idleness. In Parliament, Bacon soon won a position of respect for his weighty judgment and thoroughness, and in the lack of official advancement, he began to take some interest in the practice of his profession. But other important, if less public, occupations also engaged his attention. Bacon aspired to be a ruling and directing power among men, and during this period of enforced leisure, he set himself the task of anatomizing the hearts and minds of his fellow-beings. He drew a kind of moral map of humanity by which he might direct his course in the great voyages that were to bring him power and usefulness in the world. He saw himself sitting apart with a Machiavellian aloofness, not swayed by the passions and prejudices which make the actions of ordinary men ineffective, but by the power of his knowledge leading his poor blind fellow-creatures, the unthinking herd, into paths of comfort and safety. Much of this wisdom he distilled, drop by drop, into the epigrammatic literary form of the *Essays,* but the applications of it are to be seen all through his life.

Not until after the accession of James did Bacon begin to find himself in the important position of confidence which he had long aspired to occupy. The story of his advancement and fall are too familiar to call for discussion. It is more to the present point to turn attention to the speeches, papers, judicial charges, memorials, and similar writings which Bacon composed in the course of his multifarious business and professional activities. These were occasional papers, but many of them have a permanent interest, both as illustrations of Bacon's thought and as examples of the successful application of prose to the conduct of affairs. The earliest extant is the *Letter of Advice to Queen Elizabeth,*[3] written in 1584 when Bacon was twenty-four years old. This letter was of course gratuitously written, as one might write an essay or review to-day. Its subject is the state of religion in England, and Bacon speaks not as the friend or defender of any one side, but as the politic adviser who would show how best to control contending factions. He sets party against party with cool indifference. The Puritans he notes " are somewhat over-squeam-

[3] *Letters and Life,* I, 47-56.

ish and nice, and more scrupulous than they need"; but they are not to be too greatly discouraged since "with their careful catechizing and diligent preaching they bring forth that fruit which your most excellent Majesty is to wish and desire; namely the lessening and diminishing of the Papistical number." As a would-be friend of the government and as one who expected favors at the hands of Elizabeth, it goes without saying that Bacon supported the Establishment. One might expect to find in him some of the zeal for the Puritan cause by which his mother was distinguished, but the expectation is not realized. Young as he was, Bacon had already learned either not to have, or not to bear too strongly upon personal convictions.

A few years later Bacon continued the subject of the *Letter of Advice* in his interesting *Advertisement Touching the Controversies of the Church of England* (1589),[4] a "meditation," as Bacon calls it, probably written to clarify his own views and possibly on intimation that what he said might interest the government. Here again Bacon is the politic adviser, though much general wisdom is mingled with his counsel with respect to practical measures. Controversies, he points out, are not necessarily evil, or if evil, a necessary evil. The real question is of the proper spirit of controversy. "It is the condition of the church to be ever under trials; and there are but two trials; the one of persecution, the other of scandal and contention; and when the one ceaseth the other succeedeth."[5] The particular scandal of the church at the time Bacon was writing was the Marprelate tracts, and it was perhaps to aid the government in extricating itself from the awkward position into which Martin had put it that Bacon penned his "meditation." It is not likely that he had any special interest in

[4] *Letters and Life,* I, 74-95.

[5] *Observations on a Libel, Letters and Life,* I, 165.

matters of church government or of religion, but he wrote on these subjects merely because they happened to be among the important public questions of the day.

In these earliest of his business or professional writings, Bacon exhibits the qualities to be found in all his later productions of the same class. Mannerisms of all kinds he sedulously avoided. He made no effort to be eloquent or fine. He avoided also a technical professional style, but in doing so he made no bid for popular attention. His tendency indeed was from the start toward a too great compression and involution of thought. His mother, in a letter written in 1593, complains that she cannot understand "his enigmatical folded writing." [6] And a letter from Henry Gosnold to Bacon's brother, Anthony, in 1594, describes Bacon as arguing a case of some importance and one by which Bacon considerably raised his reputation, as follows:

"His argument, contracted by the time, seemed a *bataille serrée,* as hard to be discovered as conquered. The unusual words wherewith he had spangled his speech, were rather gracious for their propriety than strange for their novelty, and like to serve for occasions to report and means to remember his argument. Certain sentences of his, somewhat obscure, and as it were presuming upon their capacities, will I fear make some of them rather admire than commend him." [7]

But it was never part of Bacon's program to make his utterances too easily intelligible. He was of the opinion that a certain degree of obscurity added to the weight of a thought, and that a difficult style served a useful purpose in eliminating the unfit from among one's hearers or readers, enabling the writer to "single and adopt his reader." [8] A

[6] *Letters and Life,* I, 245.
[7] Ibid., I, 268.
[8] *Valerius Terminus, Works,* VI, 71.

facile style soothes, a difficult style excites the attention. But fortunately Bacon never carried these theories to extremes, and thoughtful readers will rarely find the difficulty of arriving at his meaning greater than the value of it when it is found.

In all these professional writings one notes the temperateness and restraint, the deliberate subjection of means to ends, which are throughout characteristic of Bacon. One of his favorite mottoes is the saying of Heraclitus, *Lumen siccum optima anima,* and his discussions not only of philosophical theories but of such concrete realities as Essex and Raleigh, realities of a kind to stir the coldest blood, are carried on in this dry light so highly commended. Bacon was always the cautious analyst and judge, he was never betrayed into emotion. As a public speaker he cultivated the same qualities as in writing, and though he puts it down in his *Comentarius Solutus* (1608) as something to be corrected, "To suppress at once my speaking wth panting and labor of breath and voyce,"[9] these impediments to fluent discourse could not often have been caused by depth of feeling. His manner was so prevailingly grave, deliberate, and controlled, that when on one occasion, in a debate on Charitable Trusts, the point of which has not been clearly recorded, he did "speak out of the very strings" of his heart, he noted also that it "doth alter my ordinary form of speech."[10]

Bacon's method of persuasion was to set forth clearly the grounds and reasons for a belief or opinion; and in letters of instruction, explanation, and counsel to the king, in charges to judges, in the summing up of cases, in communications relating to such public affairs as he was concerned with, Bacon felt that dignity of expression combined with thoroughness and good order in presentation were sufficient. It

[9] *Works,* IV, 93. [10] *Letters and Life,* III, 38.

was not his business to be "curious or elaborate."[11] But it was his affair to write with an eye to the proprieties of the situation, and these demanded of him soberness and solidity rather than the graces of an artful literary style. It was Bacon's endeavor to subdue and combine intractable facts and realities so that they might move together in their proper relations and in harmony. And if the test of a good style in writing be the fitness of it for its purpose, then Bacon's official and business publications cannot be regarded otherwise than as admirable models of style.

It was during the closing years of Elizabeth's reign that, discouraged at his slow progress in the world, Bacon was dallying with the thought of retiring to Cambridge to spend his life in studies and contemplations without looking back. According to his friend and literary executor, Dr. Rawley, when Bacon was sixteen years old and "whilst he was commorant in the university" his interest was aroused in philosophical thought by his dislike of the philosophy of Aristotle, "not for the worthlessness of the author, to whom he would ever ascribe all high attributes, but for the unfruitfulness of the way."[12] This interest in philosophy, begun thus early, or perhaps earlier, remained with Bacon to the end of his life. Though his professional and public activities occupied to outward appearances the greater part of his time and attention, Bacon may have spoken the truth when he declared that the contemplative planet carried him away wholly. "Business of state" he professed to have chosen merely as a means to an end: "and I was not without hope (the condition of Religion being at that time not very prosperous) that if I came to hold office in the state, I might get something done too for the good of men's

[11] *Letters and Life,* IV, 114. [12] *Works,* I, 37.

souls."[13] But men's bodies as well as their souls were the concern of Bacon's philosophy. His *Novum Organum* he declares is "for the bettering of men's bread and wine which are the characters of temporal blessings and sacraments of eternal."[14] And at another place he says that no blessing which could be conferred upon mankind seemed to him so great as the "discovery of new arts, endowments and commodities for the bettering of man's life."[15] The end of his work was "for the benefit and use of life";[16] and the task he set himself was "no mere felicity of speculation, but the real business and fortunes of the human race."[17] He hoped and planned, as he said, to "extend more widely the limits of the power and greatness of man."[18]

To describe the means by which these ends were to be attained requires some brief analysis of Bacon's system of thought. Its main principles consisted in the application of exact observation to the phenomena of nature with the intent of discovering general laws or causes, and by the intelligent use of these causes, of enabling man to acquire power over the immediately surrounding facts of his existence. With final causes and with divinity, Bacon did not concern himself. He notes several times that it was not "that pure light of natural knowledge, whereby man in paradise was able to give unto every living creature a name according to his propriety, which gave occasion to the fall; but it was an aspiring desire to attain to that part of moral knowledge which defineth of good and evil . . . which was

[13] *Letters and Life,* III, 85.
[14] Ibid., VII, 130.
[15] Ibid., III, 84.
[16] *Novum Organum, Works,* VIII, 36.
[17] Ibid., p. 53.
[18] Ibid., p. 147.

the original temptation."[19] This practical and philanthropic purpose gives to Bacon's philosophical writings a directness and reality rarely found in writings on speculative subjects. On a few occasions, particularly in the treatment of forms,[20] or "absolute actuality,"[21] the discussion waxes metaphysical, but for the most part what Bacon has to say seems more like the wisdom of a thoughtful and experienced man applied to the affairs and circumstances of life than philosophy—or if it be philosophy, then all thinking men are philosophers. But Bacon's philosophy is by no means popular in the narrower sense of that term. A lofty purpose, which he prosecuted with the most profound conviction, gives dignity to the general outlines and to the form of presentation of his system. He took, as he declares, all knowledge for his province, and in the acquisition of this knowledge, he purposed to employ a method hitherto unknown to mankind, whereby to make "philosophy and sciences both more true and more active."[22] His plan was to "commence a total reconstruction of sciences, arts, and all human knowledge, raised upon the proper foundations."[23] He felt that he had had the good fortune to happen upon a wonderful discovery, that his work was "the child of time rather than of wit," and he was filled with wonder that "the first notion of the thing, and such great suspicions concerning matters long established, should have come into any man's mind."[24] He compares himself to Columbus,[25] and like an explorer, he travels in his course "altogether a pioneer, following in no man's track, nor sharing these

[19] *Valerius Terminus, Works,* VI, 30.
[20] *Novum Organum, Works,* VIII, 168.
[21] Ibid., pp. 205-206.
[22] *Letters and Life,* VII, 120.
[23] *Novum Organum, Works,* VIII, 18.
[24] Ibid., p. 23.
[25] Ibid., p. 129.

counsels with any one."[26] He insists often that he is not to be compared with the ancients, that as he does not compete with them, he cannot detract from their greatness—"my object being to open a new way for the understanding, a way to them untried and unknown."[27] But though he declares that he "leaves the honour of the ancients untouched,"[28] the whole habit of his mind was exalted above them. He accuses the Greek philosophers of leaning "too much to the ambition and vanity of founding a sect and catching popular applause," and he agrees with the characterization of the Greeks "by the Egyptian priest," that they were always boys, without antiquity of knowledge or knowledge of antiquity. "Assuredly they have," he adds, "that which is characteristic of boys; they are prompt to prattle, but cannot generate; for their wisdom abounds in words but is barren of works. And therefore the signs which are taken from the origin and birth-place of the received philosophy are not good."[29]

It is this magnificence of purpose, this bold confidence in himself as a modern and as a discoverer which gives to Bacon's philosophizing its characteristic largeness and dignity of manner. His seriousness is so great that he feels no need for the slighter graces of speech or of learning. "First then, away with antiquities and citations or testimonies of authors . . . everything in short which is philological . . . And for all that concerns ornaments of speech, such like emptinesses, let it be utterly dismissed. Also let all those things which are admitted be themselves set down briefly and concisely, so that they may be nothing less than words. For no man who is collecting and storing up materials for shipbuilding or the like, thinks of arranging them elegantly, as in a shop, and displaying them so as to please the eye; all his

[26] *Novum Organum, Works,* VIII, 145.
[27] Ibid., p. 62.
[28] Ibid., p. 89.
[29] Ibid., p. 103.

care is that they be so arranged as to take up as little room as possible in the warehouse. And this is exactly what should be done here." [30]

These counsels of perfection fairly describe Bacon's own endeavors in his philosophical writing. Though his schemes may have been grandiose, his language is never so. Ever serious, lofty, dignified, it never loses itself in the fields of flowery eloquence. The reader who is attracted by its promising title to Bacon's *History of Life and Death* with the expectation of finding there a display of oratory will be disappointed, for Bacon never plays the part of the popular preacher, never forgets the proprieties of his subject. This *History of Life and Death* was designed to form a part of the *Great Instauration,* and as one "labouring for the perfection of arts," Bacon says he naturally took thought of the ways in which life is maintained and how it ceases, as well as "about the means of prolonging the life of man." An Elizabethan Nietzsche or Strauss might have found in this theme vast possibilities for poetic treatment, but with Bacon all passes under his gaze in the dry light of reason. Apparently he was never even tempted to yield to the allurements of the more purely literary possibilities of his subject—at least he makes no apology for neglecting them. And yet, despite the dry and scientific treatment, the reader is constantly aware that Bacon was keenly alive to the elemental grandeur of his undertaking, that he could have treated it as poetry if he had not preferred to treat it as science. In the titles and names of divisions of the discussion his imaginative grasp of the whole is specially apparent, as for example, to choose one of a number, the title "the porches of death," a section which treats of "the things which happen to men a little before and a little after the point of death." [31]

[30] *Novum Organum, Works,* VIII, 359. [31] *Works,* III, 142.

This happy faculty in choosing titles and catchwords is illustrated throughout Bacon's philosophical writings. His imagination often lends color and warmth to detail, but especially to structural detail like nomenclature. The designation of the impediments to sound thinking as Idols of the Tribe, of the Cave, of the Market Place, of the Theatre, are perhaps the best known and have been most frequently imitated, but other inventions in terminology are equally felicitous. The first general conclusion in the interpretation of nature he calls the First Vintage,[32] and other bits of picturesque nomenclature are his Instances of the Twilight,[33] Instances of the Lamp, "they are those which aid the senses," [34] Instances of the Door or Gate, "this being the name I give to instances which aid the immediate actions of the senses." [35]

When one comes to examine Bacon's philosophical writings singly, one discovers that they consist mainly of a collection of fragments. Bacon realized that his scheme implied more than one man or one generation of men could accomplish. "I was desirous," he says, "to prevent the uncertainness of my own life and times, by uttering rather seeds than plants." His purpose in the *Advancement* he declares to have been "to ring a bell to call other wits together," [36] and in the *Novum Organum* he explains his willingness to publish incomplete parts of his work as due to the fact that "he knew not how long it might be before these things would occur to any one else, judging especially from this, that he has found no man hitherto who has applied his mind to the like." [37] In consequence of this

[32] *Vindematio Prima, Works,* I, 390.
[33] *Instantias Crepusculi, Works,* I, 407.
[34] *Instantias Lampadis, Works,* I, 454.
[35] *Instantias Januae sive Portae, Works,* I, 455.
[36] *Letters and Life,* III, 301.
[37] *Works,* VIII, 19.

method of publication, one finds much repetition of thought and even of phrasing in the various works. The well-known figure in the *Advancement* of "the golden ball thrown before Atalanta, which while she goeth aside and stoopeth to take up, the race is hindered,"[38] used to illustrate the activities of those who by applying knowledge "to lucre and profession" interrupt the advancement of knowledge, occurs twice with the same application in *Valerius Terminus,* and perhaps elsewhere. And the figure of time like a river carrying down the light things but letting the heavy sink occurs a number of times. This repetition of thought and phrasing, partly due to the fact that Bacon preserved preliminary drafts of his writings, is indicative of a certain lack of literary finish and completeness in the philosophical works. The scheme was too vast, apparently, to permit the rounding out of even small sections of the whole. *The Advancement of Learning* is the most finished of the minor philosophical writings, but even here there are evident signs of haste in composition. It was first published in English in 1605 as a completed work, but later, though it was not originally intended to form part of Bacon's general philosophical scheme, it finally found a place in it as a general preparative or prolegomenon, in the form of a Latin translation under the title *De Augmentis Scientiarum.* Of the great philosophical work, the *Magna Instauratio,* only the general outlines were broadly sketched. The most important part of this work in Bacon's plan was the second division which he entitled the *Novum Organum.* For this section, the most carefully written of all Bacon's philosophical works, the language chosen was Latin, which indeed was the intention for all the parts of the *Magna Instauratio.* As the *Novum Organum* presents the method by which Bacon hoped to bring about a reform of sciences

[38] *Works,* VI, 69.

and knowledge, it occupies the place of prime importance among the philosophical writings. The third part of the *Magna Instauratio* was to consist of a collection of separate histories of the phenomena of the universe, a stupendous undertaking represented only by the *Historia Ventorum,* the *Historia Vitae et Mortis,* and the *Historia Densi et Rari.* Some notion of the comprehensiveness of Bacon's plan may be seen from his catalogue of particular histories to be supplied to the number of one hundred and thirty, including a *History of Showers, Ordinary, Stormy and Prodigious; also of Waterspouts (as they are called); and the like; History of Sleep and Dreams; History of Ticking and Feathers.* The seeming triviality of some of these proposed histories is due to the fact that Bacon wished to collect a complete store of the known facts of natural history upon which the philosopher was to operate, and in making this collection his purpose was to utilize the knowledge which unphilosophical artisans and work-people had acquired in the daily practice of their various callings. Some of the "science" which Bacon thought it worth while to record is amusingly naïve, but it would not be safe to infer that Bacon believed everything he put down. He had not the simple faith in prodigies which appears in Stowe and Camden and the chroniclers, and though his skepticism was not that of the modern scientist, he remarks that he records popular superstitions and beliefs not as truths but as matters to be examined and sifted.

Similar in character to these histories of the *Magna Instauratio* was the last work upon which Bacon was engaged, his *Sylva Sylvarum,* a collection of experiments on many subjects, written in English and full of quaint misinformation. As an appendix to his *Sylva Sylvarum,* Bacon wrote his most popular philosophical work, the *New Atlantis,* a summary in the form of fiction of some of the principles of the Baconian philosophy. One of the latest of Bacon's writings, the *New Atlantis* remained a fragment and was not published until after his death. The story is that of an ideal commonwealth, the New Atlantis, reports of which are brought back by travelers who have met with it on a journey from Peru to China and Japan, by way of the South Sea. Like most accounts of imaginary voyages since More's time, the *New Atlantis* owes something to the *Utopia*. Concrete and minute descriptions of costume and similar details are introduced to lend verisimilitude to the narrative. One of the distinguished citizens of the New Atlantis "had on him a gown with wide sleeves, of a kind of water chamolet, of an excellent azure colour, far more glossy than ours; his under apparel was green; and so was his hat, being in the form of a turban, daintily made, and not so huge as the Turkish turbans; and the locks of his hair came down below the brims of it." [39] Bacon's belief in the wealth and luxury which would result from the application of his philosophic method enabled him to indulge in the *New Atlantis* in characteristically Elizabethan opulence of description. But the main point of the treatise centers in the account of Solomon's House, a house of knowledge combining the characteristics of a museum of natural history, a scientific laboratory, and a modern university. An account of the method of experimentation in Solomon's House is given, and the experiments are of the same general kind as those collected by Bacon in the *Sylva Sylvarum*. The great quest of the New Atlantis, in the words of one of its citizens, was "only for God's first creature, which was Light: to have *Light* (I say) of the growth of all parts of the world." [40] "The end of our Foundation" (he is speaking of Solomon's House) "is the knowledge of Causes, and secret motions of things; and the enlarging of the bounds

[39] *Works*, V, 362.

[40] Ibid., p. 384.

of Human Empire, to the effecting of all things possible." [41] The sublime simplicity of this Gargantuan curriculum reminds one of the Oriental stories of the philosopher who inscribed the *omne scibile* upon the walls of his pupil's chamber and then gave him seven days in which to learn it. But Bacon's New Atlantis was not all visionary romance, and though the possible "bounds of Human Empire" seem now narrower than Bacon thought them, the task of slowly widening these bounds in Bacon's way has been assumed as its distinctive obligation by the modern world.

In Bacon's scheme of values, he assigned the first place to his public and civil duty. "I aspire," he writes to Essex, "to the conscience and commendation first of *bonus civis,* which with us is a good and true servant to the Queen, and next of *bonus vir,* that is an honest man." [42] This distinction between public and private morality is characteristic of Bacon. "For if any one charge me with seeking to be wise overmuch," he says at another place, "I answer simply that modesty and civil respect are fit for civil matters; in contemplations nothing is to be respected but Truth." [43] And again: "for when a question is *de vero,* it is simple, for there is but one truth; but when a question is *de bono,* it is for the most part comparative; for there be differing degrees of good and evil, and the best of the good is to be preferred and chosen and the worst of the evil is to be declined and avoided." [44] The practical bearing of these principles appears in Bacon's criticism of those who "speak as if their scope were only to set forth what is good, and

[41] *Works,* V, 398.
[42] *Letters and Life,* II, 191.
[43] Ibid., III, 86.
[44] Ibid., III, 308. Cf. also *Letters and Life,* VI, 157, where he speaks of a measure which he thinks to be good "both *de vero* and *ad populum.*"

not to seek forth what is possible; which is to wish, and not to propound."[45]

Next in rank after good citizenship and the private virtue of an honest man, Bacon placed the duty of exerting the powers of his mind for the enlightenment and bettering of mankind. He felt himself to be of the intellectually elect and consequently under obligation to let his light shine. And still lower than these several ideals of character and conduct, Bacon placed literary ambition. At an age when many of the young wits of his generation were flooding London with poems, plays, and pamphlets, Bacon had written nothing. He professed scorn for "knowledge which tendeth to profit or profession or glory."[46] The first edition of his *Essays* did not appear until 1597, a thin volume containing only ten essays, eked out by miscellaneous matters omitted in later editions. In the edition of 1612, the number was increased to thirty-eight, and the edition of 1625, the last with which Bacon was concerned, contains fifty-eight essays. Besides the essays, Bacon wrote no other literary works of any extent in English except his *History of Henry VII,* which has already been discussed.[47] A very popular work in Bacon's day was his *De Sapientia Veterum* (1609), allegorical interpretations of classic myths and legends. But this book, though not without a charm of its own, was originally written in Latin and never turned into English by Bacon. His remaining literary works are either fragmentary or of very brief extent. Among them may be mentioned translations of seven psalms into English verse, not notable in any respect except as the only verse written by Bacon now extant, and as illustrating a skill in the management of a variety of metrical forms which could have been the result only of considerable practice. Other verses he

[45] *Letters and Life,* III, 104.

[46] *Works,* VI, 34.

[47] See above, pp. 425-428.

composed, but seems to have considered none of them deserving of preservation. He wrote an occasional poem when Elizabeth once dined with him at Twickenham, but saves himself with the apologetic remark, "I profess not to be a poet." [48]

The first edition of his *Essays* Bacon dedicated to his brother Anthony, perhaps with the feeling that they were in a way private and personal utterances and of value to a friend, but not important enough to warrant a dedication to a great personage. Bacon declared that he published them only under compulsion, because certain manuscript copies had got abroad and passed into circulation. He fears that they will be criticised as were "the late new halfepence, which though the Silver were good, yet the peeces were small." [49] His final opinion of the *Essays,* expressed a few years before his death, shows that his estimation of them had not been greatly raised by their popularity. "As for my Essays," so he writes in a general review of his activities in 1622, "and some other particulars of that nature, I count them but as the recreations of my other studies, and in that sort purpose to continue them; though I am not ignorant that those kind of writings would yield more lustre and reputation to my name than those other which I have in hand. But I account the use that a man should seek of the publishing of his own writings before his death to be but an untimely anticipation of that which is proper to follow a man, and not to go along with him." [50] Though the *Essays* were but the recreation of his other studies, they are nevertheless the completest exemplification of Bacon's aims and methods as a writer. They are the striking instance in which Bacon permitted technic to occupy as important a place as content, and the study of the technic

[48] *Letters and Life,* III, 149.
[49] *Works,* XII, 290.
[50] Ibid., XIII, 188.

of the essays is the study of the formation of Bacon's style.

Though for mere literary virtuosity, for technic as technic, Bacon frequently expressed utter disregard, it goes without saying that he did not arrive at his command over English prose without long and exacting preliminary exercise. The basis of the style of the *Essays* is the compact, aphoristic sentence, weighted with thought and finished, but not elaborate, in form. Since Bacon regarded ornament as padding, he consistently reduced it to a minimum in the *Essays.* In the first edition the separate essays are much shorter than in the later editions, and the thoughts are expressed more concisely and epigrammatically. They bear markedly the indications of being "dispersed meditations," as loosely put together as the Orphic passages of Emerson. As Bacon revised the *Essays,* however, he amplified them, supplied connecting links in thought, and in general gave much greater rotundity and fluency to the phrasing; and in these later forms the *Essays* consequently read more easily and currently. But they never become discursive treatments of the topics they consider, the fancy and imagination are not allowed to play freely. Bacon never permits the feeling for the solidity and reality of his intellectual world to weaken. The *Essays* remain, even in their elaborated forms, compact summaries of observations. The meditations of which they were composed are the essence of Baconian wisdom, put up in neat capsules and enclosed within labeled boxes.

"The word is late," says Bacon, commenting on the title of his *Essays,* "but the thing is ancient. For Seneca's epistles to Lucilius, if one mark them well, are but essays, that is, dispersed meditations, though conveyed in the form of epistles."[51] Bacon seems to have borrowed the word

[51] *Letters and Life,* IV, 341.

from the *Essais* of Montaigne and to have been the first to use the word in this sense in English.[52] Montaigne's *Essais* had appeared in 1580, seventeen years before Bacon's first edition, which in turn antedated Florio's translation of Montaigne by six years. But Bacon's indebtedness to Montaigne was not extensive. Neither the impulse which led to the composition of the essays nor the general spirit in which they were written owed much to the garrulous Frenchman. It is not necessary to look beyond Bacon's own mind and the fashion of the times to account for his interest in collecting "dispersed meditations." Among Renascence scholars the favorite medieval method of summarizing experience and doctrine, the narrative exemplum, had been to a large extent replaced by the aphorism and wise saying. The writings of the ancients were ransacked for pithy moral observations, and these, no matter how commonplace, seemed to acquire dignity by reason of their classical origin and by virtue of the fact that they had never before been succinctly formulated in vernacular phrases. The sententious wisdom of Guevara and of English romancers like Lyly are extreme illustrations of this tendency. Wits and courtiers were infected with the fashion, and Hamlet with his tables, ready to record the observation that a man may smile and be a villain—or any other that might occur to him—and Polonius with his own collection of rules and maxims, doubtless had many a living counterpart in Elizabethan days. Robert Greene farces his romances with long miscellaneous lists of precepts and sententious sayings, quite in the manner of Bacon, but entirely lacking in relevancy, as though when graveled for lack of matter, he emptied his note-book of its available store of observations.[53] He prob-

[52] Montaigne is mentioned by name in the essay "Of Truth," the first essay in the edition of 1625. This essay does not appear in the earlier editions.

[53] See *Works,* ed. Grosart, III, 143.

ably knew that wise sayings were as acceptable a form of entertainment to his public as love-making.

To come a little closer home, we find that Bacon's mother, a learned and serious lady not incapable of quoting Greek on occasion, cultivated this same art of sententious moralizing. "Be not speedy of speech nor talk suddenly," she writes to her son, "but where discretion requireth, and that soberly then.[54] For the property of our world is to sound out at first coming, and after to contain. Courtesy is necessary, but too common familiarity in talking and words is very unprofitable, and not without hurt-taking, *ut nunc sunt tempora.*" [55] From this serious didacticism the rapid transition of Lady Bacon's letters to anxious inquiries as to her son's digestion or his bad habit of going to bed late and of rising late, or to the practical details of a gift of strawberries from Gorhambury or the first flight of her doves, may seem amusing to the modern reader. But it doubtless did not seem so to her son, for he agreed with Lady Bacon in considering the acquisition of wisdom to be one of the practical concerns of daily life.

Bacon's earliest writings contain many illustrations of his fondness for compact epigrammatic expression. In his *Letter of Advice to Queen Elizabeth* he distinguishes neatly between discontent and despair: "for it sufficeth to weaken the discontented; but there is no way but to kill the desperate . . . for among many desperate men, it is like some one will bring forth a desperate effort." [56] And some of the following might be extracts from the *Essays:*

"Laws, not refreshed with new laws, wax sour. Without change of the ill, a man cannot continue the good. To take away abuses supplanteth not good orders, but estab-

[54] That is, be hasty only after careful consideration.
[55] *Letters and Life,* I, 112.
[56] Ibid., I, 48.

lisheth them. A contentious retaining of custom is a turbulent thing, as well as innovation." [57]

"He seeketh not unity, but division, which exacteth in words that which men are content to yield in action." [58]

These generalizations were doubtless in large part the fruits of that solitariness at his place at Twickenham Park which "collecteth the mind, as shutting the eyes doth the sight," of which Bacon on one occasion speaks.[59] After they were excogitated, they were put down in note-books and preserved until an appropriate time for using them appeared. In fact they were collected very much in the same way that Bacon collected his observations of the phenomena of natural science in the external world. The thoughts were not merely spun out of Bacon's inner consciousness, but they have a kind of objective reality which results from the fact that their wisdom springs from the combination of reflection with experience.

Examples of these "forms," or thoughts neatly expressed to be employed later, together with a great variety of other detail indicative of Bacon's methods of self-discipline, may be found in one of Bacon's note-books which happens to have been preserved. It was made in 1608 and bears the title *Comentarius Solutus*.[60] A somewhat similar work is the *Promus of Formularies and Elegancies,* a miscellaneous collection probably representing Bacon's reading and his reflections during the Christmas vacation of 1594. This latter collection consists of phrases to be used in conversation, of quotations from the Latin poets, a few natural history observations, several of Erasmus's *Adagia,* and a number of neat epigrammatic turns of thought—

[57] *Life and Letters,* I, 88.
[58] Ibid., I, 89.
[59] Ibid., I, 321.
[60] Ibid., IV, 57.

for example, "Ceremonies and green rushes are for strangers."[61] To the student of Bacon as a writer, these collections are of great interest as containing suggestions for trains of thought, exercises in composition and conversation, in short all the minutiæ of self-discipline to which the literary artist must subject himself.

The methods which Bacon followed in practice he also preached by precept. "I hold the entry of commonplaces," so he writes in the *Advancement of Learning*, "to be a matter of great use and essence in studying; as that which assureth copie of invention and contracteth judgment to a strength. But this is true, that of the *methods* of common-places that I have seen, there is none of any sufficient worth; all of them carrying merely the face of a *school*, and not a *world*, and referring to vulgar matters and pedantical divisions without all life or respect to action."[62] The method by which one was to avoid the arid deserts of the school and to cultivate the rich fields of the world of life and action, Bacon has detailed elsewhere. In his *Letter of Advice to the Earl of Rutland on his Travels*, Bacon recommends "writing or meditation or both" as aids to remembrance; and by writing he means not merely summaries of what one has read, but "notes and abridgements of that which you would remember."[63] For the making of summaries or epitomes, Bacon expresses the greatest scorn.[64] "I hold collections under heads and commonplaces of far more profit and use," he writes to Sir Fulke Greville, counseling him on his studies, "because they have in them a kind of observation without which neither long life breeds experience, nor great

[61] *Works*, IV, 21.
[62] Ibid., VI, 281.
[63] *Letters and Life*, II, 13.
[64] Ibid., II, 23; and also *Works*, VI, 281, in the second book of the *Advancement of Learning*.

reading great knowledge." Then in detail Bacon shows how from particular narratives, general ideas may be deduced. From the story of Alexander in Plutarch, after observing "the variety of accidents he met withal in the course of his life," under the head of Conqueror one may note "that to begin in the strength and flower of his age; to have a way made to greatness by his father; to find an army disciplined, and a council of great captains; and to procure himself to be made head of a league against a common enemy, whereby both his quarrel may be made popular and his assistance great, are necessary helps to great conquests."[65] In the same way Bacon shows how general ideas may be derived from particular narratives under the topics War and Periods or Revolutions of States. In short, what Bacon recommends is the combination of reading with thinking, to be followed by the crystallization of the thought in the forms of language. When one recalls Bacon's eloquent defense of learning and scholarship, his own statement that he has "rather studied books than men,"[66] and then the form which his writing took, one may confidently believe that Bacon's wisdom was in no small degree attained by the method he has described. And when one considers further the solidity and reality of Bacon's thought, qualities which make it still interesting and significant, perhaps one may conclude that the "school" and the "world" are not as far apart as they are usually supposed to be. It is true that, mingled with Bacon's profounder

[65] *Life and Letters,* II, 24. It would be interesting to see how many of Bacon's "meditations" were derived in this way from his reading. A beginning could be made for Plutarch and the *Essays* by examining the numerous parallels noted by the various editors of the *Essays,* to which should be added those recently collected by Miss Goodenough, *Bacon and Plutarch, Modern Language Notes,* XII, 283-292.

[66] Ibid., VI, 27, in a letter written in 1616.

meditations, many aphorisms occur which are obvious in thought. But it was never Bacon's endeavor to astonish by the novelty or remoteness of his ideas. Apt expression when coupled with just thinking seemed to him to satisfy all reasonable demands. Aphorisms which sound trite in the sophisticated speech of the twentieth century seem not so facile in the language of the sixteenth century. Words inevitably abate their power after long use, but around Bacon's wise sayings there still lingers much of the freshness of first efforts.[67]

The preference which Bacon gave to Latin over English, in his later years, has often been regarded as indication of a deplorable lack of understanding on Bacon's part of the possibilities of his native tongue and lack of faith in the great literature which was then being written in it. But Bacon's choice of Latin was both less significant and more reasonable than it is often made to seem. In his professional activities he was of course thoroughly accustomed to the use of Latin, which thus came to him not merely as a dead literary language, but as a speech fit for affairs and business. Nevertheless in his earlier writings he used English almost exclusively, employing Latin only where the proprieties and conventions of the situation required it. Nor did he descend to the shallow pedantry of Latinizing his English in an ostentatious way. His style is a highly Latinized style—he was no advocate of Saxon simplicity—but his vocabulary is made up in the main of words which

[67] The method of deriving aphorisms from reading is fully illustrated by Sir Robert Dallington's *Aphorismes Civill and Militarie, amplified with Authorities, and exemplified with History, out of the first Quarterne of F. Guicciardine* (1613). The amplifications are drawn from various sources and the passages in Guicciardini from which the aphorisms are supposed to be derived are printed at length. It would be an easy matter to make up a set of Baconian essays from Sir Robert Dallington's aphorisms.

had become legitimized in the learned use of the language. Compared with some of the more extravagant literary Latinizers, Bacon's vocabulary seems quite simple and modern.

When he came to carry out the project of the *Magna Instauratio,* it was almost inevitable that Bacon should turn to Latin. For this work was addressed not merely to the British nation, but to the world of scholars and thinkers. International communication was still to a large extent carried on in Latin, which was extensively used in the reign of James in theological controversy. In making use of Latin, Bacon was merely taking advantage of an opportunity the lack of which scientists and scholars to-day are vainly trying to supply artificially by the invention of theoretical languages. Latin in Bacon's time was still "the general Language," as he describes it in justifying the Latin translation of the *Advancement of Learning.*[68] His purpose in putting this book into Latin was "to free it in the language" so that it might be read everywhere.[69] In sending forth one of the presentation copies of this Latin translation, he expresses the conviction that the book "will live, and be a citizen of the world, as English books are not."[70]

In the last years of his life, however, these good and reasonable motives for the use of Latin became mingled with others of baser character. As Bacon saw the prospect of realizing in any considerable degree the plans of his *Magna Instauratio* growing more remote, he turned his thoughts more and more towards the generations that were to follow him. As he saw not only present fame but also contempo-

[68] *Works,* XIII, 187.

[69] *Letters and Life,* VII, 436. At the same time he modified opinions which might be offensive to Roman Catholic readers of the Continent, his purpose being to secure as wide and sympathetic a consideration for his main points as possible.

[70] Ibid.

rary good name and reputation slipping from him, he desired more eagerly to leave something behind him at his death which should last and which men might recall with words of praise after they had forgotten his weaknesses. "For my name and memory," so he writes in his last will, "I leave it to men's charitable speeches, and to foreign nations and the next ages."[71] Writing in 1623 to his friend Tobie Matthew, Bacon says that his chief occupation was then to have those works which he had formerly published, "as that of Advancement of Learning, that of Henry 7th, that of the Essays, being retractate and made more perfect, well translated into Latin by the help of some good pens which forsake me not. For these modern languages will at one time or other play the bank-rowtes with books; and since I have lost much time with this age, I would be glad as God shall give me leave to recover it with posterity."[72] With the help of these "good pens," who did most of the work, the task was carried to completion—an unnecessary task, as time has shown, since the interest of posterity in Bacon's English writings has not been kept alive by the Latin translations of them, nor have these translations sufficient interest or distinction to make them important in their own right. They have done no harm, however, and Bacon's weakness with respect to them must simply be cast, in Sir Walter Raleigh's phrase, in the sum of human error.

With Bacon this survey of the origins of English prose may appropriately come to an end. Though he takes his place among the writers of classic English prose largely by virtue of one book, his position there is secure. His *Essays* are the earliest original writing in English prose which has

[71] *Letters and Life,* VII, 228.
[72] Ibid., VII, 429.

held a place in the general, one might almost say in the popular, interest of readers of English since the time of their composition. But whatever Bacon's relative rank may be, whether he was the greatest prose writer in his time or not, he takes an important place in the history of English prose as marking the close of the age of experiment and discovery. With him English prose has definitely found itself, has been not merely discovered but conquered. It is true that Bacon did not realize the varied possibilities of English prose as amply as some of its later masters have done, but his limitations were those which his nature, not the command of the technic of his art, imposed upon him. His profundity of thought, his poet's imagining of abstractions, above all the sense of the reality and truth of the intellectual world in which he moved and had his being, all these Bacon has adequately transferred to the forms of English speech. His writing, perhaps, lacks warmth and feeling, but in emphasizing the virtues of prose composition he also brought into relief its characteristic weakness. Bacon's endeavor was to be honest and clear in writing, to avoid the self-deception and the floundering to which human nature is prone. He takes his stand with the moderns upon a platform of independent thinking and an independent and intelligent mastery of his art. Like the writer with whom this discussion began, to attain freedom Bacon became something of an iconoclast. Wiclif scorned to quote "holy doctors," and Bacon would away with the intellectual support of the ancients so dearly loved of all Renascence writers and scholars, away also with their superficial ornament. Both were moderns in their day, though Wiclif's reaction against medievalism and scholastic authority naturally seems much more remote from present interest than Bacon's rejection of philosophical abstractions in favor of truth as realized in experience, and of classical oratorical authority in favor of less literary and external standards of expression.

Bacon is distinctly with the moderns in his attitude toward the technic of writing. For technical skill as a means to a reasonable end, he had the highest respect. But technical skill as an exercise in virtuosity, or employed merely to realize the dream of an English style as good as that of Cicero, or of Cæsar or of Tacitus, seemed to him worthless and even reprehensible. The message came first in his estimation, and the arts of style were to be employed to make the message clear and effective, never to make it more pleasing than in justice it should be. This distrust of fine writing in English prose has not grown weaker with the passing of time. Prose has been, as Bacon would have it be, the servant of mankind, not merely an ornament of his state or a solace for his idler moments. As it has had various tasks to perform, so English prose has been made flexible to its different applications. Bacon had no theory of a fixed and standard form of prose, of an elaborated professionally literary style such as the Euphuists and Arcadianists, or such even as learned writers like Hooker, set up as their ideal. With Bacon prose took its place among the practical, not the theoretical virtues. It was not something to be imposed upon English life and culture, it was an inherent and changing element in that developing life and culture, an emanation not an acquisition. Time alone, it is true, could have made possible such opinions as Bacon held. He could rest satisfied with the product of the life of his day because English culture had at last reached the age of maturity. It had assimilated much in the generations since Wiclif and Chaucer, and it had learned by many errors as well as by some successes. Bacon's wisdom was manifested in his realization of the riches which lay at his very door. He saw himself not as a dæmonic being, rapt with a divine frenzy into the fiery clouds of inspiration and speaking and writing a language, not of men but of the gods. His Pegasus was his intelligence, a well-disciplined and governed intelligence. He placed English prose where English writers ever since have labored to keep it, in the everyday world of established experience, of good order, and of sound sense. The source of eloquence in prose he found not in the elevation of art above nature, but in the just expression of all that is best and most worthy of expression within the heart and mind of man.

INDEX